THE CUBS CHRONOLOGY

A CHRONOLOGICAL HISTORY OF THE CHICAGO CUBS

TIM STEELE

STELLAR PRESS
ST. LOUIS, MISSOURI

This book is dedicated to
MOM AND DAD
who are not Cubs fans.

And to my wife, Suzi, whose not-always-infinite patience has been tried for more years than I care to remember but whose understanding and guidance have kept me focused in the right direction.

The Cubs Chronology
By Tim Steele

ISBN 0-9708422-9-5

PRINTED IN THE UNITED STATES OF AMERICA

Published and distributed by Stellar Press
634 N. Grand Blvd.
Suite 10-6
St. Louis, Missouri 63103
1-877-572-8835
www.stellarpress.com

CONTENTS

ACKNOWLEDGEMENTS

This book couldn't have been produced without the legions of correspondents, scholars and professionals who have shared information, uncovered material or generally kept me focused for the past year:

Many thanks to the **Chicago Cubs**, the **National Baseball Hall of Fame**, the **St. Louis Cardinals**, the **New York Yankees**, the **Detroit Tigers**, the **Oakland Athletics**, the **New York Mets**, the **San Diego Padres**, the **Chicago Tribune**, the **St. Louis Post-Dispatch**, the **St. Louis Globe Democrat**, the **St. Louis County Library**, **Northwestern University**, the **University of Missouri St. Louis**, the **Society for American Baseball Research**, the **Sporting News**, the **New York Times**, the **Major League Baseball Players Association**, **Major League Baseball**, **Ken Holtzman**, **Jim Hunstein**, my editor, **Ken Christian**, and everyone at **Stellar Press**.

INTRODUCTION

The Cubs Chronology is the second in a broad (well, we can hope) series of chronologically-based baseball books. After completing *The Cardinals Chronology*, it seemed natural that *The Cubs Chronology* would follow, since the two ballclubs represent the oldest (and longest) rivalry in professional sports. The Cubs and Cards first hooked up in a hotly contested post-season series in 1885 which ended in a disputed tie. Although the two clubs' fortunes have polarized over the last several decades, that bitter rivalry is still there.

Why a chronology?

Ever stand in the "Sports" section at Barnes & Noble looking for a book on baseball history? What do you see? Shelves and shelves of historical perspective, all written by prominent journalists or ghostwriters posing as ballplayers or both. Spin city. Or gigantic volumes full of esoteric statistics in eye-straining, five-point text. Snooze-o-rama. Sure, that stuff is fine for stat nerds and Yankeephiles, but what about the rest of us? We want the highlights. We want to be entertained. What made the ballclub great? What was responsible for its decline? We want to *absorb* without being bored to tears by some pompous windbag force-feeding us convoluted, mind-numbing analysis. Oh, the humanity!

Give me a *chronology*. Allow me to imagine what's happening. Allow me to visualize. Give me the facts. Let me formulate my own perspective, without a lot of over-analyzed piffle. Under what circumstances did Babe Ruth call, or not call, his shot? How is it possible that my beloved Cubbies led the National League for 150 days and then crapped out the last two weeks of the '69 season? How could Mr. Maddux leave the green pastures of Wrigley for the brown fields of Turner Field? Was Leo Durocher really a genius—or just an obnoxious, overrated self-promoter? Give me the facts!

Somewhere between monotonous statistics and embarrassing "I remember when it was just a game" dissertations lies the chronology. Easy to read, easy to learn, always entertaining. Whether it's baseball or world history, chronological books are the best way to understand the past because they allow you to visualize a particular milestone and put it into the perspective of current events.

The facts, I say! Give me the facts! Let me formulate my *own* opinion! Give me details that won't push the limits of my attention span! Or patience!

At least that's what *I* think. Enjoy.

-Tim Steele, 2003

"Wrigley Field is a Peter Pan of a ballpark.
It has never grown up and it has never grown old.
Let the world race on - they'll still be playing day
baseball in the friendly confines of Wrigley Field,
outfielders will still leap up against the vines...
and the Cubs...well, it's the season of hope.
This could be the Cubbies' year."

-E.M. Swift

THE CHRONOLOGY

1832 - 2003

WORTH QUOTING - "Chicago Cubs fans are the greatest fans in baseball. They've got to be."
-Bill Buckner, 1986

1832-1870

October 23, 1832 - William A. Hulbert is born in Burlington Flats, New York.

September 2, 1850 - Albert Goodwill Spalding is born in Byron, Illinois.

April 11, 1852 - Cap Anson is born in Marshalltown, Iowa.

November 20, 1869 - Clark Griffith is born in Clear Creek, Missouri.

April 25, 1870 - The Chicago White Stockings, the first generation of the team that will become the Cubs, begins spring training in New Orleans. The White Stockings play in the newly-created National Association of Baseball Players, an amateur league.

The Cincinnati Reds, baseball's oldest organized team, also begins a series of exhibitions in New Orleans.

July 23, 1870 - Chicago baseball makes the national news for the first time. Five thousand fans jam Dexter Park to see the White Stockings play the visiting New York Mutuals.

Mutuals pitcher Rynie Wolters holds the White Stockings to three singles, beating them 9-0 for the first shutout in recorded baseball history. From now on, the New York Herald will use the term "Chicagoed" to signify a shutout - the term will last until the turn of the century.

1871

Principle Owner and President: David Gage; **Manager:** Jimmy Wood; **Ballpark:** Lake Park; **Attendance:** 69,000; **Finish:** 3rd (20-9); **Recap:** Led by manager-second baseman Jimmy Wood, who bats a robust .378, and pitcher Goerge Zettlein, who goes 18-9, the White Stockings nearly capture the National Association's first pennant. Unfortunately, the Great Chicago Fire wipes out the club's ballpark, equipment, uniforms, several of the players' houses, and many of the banks holding their cash. The Whites are forced to finish the season on the road, dropping three games in a row, and slipping to third.

P	PLAYER	R	HR	RBI	SB	AVE
1B	Bub McAtee	34	0	10	-	.274
2B	Jimmy Wood	45	1	29	-	.378
SS	Ed Duffy	30	0	15	-	.231
3B	Ed Pinkham	27	1	17	-	.263
RF	Joe Simmons	29	0	17	-	.217
CF	Mart King	23	2	16	-	.208
LF	Fred Treacey	39	4	33	-	.339
C	Charlie Hodes	32	2	25	-	.277
P	George Zettlein	23	0	18	-	.250
UT	Tom Foley	18	0	13	-	.262
IF	Mike Brannock	2	0	0	-	.071

T	PITCHER	W-L	SV	SO	SH	ERA
R	George Zettlein	18-9	0	22	0	2.73
L	Ed Pinkham	1-0	1	0	0	3.48

March 1 - The Windy City is awarded its first professional baseball team. The National Association of *Professional* Baseball Players is created at Collier's Saloon in New York City. The Chicago White Stockings, the team that will eventually become the Cubs, joins the Philadelphia Athletics, Boston Red Stockings, Brooklyn Eckfords, Cleveland Forest Citys, Rockford (Illinois) Forest Citys, New York Mutuals, Washington (D.C.) Nationals, Washington (D.C.) Olympics, and Troy (New York) Haymakers. Playing rules will be the same

as the amateur game with the exception of player compensation. Second baseman Jimmy Wood is chosen to be the Whites' player-manager.

April 29 - The White Stockings' brand new ballpark, Lake Park, opens for an exhibition between the club and a hand-picked nine in front of 1,500 fans. The ballpark is heralded as one of the finest in the country. It seats 6,500.

June 5 - Ten thousand fans jam Union Grounds in Brooklyn for a game between the White Stockings and New York Mutuals. Five of the old National Association's Eckfords play for Chicago while several former Brooklyn Atlantics, also an old NAclub, play for the Mutuals. Chicago loses, 8-5, making 19 errors. It's the Whites' first loss of the season after seven straight wins.

August 28 - Whites pitcher George Zettlein holds the powerful Athletics to just four hits in a 6-3 triumph at Philadelphia. It's the least amount of runs that Philly has scored this season.

September 5 - The race for the pennant heads into the home stretch. The league-leading Whites lose to the second-place Red Stockings 6-3, blowing a 3-0 lead. First baseman Charley Gould smacks a grand slam for Boston in a six-run fifth inning. Chicago will rebound to take tomorrow's game.

October7 - The Chicago Fire breaks out in Mrs. O'Leary's barn at 10 o'clock. Whether the kerosene lamp was kicked over by a clumsy cow or by Louis Cohn during a craps game, the fire wipes out Lake Park and all of the Whites' equipment. The team was to take on the visiting Rockford club the next day; winning the best-of-three series with the Forest Citys would have clinched the pennant for Chicago.

The Great Chicago Fire also leveled many of the players'homes and wiped out their bank accounts.

WORTH NOTING- The Cubs first surfaced as a member of the National Association of Professional Baseball Players in 1871 and were called the White Stockings. From then until 1902, when they officially became known as the Cubs, they were called, directly or indirectly, the Colts, the Ex-Colts, the Rainmakers, Cowboys, Rough Riders, Desert Rangers, Orphans, Remnants, Recruits, Panamas, Zephyrs, Nationals, Trojans, and Spuds.

October 21 - The Whites meet the Haymakers in Troy, New York for the first time this season. Thanks to the fire in Chicago, the Whites are playing their first game since September 29. They beat the home team 11-5 but will lose the next game. The rest of the series will be rained out.

October 30 - The White Stockings take on the Philadelphia Athletics for all the marbles at Brooklyn's Union Grounds. The National Association's Championship Committee has determined that today's game will decide the winner of the pennant. Chicago, who has been on the road since the fire, appears on the field in a variety of different uniforms. Theirs were destroyed in the blaze. The Athletics win 4-1, with the final putout recorded by Nate Berkenstock, a 40-year old retired amateur who is appearing in his only professional game. Born in 1831, Berkenstock is the oldest player to appear in a NAgame.

The devastated White Stockings will disband this winter, resurfacing in 1874.

1872-1873

May 29, 1872 - The first baseball game to be played in Chicago since the Great Fire is played on the new grounds of the Chicago Base Ball Association, 23rd Street Grounds. The Baltimore Canaries defeat the Cleveland Forest Citys 5-3 before 4,000 fans.

August 16, 1873 - The Windy City is buzzing again after it is announced that the White Stockings have regrouped under new owner William Hulbert and will re-enter the National Association this year. The new club will loot the Philadelphia Athletics of six regulars: Levi Meyerle, Jim Devlin, Ferby Malone, Ned Cuthbert, and former Chicago stars George Zettlein and Jimmy Wood. Wood will lose his right leg to an infection, ending his career, but the other five combined with newcomers Davy Force, John Glenn, and Paul Hines make the Whites the early-season favorites.

1874

Principle Owner and President: William Hulbert; **Manager:** Fergie Malone (18-18) / Jimmy Wood (10-13); **Ballpark:** 23rd Street Grounds; **Attendance:** 66,000; **Finish:** 5th (28-31); **Recap:** Despite the hitting of Levi Meyerle, who paces the National Association with a .394 average, the rebuilt White Stockings underachieve and sink to fifth.

P	PLAYER	R	HR	RBI	SB	AVE
1B	John Glenn	33	0	33	-	.283
2B	Levi Meyerle	65	1	47	-	.394
SS	John Peters	69	1	25	-	.289
3B	Davy Force	61	0	26	-	.313
RF	Fred Treacey	18	0	12	-	.189
CF	Paul Hines	47	0	34	-	.295
LF	Ned Cuthbert	65	2	22	-	.269
C	Fergie Malone	33	0	29	-	.251
P	George Zettlein	26	0	18	-	.193
C	(?) Gilroy	4	0	7	-	.211
C	Terry Connell	0	0	0	-	.000
P	Dan Collins	1	0	0	-	.083

T	PITCHER	W-L	SV	SO	SH	ERA
R	George Zettlein	27-30	0	26	3	2.42
-	Dan Collins	1-1	0	0	0	4.91
R	Davy Force	0	0	0	0	15.43

March 1 - The first home game in Chicago since the Great Fire in 1871 is played at the Whites' new ballpark, the 23rd Street Grounds, before 4,000 fans.

George Zettlein defeats the Philadelphia Athletics 4-0. The Athletics strand 21 baserunners.

June 15 - Using his controversial curve-ball, the Athletics' Candy Cummings fans six consecutive White Stockings in an 8-6 victory at Philadelphia.

June 18 - The White Stockings are on the wrong end of an ugly 38-1 whipping by the Mutuals in New York. The Mutes collect 33 hits; the Whites commit 36 errors.

June 27 - The ugliness continues in Boston; Red Stockings pitcher Al Spalding collects six hits en route to a 29-6 victory over Chicago.

July 4 - The White Stockings celebrate Independence Day with a 17-16 victory over the visiting Boston Red Stockings before 10,000 screaming fans. It's Chicago's first home game after a grueling four-week road trip to the east coast.

July 15 - Before a Chicago home game with the Philadelphia Pearls, umpire William McLean is approached by Philadelphia utility player John Radcliffe who offers him $175 if he'll help Chicago win the game. Reportedly, Philadelphia's Candy Cummings, Bill Craver, Nat Hicks, and Denny Mack are in on the plot.

Radcliffe will be expelled in September.

September 14 - The middle-of-the-pack Chicagoes defeat the first-place Red Stockings in Boston, battering ace Al Spalding for 22 hits in a 10-0 victory behind George Zettlein. Boston shortstop George Wright makes three errors.

1875

Principle Owner and President: William Hulbert; **Manager:** Jimmy Wood; **Ballpark:** 23rd Street Grounds; **Attendance:** 60,323; **Finish:** Sixth (30-37); **Recap:** The loss of star infielders Levi Meyerle and Davy Force and steady veteran Ned Cuthbert doom the White Stockings to sixth place.

P	Player	R	HR	RBI	SB	AVE
1B	Jim Devlin	60	0	40	-	.289
2B	Paul Hines	45	0	36	-	.328
SS	John Peters	40	0	34	-	.286
3B	Warren White	37	0	23	-	.247
RF	Oscar Bielaski	21	0	11	-	.239
CF	Scott Hastings	43	0	30	-	.254
LF	John Glenn	46	0	27	-	.244
C	Dick Higham	44	0	12	-	.236
P	Mike Golden	16	0	14	-	.258
P	George Gettlein	7	0	9	-	.218
UT	Paddy Quinn	12	0	1	-	.230
UT	Joe Miller	8	0	1	-	.148
IF	George Keerl	2	0	3	-	.130
IF	Fred Waterman	2	0	3	-	.300

T	Pitcher	W-L	SV	SO	SH	ERA
R	George Zettlein	17-14	0	18	6	1.28
R	Jim Devlin	7-16	0	23	0	1.93
R	Mike Golden	6-7	0	14	1	1.89

May 6 - The St. Louis Browns defeat the White Stockings by a score of 10-0 in front of 5,000 fans at Grand Avenue Grounds (later called Sportsman's Park) in St. Louis. George Bradley tosses a four-hitter.

May 8 - The Browns beat the Whites 4-3, holding them scoreless through the first eight innings. The 17-inning scoring drought is the longest in baseball history to date.

May 11 - Chicago gains a bit of revenge, shutting out the Browns 1-0. It's the lowest-scoring game in baseball history so far. Each team is held to six hits.

June 19 - Paul Hines drives home Jim Devlin with a sacrifice fly in the 11th inning to give the Chicagoes a 1-0 victory vs. the Hartford Dark Blues. Sportswriter Harry Chadwick writes that it is "the finest display of baseball playing and the most exciting contest yet recorded in the annals of the national game."

July 5 - Fifteen thousand screaming cranks, the largest crowd in St. Louis history so far, jam Grand Avenue Grounds to watch the Browns pummel the visiting White Stockings 13-2. In the stands are members of the Washington ballclub, who find out after the game that there is no money to pay their way back to Washington. The club is disbanded then and there. The Browns pay the team's way back home.

July 20 - The Chicago Tribune posts a rumor that the Boston Reds are to disband at the end of the season, with Harry Wright defecting to the Cincinnati club with brother George in tow. According to the Trib, the White Stockings have secretly signed Boston stars Al Spalding, Deacon White, Cal McVey, and Ross Barnes.

July 28 - Athletics hurler Joseph Borden tosses the first no-hitter in professional baseball history, a 4-0 gem over the White Stockings. The game takes 95 minutes to play.

September 25 - Philadelphia pounds Chicago 15-6, aided by second baseman

Albert Goodwill Spalding

Paul Hines's 10 errors.

October 24 - The Tribune, in an editorial, calls for the formation of a new professional league that includes the Chicago, Cincinnati, Louisville, Philadelphia, New York, Boston and Hartford clubs. "Unless the present Professional Association leadership adopts rules to limit the number of teams allowed to participate in the championship season," the Tribune writes, "all clubs will go broke."

1876

Principle Owner and President: William Hulbert; **Manager:** Al Spalding; **Ballpark:** 23rd Street Grounds; **Attendance:** 65,441; **Finish:** First (52-14); **Recap:** The National League is born on February 2 in New York by White Stockings president William Hulbert. Hulbert's careful planning notwithstanding, the National League is not a resounding success in its first year, mostly because his White Stockings run away with the pennant at a .790 clip, preventing any of the other teams to turn a profit. Spalding's arm and the greatest offensive infield in major league history are much of the reason that the team never loses more than two games in a row.

P	Player	R	HR	RBI	SB	AVE
1B	Cal McVey	62	1	53	-	.347
2B	Ross Barnes	126	1	59	-	.429
3B	Cap Anson	63	2	59	-	.356
SS	John Peters	70	1	47	-	.351
RF	Bob Addy	36	0	16	-	.282
CF	Paul Hines	62	2	59	-	.331
LF	John Glenn	55	0	32	-	.304
C	Deacon White	66	1	60	-	.343
P	Al Spalding	54	0	44	-	.312
OF	Oscar Bielaski	24	0	10	-	.209
OF	Fred Andrus	6	0	2	-	.306

T	Pitcher	W-L	SV	SO	SH	ERA
R	Al Spalding	47-12	0	39	9	1.75
R	Cal McVey	5-2	2	9	0	1.52
R	Deacon White	0-0	1	3	0	0.00
R	Ross Barnes	0-0	0	0	0	20.25
R	John Peters	0-0	1	0	0	0.00

February 2 - Chicago president William Hulbert organizes a meeting at the Grand Central Hotel on lower Broadway in New York to establish a new league. The other owners, as well as the press, believe its purpose is simply to address reforms, particularly the unstable finances of many clubs and the need for rule changes. But the announced reason for the meeting is a ploy; the owners find themselves trapped behind locked doors so that Hulbert can pitch his new concept.

The cornerstone of the new league is the elimination of players from any position of authority in team affairs, turning power over to the owners. Hulbert outlines reforms that would address player drunkenness, gambling and incompetent leadership.

Hulbert's real reasons, however, may be a bit more self-serving; the White

Stockings secretly signed away four of the Boston Reds' biggest stars - Al Spalding, Deacon White, Cal McVey, and Ross Barnes - as well as Philadelphia's Cap Anson, and recognizes that the other owners are intending to expel Chicago from the National Association.

Hulbert successfully sways the owners, promising greater profits and greater respect for the game. The National League is formed, with rules targeting well-heeled Victorian sports fans rather than the riffraff that normally populates the stands (no beer or whiskey allowed, no Sunday games, no drunkenness or swearing), in order to extract a fifty cents admission fee instead of a quarter.

To win the support of the four eastern clubs Hulbert needs to tip the votes in his favor, he nominates William Bulkeley of Hartfort as the league's first president and Washington's Nick Young as secretary.

February 12 - Al Spalding moves from Rockford, Illinois, to Chicago with his brother, J. Walter, and opens "a large emporium where they will sell all kinds of baseball goods." The Spalding sporting goods company is launched.

April 24 - Spalding, who has been named manager, pitches the National League's first shutout, a 4-0 whitewashing at Louisville on Opening Day.

April 27 - Spalding tosses another shutout over the Grays, beating them 10-0.

May 2 - Second baseman Ross Barnes hits the first National League home run, an inside-the-park dinger off Cincinnati's Cherokee Fisher. Barnes also triples, singles, and steals two bases, scoring four runs.

May 5 - The White Stockings lose their first game, 1-0, to George Bradley of St. Louis. Spalding takes the loss.

WORTH NOTING - Outfielder Bob Addy, who played for the White Stockings in 1876, is credited with being the first player to slide into a base, which he did during a game in 1866 while playing for the amateur Rockford, Illinois club.

May 30 - In Boston, 14,000 pack South End Grounds to welcome four former Reds, now members of the White Stockings, for the first time since they defected. The crowd is called "the largest that ever attended a baseball match in the world." Chicago triumphs, 5-1.

June 27 - The Athletics score four runs in the ninth to pull out a 14-13 victory over the White Stockings at Jefferson Street Grounds in Philadelphia. Former White Stocking Davy Force, the Athletics' shortstop, goes 6-for-6 against Spalding.

July 8 - The Boston Herald publishes the mid-season batting averages, showing that Ross Barnes leads the way with 2.1 hits per game.

July 22 - Cal McVey goes 6-for-7 in a 30-7 drubbing of Louisville. The Whites tally 31 hits off starter John Ryan (and Ryan contributes 10 wild pitches) and score a runner in every inning but the second. It's the first of 40 20-run games for the Chicago franchise, a major league record).

July 25 - Cal McVey goes 6-for-7 for the second consecutive day. It gives him a record 15 hits in three games. The offensive explosion helps the White Stockings defeat Cincinnati 23-3.

July 27 - Not to be outdone, Ross Barnes

WORTH QUOTING - "Baseball gives... a growing boy self-poise and self-relieance. Baseball is a man maker."
-Albert Goodwill Spalding

goes 6-for-6 during a 17-3 thrashing of Cincinnati. The White Stockings have scored 88 runs in their last four games.

August 4 - Losing by a wide margin with rain threatening in the fifth, Louisville begins to stall. They make one error after another until the umpire decides to forfeit the game to Chicago. The league will later rule the contest a "no game."

September 11 - Athletics president G.W. Thompson informs Hulbert that the Athletics cannot afford to make their final western trip, suggesting that Chicago and St. Louis travel to Philadelphia instead. Hulbert declines.

The Athletics and New York Mutuals, who also could not finish the season, are expelled unanimously.

September 26 - The White Stockings clinch the National League's first pennant, beating Hartford 7-6. McVey, Spalding's backup pitcher, gets the victory.

December 10 - William Hulbert is elected National League president.

1877

Principle Owner and President: William Hulbert; **Manager:** Al Spalding; **Ballpark:** 23rd Street Grounds; **Attendance:** 46,454; **Finish:** 5th (26-33); **Recap:** Despite retaining its championship lineup, the White Stockings do not repeat in 1877, mostly because of Ross Barnes's demise as an offensive force due to illness and the elimination of the fair-foul hit, and because Spalding decides he's had enough of pitching and relegates himself to first base, leaving the mound chores to washed-up St. Louis veteran George Bradley. The White Stockings do not hit a single home run in 1877.

P	PLAYER	R	HR	RBI	SB	AVE
1B	Al Spalding	29	0	35	-	.256
2B	Ross Barnes	16	0	5	-	.272
SS	John Peters	45	0	41	-	.317
3B	Cap Anson	52	0	32	-	.337
RF	Paul Hines	44	0	23	-	.280
CF	Dave Eggler	20	0	20	-	.265
LF	John Glenn	31	0	20	-	.228
C	Cal McVey	58	0	36	-	.368
P	George Bradley	31	0	12	-	.243
UT	Harry Smith	7	0	3	-	.202
OF	Jimmy Hallinan	17	0	11	-	.281
OF	Charlie Eden	9	0	5	-	.218
OF	Charlie Waitt	2	0	2	-	.098
P	Laurie Reis	3	0	1	-	.125

T	PITCHER	W-L	SV	SO	SH	ERA
R	George Bradley	18-23	0	59	2	3.31
R	Cal McVey	4-8	2	20	0	4.50
R	Laurie Reis	3-1	0	11	1	0.75
R	Al Spalding	1-0	1	2	0	3.27
R	Dave Rowe	0-1	0	0	0	18.00

January 15 - Al Spalding officially proposes a "League Alliance" in which independent teams would affiliate with the National League and the National League would honor their contracts. Spalding also proposes that all contracts signed after March 15 would be honored.

May 8 - Despite the elimination of the "fair foul hit" rule, Ross Barnes goes 2-for-4 in Chicago's opener. The rule, which Barnes exploited in 1876 to pad a .429 average, allowed for a ball that struck the infield in fair territory but bounced foul was still ruled a hit.

The new rule states that a ball striking first in fair territory and then moving into foul ground is declared foul. This new rule will change the game dramatically.

May 12 - The White Stockings commit 21 errors, including passed balls and wild pitches, losing to Boston 18-9.

May 17 - The new "lively ball", produced by Spalding's sporting goods company, is officially adopted by the National League.

June 5 - Spalding makes his last start as a pitcher, failing to retire any of the five Cincinnati batters he faces. Bob Addy, Spalding's ex-teammate at Hartford, knocks him out of the box - literally - with a line drive to the chest.

July 13 - George Bradley, acquired from St. Louis over the winter, steps aside after pitching in 88 consecutive games. Cal McVey makes the start for Chicago. Bradley plays third base. Spalding plays first base and Cap Anson, normally the third baseman, catches. Chicago beats Hartford 6-3.

July 20 - William Hulbert sends slumping outfielder Paul Hines a memo threatening him with a release for poor play.

August 6 - The new National League rule calling for the home team to submit three names of approved local men as a possible umpire is tested in Louisville today; McVey reaches into a hat before the White Stockings' game with the Grays and pulls out a slip with Dan Devinney's name on it. Devinney, who on August 1 charged St. Louis manager George McManus with trying to bribe him, is deemed undesirable. McVey reaches into the hat again and finds that all three slips have Devinney's name on it.

The White Stockings demand a new umpire, then snap the Grays' six-game winning streak by a score of 7-2.

August 7 - Chicago scores 13 runs in the second inning on their way to a 21-7 pounding of Cincinnati. The rally still stands for runs scored in the second inning.

September 9 - Frank Chance is born in Fresno, California.

November 17 - The White Stockings lease Lake Front Park, located downtown at the corner of Michigan Avenue and Randolph Street. It's the same site that was used by the White Stockings'National Association club in 1871 before the Great Chicago Fire.

December 6 - Hulbert is re-elected president of the NL during this season's Winter Meetings. Hartford is expelled from the league.

1878

Principle Owner and President: William Hulbert; **Manager:** Bob Ferguson; **Ballpark:** Lake Front Park; **Attendance:** 58,691; **Finish:** Fourth (30-30); **Recap:** Cal McVey's defection to Cincinnati and a cast of mediocre newcomers plunge the White Stockings to the bottom of the pack in 1878. Despite a good season by first baseman Joe Start, who leads the league in hits with 100, the Chicagoes finish fourth.

P	PLAYER	R	HR	RBI	SB	AVE
1B	Joe Start	58	1	27	-	.351
2B	Bill McClellan	26	0	29	-	.224
SS	Bob Ferguson	44	0	39	-	.351
3B	Frank Hankinson	38	1	27	-	.267
RF	John Cassidy	33	0	29	-	.266
CF	Jack Remsen	32	1	19	-	.232
LF	Cap Anson	55	0	40	-	.341
C	Bill Harbidge	32	0	37	-	.296
P	Terry Larkin	33	0	32	-	.288

WORTH QUOTING - "The genius of our institutions is democratic; Base Ball is a democratic game."

-Albert Goodwill Spalding

Cap Anson

P	Player	R	HR	RBI	SB	AVE
UT	Jim Hallinan	14	0	2	-	.284
C	Phil Powers	2	0	2	-	.161
P	Laurie Reis	2	0	0	-	.150
C	Bill Traffley	1	0	1	-	.111
OF	Bill Sullivan	1	0	0	-	.167

T	Pitcher	W-L	SV	SO	SH	ERA
R	Terry Larkin	29-26	0	163	1	2.24
R	Laurie Reis	1-3	0	8	0	3.25
R	Frank Harkinson	0-1	0	4	0	6.00

April 20 - New Lake Front Park is christened with a practice game vs. a local nine. The White Stockings will play here for eight years.

May 6 - Chicago beats Indianapolis 3-1, making just one error and rolling four double plays.

June 12 - The White Stockings beat Milwaukee 1-0; right fielder John Cassidy throws out a runner at home for a double play in the bottom of the 10th to preserve the victory.

August 31 - Al Spalding comes out of retirement to play second base in a game vs. Boston. He goes 2-for-4 in a 5-2 White Stockings loss.

September2 - The White Stockings play a benefit game in Chicago for yellow fever victims in Memphis, Tennessee. The game raises $682.

September 4 - Providence righthander John Montgomery Ward shuts Chicago out for the second straight game, hurling a 9-0 four-hitter.

1879

Principle Owner and President: William Hulbert; **Manager:** Cap Anson (41-21) / Silver Flint (5-12); **Ballpark:** Lake Front Park; **Attendance:** 67,687; **Finish:** Fourth (46-33); **Recap:** Cap Anson takes over as manager and finds some welcome roster additions, including outfielder Abner Dalrymple, catcher Silver Flint and third baseman Ned Williamson. Although initially predicting a pennant for itself, the White Stockings finish fourth due in part to a kidney ailment that sidelines Anson for half the season and a line drive off the head of ace pitcher Terry Larkin that ends his career.

P	Player	R	HR	RBI	SB	AVE
1B	Cap Anson	40	0	34	-	.217
2B	Joe Quest	38	0	22	-	.207
SS	John Peters	45	1	31	-	.245
3B	Ned Williamson	66	1	36	-	.294
RF	Orator Shafffer	53	0	35	-	.304
CF	George Gore	43	0	32	-	.263
LF	Abner Dalrymple	47	0	23	-	.291
C	Silver Flint	46	1	41	-	.284
P	Terry Larkin	26	0	18	-	.219
P	Frank Hankinson	14	0	8	-	.181
UT	Jack Remsen	14	0	8	-	.217
IF	Lew Brown	2	0	3	-	.286
OF	Bill Harbidge	2	0	1	-	.111
IF	John Stedronsky	1	0	0	-	.083

T	PITCHER	W-L	SV	SO	SH	ERA
R	Terry Larkin	31-23	0	142	4	2.44
R	Frank Hankinson	15-10	0	69	2	2.50

June 2 - The White Stockings are no-hit in seven innings by J.Lee Richmond, Brown University baseball star, who is making his pro debut with the Worcester Ruby Legs, a minor league team. Worcester wins 11-0. Since there are currently no rules prohibiting college athletes to play for professional teams, Brown returns to school and pitches the Bears past Yale 3-2 for the college championship.

June 14 - Catcher Silver Flint hits the ball over the left field fence in the ninth inning of a game at Putnam Grounds in Troy, New York. He takes only three bases because he wants the Trojan catcher to play close behind the next batter, giving the hitter a better chance. Troy wins anyway, 10-9.

August 13 - The Cincinnati Reds refuse to play a makeup game with the White Stockings because of poor field conditions after a downpour. The visiting Chicagoes appoint one of their traveling party as umpire, who declares a 9-0 forfeit victory for the White Stockings. The victory will be held up during the Winter Meetings in December.

August 15 - Cap Anson plays his final game of the year, deciding to sit out the rest of the season to recuperate from a kidney ailment. Chicago, who has been in first place, will slip to fourth due to Anson's sickness and pitcher Terry Larkin's sore arm.

September 9 - Boston's Tommy Bond shuts out Chicago 10-0 for his 11th whitewash of the season. It's the third year in a row that Bond has led the league in shutouts.

October 2 - Chicago violates the league's new Reserve Clause, signing Troy's Fred Goldsmith. The league approved the new rule, allowing each club to reserve five players with whom the other clubs cannot negotiate, on September 30.

October 16 - Chicago signs star Mike "King" Kelly, who is on a California tour with the White Stockings, for next season. Kelly's present club, the Cincinnati Reds, are disbanding.

1880

Principle Owner and President: William Hulbert; **Manager:** Cap Anson; **Ballpark:** Lake Front Park; **Attendance:** 66,708; **Finish:** First (67-17); **Recap:** The White Stockings win the pennant with the highest winning percentage (.798) in major league history. The emergence of King Kelly, rookie shortstop Tom Burns and pitchers Larry Corcoran and Fred Goldsmith augments the stellar contributions of George Gore, Abner Dalrymple, and Cap Anson.

P	PLAYER	R	HR	RBI	SB	AVE
1B	Cap Anson	54	1	74	-	.337
2B	Joe Quest	37	0	27	-	.237
SS	Tom Burns	47	0	43	-	.309
3B	Ned Williamson	65	0	31	-	.251
RF	King Kelly	72	1	60	-	.291
CF	George Gore	70	2	47	-	.360
LF	Abner Dalrymple	91	0	36	-	.330
C	Silver Flint	30	0	17	-	.162
P	Larry Corcoran	41	0	25	-	.231
P	Fred Goldsmith	27	0	15	-	.261
UT	Tommy Beals	4	0	3	-	.152
OF	Tom Poorman	3	0	0	-	.200
P	Charlie Guth	0	0	0	-	.250

T	PITCHER	W-L	SV	SO	SH	ERA
B	Larry Corcoran	43-14	2	268	4	1.95
R	Fred Goldsmith	21-3	1	90	4	1.75
R	Tom Poorman	2-0	0	0	0	2.40
-	Charlie Guth	1-0	0	7	0	5.00
R	King Kelly	0-0	0	1	0	0.00
R	Tom Burns	0-0	0	1	0	0.00

May 1 - On Opening Day in Cincinnati, the White Stockings spoil the official opening of new Bank Street Grounds by beating the Reds 4-3 with two runs in the bottom of the ninth. It's the first time a professional game has ended in "sudden death" as the old rules required that the full inning be played in its entirety even if the team batting was ahead. The rule that the visiting team bats last still applies.

May 7 - Center fielder George Gore goes 6-for-6 with five runs scored in a 20-7 Chicago victory over Cincinnati.

May 20 - Manager Cap Anson sets up baseball's first pitching rotation, using Larry Corcoran and Fred Goldsmith in alternate games to keep them rested.

May 27 - Goldsmith shuts out the Buffalo Bisons on two hits, winning 11-0. It's Chicago's 13th straight win, a new NL record.

May 29 - Boston ends Chicago's winning streak, beating them 11-10. Legendary star George Wright, who has jumped from Providence illegally, scores two runs. Wright will not play again for Boston because of protests from the Grays, who have him "reserved."

June 4 - Corcoran and Monte Ward of the Grays battle to a 1-1 tie after 16 innings; the game is called for darkness. The 16-inning affair will be the longest in NL history until August 17, 1882, when Ward will beat Detroit 1-0 in 18 frames.

June 26 - Gore, Corcoran, and Abner Dalrymple, all lefthanded batters, cross over and bat righthanded against lefty Lee Richmond of Worcester. Each get a hit and Chicago wins 4-0.

July 8 - The White Stockings win their 21st game in a row, beating Providence 5-4. The streak will be beaten just once, by the New York Giants in 1916. Chicago is currently 35-3, outdistancing Providence, who is 21-16.

July 10 -The Cleveland Blues snap Chicago's winning streak, 1-0. The game is scoreless until the bottom of the ninth, when shortstop Jack Glasscock walks and second baseman Fred Dunlap rips a home run to center field. A post-game debate ensues as to whether Dunlap is awarded a home run or whether the game ends when Glasscock touches the plate under the sudden-death rule.

July 27 - Joe Tinker is born in Muscotah, Kansas.

August 12 - The White Stockings suffer their first defeat at Lake Front Park after 21 straight victories, losing to Providence 6-4. Chicago's last home defeat was on August 25, 1879.

August 19 - Larry Corcoran hurls a 6-0 no-hitter vs. Boston. It's Corcoran's third start in three days.

September 30 - Chicago closes the season by winning for the 67th time against just 17 defeats, establishing a record-setting winning percentage (.798).

WORTH QUOTING - "Professional baseball is on the wane. Salaries must come down or the interest of the public must be increased in some way. If one or the other does not happen, bankruptcy stares every team in the face."

-Albert Goodwill Spalding, 1881

1881

Principle Owner and President: William Hulbert; **Manager:** Cap Anson; **Ballpark:** Lake Front Park; **Attendance:** 82,000; **Finish:** First (56-28); **Recap:** Although the White Stockings don't come close to their record-setting pace of 1880, they win the pennant again thanks to the hot hitting of Cap Anson, who leads the league in hits (137), RBI (82) and average (.399) and the sensational pitching of Corcoran, who paces the NLin wins (31).

P	Player	R	HR	RBI	SB	AVE
1B	Cap Anson	67	1	82	-	.399
2B	Joe Quest	35	1	26	-	.246
SS	Tom Burns	41	4	42	-	278
3B	Ned Williamson	56	1	48	-	.268
RF	King Kelly	84	2	55	-	.323
CF	George Gore	86	1	44	-	.298
LF	Abner Dalrymple	72	1	37	-	.323
C	Silver Flint	46	1	34	-	.310
P	Larry Corcoran	25	0	9	-	.222
P	Fred Goldsmith	24	0	16	-	.241
OF	Hugh Nicol	13	0	7	-	.204
IF	Andy Piercy	1	0	0	-	.250

T	Pitcher	W-L	SV	SO	SH	ERA
B	Larry Corcoran	31-14	0	150	4	2.31
R	Fred Goldsmith	24-13	0	76	5	2.59
R	Ned Williamson	1-1	0	2	0	2.00

March 8 - During the NLSpring Meetings, a newspaper reporter gets the various owners to predict the winner for the coming season. Chicago is the consensus choice, claiming five votes.

May 14 - During a game with the Worcester Ruby Legs at Lake Front Park, Tommy Burns slaps a liner that rolls up onto the clubhouse platform in the outfield, where owner William Hulbert's dog is sleeping. Burns circles the bases as Worcester outfielder Buttercup Dickerson fights the dog for the ball.

May 20 - King Kelly solidifies his reputation as a cheater by cutting third base by almost 30 feet to score from second on a groundout in a 5-4 Chicago win over Boston. The umpire misses the cheat.

WORTH QUOTING - "We always wore the best uniforms that money could get, Spalding saw to that. We had big wide trousers, tight-fitting jerseys, with the arms cut out clear to the shoulder, and every man had on a different cap. We wore silk stockings. When we marched on a field with our big six-footers out in front it used to be a case of 'eat 'em up, Jake.' We had most of 'em whipped before we threw a ball. They were scared to death."

-King Kelly, on the Chicago White Stockings of 1882

June 25 - George Gore steals seven bases in a White Stockings win vs. Providence. Gore steals second five times and third twice, scoring five times in five at-bats. Billy Hamilton will tie this record on August 31, 1894.

June 30 - The Whites eke out an ugly 4-1 win over Troy. There are many delays and 217 called balls in the game, which still takes only 2 1/2 hours to play.

July 21 - Johnny Evers is born in Troy, New York.

August 11 - Chicago pummels the new Detroit Wolverines 17-0. Fred Goldsmith is the victor in the league's most lopsided game of the season.

August 23 - Larry Corcoran, who is monitoring the Recreation Park turnstile count, is called into the game after Goldsmith is knocked from the box in the third inning. Corcoran hurls nine innings as the White Stockings take the game in twelve, 8-6.

WORTH NOTING - In 1882, the National League put into play William Hulbert's idea of color-coordinating players based upon their position. Under the new system, every player on every team wore white pants and white ties, with each team being distinguished by different-colored socks. Cap and shirt colors were determined by position: light blue for pitchers, scarlet for catchers, scarlet and white for first baseman, orange and black for second basemen, maroon for shortstops, blue and white for third basemen, red and black for center fielders, white for left fielders, and gray for right fielders. Hulbert was probably under pressure from Al Spalding, whose sporting goods company was responsible for creating the uniforms. The scheme was scrapped after a year.

September16 - Chicago beats Boston 4-0, clinching another pennant.

October 1 - The independent New York Metropolitans beat the NL-Champion White Stockings 7-4 in a postseason exhibition. The Mets are the only "minor league" team to have won more than one game vs. a NL club. Obviously campaigning for a NL berth, they'll finish 18-43 vs. league competition.

1882

Principle Owner and President: Al Spalding; **Manager:** Cap Anson; **Ballpark:** Lake Front Park; **Attendance:** 125,452; **Finish:** First (55-29); **Recap:** Trailing Providence by three games with 16 to go, Anson benches second right fielder Hugh Nicol, moves King Kelly to short, Tom Burns to second, and Joe Quest to right, and the team responds with a 15-1 streak and another pennant.

P	PLAYER	R	HR	RBI	SB	AVE
1B	Cap Anson	69	1	83	-	.362
2B	Tom Burns	55	0	48	-	.248
SS	King Kelly	81	1	55	-	.305
3B	Ned Williamson	66	3	60	-	.282
RF	Hugh Nicol	19	1	16	-	.199
CF	George Gore	99	3	51	-	.319
LF	Abner Dalrymple	96	1	36	-	.295
C	Silver Flint	48	4	44	-	.251
P	Fred Goldsmith	23	0	19	-	.230
P	Larry Corcoran	23	1	24	-	.207
IF	Joe Quest	24	0	15	-	.201
IF	Milt Scott	1	0	0	-	.400

T	PITCHER	W-L	SV	SO	SH	ERA
R	Fred Goldsmith	28-17	0	109	4	2.42
B	Larry Corcoran	27-12	0	170	3	1.95
R	Ned Williamson	0-0	0	0	0	6.00

April 10 - Chicago president William Hulbert dies of a heart attack in Chicago. A.H. Soden, president of the Boston club, is appointed by the National League as a temporary replacement. Al Spalding takes over the White Stockings.

May 5 - Cap Anson is called out at first for walking back to the base after a foul ball, instead of running, as the rule specifies. The rule will be amended after the season.

May 10 - Around 1,000 fans watch the Chicago home opener for free from a nearby viaduct. Chicago officials will attempt to correct this "unfair opportunity to beat the gate" by installing a high fence.

July 8 -The White Stockings move into first place with a 3-0 victory vs. Troy. It's Chicago's ninth win in a row.

July 24 - The Whites beat Cleveland 35-4, setting a NL record for runs scored. Chicago will best its own record on June 29, 1897, racking up 36 against Louisville.

September 9 - The White Stockings defeat Troy 24-1 in eight innings. Five Chicago players get four hits apiece.

September 14 - Chicago leapfrogs Providence into first place by beating them 6-2. The White Stockings will retain their hold on the league lead for the rest of the season.

September 20 - Larry Corcoran hurls his second career no-hitter, beating Worcester 5-0. The Ruby Legs will be out of the NL by the end of the year.

September 30 - The day after the pennant is clinched, the White Stockings install 16-year-old Milton Scott at first base in a game against Buffalo. Scott goes 2-for-5 in Chicago's 6-5 victory at Lakefront Park. Scott is the youngest player ever to suit up for Chicago.

October 6 - The White Stockings lose the first game in the first-ever post-season championship series between two different professional leagues, a 4-0 decision to the new American Association's Cincinnati Red Stockings.

October 7 - Chicago returns the favor, shutting out Cincinnati 2-0. After the game, Cincinnati cancels the rest of the season to avoid being expelled by the league.

1883

Principle Owner and President: Al Spalding; **Manager:** Cap Anson; **Ballpark:** Lake Front Park; **Attendance:** 124,880; **Finish:** Second (59-39); **Recap:** In contrast to the chaos caused by the defection of National Leaguers to the new American Association, the White Stockings manage to keep their entire roster except for outfielder Hugh Nicol. King Kelly returns to right field and Tom Burns to shortstop, making way for new second baseman Fred Pfeffer. Chicago starts slowly, losing four of its first six games with Detroit, but rights itself and finishes a close second, four games behind Boston.

P	PLAYER	R	HR	RBI	SB	AVE
1B	Cap Anson	70	0	68	-	.308
2B	Fred Pfeffer	41	1	45	-	.235
SS	Tom Burns	69	2	67	-	.294
3B	Ned Williamson	49	2	59	-	.276
RF	King Kelly	92	3	61	-	.255
CF	George Gore	105	2	52	-	.334
LF	Abner Dalrymple	78	2	37	-	.298
C	Silver Flint	57	0	32	-	.265
P	Larry Corcoran	40	0	25	-	.209
P	Fred Goldsmith	38	1	16	-	.221
OF	Billy Sunday	6	0	5	-	.241

T	PITCHER	W-L	SV	SO	SH	ERA
B	Larry Corcoran	34-20	0	216	3	2.49
R	Fred Goldsmith	25-19	0	82	2	3.15
R	Cap Anson	0-0	1	0	0	0.00
R	Ned Williamson	0-0	0	1	0	9.00
R	King Kelly	0-0	0	0	0	0.00

April 24 - Terry Larkin, who pitched for the White Stockings in 1878-79, shoots his wife and a policeman and attempts to take his own life. Larkin, suffering from depression, fails in the attempt and tries again the next day. He will survive and play for several teams next year before retiring. Larkin won 29 games for the Whites in '78 and 31 in '79.

May 5 - Spectacular new Lake Front Park (Version II) is inaugurated with a 3-2 loss to Detroit. The new park features 41 uniformed attendants. Detroit scores with two out in the bottom of the ninth to take the game.

May 22 - Future evangelist Billy Sunday goes 0-for-4 in his major league debut, fanning four times.

May 30 - The Whites thump the Phillies 15-8 in Game 1 and 22-4 in Game 2 of a doubleheader in Philadelphia.

June 2 - Chicago loses an ugly 22-7 affair to New York, committing 20 errors. The

Gothams commit 10. Only one player on each team plays error-free.

July 3 - The White Stockings defeat the Buffalo Bisons 31-7. Cap Anson and Abner Dalrymple lead the way with five hits apiece and Dalrymple scores five times. Each Chicago player gets a hit and scores at least three times. The Whites total 14 doubles, a major league record.

September 6 - Chicago scores a record 18 runs in the seventh inning of a 26-6 victory vs. Detroit. In the inning shortstop Tom Burns goes 3-for-3 with two doubles and a homer to score three runs, all records. Burns, Fred Pfeffer, and Ned Williamson become the first players to tally three hits in one inning, setting another record. Burns and Williamson score three times in the seventh, setting yet another mark. Nine different players score three runs or more in the contest. The White Stockings outscore the Wolverines 53-8 in the three game series.

September 10 - The White Stockings' winning streak is snapped at 11 by Boston by a a score of 4-2.

September 11 - Botson moves into first place for good by beating Chicago 3-2.

1884

Principle Owner and President: Al Spalding; **Manager:** Cap Anson; **Ballpark:** Lake Front Park; **Attendance:** 87,667; **Finish:** T-Fourth (62-50); **Recap:** Prior to the 1884 season, Al Spalding talks the league into changing the ground rule at Lake Front Park that defines a ball hit over what are the shortest left and right field fences in the majors, 196 and 180 feet, as doubles. With the drives now ruled as home runs, the White Stockings produce 142 round-trippers - the most until the 1927 Yankees come along. Ned Williamson, who hit two in 1883, leads the NL with 27. Despite the asterisk-worthy show of power, the Whites finish fourth.

P	PLAYER	R	HR	RBI	SB	AVE
1B	Cap Anson	108	21	102	-	.335
2B	Fred Pfeffer	105	25	101	-	.289
SS	Tom Burns	54	7	44	-	.245
3B	Ned Williamson	84	27	84	-	.278
RF	King Kelly	120	13	95	-	.354
CF	George Gore	104	5	34	-	.318
LF	Abner Dalrymple	111	22	69	-	.309
C	Silver Flint	35	9	45	-	.204
P	Larry Corcoran	43	1	19	-	.243
OF	Billy Sunday	25	4	28	-	.222
P	John Clarkson	16	3	17	-	.262
IF	Walt Kinzie	4	2	8	-	.159
P	Fred Goldsmith	11	2	6	-	.136
P	Joe Brown	6	0	3	-	.213

T	PITCHER	W-L	SV	SO	SH	ERA
B	Larry Corcoran	35-23	0	272	7	2.40
R	Fred Goldsmith	9-11	0	34	1	4.26
R	John Clarkson	10-3	0	102	0	2.14
-	Joe Brown	4-2	0	27	0	4.68
--	Tom Lee	1-4	0	14	0	3.77

January 4 - Larry Corcoran, who earlier had jumped to the fledgling Union Association, re-signs with the White Stockings.

May 23 - Corcoran tosses a one-hitter, beating Cleveland 5-0.

May 29 - The White Stockings take advantage of a new rule declaring that balls hit over Lake Front Park's short right field fence are to be called home runs (rather than doubles, as they had been ruled), five players hit homers on Opening Day against the Detroit Wolverines. Chicago will hit 142 round-trippers during the season, setting a record that will hold until the 1927 New York Yankees hit158.

May 30 - In the nightcap of a doubleheader vs. Detroit, third baseman Ned Williamson swats a record three home runs in a 12-2 victory. Williamson will hit 27 this year, a major league record until Babe Ruth hits 29 for the Boston Red Sox in 1919.

June - Cap Anson protests the appearance of African-American Moses Fleetwood Walker in the lineup during and exhibition match vs. the American Association's Toledo Blue Stockings.

Toledo manager Charlie Morton threatens that there will be no game without Walker, even though Walker is nursing a sore hand. Anson decides to play the game instead of losing the team's cut of the gate receipts. Despite a .263 batting average, Walker will be released two weeks later.

June 9 - Billy Sunday homers for the third time in three games. He'll hit four all year.

June 16 - Ambidextrous Corcoran pitches right-handed and left-handed during a 20-9 loss to Buffalo.

June 24 - A Chicago court rules that Lake Front Park may continued to be used for the rest of the season even though it illegally blocks the lake view.

June 27 - Corcoran snaps the Providence Grays' 10-game winning streak with a 6-0 no-hitter. It's Corcoran's third no-hitter.

June 30 - King Kelly homers with two outs in the bottom of the ninth to defeat Providence 5-4.

July 4 - Tommy Burns hits two home runs in a 22-3 victory over the Phillies at Lake Front Park.

August 5 - Deaf-mute pitcher Thomas Lynch's major league debut goes well until the eighth inning, when his arm gives out. First baseman Cap Anson switches positions with Lynch when the umpire refuses to let him leave the game. Anson surrenders five runs and loses the game to Cleveland 8-5. Lynch will never play another game.

August 6 - Anson smacks three homers during a 13-4 victory over Cleveland. Cap has five homers in two games, a major league record.

September 16 - Fred Pfeffer collects five hits and George Gore homers twice in a 17-0 beating of Boston at Lake Front Park.

1885

Principle Owner and President: Al Spalding; **Manager:** Cap Anson; **Ballpark:** West Side Park; **Attendance:** 117,519; **Finish:** First (87-25); **Recap:** The White Stockings move into brand new West Side Park, returning to the pitch-and-run game that won them so many pennants in the past. And indeed they do, finishing two lengths in front of New York.

Four Whites score 100 or more runs and John Clarkson leads the league in innings pitched (623), complete games (68), wins (53), strikeouts (308) and shutouts (10). Clarkson's 53 wins are the second-highest total in history. It's the first of eight straight seasons with at least 25 victories for the future Hall of Famer.

P	PLAYER	R	HR	RBI	SB	AVE
1B	Cap Anson	100	7	108	-	.310
2B	Fred Pfeffer	90	5	73	-	.241
SS	Tom Burns	82	7	71	-	.272
3B	Ned Williamson	87	3	65	-	.238
RF	King Kelly	124	9	75	-	.288
CF	George Gore	115	5	57	-	.313
LF	Abner Dalrymple	109	11	61	-	.274
C	Silver Flint	27	1	17	-	.209
P	John Clarkson	34	4	32	-	.216
OF	Billy Sunday	36	2	20	-	.256
P	Jim McCormick	13	0	16	-	.223
UT	Sy Sutcliffe	5	0	4	-	.186

1 8 8 5

T	Pitcher	W-L	SV	SO	SH	ERA
R	John Clarkson	53-16	0	308	10	1.85
R	Jim McCormick	20-4	0	88	3	2.43
-	Ted Kennedy	7-2	0	36	0	3.43
B	Larry Corcoran	5-2	0	10	1	3.64
R	Fred Pfeffer	2-1	2	13	0	2.56

April 1 - Al Spalding's Sporting Goods store opens in New York.

June 6 - The White Stockings inaugurate their new ballpark, West Side Park, with a 9-2 victory over the expansion St. Louis Maroons. More than 10,000 fans are on hand.

June 20 - John Clarkson tosses a 5-0 one-hitter over the Buffalo Bisons.

June 25 - The White Stockings suffer their first loss at new West Side park, 2-0 to Philadelphia, after 18 straight victories.

July 1 - Shortstop Tommy Burns launches a 500-foot homer as Chicago whips Boston 24-10. The 34 combines runs are a season high.

July 9 - George Gore rips three doubles and two triples off Providence ace Old Hoss Radbourn.

July 11 - The White Stockings release pitcher Larry Corcoran. The slumping former ace averaged 34 wins the last five seasons.

July 27 - Clarkson hurls an 8-0 no-hitter vs. the Providence Grays.

August 1 - The New York Giants defeat the White Stockings 7-6 in front of 13,427 fans at the Polo Grounds. It's the largest paying crowd to date.

September 4 - Cap Anson homers in the sixth and seventh innings to lead the Whites to a 12-4 victory over Buffalo.

September 25 - The Providence Grays make 20 errors and the Whites tally 26 hits in a 21-3 Chicago victory. The game is played in Milwaukee.

September 29 - Over 10,000 fans pack West Side Park for today's game against the Giants. Since the ballpark has a capacity of only 6,000, a standing-room crowd rings the outfield and it is declared that if a ball is hit into the crowd it is ruled a ground-rule double.

October 12 - The periodical *Mirror of American Sports* offers a $1,000 prize for the winner of the "America's Championship Series," pitting the National League-Champion White Stockings against the St. Louis Browns, champions of the American Association.

October 14 - World Series Game 1

The first official post-season game in history gets underway on a Wednesday at windy West Side Park. Before the game a series of running and throwing contests are held for the amusement of the fans. Chicago third baseman Ned Williamson wins the long-throw contest with a toss of 400 feet four inches and second baseman Fred Pfeffer rounds the bases in just under 16 seconds, defeating five other contestants.

The contest begins at 3 o'clock. The Browns draw first blood: first baseman Charlie Comiskey walks in the second inning and scores on three consecutive errors.

St. Louis scores four more runs in the fourth on hits by second baseman Yank Robinson and third baseman Arlie Latham and three more errors. The Whites score a single run in the bottom of the frame.

In the eighth, George Gore reaches on a base on balls and scores on singles by King Kelly and Cap Anson. Pfeffer follows with a three-run homer, tying the game.

The game ends tied 5-5, called by umpire Dave Sullivan for darkness. The Browns and White Stockings will travel to St. Louis for Games 2, 3 and 4, then take the series on the road - barnstorming through Pittsburgh and Cincinnati.

The original agreement between team president Al Spalding and St. Louis owner Chris Von der Ahe calls for a 10-game series, with games in Baltimore, Philadelphia and Brooklyn, but cold weather will amend the schedule.

October 15 - World Series Game 2
Game 2 of the championship series is an ugly affair, to say the least. National League umpire Dave Sullivan, who officiated the first contest, is given prior approval by Charlie Comiskey to work Game 2 in St. Louis. It's an endorsement he'll live to regret.

The trouble starts in the first inning, when Sullivan calls King Kelly out on a steal attempt (he is clearly safe) and finds himself the victim of taunts and hoots from the St. Louis crowd - and jeers and profanity from the Chicago bench.

In the third, Sullivan declares Dave Foutz's hit down the right field line foul; the Browns'pitcher, thinking he's hit a sure two-bagger, is called back. The ruling is greeted by a loud chorus of boos from the Sportsman's Park grandstand (and not a few epithets from the Browns'dugout).

The arbiter then calls Sam Barkley out on a ball pitched well above his head. The home field fans respond with another round of hissing and cursing.

The worst is yet to come. In the sixth, Billy Sunday pinch hits with two outs for Chicago catcher Silver Flint, raps out a double to right and moves to third on a passed ball. King Kelly bounces a slow roller to shortstop Bill Gleason, who briefly bobbles the ball before gunning it to first. Sullivan calls the King safe; the White Stockings score the go-ahead run.

John Clarkson

The crowd is stunned. Comiskey decides he's had enough and demands that Anson agree to a new umpire. The Chicago manager refuses; a long quarrel follows.

While Anson and Comiskey argue, Sullivan walks over to the visitors' bench, puts his coat on, and sits down.

Even Missouri congressman John O'Neill gets into the act, stepping down from the grandstand and joining in the fracas.

Play is finally restored after Sullivan pulls his watch; O'Neill remains on the field. Kelly steals second and takes third on a wild pitch. A base hit by Anson knocks him in. Fred Pfeffer forces Anson and steals second base. Ned Williamson follows with a slow grounder up the first base line that kicks off the bag. Pfeffer comes in to score the go-ahead run; Williamson is ruled safe.

Comiskey, citing some vague American

WORTH QUOTING - "It depends on the length of the game."
-King Kelly, when asked if he drinks while playing baseball

Association rule, insists that Williamson's ball should be declared foul. Sullivan is indignant; another shouting match develops. Having had enough, Comiskey calls his men off the field.

A few of the spectators rush the field; one crowd gathers around Anson, a second follows Sullivan - escorted by policemen - off the field. The umpire will later rule the game a 9-0 forfeit to Chicago.

October 16 - World Series Game 3
Ill feelings disappear for the most part in Game 3. Managers Anson and Comiskey agree on the choice of Harry McCaffrey as umpire and he officiates the contest smoothly.

The Browns jump out to a 5-1 lead in the first inning thanks to an error, a walk, a wild pitch, a single, a double and a triple.

St. Louis scores two more runs in the bottom of the sixth and go on to win 7-4.

Starter Bob Caruthers yields just eight hits, fanning seven. The White Stockings commit 12 costly errors - mostly on fly balls.

October 17 - World Series Game 4
Chicago manager Cap Anson refuses to allow Harry McCaffrey to umpire today's game. The two sides settle on a local merchant, William Medart. By the end of the game, the impromptu arbiter will declare that he'll never again be put into such a position.

Game 4 is one of the most exciting at Sportsman's Park this season. The Browns take a 1-0 lead in the third when Latham bunts safely, steals second and scores on a sacrifice fly.

In the fifth, shortstop Tommy Burns singles, moves to second on a passed ball and takes third on a ground ball to Sam Barkley at second. Abner Dalrymple follows with a two-run homer, giving the White Stockings a 2-1 lead.

Arlie Latham opens the eighth by reaching first on an error. He takes second on a passed ball, third on a fielder's choice and scores on Bob Caruthers's single to left. When Latham crosses the plate with the tying run, the grandstand - quiet for most of the game - leaps to its feat with a loud cheer.

Gleason next rolls a grounder to short; Caruthers is out but Pfeffer's relay throw to first is over Anson's head and into the stands. Gleason streaks to third. Center fielder Curt Welch, next up, sends a hot shot down the third base line; Gleason tallies the go-ahead run.

Bad mojo in the ninth. Burns opens the inning with an infield single off the glove of second baseman Barkley. Pitcher Jim McCormick pops to Charlie Comiskey; the first baseman drops the ball. Burns sprints for third; Comiskey retrieves the ball and fakes a throw to third baseman Latham. McCormick is caught off first; Comiskey tags him out.

McCormick, however, refuses to remove himself from first base, insisting he's safe. Billy Sunday bolts from the bench to argue the call. Medart calls the little outfielder a liar and orders him to shut up or be thrashed; Sunday is dragged off the field by his teammates.

At this point, McCormick, his face red with anger, jumps off the bag at first and makes a beeline for Medart. King Kelly heads him off; order is eventually restored. The Browns hold on for a 3-2 victory.

October 22 - World Series Game 5
Game 5 takes place on a windy, cold day in Pittsburgh. Both teams play apathetically;

the Browns commit seven errors and suffer a 9-2 loss. Only 500 chilly cranks witness the contest; the game is called in the seventh because of darkness.

Due to frigid temperatures, owners Chris Von der Ahe and Al Spalding agree to shorten the post-season schedule to a seven-game series ending in Cincinnati on October 24.

October 23 - World Series Game 6
Jim McCormick beats the Browns 9-2 on two hits in front of about 1,500 Cincinnatians. Game 6 isn't pretty - the two sides combine for 17 errors.

The game sets a major league record for a World Series played in most cities (4). It will be tied by St. Louis and New York in 1888.

October 24 - World Series Game 7
With John Clarkson running late, Cap Anson turns to Game Six starter Jim McCormick to work the final game.

The Browns batter the righthander for 13 hits, taking a 14-3 victory. The White Stockings make matters worse with a horrendous display of fielding, finishing the game with 17 miscues, three by McCormick himself.

The game is called in the eighth because of darkness. The series ends in a tie. Chris Von der Ahe, insisting that the Game 2 forfeit doesn't count, declares his club the champions and generously gives the full portion of the proceeds to his players.

Each club receives $500.

WORTH NOTING- The White Stockings' World Series opponents in 1885 are the St. Louis Browns, managed by **Charlie Comiskey**. The Browns finish with a 79-33 (.705) record, leading the American Association in complete games (111), shutouts (11), and ERA(2.44).

P	PLAYER	R	HR	RBI	SB	BA
1B	Charlie Comiskey	68	2	44	-	.256
2B	Sam Barkley	67	3	53	-	.268
SS	Bill Gleason	79	3	53	-	.252
3B	Arlie Latham	84	1	34	-	.206
RF	Hugh Nicol	59	0	45	-	.207
CF	Curt Welch	84	3	69	-	.271
LF	Tip O'Neill	44	3	38	-	.350
C	Doc Bushong	42	0	21	-	.267

T	PITCHER	W	L	SV	SH	ERA
R	Bob Caruthers	40	13	0	6	2.07
R	Dave Foutz	33	14	0	2	2.63
R	Jumbo McGinnis	6	6	0	3	3.38

1886

Principle Owner and President: Al Spalding; **Manager:** Cap Anson; **Ballpark:** West Side Park; **Attendance:** 142,438; **Finish:** First (90-34); **Recap:** With the league expanding to 124 games in 1886, Cap Anson brings in rookie Jocko Flynn to join John Clarkson and Jim McCormick in an unprecedented three-man rotation. The move pays off in yet another pennant, with King Kelly and Anson himself supplying most of the offense.

The White Stockings also agree to another challenge by the American Association's winners, the St. Louis Browns, losing the best-of-seven series in six hotly contested games.

P	PLAYER	R	HR	RBI	SB	AVE
1B	Cap Anson	117	10	147	29	.371
2B	Fred Pfeffer	88	7	95	30	.264
SS	Ned Williamson	69	6	58	13	.216
3B	Tom Burns	64	3	65	15	.276
RF	Jimmy Ryan	58	4	53	10	.306
CF	George Gore	150	6	63	23	.304
LF	Abner Dalrymple	62	3	26	16	.233
C	King Kelly	155	4	79	53	.388
P	John Clarkson	21	3	23	2	.233
C	Silver Flint	30	1	13	1	.202
P	Jocko Flynn	40	4	19	9	.200
P	Jim McCormick	17	2	21	1	.236
OF	Billy Sunday	16	0	6	10	.243
UT	Prunes Moolic	9	0	2	0	.143

T	PITCHER	W-L	SV	SO	SH	ERA
R	John Clarkson	36-17	0	313	3	2.41
R	Jim McCormick	31-11	0	172	2	2.82
R	Jocko Flynn	23-6	1	146	2	2.24
L	Jimmy Ryan	0-0	1	15	0	4.63
R	Ned Williamson	0-0	1	1	0	0.00

February 5 - Trial begins for a patent dispute between sporting goods companies Thayer & Wright and Al Spalding's A.G. Spalding & Brothers. Thayer is a Harvard pitcher who claims to have invented the catcher's mask that Spalding is selling in his stores; Wright is George Wright, Spalding's former teammate in Boston.The court will eventually rule in Thayer's favor, resulting in royalties for the former pitcher on masks sold by Spalding's company.

April 30 - Chicago beats the new Kansas City Cowboys at their home park, Association Park, by a score of 6-5 in 13 innings. It's the first National League game played in Kansas City. The game is recreated for fans back in Chicago on a board outside the Central Music Hall.

May 28 - Chicago scores 18 unearned runs in a 20-0 whitewashing of the Washington Nationals. It's the most one-sided shutout in team history.

June 22 - A livid Cap Anson is fined $110 by umpire John Gaffney, a record for one game, during a 5-4 Chicago loss in Detroit.

July 1 - Jim McCormick raises his record to 16-0 after beating New York 7-3.

July 20 - Cap Anson, Jimmy Ryan, and Abner Dalrymple homer in the third, the first time three players have homered in one inning, during a 20-4 drubbing of the St. Louis Maroons.

July 22 - A story is published that owner Al Spalding has hired detectives to shadow the Chicago players and report their drinking habits. Seven players are fined $25 apiece for breaking Spalding's drinking rule.

August 24 - Anson scores six runs in Chicago's 18-6 victory over Boston.

September 1 - Washington Nationals pitcher Cannonball Crane walks 14 and unleashes five wild pitches in a 15-2 loss to the White Stockings. He also makes an error.

September 10 - The Whites beat Detroit 14-8 despite a record 15 total bases by Wolverines first baseman Dan Brouthers. Big Dan knocks three homers, a double and a single.

September 25 - St. Louis Browns owner Chris Von der Ahe formally challenges Al Spalding to another World's Championship Series.

Although the pennant race is yet to be determined, Spalding accepts the challenge and proposes a nine-game series with the winning club getting the total gross of gate receipts. Von der Ahe will agree but proposes a best-of-seven series instead.

October 9 - The White Stockings officially clinch the pennant, beating Boston 12-3 on the final day of the season.

October 18 - World Series Game 1

A dark, stormy morning makes early prospects for a game today slim. Von der Ahe meets Spalding in his Chicago office to discuss the Browns owner's idea of a three-man umpiring staff for today's contest. It's decided that just one arbiter will be used today, as usual, but the concept will be tested tomorrow.

The thunder clouds pass by noon and at two o'clock the Browns climb into their carriages - fully dressed - in front of their hotel, the Tremont House, where a crowd of about 5,000 has gathered to catch a glimpse of the American Association champs.

The crowd hoots and hisses and throws vegetables at them as they make their way to West Side Park.

The Browns take fielding practice for about fifteen minutes before the White Stockings make their grand entrance - at the extreme eastern corner of the park - in single file with their bats on their shoulders like muskets and headed by a large brass band. The crowd - 6,000 strong - stands and roars with admiration. .

Association arbiter John McQuade, brought to Chicago by Von der Ahe, is agreed upon for the opener. Cheerful and always smiling, McQuade wins over the home crowd almost immediately.

Chicago takes a 2-0 lead in the first inning on an error by center fielder Curt Welch and an RBI single by second baseman Fred Pfeffer.

It's all that starter John Clarkson needs; the big righthander stifles the Browns on just five hits, winning 6-0.

The White Stockings put the game out of reach in the eighth, scoring three runs on two hits and two errors.

The ill feelings that sullied last year's Series seem to have disappeared. The only disagreeable show of feeling is on the part of the home crowd, who hoots and jeers at the Browns all day. The worst of it - oddly - is from the pressbox.

October 19 - World Series Game 2

The Browns turn the tables on Cap Anson's champion White Stockings, burying them 12-0 behind Bob Caruthers'one-hitter.

First baseman Charlie Comiskey's squad pounds Jim McCormick for 13 hits. Left fielder Tip O'Neill leads the charge with three safeties - a single and two home runs.

Caruthers, Comiskey and right fielder Dave Foutz collect two hits apiece. Caruthers misses two homers by inches, both caroming off the right field fence.

Von der Ahe's three-man umpire experiment is utilized during the game, with John Kelly - an ex-umpire now managing the Louisville Eclipse - joining John McQuaid and Joe Quest on the field. McQuaid is chosen by Chicago and Quest by St. Louis, with Kelly serving as "referee" in case of a deadlock decision.

The system is tested almost immediately. Browns third baseman Arlie Latham, opening the game with a walk, is sent diving back to first base on McCormick's pickoff attempt. Anson slaps Latham with the tag and McQuaid calls him out. Quest protests, saying that Latham is back in time. Kelly agrees.

The Browns pile up the runs largely without incident until the fifth when McCormick smacks Curt Welch to the ground as he's tallying the team's third run of the inning.

Welch leaps to his feet and lunges at

WORTH NOTING- The Cubs' World Series opponents in 1886 are the St. Louis Browns, managed by **Charlie Comiskey**. The Browns finish with a 93-46 (.669) record, leading the American Association in runs (944), hits (1365), average (.273), stolen bases (336), and ERA(2.49).

P	PLAYER	R	HR	RBI	SB	BA
1B	Charlie Comiskey	95	3	76	41	.254
2B	Yank Robinson	89	3	71	51	.274
SS	Bill Gleason	97	0	61	19	.269
3B	Arlie Latham	152	1	47	60	.301
RF	Hugh Nicol	52	0	19	38	.206
CF	Curt Welch	114	2	95	59	.281
LF	Tip O'Neill	106	3	107	9	.328
C	Doc Bushong	56	1	31	12	.223

T	PITCHER	W	L	SV	SH	ERA
R	Dave Foutz	41	16	1	11	2.11
R	Bob Caruthers	30	14	0	2	2.32
R	Nat Hudson	16	10	1	0	3.03

WORTH QUOTING - "We shall no longer endure the criticism of the respectable people because of drunkenness in the Chicago nine."
-Al Spalding, 1886

McCormick. King Kelly wrestles the outfielder away.

After the game, the Browns are wined and dined all over the Windy City; Von der Ahe spends most of the evening in his hotel room opening fan mail and reading congratulatory telegrams (more than 100 cables are sent to his room, chiefly from St. Louis but many from New York, Philadelphia, Boston, Pittsburgh, Cincinnati, and other cities).

October 20 - World Series Game 3

Caruthers, a native Chicagoan, is given permission to start today's game, too. But the righthander is ripped for 11 hits, including two homers, suffering an 11-4 loss. King Kelly and Tom Burns touch Caruthers for three hits apiece; George Gore and Jimmy Ryan collect two.

It's ugly from the very beginning. The White Stockings take a 2-0 lead in the first inning on four walks and a fielder's choice.

The Browns cut the lead to 2-1 in the second; catcher Doc Bushong drives in second baseman Yank Robinson with a single.

Kelly's towering two-run blast over the right field fence widens the lead to 4-1.

Parisian Bob's arm is shot by the sixth. A triple, single and error lead to two more runs. The Chicagoes score three more in the seventh on three hits and three errors and two in the eighth on a homer by George Gore.

The game is called in the eighth because of darkness.

October 21 - World Series Game 4

The White Stockings, apparently having learned nothing from Bob Caruthers' performance yesterday, announce that John Clarkson will take the pitcher's box for the second day in a row.

The contest begins at 3:00 before around 12,000 crazed Sportsman's Park cranks. The White Stockings open the game in familiar fashion, tallying three quick runs off a very shaky Dave Foutz.

The Browns score their first run in the second. Shortstop Bill Gleason and Charlie Comiskey reach on consecutive errors by second baseman Fred Pfeffer. Foutz drives in Gleason with a two-bagger to left.

St. Louis tallies another run in the third. Bob Caruthers reaches on third baseman Ned Williamson's fumble and scores on Tip O'Neill's triple.

The Browns go ahead in the bottom of the fifth. With one out, Bushong walks and Latham singles. Caruthers sends a fly to Ryan in right; Bushong advances to third. Clarkson walks O'Neill intentionally, loading the bases.

Clarkson gets two quick strikes on Gleason; the shortstop whacks the next pitch up the middle, scoring Bushong and Latham.

The crowd erupts with a roar - standing and clapping and yelling. Hats and umbrellas are tossed into the air; men embrace and women wave their handkerchiefs. The game is stalled for a few minutes until the cheering stops.

It erupts again as Comiskey drills a single into center, scoring O'Neill. Pool tickets, some of them worth over $100, are thrown to the Browns'manager.

The mood darkens in the top of the next inning, however, as the White Stockings tie the score.

But in the Browns' half of the frame, Pfeffer drops a pop-up with the bases loaded, allowing Bushong and Robinson to cross the plate, and Gleason lines another clutch single to center, scoring Caruthers.

Umpire Joe Quest makes an attempt to call the game after the inning but Anson protests, demanding another chance to bat. Foutz retires the White Stockings in order.

The delirious crowd - biggest of the year - charges onto the field to congratulate the home team; several players are carried around the field and out of the ballpark.

October 22 - World Series Game 5
The Series is tied at two wins apiece. Around 10,000 cranks file into Sportsman's Park to catch today's game. Chris Von der Ahe's successful three-man umpiring crew of Joe Quest, John McQuade and John Kelly is employed for Game 5.

With Jim McCormick and John Clarkson drained - and reserve righthander Jocko Flynn back in Chicago with a bum arm - Chicago president Al Spalding announces that a lefthander named Baldwin - who reportedly fanned 19 in a game for Duluth of the Northwestern League - has been signed to pitch Game 5 for Chicago.

Von der Ahe instantly files a grievance with the umpiring crew, arguing that Spalding had refused to let him engage Louisville lefty Toad Ramsey (38-27, 2.45) before the start of the Series. The umpires rule against Chicago; Anson is forced to put shortstop Ned Williamson in the box.

Williamson is wild in the first inning, allowing two runs. Anson replaces him with right fielder Jimmy Ryan. Ryan is battered for eight runs and nine hits over six innings. The Browns cruise to an easy 10-3 triumph.

In the bottom of the fourth - with the Browns leading 7-2 - the White Stockings' frustration becomes evident when first baseman Anson, bored with Arlie Latham's habit of fouling off pitch after pitch after pitch, positions himself beside the grandstand in order to catch one of the third baseman's pops.

Latham tries to foil the strategy by pushing a grounder through the vacancy at first base but second baseman Fred Pfeffer scoops up the ball and beats him to the bag.

Browns starter Nat Hudson is terrific, allowing just two infield singles and a double, fanning two. The Browns take a three-games-to-two Series advantage. One more win will give St. Louis the championship.

October 23 - World Series Game 6
A dark bank of thunderstorm clouds moves slowly over St. Louis at game time, threatening to postpone the match. Most of the 11,500 in attendance are equipped with umbrellas and raincoats.

Not a drop falls, however, and, at 2:15 p.m., local dignitary Clay Sexton joins Browns owner Chris Von der Ahe on the field, giving a pregame speech and presenting catcher Doc Bushong with a silver tea set donated by the Merchants'Exchange.

Grace Pierce is announced as the umpire - to a chorus of boos (Pierce has been criticized in the local press for favoring the visitor each time he's engaged to officiate a Browns game).

The White Stockings take a 1-0 lead in the top of the second on two singles and a passed ball. Fred Pfeffer leads off the fourth with a solo shot into the right field seats - on the very first pitch - to give Chicago a 2-0 advantage. John Clarkson, meanwhile, is brilliant; the Browns have yet to reach base.

Pfeffer is safe again in the sixth when his grounder sneaks through the right side of the infield; he hustles around to third when the ball gets by right fielder Dave Foutz. Williamson's sacrifice fly brings him in.

The game - and the series - unravels for Clarkson and the White Stockings in the eighth. Charlie Comiskey leads off with a base hit to right. Welch follows with an infield single. Comiskey moves to third on a passed ball and scores on a sacrifice fly. With on out, Bushong walks. Latham sends a ball over the head of left fielder Abner Dalrymple, scoring Welch and Bushong. The game is tied, 3-3.

Caruthers works out of a jam in the ninth, fanning left fielder Abner Dalrymple to retire the side and preserve the tie. The Browns are checked in the bottom of the inning, thanks in part to Jimmy Ryan's leaping grab of Tip O'Neill's line drive. The game moves into extra innings.

Caruthers, tiring but determined, retires Chicago in order in the top of the 10th.

Curt Welch opens the Browns' half of the frame with a single to center. Dave Foutz next bounces a ball just out of Clarkson's reach; shortstop Williamson fumbles it and everyone is safe.

Robinson moves the runners to second and third with a sacrifice. The Series-winning run stands at third with one out. Bushong is the batter.

Clarkson, now visibly shaken, delivers a wild pitch over catcher King Kelly's head. Kelly, mortified, is frozen; Welch gallops home, sliding in with the series-winning run.

The hysterical Sportsman's Park horde rushes the field. The players are lifted and carried around the ballpark.

About 8,000 remain on the field until the Browns reappear from the dressing room, offering trinkets, mugs of beer and winning pool ticket stubs.

The scene won't soon be forgotten - nor will the contest. Game 6 of the 1886 World Series, featuring Curt Welch's "$15,000 Slide (the players actually split about $14,000)," will become legendary - quite possibly the greatest moment in Browns history.

Von der Ahe, knowing the monetary benefits of a championship, sends a note to Al Spalding, inviting him to participate in a final exhibition series in Cincinnati. Spalding politely backs out.

WORTH QUOTING - "He was a whole-souled, genial fellow with a host of friends and but one enemy, that one being himself. Time and again, I have heard him say that he would never be broke, but money slipped through Mike's fingers as water slips through the meshes of a fisherman's net, and he was as fond of whiskey as any representative of the Emerald Isle."

-Cap Anson on King Kelly

1887

Principle Owner and President: Al Spalding; **Manager:** Cap Anson; **Ballpark:** West Side Park; **Attendance:** 217,070; **Finish:** Third (71-50); **Recap:** After the baffling post-season loss to the Browns in 1886, a mortified Al Spalding sells or releases King Kelly, George Gore and Jim McCormick, laying the blame of defeat squarely on their shoulders. As a result, the White Stockings start the season 11-15 and end May nine games behind Detroit. Chicago gains six games in July but falls back in August, finishing third.

With the departure of the three veterans and the addition of such young players as Tom Daly and Marty Sullivan, the Chicago press begins calling the team the "Colts."

P	Player	R	HR	RBI	SB	AVE
1B	Cap Anson	107	7	102	27	.347
2B	Fred Pfeffer	95	16	89	57	.278
SS	Tom Burns	57	3	60	32	.264
3B	Ned Williamson	77	9	78	45	.267
RF	Billy Sunday	41	3	32	34	.291
CF	Jimmy Ryan	117	11	74	50	.285
LF	Marty Sullivan	98	7	77	35	.284
C	Tom Daly	45	2	17	29	.207
P	John Clarkson	40	6	25	6	.242

P	Player	R	HR	RBI	SB	AVE
C	Silver Flint	22	3	21	7	.267
P	George Van Haltren	30	3	17	12	.203
UT	Del Darling	28	3	20	19	.319
P	Mark Baldwin	18	4	17	4	.187
UT	Bob Pettit	29	2	12	16	.261

T	Pitcher	W-L	SV	SO	SH	ERA
R	John Clarkson	38-21	0	237	2	3.08
R	Mark Baldwin	18-17	1	164	1	3.40
L	George Vn Haltren	11-7	1	76	1	3.86
L	Jimmy Ryan	2-1	0	14	0	4.20
L	Shadow Pyle	1-3	0	5	0	4.73

February 8 - King Kelly meets with Al Spalding to discuss his contract. Kelly, whose .388 bating average won the NL championship last year, wants the $375 bonus that Spalding promised for good behavior. Spalding refuses, citing the $225 he fined Kelly for excessive drinking in 1886. An enraged Kelly threatens to jump the team.

February 14 - Boston owner James B. Billings offers Kelly a $2,000 salary and $3,000 signing bonus if he can purchase the Chicago slugger from Spalding.

February 16 - The White Stockings sell Kelly to Boston for $10,000, more than twice the amount ever paid for a player. Billings is true to his word, and with the bonus, salary, and sales price, Kelly is dubbed the "15,000 beauty."

February 26 - Grover Cleveland "Pete" Alexander is born in Elba, Nebraska.

April 19 - An 11-year-old, Willie Hahn, is signed to a regular league contract to become the Whites'mascot.

April 21 - Joe McCarthy is born in Philadelphia, Pennsylvania.

May 18 - Rookie Marty Sullivan ties a record with five errors in right field during an 11-4 loss to Washington.

May 30 - The White Stockings walk 17 times in a 12-11 victory over the Giants. New York starter Bill George sets a major league record with 16 bases on balls.

June 27 - Rookie George Van Haltren ties the record with 16 walks in his major league debut, a 17-11 loss to Boston.

July 19 - Cap Anson refuses to play an exhibition match with the International League's Newark club until their starting pitcher, George Stovey, an African-American, is removed from the lineup. Stovey, the league's top pitcher, is currently under negotiations to be acquired by the New York Giants. His battery mate for the game is scheduled to be Moses Fleetwood Walker, also an African-American. It's the second time Anson has refused to play against Walker, having done so in 1884.

Stovey complains of illness and backs out of the game; Walker is benched. Neither will be signed to a major league contract. The International League will ban black players the very next day.

August 15 - Chicago defeats Detroit 6-4 behind John Clarkson to move into a first-place tie with the Wolverines.

August 16 - Detroit scores five runs in the fourth inning to beat Chicago 5-3 and regain sole possession of first place.

September 5 - Second-place Chicago and first-place Detroit meet for their final series of the year. Chicago wins the opening game of the series 11-7; Clarkson wins his ninth of the year versus the Wolverines, a record by a pitcher against a pennant-winning team.

September 7 - Detroit sweeps a doubleheader with the White Stockings, beating them 8-2 and 8-4. Chicago is now seven games behind.

September 12 - Center fielder Jimmy Ryan goes 6-for-6 and pitches the final three innings to beat the Phillies 16-13.

September 14 - Cap Anson goes 3-for-5, giving him 17 hits in the last five games.

September 28 - Former White Stocking Abner Dalrymple, now with Pittsburgh, smacks two dramatic homers in front of his old fans at West Side Park, one to tie the game for the Alleghenys and one to win it 3-2 in the 10th inning. These are Dalrymple's only home runs this season.

October 29 - Despite pledging to play for John Montgomery Ward's new Players League in 1888, Ned Williamson and Silver Flint re-sign with Chicago.

1888

Principle Owner and President: Al Spalding; **Manager:** Cap Anson; **Ballpark:** West Side Park; **Attendance:** 228,906; **Finish:** Second (77-58); **Recap:** Led by lefthander Gus Krock's 25 wins, Jimmy Ryan's 16 homers and Cap Anson's 84 RBIs, the White Stockings finish second to the New York Giants. Anson's batting title will be his last.

P	Player	R	HR	RBI	SB	AVE
1B	Cap Anson	101	12	84	28	.344
2B	Fred Pfeffer	90	8	57	64	.250
SS	Ned Williamson	75	8	73	25	.250
3B	Tom Burns	60	3	70	34	.238
RF	Hugh Duffy	60	7	41	13	.282
CF	Jimmy Ryan	115	16	64	60	.332
LF	Marty Sullivan	40	7	39	9	.236
C	Duke Farrell	34	3	19	8	.232
P	Gus Krock	9	1	11	1	.164
UT	George Van Haltren	46	4	34	21	.283
C	Tom Daly	34	0	29	10	.192
OF	Bob Pettit	23	4	23	7	.254
P	Mark Baldwin	11	1	5	4	.151
C	Silver Flint	6	0	3	1	.182

T	Pitcher	W-L	SV	SO	SH	ERA
L	Gus Krock	25-14	0	161	4	2.44
R	Mark Baldwin	13-15	0	157	2	2.76
L	George Vn Haltren	13-13	1	139	4	3.52
R	John Tener	7-5	0	39	1	2.74
R	George Borchers	4-4	0	26	1	3.49

March 20 - Al Spalding announces that he will take the Colts and a team of National League All-Stars on an around-the-world baseball tour next winter.

April 3 - The Colts sell John Clarkson to Boston for $10,000. With the $10,000 acquisition of King Kelly last year, the Beaneaters now sport a "$20,000 Battery."

April 9 - Hippo Vaughn is born in Weatherford, Texas.

June 12 - Center fielder Jimmy Ryan homers in the first inning then is brought in to pitch with the bases loaded in the second. He shuts the Giants out the rest of the way, winning 4-2.

June 21 - George Van Haltren hurls a 1-0 6-inning no-hitter over the Pittsburgh Alleghenys. Van Haltren actually pitches a hitless seventh but rain ends the game in the bottom half of the inning.

July 21 - Jimmy Ryan hits for the cycle during a 21-17 win over Detroit.

July 28 - Ryan connects for two triples, two singles, and a home run and hurls seven innings to beat Detroit 21-17. The Colts trail the Wolverines and New York Giants by 2 1/2 games.

August 24 - Cap Anson goes 5-for-5 and Jimmy Ryan is 4-for-5 in a 14-4 win over Detroit.

September12 - The Colts pick up a forfeit win vs. the Giants when catcher Buck Ewing is injured in the fifth and cannot finish the game. New York has no uniformed substitutes available, so the team simply leaves the grounds.

November 4 - Spalding's Around-the-World tour commences with a quick game in San Francisco, with the "All-Americans" whipping the Colts 14-4 before a crowd of 10,500.

December 5 - The tourists play their first game overseas, before 5,000 Australians in Sydney.

1889

Principle Owner and President: Al Spalding; **Manager:** Cap Anson; **Ballpark:** West Side Park; **Attendance:** 149,175; **Finish:** Third (67-65); **Recap:** The ho-hum Colts finish third, 19 games behind New York, despite strong seasons from Cap Anson, Jimmy Ryan and George Van Haltren.

P	PLAYER	R	HR	RBI	SB	AVE
1B	Cap Anson	100	7	117	27	.311
2B	Fred Pfeffer	85	7	77	45	.228
SS	Ned Williamson	41	1	30	2	.237
3B	Tom Burns	64	4	66	18	.242
RF	Hugh Duffy	144	12	89	52	.295
CF	Jimmy Ryan	140	17	72	45	.307
LF	George Van Haltren	126	9	81	28	.309
C	Duke Farrell	66	11	75	13	.248
P	Ad Gumbert	30	7	29	2	.288
IF	Charlie Bastian	19	0	10	1	.135
P	John Tener	18	1	19	2	.273
P	Frank Dwyer	14	1	6	0	.200
P	Bill Hutchison	14	1	7	2	.158
C	Del Darling	14	0	7	5	.192

T	PITCHER	W-L	SV	SO	SH	ERA
R	Bill Hutchison	16-17	0	136	3	3.54
R	John Tener	15-15	0	105	1	3.64
R	Frank Dwyer	16-13	0	63	0	3.59
R	Ad Gumbert	16-13	0	91	2	3.62
L	Gus Krock	3-3	0	16	0	4.90

January 1 - Al Spalding's touring baseball clubs play a game in Melbourne, Australia; the Colts beat the All-Americans 9-8.

February 9 - The touring group plays an exhibition near the Pyramids outside Cairo, Egypt. The All-Americans beat Chicago 10-6.

February 19 - The first American baseball game is played in Europe, with Spalding's tourists playing in Naples, Italy.

February 22 - The tourists take Rome, with the Chicagoes edging All-America 3-2 at the Villa Borghesi before a crowd that includes Italy's King Humbert.

March 8 - The All-Americans beat the Colts at the Parc Aristotique in Paris. Chicago shortstop Ned Williamson injures his knee sliding on the cinder field, ending his days as a top performer.

March 12 - The tourists play a game at the Surrey County Cricket Club in Kensington Oval, London, England. The Prince of Wales is in the crowd.

March 22 - The All-Americans beat the Colts 7-6 at Old Trafford Cricket Stadium in Manchester. The Manchester Guardian writes that "the general verdict of the more than 1,000 spectators was that the American game was 'slow'and 'wanting in variety'".

March 27 - The final tour game is played in Dublin, Ireland. The Colts and All-Stars will return to America the next day after playing 28 games overseas.

April 15 - The Colts and All-Americans are invited to the White House to meet President Benjamin Harrison. Harrison is a great baseball fan and will attend many of the Washington Nationals' games this season.

July 14 - Spalding's proposal for classifying minor leagues is published. The plan calls for strict salary and draft-price guidelines according to the class of the leagues, and will serve as a foundation into the next century.

August 9 - Hugh Duffy hits two inside-the-park home runs, setting a Cubs record.

1890

Principle Owner and President: Al Spalding; **Manager:** Cap Anson; **Ballpark:** West Side Park; **Attendance:** 102,536; **Finish:** Second (84-53); **Recap:** Despite nearly every one of Cap Anson's key players defecting to the new Players League, Chicago finishes second, six games behind the Brooklyn Bridegrooms.

P	PLAYER	R	HR	RBI	SB	AVE
1B	Cap Anson	95	7	107	29	.312
2B	Bob Glanalvin	43	4	26	30	.268
SS	Jimmy Cooney	114	4	52	45	.272
3B	Tom Burns	86	5	86	44	.277
RF	Jim Andrews	32	3	17	11	.188
CF	Walt Wilmot	114	13	99	76	.278
LF	Cliff Carroll	134	7	65	34	.285
C	Mal Kittridge	46	3	35	7	.201
P	Bill Hutchison	28	2	27	6	.203
UT	Howard Earl	57	7	51	17	.247
UT	Tom Nagle	21	1	11	4	.271
P	Pat Luby	27	3	17	3	.267
IF	Pete O'Brien	15	3	16	4	.283
OF	Elmer Foster	20	5	23	18	.248

T	PITCHER	W-L	SV	SO	SH	ERA
R	Bill Hutchison	42-25	2	289	5	2.70
R	Pat Luby	20-9	1	85	0	3.19
R	Ed Stein	12+6	0	65	1	3.81
L	Mike Sullivan	5-6	0	33	0	4.59
R	Roscoe Coughlin	4-6	0	29	0	4.26

April 19 - Wild Bill Hutchison beats Cincinnati 5-4 on Opening Day at West Side Park, the first of 65 complete games out of 66 starts. He'll also relieve five times, compiling 603 total innings. The National League's largest Opening Day crowd, 6,311, is on hand.

May 8 - Losing 9-4, the Colts score 12 runs in the sixth and go on to beat the Reds 18-9.

May 23 - The National League throws out a 10-8, 10-inning Chicago victory at Philadelphia because the umpire admits he made an error in not allowing the Phillies to send outfielder Billy Grey in as a sub during the contest.

May 30 - Hutchison hurls both ends of a doubleheader, winning 5-1 and 7-3. He completes both games.

June 2 - The Colts lose 20-7 to Cleveland; Spiders outfielder Ed Delahanty goes 6-for-6 with five runs scored.

July 15 - Al Spalding helps to bail out New York Giants owner John B. Day, who is threatening to fold the team if he can't come up with $80,000 to meet expenses.

August 16 - The Colts hit two grand slams during a 13-run fifth inning vs. the Pittsburgh Pirates. Tommy Burns and Malachi Kittridge do the damage.

September 30 - Walt Wilmot becomes the first of just two players to be hit by a batted ball twice in one game.

October 3 - Pat Luby wins his 17th straight start, beating Amos Rusie and the Giants 3-2.

1891

Principle Owner and President: Al Spalding; **Manager:** Cap Anson; **Ballpark:** South Side Park / West Side Park; **Attendance:** 201,188; **Finish:** Second (82-53); **Recap:** With the return of

Chicago's star players from the defunct Players League, Chicago leads the pack until September, when the club is overtaken by Boston in a late September rally. Cap Anson accuses the Giants of losing a four-game series to Boston on purpose because New York wanted an eastern club to win the pennant. The Colts'second-place finish will be their best of the decade.

P	PLAYER	R	HR	RBI	SB	AVE
1B	Cap Anson	81	8	120	17	.291
2B	Fred Pfeffer	93	7	77	40	.247
SS	Jimmy Cooney	84	0	42	21	.245
3B	Bill Dahlen	114	9	76	21	.260
RF	Cliff Carroll	87	7	80	31	.256
CF	Jimmy Ryan	110	9	66	27	.277
LF	Walt Wilmot	102	11	71	42	.279
C	Mal Kittridge	26	2	27	4	.209
P	Bill Hutchinson	27	2	25	5	.185
UT	Tom Burns	36	1	17	18	.226
P	Ad Gumbert	18	0	16	4	.305
P	Pat Luby	19	2	24	3	.245
UT	Pop Schriver	15	1	21	1	.333
C	Bill Bowman	2	0	5	0	.089

T	PITCHER	W-L	SV	SO	SH	ERA
R	Bill Hutchison	44-19	1	261	4	2.81
R	Ad Gumbert	17-11	0	73	1	3.58
R	Pat Luby	8-11	1	52	0	4.76
R	Ed Stein	7-6	0	38	1	3.74
R	Tom Vickery	6-5	0	39	0	4.07

March 25 - Al Spalding retires from the team's presidency and from active participation on the National League's board of directors. James A. Hart, the team's business manager, takes over. Spalding still retains his club stock.

May 5 - Pittsburgh star Pete Browning has a game to forget when he bunts into a triple play in the top of the sixth inning and makes an error to allow the only run to score in the bottom of the frame in a 1-0 loss to the Colts. Browning achieved fame in 1884 when Louisville craftsman Bud Hillerich created a new bat for the Grays' outfielder - the Louisville Slugger.

June 13 - The Colts lose to the Giants 8-7 before a record 22,289 at the Polo Grounds.

July 1 - Jimmy Ryan hits for the cycle during a game with the Cleveland Spiders.

July 25 - Right fielder Cliff Carroll homers over the fence to cap a four-run rally in the bottom of the ninth as the Colts defeat the Cleveland Spiders 15-14 in Cleveland. Carroll is only credited for a double, however, as the winning run scores from second base (under current rules, the game would end 16-14).

August 7 - A wild pitch by former Chicago ace John Clarkson allows the winning run to score in the 10th inning as the Colts defeat the Beaneaters 6-5. It's the fourth straight game that Chicago has beaten Boston in extra innings.

August 22 - Left fielder Walt Wilmot draws six walks from Cleveland hurlers Lee Viau and Cy Young, setting a major league record. Boston's Jimmie Joxx (June 16, 1938) and Cleveland's Andre Thornton (May 2, 1984) will tie the mark.

August 25 - The Colts crush the Brooklyn Bridegrooms 28-5. Pitcher Pat Luby hits two home runs in the game.

August 31 - Bill Hutchison and New York's Hoosier Thunderbolt, Amos Rusie, battle to an 11-inning 0-0 tie.

September 4 - Cap Anson, who has been teased about his age (39) all season, shows that he can be a good sport, showing up for today's game with Boston wearing a wig and a long white beard. The delighted home crowd is even happier when the Colts beat the Beaneaters 5-3 to stretch their National League lead to seven games.

September 14 - Hutchison earns his 40th win, beating the Beaneaters 7-1.

September 15 - The Colts beat Boston for the second day in a row. The Sporting News proclaims that the Beaneaters "might as well give up all hope of flying the flag." The next day, however, Kid Nichols will beat Chicago, launching an 18-game win streak that will propel them to the top of the standings.

September 28 - The New York Giants begin a makeup five-games-in-three-days series with the Beaneaters in Boston without three of their best players, including ace pitcher Rusie. The Beaneaters will sweep all five games to leapfrog the Colts into first place.

September30 - Colts president James Hart formally protests the makeup games played by the Giants in Boston - Chicago sportswriters have asserted that the eastern clubs have purposely let the Beaneaters win the games, especially after four Giants are called out at home plate in the final game, a 5-3 Boston win.

November 11 - The National League dismisses Hart's collusion charge, officially giving the pennant to Boston.

1892

Principle Owner and President: James Hart; **Manager:** Cap Anson; **Ballpark:** South Side Park; **Attendance:** 109,067; **Finish:** Seventh / Eighth (31-39 / 39-37); **Recap:** A bad season gets off to a bad start when Al Spalding announces he's stepping down as president in favor of business manager John Hart, a move that embitters Cap Anson, who has never liked Hart.

With the disbanding of the rival American Association, the National League incorporates a few of the AA's clubs and expands to 12, then splits the season into two halves in order to provide a post-season championship series. The Colts tumble to seventh in the first half of the season and eighth in the second half. Part of the responsibility for the disastrous finish rests squarely with Anson, who slumps for most of the year. In addition, Anson allows Fred Pfeffer to finish his career in his home town of Louisville and installing Jimmy Canavan in his place (Canavan's .166 average is the worst ever for a major leaguer with 400 or more at-bats).

P	Player	R	HR	RBI	SB	AVE
1B	Cap Anson	62	1	74	13	.272
2B	Jimmy Canavan	48	0	32	33	.166
SS	Bill Dahlen	114	5	58	60	.291
3B	Jiggs Parrott	38	2	22	7	.201
RF	Sam Dungan	46	0	53	15	.284
CF	Jimmy Ryan	105	10	65	27	.293
LF	Walt Wilmot	47	2	35	31	.216
C	Pop Schriver	40	1	34	4	.224
P	Bill Hutchison	23	1	22	8	.217
UT	George Decker	32	1	28	9	.227
IF	Jimmy Cooney	18	0	20	10	.172
C	Mal Kittridge	19	0	10	2	.179
P	Ad Gumbert	18	1	8	5	.236
P	Pat Luby	14	2	20	3	.190

T	Pitcher	W-L	SV	SO	SH	ERA
R	Bill Hutchison	37-36	0	316	5	2.74
R	Ad Gumbert	22-19	0	118	0	3.41
R	Pat Luby	10-16	1	64	1	3.13
L	Harry DeMiller	1-1	0	15	0	3.13

January 9 - A newspaper quotes Cap Anson as saying, "I don't care if they can't field a little bit. In my experience I have found that a man can be taught to almost stop cannon balls, but it is a very difficult task to teach them to line 'em out."

April 19 - Tony Mullane of the Cincinnati Reds shuts the Colts out on one hit, 3-0.

May 7 - Bill Hutchison loses a no-hitter in the ninth on Orator Jim O'Rourke's single,

West Side Park

settling for an 8-0 one-hitter over the Giants.

May 21 - The Colts beat Pud Galvin and the Pirates 1-0, the team's 11th straight victory. Galvin allows just two hits in the loss.

May 28 - Jimmy Ryan draws five walks off New York ace Amos Rusie in a 10-4 Chicago win. Rusie walks 10 in the game.

June 30 - Ad Gumbert hurls 20 innings, only to end up with a 7-7 tie vs. the Cincainnati Reds at South Side Park.

July 11 - The Boston Beaneaters show up for today's game with the Colts in outlandish costumes and beards. The bearded Beaneaters win 3-2.

August 15 - Ryan's 29-game hitting streak is snapped during a 9-2 loss to the Baltimore Orioles. The streak began on July 9th.

August 18 - Slumping Cap Anson has a big day, tallying five hits including two triples and a double, but the Colts lose 7-5 to the Brooklyn Bridegrooms.

September 28 - Bill Hutchison pitches both ends of a doubleheader with Louisville, winning the first contest 5-4 and losing the second 5-3.

1893

Principle Owner and President: James Hart; **Manager:** Cap Anson; **Ballpark:** West Side Park; **Attendance:** 223,500; **Finish:** Ninth (56-71); **Recap:** The Colts move to a new ballpark, West Side Grounds, located at Polk and Lincoln. They'll remain there until moving into Wrigley Field in 1916. Despite a ninth-place finish, the Colts draw 223,500 fans in 1893, nearly doubling last year's total and second-best in the NL.

P	Player	R	HR	RBI	SB	AVE
1B	Cap Anson	70	0	91	13	.314
2B	Bill Lange	92	8	88	47	.281
SS	Bill Dahlen	113	5	64	31	.301
3B	Jiggs Parrott	54	1	65	25	.244
RF	Sam Dungan	86	2	644	11	.297
CF	Jimmy Ryan	82	3	30	8	.299
LF	Walt Wilmot	69	3	61	39	.301
C	Mal Kittridge	32	2	30	3	.231
P	Bill Hutchison	14	0	25	2	.253
UT	George Decker	57	2	48	22	.271
C	Pop Schriver	49	4	34	4	.284
UT	Llewellyn Camp	37	2	17	30	.263
P	Willie McGill	18	0	13	5	.234
IF	Charlie Irwin	14	0	13	4	.305

T	Pitcher	W-L	SV	SO	SH	ERA
R	Bill Hutchison	16-24	0	80	2	4.75
L	Willie McGill	17-18	0	91	1	4.61
R	Hal Mauck	8-10	0	23	1	4.41
L	Fritz Clausen	6-2	1	31	0	3.08
L	Gus McGinnis	2-5	0	13	0	5.35

June 14 - Giants shortstop "Gorgeous George" Davis becomes the first player in history to hit a homer and a triple in the same inning during an 11-10 win over the Colts.

The feat will be matched in 1926 by Detroit Tigers outfielder Fatty Fothergill.

July 13 - After Joe Kelley of the Orioles homers in a game at West Side Park, his bat disappears. The game is held up at Kelley's next at-bat until his bat is found - in a pile of bats in front of the Colts'dugout.

July 14 - The Colts batter the Orioles 10-2; Baltimore starter Tony Mullane pitches the last inning left-handed.

August 6 - Jimmy Ryan is injured in a train accident and is lost for the season.

August 20 - Chicago catcher Malachi Kittridge fails to call time before dusting off the plate; the Washington runner scores from third.

August 24 - Umpires move the Polo Grounds diamond 45 feet closer to the grandstand after a downpour floods the outfield. The Colts defeat the Giants 10-4.

1894

Principle Owner and President: James Hart; **Manager:** Cap Anson; **Ballpark:** West Side Park; **Attendance:** 239,000; **Finish:** Eighth (57-75); **Recap:** About the only thing Chicago fans have to cheer about in 1894 is the hitting of Cap Anson, a 42-game hitting streak by shortstop Bill Dahlen, and the play of young center fielder Bill Lange, who will average over .339 for the next six seasons. Anson hits a healthy .388 but finishes a distant sixth behind Boston outfielder Hugh Duffy's .440.

Of note is the record of second-year pitcher (and future Washington Senators owner) Clark Griffith, who leads the team with 21 victories and whose ERA(4.92) is 70 points below the team's mark.

P	Player	R	HR	RBI	SB	AVE
1B	Cap Anson	82	5	99	17	.388
2B	Jiggs Parrott	82	3	64	30	.248
SS	Bill Dahlen	149	15	107	42	.357
3B	Charlie Irwin	84	8	95	35	.289
RF	Jimmy Ryan	132	3	62	11	.361
CF	Bill Lange	84	6	90	65	.328
LF	Walt Wilmot	134	5	130	74	.330
C	Pop Schriver	55	3	47	9	.275
UT	George Decker	74	8	92	23	.313
C	Mal Kittridge	36	0	23	2	.315
P	Clark Griffith	27	0	15	6	.232
P	Bill Hutchison	30	6	16	2	.309
P	Scott Stratton	29	3	23	3	.375

T	Pitcher	W-L	SV	SO	SH	ERA
R	Bill Hutchison	14-16	0	59	0	6.06
R	Clark Griffith	21-14	0	71	0	4.92
L	Willie McGill	7-19	0	58	0	5.84
R	Adonis Terry	5-11	0	39	0	5.84
R	Scott Stratton	8-5	0	23	0	6.03

June 7 - Brooklyn's Ed Stein tosses a seven-inning no-hitter to beat the Colts 1-0. The day before the Bridegrooms' Brickyard Kennedy held Chicago to just one hit in a 5-0 whitewash.

June 24 - The Colts push across five runs in the top of the ninth to take a lead over Baltimore, but the raucous Orioles storm back with three runs in the bottom of the inning to snatch an 11-10 win.

June 27 - Chicago defeats Baltimore 13-4, the first time in 24 games the slugging Orioles are held to less than seven runs.

July 25 - George Decker allegedly slugs a 520-foot home run at West Side Park during a 24-6 thumping of the Pirates. Jimmy Ryan scores a record six runs in the game.

August 1 - The Colts crush St. Louis 26-8, with Cap Anson and George Decker each going 5-for-7 with a home run. Jimmy Ryan scores five runs.

August 5 - A fire breaks out at West Side Park with Anson at bat in the sixth; hundreds are injured as the sold-out crowd stampedes, tearing down barbed wire fencing that had been put up to prevent drunken fans from charging the umpire. The game is called; Chicago wins 8-1.

August 7 - Shortstop Bill Dahlen's record 42-game hitting streak is snapped during a 13-11 win over Cincinnati. Left fielder Walt Wilmot steals four bases for the second straight day, going 5-for-5.

August 22 - With the Colts trailing 8-2 in the eighth, Lange decides to lighten the mood by walking to the plate wielding a 6-foot bat that had been given to Ryan by a New York theater manager.

Neither the umpire nor the Giants object, and Lange grounds to first baseman Jack Doyle, who boots the ball. New York holds on to win, 8-5.

August 24 - In a pre-game publicity stunt, catcher Pop Schriver catches a ball dropped from the top of the Washington monument. The Colts beat the Nationals later that day, 10-5.

September 3 - The Louisville Courier-Journal, in a story about Cap Anson, describes the 42-year-old manager as a "wholesome example to the young ballplayers" who "smokes three cigars a day."

September 16 - George Decker triples and homers twice, hitting for the cycle in a 13-5 Chicago win over Brooklyn.

September20 - The Colts score 10 runs in the first inning of a 20-4 victory over the Phillies.

1895

Principle Owner and President: James Hart; **Manager:** Cap Anson; **Ballpark:** West Side Park; **Attendance:** 382,300; **Finish:** Fourth (72-58); **Recap:** With Clark Griffith and Bill Lange leading the way, the Colts rise to fourth in the standings. Lange bats .389 and finishes in the top five in average, on-base percentage (.456), home runs (10) and stolen bases (67).

Griffith wins 26, and finishes fifth in the NL with 39 complete games. Third baseman Bill Everett sets the major league record for average (.358) by a rookie with 400 or more at-bats.

P	PLAYER	R	HR	RBI	SB	AVE
1B	Cap Anson	87	2	91	12	.335
2B	Ace Stewart	52	8	76	14	.241
SS	Bill Dahlen	106	7	62	38	.254
3B	Bill Everett	129	3	88	47	.358
RF	Jimmy Ryan	83	6	49	18	.317
CF	Bill Lange	120	10	98	67	.389
LF	Walt Wilmot	86	8	72	28	.283
C	Tim Donahue	29	2	36	5	.269
UT	George Decker	51	2	41	11	.276
C	Mal Kittridge	30	3	29	6	.226
P	Clark Griffith	20	1	27	2	.319
P	Adonis Terry	18	1	10	1	.219
P	Bill Hutchison	12	0	11	1	.198

T	PITCHER	W-L	SV	SO	SH	ERA
R	Clark Griffith	26-14	0	79	0	3.93
R	Adonis Terry	21-14	0	88	0	4.80
R	Bill Hutchison	13-21	0	85	0	4.73
R	Doc Parker	4-2	0	9	1	3.68
L	Danny Friend	2-2	0	10	0	5.27

January 25 - In a newspaper interview the ever-quotable Cap Anson notes that "nobody likes to see a play made with the aid of gloves." Anson, a first baseman, says that only catchers should be permitted to wear gloves. The National League will later restrict the size of gloves for all fielders, except catchers and first basemen, to 10 ounces, with a maximum circumference of 14 inches around the palm.

May 20 - Colts ace Clark Griffith goes 5-for-6 in a 24-6 battering of Philadelphia. Third baseman Bill Everett, a rookie, tallies four hits and five runs. Asa Stewart hits an inside-the-park grand slam. The Phillies commit 13 errors in the game.

July 2 - The Colts are pummeled for 11 runs in the first inning in a 15-9 loss to the St. Louis Browns.

WORTH NOTING - Between the ages of 41 and 44, Cap Anson hit at least .314 and drove in at least 91 a season. No other player in major league history has batted .300 four times after the age of 40.

July 17 - Chicago scores 12 runs in the fourth in a 12-7 triumph over the Phillies. The Colts score five more in the bottom of the seventh and are still batting when Philadelphia decides to forfeit.

November15 - Cap Anson makes his stage debut in the play "A Runaway Colt" on Broadway. Anson forgets a few lines but receives good notices.

December 28 - Shortstop Bill Dahlen breaks his arm in a fall. He'll recover in time to bat .352 with 137 runs scored for the Colts in 1896.

1896

Principle Owner and President: James Hart; **Manager:** Cap Anson; **Ballpark:** West Side Park; **Attendance:** 317,500; **Finish:** Fifth (71-57); **Recap:** The also-ran Colts finish 18 1/2 games behind the pennant-winning Baltimore Orioles. Bill Lange finishes with 84 stolen bases, good enough for second in the league and shortstop Bill Dahlen emerges as an offensive force. At age 46, Cap Anson becomes the oldest player to post a .300 average for a full season.

P	PLAYER	R	HR	RBI	SB	AVE
1B	Cap Anson	72	2	90	24	.331
2B	Fred Pfeffer	45	2	52	22	.244
SS	Bill Dahlen	137	9	74	51	.352
3B	Bill Everett	130	2	46	46	.320
RF	Jimmy Ryan	83	3	86	29	.305
CF	Bill Lange	114	4	92	84	.326
LF	George Decker	68	5	61	20	.280
C	Mal Kittridge	17	1	19	6	.223
C	Tim Donahue	27	0	20	11	.218
UT	Barry McCormick	22	1	23	9	.220
P	Clark Griffith	22	1	16	3	.267

T	PITCHER	W-L	SV	SO	SH	ERA
R	Clark Griffith	23-11	0	81	0	3.54
L	Danny Friend	18-14	0	86	1	4.74
R	Adonis Terry	15-14	0	74	1	4.28
R	Buttons Briggs	12-8	1	84	0	4.31
R	Doc Parker	1-5	0	15	0	6.16

January 14 - Outfielder Walt Wilmot, charged for violating the Sabbath law by playing Sunday baseball last year, is acquitted by a Chicago jury. It's a landmark case; the Illinois Blue Law forbidding work on Sunday will soon be toppled.

March 7 - A Chicago writer, quoted in the New York Clipper, refers to shortstop Bill Dahlen as "one of the few now in the league who came blood-new from a punky little league and became a good thing at first jump."

April 27 - Rogers Hornsby is born in Winters, Texas.

May 8 - Clark Griffith's quick thinking preserves a 5-3 victory for the Colts. In the top of the ninth, Philadelphia third baseman Billy Nash starts an argument with the umpire over a called strike. Griffith tosses a pitch that bounces off the preoccupied Nash's bat, resulting in a double play.

May 13 - Tied 4-4 with Chicago, the Boston Beaneaters begin to stall for darkness in the bottom of the 11th inning. Umpire Tim Keefe awards a forfeit victory to the Colts.

June 19 - In the seventh inning of an 8-3 Chicago victory, umpire Tom Lynch changes a close call at first base and Cleveland manager-first baseman Patsy Tebeau explodes, earning him an ejection. Tebeau, however, refuses to leave the field, sparking a near-riot in the stands. Lynch storms off the field; the game is finished with Dahlen and Spiders pitcher Cy Young alternating as umpires.

July 13 - Philadelphia's Ed Delahanty smacks four home runs, all inside-the-park, off Adonis Terry in a 9-8 loss to the Colts. The record still stands.

August 2 - In the sixth inning of a 2-1 loss to Louisville, catcher Tim Donahue is spiked by third baseman Billy Clingman while tagging him out. Donahue tries to retaliate by hurling the ball at Clipman but the umpire wrestles it away.

August 11 - Adonis Terry shuts out Cincinnati 6-0. It's the first whitewash of the season suffered by the Reds.

August 31 - Win Mercer of the Washington Nationals shuts out Chicago, 1-0 in 11 innings. It's the first shutout by a Washington pitcher since September 17, 1893.

1897

Principle Owner and President: James Hart; **Manager:** Cap Anson; **Ballpark:** West Side Park; **Attendance:** 327,160; **Finish:** Ninth (59-73); **Recap:** A ninth-place finish is all club president James Hart needs as an excuse to fire Cap Anson, who has been a nuisance since he took over the club in 1892. Anson doesn't help himself by slumping to .285 in his final season.

P	PLAYER	R	HR	RBI	SB	AVE
1B	Cap Anson	67	3	75	11	.285
2B	Jim Connor	40	3	38	10	.291
SS	Bill Dahlen	67	6	40	15	.290
3B	Bill Everett	63	5	39	26	.314
RF	Jimmy Ryan	103	5	85	27	.300
CF	Bill Lange	119	5	83	73	.340
LF	George Decker	72	5	63	11	.290
C	Mal Kittridge	25	1	30	9	.202
IF	Barry McCormick	87	2	55	44	.267
UT	Nixey Callahan	60	3	47	12	.292
UT	Walter Thornton	39	0	55	13	.321
C	Tim Donahue	28	0	21	3	.239

T	PITCHER	W-L	SV	SO	SH	ERA
R	Clark Griffith	21-18	1	102	1	3.72
L	Danny Friend	12-11	0	58	0	4.52
R	Nixey Callahan	12-9	0	52	1	4.03
R	Buttons Briggs	4-17	0	60	0	5.26
L	Walter Thornton	6-7	0	55	0	4.70

May 4 - It's Cap Anson Day in Chicago; Pop catches the game and singles in the Colts'5-2 victory.

June 29 - The Colts crush the Louisville Grays 36-7, setting a National League record for runs scored. Scoring in every inning, Chicago tallies 32 hits, led by third baseman Barry McCormick's 6-for-8 day. Major league records are set when 71 players come to bat for Chicago and 10 players score two or more runs. Four different players score six runs in the game.

July 17 - The Baltimore Orioles pummel the Colts 20-2. Third baseman Wee Willie Keeler gets five hits and scores five runs to lead the Orioles.

July 18 - Anson collects a fourth-inning single for his 3,000th hit, in a 6-3 defeat of Baltimore. The newspapers, however, are unaware of the significance of the feat and it goes unpublished.

August 13 - Clark Griffith beats Cincinnati 2-0, his 104th career win and first career shutout.

October 3 - Anson's final day in the big leagues is a memorable one. He helps Chicago split a doubleheader with St. Louis by slugging two home runs in the first game and stealing a base in the nightcap. The 45-year old Anson's career has spanned 26 years.

1898

Principle Owner and President: James Hart; **Manager:** Tom Burns; **Ballpark:** West Side Park; **Attendance:** 424,352; **Finish:** Fourth (85-65); **Recap:** With Anson out of the picture, the Chicago papers begin calling the team the Orphans. Although fans, for the most part, resent the firing of Pop, the team draws a club-record 424,352 fans for the year. The crowds generally get their money's worth as the club rises to fourth in the standings, thanks chiefly to the pitching of Clark Griffith, whose 1.88 ERAleads the NL.

The Orphans turn 149 double plays this season, a record that will not be surpassed until the Cardinals turn 153 in 1917.

P	PLAYER	R	HR	RBI	SB	AVE
1B	Bill Everett	102	0	69	28	.319
2B	Jim Connor	51	0	67	11	.226
SS	Bill Dahlen	96	1	79	27	.290
3B	Barry McCormick	76	2	78	15	.247
RF	Sam Mertes	45	1	47	27	.297
CF	Bill Lange	79	5	69	22	.319
LF	Jimmy Ryan	122	4	79	29	.323
C	Tim Donahue	52	0	39	17	.220
P	Walter Thornton	34	0	14	8	.295
OF	Danny Green	26	4	27	12	.314
P	Nixey Callahan	27	0	22	3	.262
UT	Frank Isbell	17	0	8	3	.233
T	**PITCHER**	**W-L**	**SV**	**SO**	**SH**	**ERA**
R	Clark Griffith	24-10	0	97	4	1.88
R	Nixey Callahan	20-10	0	73	2	2.46
L	Walter Thornton	13-10	0	56	2	3.34
R	Walt Woods	9-13	0	26	3	3.14
L	Matt Kilroy	6-7	0	18	0	4.31

January 31 - Cap Anson is officially fired as the Colts' manager after 19 seasons. Anson managed the team to 1,288 victories and five pennants. Infielder Tommy Burns will take over; sportswriters will refer to the team as the Orphans until 1902.

Anson will be hired to manage the New York Giants on June 11 and quit on July 7 after being criticized for being unable to handle "modern" ballplayers.

April 16 - The Sportsman's Park grandstand catches fire during a game between the Browns and Orphans in St. Louis. The crowd of 6,000 stampedes; 40 people are injured. Browns manager Tim Hurst, players, and contracted workmen work all night to restore part of the stands for the next day's game, borrowing wood from a nearby circus.

May 24 - The Orioles beat Chicago 15-13 in the highest-scoring game of the season. Chicago pitchers yield 36 hits, 10 walks and three hit batsmen. Starter Clark Griffith is ejected for obscenity directed at umpire Tom Lynch.

May 25 - Chicago rebounds against Baltimore rookie Frank Kitson, scoring 20 runs. Kitson hurled a shutout in his major league debut six days ago.

June 6 - Bill Dahlen's three triples lead the Orphans to a 15-2 triumph at Brooklyn.

June 9 - New York starter Ed Doheny fans 12 Orphans but walks seven and throws five wild pitches to give Chicago a 10-8 win.

June 22 - Walt Woods loses his second 14-inning game in three starts, 6-5 to Boston. The Beaneaters' Ted Lewis relieves starter Vic Willis with two outs in the first inning and pitches the rest of the way for the win.

July 15 - Ugliness in Baltimore: third baseman Barry McCormick accuses first baseman Bill Everett of making a poor throw, sparking a fistfight on the field. A Baltimore spectator, trying to break up the fight, is punched. McCormick storms off the field and the Orphans lose 10-9.

August 21 - Walter Thornton, who also platoons in the outfield, hurls a 2-0 no-hitter over the Brooklyn Bridegrooms.

August 28 - Charlie Grimm is born in St. Louis, Missouri.

August 30 - Concerned about on-field fighting and the deterioration of the game, the New York press calls for the return of Al Spalding because he "worked so long and well to place it (baseball) upon a high plane."

Clark Griffith tosses a three-hit 1-0 shutout vs. the Giants.

Kiki Cuyler is born in Harrisville, Michigan.

September 16 - Jimmy Ryan leads off a game vs. Philadelphia with a home run for the 17th time in his career, the highest total for any 19-century player. The Orphans triumph, 10-5.

October 9 - The Orphans' Jack Taylor beats the Browns' Jack Taylor 5-4. Chicago's Taylor is a rookie who won 28 games for the Western League's Milwaukee club this season.

1899

Principle Owner and President: James Hart; **Manager:** Tom Burns; **Ballpark:** West Side Park; **Attendance:** 352,130; **Finish:** Eighth (75-73); **Recap:** Despite a fine performance by the club's starting three, Clark Griffith (22 wins), Nixey Callahan (21) and Jack Taylor (18), the Orphans slump to eighth place, 26 games behind the champion Brooklyn Bridegrooms. Bill Lange retires after the season, due to his prospective father-in-law's disapproval of ball players.

P	PLAYER	R	HR	RBI	SB	AVE
1B	Bill Everett	87	1	74	30	.310
2B	Barry McCormick	48	2	52	14	.258
SS	Gene Demontreville	43	0	40	26	.281
3B	Harry Wolverton	50	1	49	14	.285
RF	Danny Green	90	6	56	18	.295
CF	Bill Lange	81	1	58	41	.325
LF	Jimmy Ryan	91	3	68	9	.301
C	Tim Donahue	39	0	29	10	.248
OF	Sam Mertes	83	9	81	45	.298
IF	Jim Connor	26	0	24	6	.205
C	Frank Chance	37	1	22	10	.286
UT	George Magoon	24	0	21	5	.228
P	Nixey Callahan	21	0	18	9	.260

1 8 9 9 - 1 9 0 0

T	Pitcher	W-L	SV	SO	SH	ERA
R	Jack Taylor	18-21	0	67	1	3.76
R	Clark Griffith	22-14	0	73	0	2.79
R	Nixey Callahan	21-12	0	77	3	3.06
R	Ned Garvin	9-13	0	69	4	2.85
R	Bill Phyle	1-8	1	10	0	4.20

March 17 - Charlie Root is born in Middletown, Ohio.

April 14 - The Orphans beat Louisville 15-1 behind Clark Griffith on Opening Day.

April 30 - Chicago sets a new attendance record as 27,000 pile into West Side Park to watch Nixey Callahan shut out the St. Louis Browns 4-0.

July 9 - Andrew Brennan, a neighbor of West Side Park, is granted the right by Chicago's Judge Dunn to sell rooftop seats on his house on game days.

October 2 - Louisville's Rube Waddell fans 13 Orphans in an eight-inning 6-1 victory at Chicago.

October 8 - Jack Taylor hurls his first shutout, 11-0, in the morning game of a doubleheader against Louisville, The second game isn't played until late that afternoon, and is called in the fifth inning of the second game because of darkness with Chicago winning 7-3.

1900

Principle Owner and President: James Hart; **Manager:** Tom Loftus; **Ballpark:** West Side Park; **Attendance:** 248,577; **Finish:** Fifth (65-75); **Recap:** The Colts kick off the new century with a fifth-place finish, 19 games out of first. Don't blame it on the pitching: the staff's 3.23 earned run average is second only to Pittsburgh's 3.06 mark.

P	Player	R	HR	RBI	SB	AVE
1B	John Ganzel	29	4	32	5	.275
2B	Cupid Childs	67	0	44	15	.241
SS	Barry McCormick	35	3	48	8	.219
3B	Bill Bradley	63	5	49	14	.282
RF	Jimmy Ryan	66	5	59	19	.277
CF	Danny Green	63	5	49	28	.298
LF	Jack McCarthy	68	0	48	22	.294
C	Tim Donahue	21	0	17	8	.236

P	Player	R	HR	RBI	SB	AVE
UT	Sam Mertes	72	7	60	38	.295
IF	Billy Clingman	15	0	11	6	.208
C	Frank Chance	26	0	13	8	.295
UT	Charlie Dexter	7	2	20	2	.200
P	Nixey Callahan	16	0	9	5	.235

T	Pitcher	W-L	SV	SO	SH	ERA
R	Nixey Callahan	13-16	0	77	2	3.82
R	Clark Griffith	14-13	0	61	4	3.05
R	Ned Garvin	10-18	0	107	1	2.41
R	Jack Taylor	10-17	1	57	2	2.55
R	Jock Menefee	9-4	0	30	0	3.85

April 26 - Lewis "Hack" Wilson is born in Ellwood City, Pennsylvania.

April 27 - The Orphans beat the Cardinals 6-5 on Opening Day in Chicago.

May 26 - The Orphans beat the Brooklyn Superbas 1-0 in 95 minutes.

June 19 - Clark Griffith and Pittsburgh's Rube Waddell hook up in a classic pitching duel. The game is scoreless until the 14th, when Griffith's double off Waddell drives in the game's only run.

Rube will join the Orphans for the 1901 season.

September 12 - Rookie third baseman Sammy Strang breaks into the majors with seven hits in a doubleheader vs. the Giants.

October 8 - The Reds and Orphans set a record for fielding ineptitude that stands to this day: Chicago makes 17 errors and Cincinnati 8 as the Reds sweep a doubleheader 13-4 and 9-1.

December 20 - Gabby Hartnett is born in Woonsocket, Rhode Island.

1901

Principle Owner and President: James Hart; **Manager:** Tom Loftus; **Ballpark:** West Side Park; **Attendance:** 205,071; **Finish:** Sixth (53-86); **Recap:** The defection of Clark Griffith and several others to the new American League's cross-town White Sox reduces the club to a 53-86 finish and gives them a new nickname: the Remnants.

Al Spalding, still the majority stockholder despite a thriving sporting goods business, publicly insists that the team be called the Colts in an attempt to at least salvage their nicknames since they can't put a noteworthy product on the field. A solution will present itself in 1902 when the Chicago Daily News suggests a new name: the Cubs.

P	Player	R	HR	RBI	SB	AVE
1B	Jack Doyle	19	0	39	11	.241
2B	Cupid Childs	23	0	21	3	.257
SS	Barry McCormick	45	1	32	12	.234
3B	Fred Raymer	41	0	43	18	.233
RF	Frnk Chance	37	0	36	30	.289
CF	Danny Green	82	6	61	31	.313
LF	Topsy Hartsel	111	7	54	41	.335
C	Johnny King	25	0	21	7	.265
UT	Charlie Dexter	46	1	66	22	.267
UT	Mike Kahoe	21	1	21	5	.224
IF	Pete Childs	23	0	14	4	.229
UT	Jock Menefree	19	0	13	4	.257
OF	Cozy Dolan	29	0	16	3	.263

T	Pitcher	W-L	SV	SO	SH	ERA
L	Rube Waddell	14-14	0	168	0	2.80
R	Jack Taylor	13-19	0	68	0	3.36
R	Tom Hughes	10-23	0	225	1	3.24
R	Jock Menefree	8-12	0	55	0	3.81
R	Mal Eason	8-17	0	68	1	3.58

June 4 - Five Colts are picked off in a game vs. Brooklyn.

July 1 - Jack Doyle jumps into the stands at the Polo Grounds to challenge a heckler and reinjures his hand, which he had broken several weeks earlier. The Colts lose 6-4 to the Giants'Dummy Taylor.

WORTH QUOTING - "Baseball as at present conducted is a gigantic monopoly, intolerant of opposition and run on a grab-all-there-is-in-sight policy that is alienating its friends and disgusting the very public that has so long and cheefully given it the support that it has withheld from other forms of amusement."

-Cap Anson, 1900

April 26 - The Reds beat the Colts 8-7 on Opening Day at West Side Park.

September 21 - Long Tom Hughes and Boston's Bill Dineen match scoreless innings until the 16th, when the Colts score on an error, hit batsman, a forceout and a single.

December 3 - Such is the respect for Al Spalding that he is elected by no less than four clubs to serve as president in order to fend off infighting and lack of leadership within each organization. Two days later, a court will void the election and forbid him from serving.

1902

Principle Owner and President: James Hart; **Manager:** Frank Selee; **Ballpark:** West Side Park; **Attendance:** 263,700; **Finish:** Fifth (68-69); **Recap:** With Johnny Kling showing capability behind the plate, new manager Frank Selee moves Frank Chance to first base. Chance, who initially fights the move, will eventually become the league's best first baseman. Selee also installs rookie Joe Tinker at shortstop and, in September, removes veteran second baseman Bobby Lowe in favor of rookie

Johnny Evers, forming the legendary Tinker-to-Evers-to-Chance double play combination.

P	Player	R	HR	RBI	SB	AVE
1B	Frank Chance	40	1	31	28	.284
2B	Bobby Lowe	41	0	31	16	.246
SS	Joe Tinker	54	2	54	28	.273
3B	Germany Schaefer	32	0	14	12	.196
RF	Davy Jones	41	0	14	12	.305
CF	Johnny Dobbs	31	0	35	3	.302
LF	Jimmy Slagle	64	0	28	40	.315
C	Johnny Kling	50	0	57	23	.286
UT	Charlie Dexter	30	2	26	13	.226
UT	Jock Menefree	24	0	15	4	.231
OF	Darkin Miller	17	0	13	10	.246
UT	Art Williams	17	0	14	9	.231
OF	Bunk Congalton	14	1	24	3	.223

T	Pitcher	W-L	SV	SO	SH	ERA
R	Jack Taylor	23-11	1	83	7	1.33
R	Jock Menefree	12-10	0	60	4	2.42
R	Pop Williams	11-16	0	94	1	2.52
R	Carl Lundgren	9-9	0	68	1	1.97
L	Jim St. Vrain	4-6	0	51	1	2.08

March 27 - The Chicago Daily News first suggests that the team, still referred to as the Colts, Orphans or Remnants, be called the Cubs. It will still take a few more years for the name to catch on.

April 3 - Cubs owner James Hart is selected as part of a three-man interim committee to run the National League. Arthur Soden (Boston) and John T. Brush (New York) make up the rest of the triumvirate.

April 19 - The Cubs take advantage of seven walks in the fourth inning by righty Bob Ewing, who is making his major league debut, to beat Cincinnati 9-5.

April 21 - The Cubs beat the Cardinals 4-3 on Opening Day at West Side Park.

April 27 - Manager Frank Selee suggests that rookie pitcher Jimmy St. Vrain, a dreadful hitter, go up to bat lefthanded during a game against the Pirates. St. Vrain manages to make contact, grounding to Pittsburgh shortstop Honus Wagner, and runs as fast as he can - to third base. An astonished Wagner throws him out. The Cubs lose 2-0.

May 7 - After Jack Taylor bests Christy Mathewson and the Giants 4-0 in Chicago, New York manager Horace Fogel demands that the distance from the mound to home plate be measured. The distance is found to be 15 inches short; two games are ordered replayed.

September 1 - The legendary double play combination of (Joe) Tinker, (Johnny) Evers, and (Frank) Chance appears on the field together for the first time, but not in the positions that will earn them their Hall of Fame credentials. Evers makes the start as shortstop, with Tinker playing third.

September13 - Tinker, Evers, and Chance play their first game at their immortal positions of shortstop, second, and first base. Germany Schaefer makes the start at third.

1903

Principle Owner and President: James Hart; **Manager:** Frank Selee; **Ballpark:** West Side Park; **Attendance:** 386,205; **Finish:** Third (82-56); **Recap:** The Cubs rise to third behind the sensational play of young Joe Tinker, Johnny Evers and Frank Chance, and the pitching of rookie Jake Weimer and veterans Jack Taylor and Bob Wicker. More intriguing is a post-season deal that sends Taylor, who is accused of deliberately throwing a couple of City Series games with the White Sox, to St. Louis for rookie Mordecai "Three Finger" Brown. Brown, given the nickname due to the loss of two fingers in a childhood farm accident, will compile six straight 20-win seasons, a lifetime ERA of

2.06, and, most importantly, become the backbone of the team's late-decade dynasty.

P	PLAYER	R	HR	RBI	SB	AVE
1B	Frank Chance	83	2	81	67	.327
2B	Johnny Evers	70	0	52	25	.293
SS	Joe Tinker	67	2	70	27	.291
3B	Doc Casey	56	1	40	11	.290
RF	Dick Harley	72	0	33	27	.231
CF	Davy Jones	64	1	62	15	.282
LF	Jimmy Slagle	104	0	44	33	.298
C	Johnny Kling	67	3	68	23	.297
IF	Otto Williams	14	0	13	8	.223
UT	Tommy Raub	6	0	7	3	.226
IF	Bobby Lowe	14	0	15	5	.267
OF	Jack McCarthy	11	0	14	8	.277
OF	Johnny Dobbs	8	0	4	0	.230

T	PITCHER	W-L	SV	SO	SH	ERA
R	Jack Taylor	21-14	1	83	1	2.45
L	Jake Weimer	20-8	0	128	3	2.30
R	Bob Wicker	20-9	1	110	1	3.02
R	Carl Lundgren	11-9	3	67	0	2.94
R	Jock Menefee	8-10	0	39	1	3.00

Frank Chance

February 5 - The Cubs and American League rival White Sox announce a 15-game pre-season City Series. It will be the first cross-town pre-season exhibition in ML history.

April 22 - The Cubs lose to the Reds 5-3 on Opening Day at West Side Grounds.

May 6 - The Cubs score nine runs in the ninth to beat Deacon Phillippe and the Pirates 11-4.

July 2 - Pitcher Jack Doscher makes his major league debut for the Cubs, becoming the first son of a former major leaguer to also play in the big leagues. Jack's father, Herm, was a journeyman third baseman from 1872-1882, posting a career batting average of .225.

September 17 - The Cubs find themselves on the wrong end of a no-hitter - 10-0 to Philadelphia's Chick Fraser.

November17 - During an interview with a Chicago newspaper reporter, Joe Tinker says that it is "impossible to fix a major league game."

December 12 - During the post-season City Series, the Cubs' Jack Taylor is ridiculed by the press for losing three games to the Sox. He is overheard to say, "Why should I win? I get $100 from (owner James) Hart for winning and $500 for losing." He will be traded to the Cardinals over the winter for righthander Mordecai "Three Finger" Brown.

1904

Principle Owner and President: James Hart; **Manager:** Frank Selee; **Ballpark:** West Side Park; **Attendance:** 439,100; **Finish:** Second (93-60); **Recap:** The major leagues expand to the 154-game schedule that will last until the early 1960s. The

WORTH NOTING - Jimmy Slagle and Frank Chance combine to steal 100 bases in 1903.

Cubs win 93 games, finishing second behind John McGraw's powerful New York Giants. Outfielders Frank "Wildfire" Schulte and Solly Hoffman join the club this year. Both will play an important role in the team's future success - Schulte as the regular left fielder and Hoffman as a versatile utility player.

P	PLAYER	R	HR	RBI	SB	AVE
1B	Frank Chance	89	6	49	42	.310
2B	Johnny Evers	49	0	47	26	.265
SS	Joe Tinker	55	3	41	41	.221
3B	Doc Casey	71	1	43	21	.268
RF	Davy Jones	44	3	39	14	.244
CF	Jack McCarthy	36	0	51	14	.264
LF	Jimmy Slagle	73	1	31	28	.260
C	Johnny Kling	41	2	46	7	.243
UT	Shad Berry	29	1	26	12	.262
UT	Otto Williams	21	0	8	9	.200
P	Bob Wicker	17	0	9	4	.219
C	Jack O'Neill	8	1	19	1	.214
OF	Harry McChesney	9	0	11	2	.261

T	PITCHER	W-L	SV	SO	SH	ERA
L	Jake Weimer	20-14	0	177	5	1.91
R	Buttons Briggs	19-11	3	112	3	2.05
R	Carl Lundgren	17-10	1	106	2	2.60
R	Bob Wicker	17-8	0	99	4	2.67
R	Mordecai Brown	15-10	1	81	4	1.87

April 21 - The Cubs are victorious on Opening Day in Chicago, beating the Cardinals 4-1.

May 14 - Jack McCarthy steps on an umpire's broom behind the plate as he goes up to bat and sprains his ankle. National League President Harry Pulliam will later order arbiters to use pocket-sized whisk brooms to brush off the plate. The American League will follow suit in 1905.

May 30 - Frank Chance is beaned three times by Jack Harper of the Reds during the first game of a doubleheader. The third time he is hit in the head and knocked unconscious. He is revived and continues to play. In the second game, Chance is plunked twice by Win Kellum, giving him a record five hit by pitched balls for the day. The Cubs and Reds split the twinbill.

June 11 - Bob Wicker holds the Giants hitless for 11 innings before losing in the 12th, 1-0.

June 13 - Frank Chance hits for the cycle in a 3-2 win over Christy Mathewson and the Giants in New York.

1905

Principle Owner and President: James Hart; **Manager:** Frank Selee / Frank Chance; **Ballpark:** West Side Park; **Attendance:** 509,900; **Finish:** Third (92-61); **Recap:**In July, the Cubs announce that James Hart and Al Spalding have sold the franchise to Charles Taft of Cincinnati. Taft installs Charles Murphy as president. In September, Frank Selee is diagnosed with tuberculosis, and Murphy insists that he step down for health reasons. Murphy's next move is a pivotal one - installing Frank Chance as the team's new skipper.

P	PLAYER	R	HR	RBI	SB	AVE
1B	Frank Chance	92	2	70	38	.316
2B	Johnny Evers	44	1	37	19	.276
SS	Joe Tinker	70	2	66	31	.247
3B	Doc Casey	66	1	56	22	.232
RF	Billy Maloney	78	2	56	59	.260
CF	Jimmy Slagle	96	0	37	27	.269
LF	Wildfire Schulte	67	1	47	16	.274
C	Johnny Kling	26	1	52	13	.218
UT	Solly Hoffman	43	1	38	15	.237
UT	Jack McCarthy	16	0	14	8	.276
C	Jack O'Neill	16	0	12	6	.198

T	Pitcher	W-L	SV	SO	SH	ERA
R	Mordecai Brown	18-10	0	89	4	2.17
L	Jake Weimer	18-12	1	107	2	2.27
R	Ed Reulbach	18-14	1	152	5	1.42
R	Carl Lundgren	13-5	0	69	3	2.24
R	Bob Wicker	13-7	0	86	4	2.02

February 25 - While most clubs travel to Florida, Texas or Louisiana, the Cubs arrive in Santa Monica, California, for spring training.

April 19 - It's another Opening Day victory for the Cubs, as they beat the Reds 5-1 at West side Park.

April 26 - Outfielder Jack McCarthy cuts down three runners at home, becoming the second outfielder in history to complete three double plays in one game. The Cubs beat the Pirates 2-1.

June 13 - For eight innings, Three Finger Brown and the Giants'Christy Mathewson match no-hitters. The Giants break out with two hits in the ninth to win 1-0; Mathewson finishes his no-hitter.

June 24 - In St. Louis, rookie Ed Reulbach beats the Cardinals' Jack Taylor, a former Cub, in 18 innings by a score of 2-1.

July 12 - Three Finger Brown beats Mathewson 8-1, the first of nine straight wins over the Giants' ace. Brown will win 14 of his 28 career starts vs. Mathewson.

July 27 - Leo Durocher is born in West Springfield, Massachusettes.

July 31 - James Hart sells the Cubs to Cincinnati Reds owner Charles Taft for $125,000. Taft, brother of future President William Howard Taft, installs Charles Murphy as president.

August 24 - Ed Reulbach beats the Phils' Tully Sparks 2-1 in 20 innings. Reulbach sets the major league record for most innings pitched in a game.

September 14 - Enraged over Johnny Evers' decision to take a taxicab to the ballpark before an exhibition match in Washington, Indiana, leaving his teammates in the hotel lobby, Joe Tinker decks the second baseman on the field during the game. It will be 33 years before the two speak to each other again.

December 16 - The Cubs trade Jack McCarthy and outfielder Billy Malone, third baseman Doc Casey and pitcher Buttons Briggs to the Dodgers for outfielder Jimmy Sheckard.

1906

Principle Owner and President: Charles W. Murphy; **Manager:** Frank Chance; **Ballpark:** West Side Park; **Attendance:** 654,300; **Finish:** First (116-36); **Recap:** New manager Frank Chance is busy during the off-season, making a series of moves that will push the Cubs to not only the top of the league but into the history books as perhaps the greatest baseball team of all time. The most important transactions see outfielder Jimmy Sheckard acquired from the Dodgers and third baseman Harry Steinfeldt obtained from the Reds. Another deal brings pitcher Orval Overall from Cincinnati; Overall goes 12-3 down the stretch for Chicago. The Cubs compile the century's greatest won-lost percentage (.763) in the first of three straight pennants, finishing 20 games ahead of New York. Chicago lead the league in hitting (.262) and runs scored (705), ERA (1.75) and shutouts (30). The Cubs are also the first team to finish with less than 200 errors.

WORTH NOTING - Three Finger Brown's career ERA of 2.06 is third-best in major league history, behind Ed Walsh (1.82) and Addie Joss (1.89).

P	PLAYER	R	HR	RBI	SB	AVE
1B	Frank Chance	103	3	71	57	.319
2B	Johnny Evers	65	1	51	49	.255
SS	Joe Tinker	75	1	64	30	.233
3B	Harry Steinfeldt	81	3	83	29	.327
RF	Wildfire Schulte	77	7	60	25	.281
CF	Jimmy Slagle	71	0	33	25	.239
LF	Jimmy Sheckard	90	1	45	30	.262
C	Johnny Kling	45	2	46	14	.312
C	Pat Moran	22	0	35	6	.252
UT	Solly Hoffman	30	2	20	13	.256
UT	Doc Gessler	8	0	10	4	.253
IF	Pete Noonan	0	0	0	0	.333
C	Tom Walsh	0	0	0	0	.000

T	PITCHER	W-L	SV	SO	SH	ERA
R	Mordecai Brown	26-6	3	144	9	1.04
L	Jake Pfiester	20-8	0	153	4	1.56
R	Ed Reulbach	19-4	3	94	6	1.65
R	Carl Lundgren	17-6	2	103	5	2.21
R	Orval Overall	12-3	1	94	2	1.88

March 6 - The Cubs put the final piece to their dynasty in place, acquiring line drive-hitting third baseman Harry Steinfeldt from the Reds for rookie third baseman Hans Lobert and lefthander Jake Weimer. Lobert, no slouch himself, will bat .274 over a 14-year career with a high of .327 in 1912, leading the NL in fielding in 1913 and 1914.

April 18 - The Cubs launch their historic season with an 11-1 crushing of the Cardinals on Opening Day in Chicago.

April 28 - Frank Chance steals home in the ninth to give the Cubs a 1-0 win over Cincinnati. Meanwhile, Pittsburgh skipper Fred Clarke steals home during a 10-1 romp over St. Louis; it's the only time in history two managers steal home on the same day.

June 2 - The Cubs send pitcher Bob Wicker and $2,000 to the Reds for Orval Overall, a 225-pound righthander. Currently 4-5, Overall will go 12-3 for the Cubs.

June 7 - The Cubs pound Christy Mathewson and Joe McGinnity for 11 runs in the first inning of a 19-0 rout of the Giants. Mathewson helps the cause with six walks.

July 1 - The Cubs re-acquire pitcher Jack Taylor from the Cardinals in exchange for backup catcher Pete Noonan, rookie pitcher Fred Beebe, and cash. Taylor will go 12-3 the rest of the way.

August 7 - Chicago earns a forfeit victory when Giants manager John McGraw refuses to let umpire James Johnstone, who had ejected him from the game the day before, enter the Polo Grounds.

August 13 - Jack Taylor is knocked from the box in the third inning of today's game with Brooklyn, ending a record string of 187 straight complete games (including 15 relief appearances in which he finished each game) that began on June 20, 1901. The Brakeman will fail to finish just eight of his 286 career starts.

September 1 - With the umpires sick from food poisoning, pitcher Carl Lundgren and St. Louis catcher Pete Noonan umpire today's 8-1 Cubs victory in Chicago.

October 4 - The Cubs record their 116th win - still a major league record - by beating Pittsburgh 4-0 at Forbes Field. The win also gives them a 60-15 road record, a winning percentage (.800) that has never been matched.

October 9 - World Series Game 1

The Cubs are favored over the "Hitless Wonders" White Sox as the World Series opens at West Side Park. The two teams will alternate parks each game.

White Sox lefthander Nick Altrock outpitches Three Finger Brown in a bitterly cold 2-1 contest, attended by 12,693 at West Side Park. The South Siders score the winning run in the sixth, when George Rohe triples and scores when catcher Johnny Kling drops the relay throw from Brown.

October 10 - World Series Game 2
In Comiskey Park, Ed Reulbach tosses a one-hitter, the first of just five in World Series history, as the Cubs roll 7-1. The Cubs tally three runs in the second off lefty Doc White while getting only one ball out of the infield - a single to left field by Harry Steinfeldt.

Two bunts, an infield hit, and an error lead to the three runs. The Cubs score another run in the third, when Frank Chance stealing second and streaking home on a throwing error, and another in the sixth, with Joe Tinker coming home on a bad throw while stealing third.

October 11 - World Series Game 3
Ed Walsh hurls a two-hitter and the White Sox win 3-0 to take a two-games-to-one advantage. Jack Pfiester pitches shutout ball in eight of his nine innings, but gives up a bases-clearing triple to George Rohe in the sixth.

October 12 - World Series Game 4
Three Finger Brown evens the series with a two-hitter, holding the Sox hitless until the sixth, when Eddie Hahn singles up the middle. The Cubs win 1-0, scoring their only run in the sixth when left fielder Hahn loses a fly ball in the sun and it falls for a single and Johnny Evers delivers a two-out RBI hit.

WORTH NOTING- The Cubs' World Series opponents in 1906 are the Chicago White Sox, managed by **Fielder Jones**. The Hitless Wonders finish with a 93-58 (.616) record, leading the American League in shutouts (32) but finishing last in hitting (.230).

P	PLAYER	R	HR	RBI	SB	BA
1B	Jiggs Donahue	70	1	57	36	.257
2B	Frank Isbell	71	0	57	37	.279
SS	George Davis	63	0	80	27	.277
3B	Les Tannehill	26	0	33	7	.183
RF	Bill O'Neill	37	1	21	19	.248
CF	Fielder Jones	77	2	34	26	.230
LF	Eddie Hahn	80	0	27	19	.227
C	Billy Sullivan	37	1	33	10	.214

T	PITCHER	W	L	SV	SH	ERA
R	Frank Owen	22	13	2	7	2.33
L	Nick Altrock	20	13	1	4	2.06
L	Doc White	18	6	0	7	1.52
R	Ed Walsh	17	13	3	10	1.88
R	Roy Patterson	10	7	1	3	2.09

October 13 - Game Five @ Chicago
Game Five at West Side Grounds draws a series-best 23,257 fans, thanks to the deadlock and warmer weather. Despite the large crowd and the presence of a couple of large bear cubs, the White Sox roll to an 8-6 win over Ed Reulbach. Thanks to a rule declaring any ball hit into the crowd ringing the outfield a double, 11 two-baggers are hit o the day.

October 14 - Game Six @ Chicago
Pitching on one day's rest, Three Finger Brown allows seven six runs and eight hits in just under two innings and the Sox take the series, 8-3 at South Side Park. The Sox are helped when a South Side policeman kicks Wildfire Schulte as he tracks down a

WORTH QUOTING - "You do things my way or you meet me after the game."
-Frank Chance

Mordecai Centennial "Three Finger" Brown

fly ball off the bat of shortstop George Davis in the first that falls for a double. The Cubs fight back from a 7-1 deficit and even load the bases in the ninth, but Schulte grounds to first to end the game, and the series. It's one of the biggest upsets in baseball history.

1907

Principle Owner and President: Charles W. Murphy; **Manager:** Frank Chance; **Ballpark:** West Side Park; **Attendance:** 422,550; **Finish:** First (107-45); **Recap:** After a 17-game New York winning streak, the Cubs and Giants have identical 24-7 records on May 20. But the Cubbies catch fire and make a mockery of the pennant race after that. Again, the pitching staff is the league's best, compiling a 1.73 ERA and NL-best 32 shutouts.

The Cubs win 107 games despite a batting order that features no more than 2 homers or 70 RBIs from any of its batters. They score just 3.8 runs per game, the fewest of any pennant winner in history.

P	Player	R	HR	RBI	SB	AVE
1B	Frank Chance	58	1	50	35	.293
2B	Johnny Evers	66	2	51	46	.250
SS	Joe Tinker	36	1	36	20	.221
3B	Harry Steinfeldt	52	1	70	19	.266
RF	Wildfire Schulte	44	2	32	7	.287
CF	Jimmy Slagle	71	0	32	28	.258
LF	Jimmy Sheckard	76	1	36	31	.267
C	Johnny Kling	44	1	43	9	.284
UT	Solly Hoffman	67	1	36	29	.268
C	Pat Moran	8	1	19	5	.227
UT	Del Howard	10	0	13	3	.230
R	Newt Randall	6	0	4	2	.205
UT	Kid Durbin	2	0	0	0	.333

T	Pitcher	W-L	SV	SO	SH	ERA
R	Orval Overall	23-8	3	141	8	1.68
R	Mordecai Brown	20-6	3	107	6	1.39
R	Carl Lundgren	18-7	0	84	7	1.17
R	Ed Reulbach	17-4	0	96	4	1.69
L	Jack Pfiester	15-9	0	90	3	1.15

April 11 - The Cubs beat the Cardinals 6-1 in the season opener at West Side Park.

May 21 - Umpires Hank O'Day and Bob Emslie are mobbed by the crowd, spurred on by Giants manager John McGraw, after a game with the Cubs at the Polo Grounds. The two arbiters require police protection as they leave the stadium.

July 8 - Frank Chance requires a police escort himself after a 5-0 Cubs win in Brooklyn. Bombarded by bottles throughout the game, Chance hurls one back into the stands, hitting a small boy.

September 1 - Down 2-0, St. Louis scores seven runs off Ed Reulbach to beat the Cubs in Chicago. The Cubbies will be shut out twice the next day by the last-place Cards.

October 8 - World Series Game 1
Game one ends in a tie, called for darkness

in the 12th, as the Cubs rally for two runs in the ninth at West Side Grounds after allowing three to cross the plate in the eighth. Chicago loads the bases on a single, a hit batsman, and an error. Frank Chance scores on a Wildfire Schulte groundout, then Detroit catcher Boss Schmidt drops Del Howard's third strike, and Harry Steinfieldt streaks home to tie the game. Johnny Evers then tries to steal home but is thrown out.

Schmidt will be later accused of dropping the ball on purpose, since the World Series purses are larger if more than four games are played (leading to the current rule that the World Series shares are based on the first four games, rather than the whole series).

WORTH NOTING- The Cubs' World Series opponents in 1907 are the Detroit Tigers, managed by **Hughie Jennings**. The Tigers finish with a 92-58 (.613) record, leading the American League in runs (694), hits (1383), and batting average (.266).

P	PLAYER	R	HR	RBI	SB	BA
1B	Claude Rossman	60	0	69	20	.277
2B	Red Downs	28	1	42	3	.219
SS	Charley O'Leary	61	0	34	11	.241
3B	Bill Coughlin	80	0	46	15	.243
RF	Ty Cobb	97	5	119	49	.350
CF	Sam Crawford	102	4	81	18	.323
LF	Davy Jones	101	0	27	30	.273
C	Boss Schmidt	32	0	23	8	.244

T	PITCHER	W	L	SV	SH	ERA
R	Bill Donovan	25	4	1	3	2.19
L	Ed Killian	25	13	0	3	1.78
R	George Mullin	20	20	3	5	2.60
L	Ed Siever	19	10	1	3	2.16
R	John Eubank	2	3	0	1	2.67

October 9 - World Series Game 2

Jack Pfiester scatters nine hits to beat the Tigers 3-1, aided by several great defensive plays by his teammates. Pfiester gets himself into trouble in the first, allowing the first two batters to single, but he fans Sam Crawford and gets Ty Cobb to ground into a double play. In the fourth, Cobb leads off with a single and moves to third on a single by Claude Rossman, but Rossman is gunned down by Wildfire Schulte as he tries for a double and Cobb is stranded on third.

In the fifth, Jimmy Sheckard makes a leaping catch against the left field fence, saving a run. In the seventh, Sheckard makes a shoestring catch and Johnny Kling throws out Charley O'Leary trying to steal. Kling stops another rally in the eighth when he throws out Davy Jones trying to steal with runners on first and third and two out. In the ninth, the Tigers put the leadoff man on for the seventh time in the game, but Bill Coughlin lines into a double play.

October 10 - World Series Game 3

Ed Reulbach tosses a six-hitter as the Cubs take a two-games-to-none lead with a 5-1 win. Reulbach retires the first 10 batters until Germany Schaefer beats out a bunt hit in the fouth.

The Cubs' outstanding defense again protects an early lead. In the fifth, the Tigers put runners on first and third with none out, but Charley O'Leary lines to Joe Tinker, who tags the runner for an unassisted double play.

In the sixth, the Tigers put the first two runners on again, but the Cubs turn a double play and Jimmy Slagle catches a deep fly for the final out. In the seventh, Bill Coughlin rips a line drive off Reulbach's shin but Joe Tinker fields the ball and gets him at first. Hurt but not out, Reulbach stays in the game.

October 11 - World Series Game 4

The World Series shifts to Detroit where just 11,306 despondent fans show up for a rainy 6-1 loss. The Tigers actually take a

1-0 lead off Orval Overall in the fourth when Ty Cobb triples with two out and scores on a single by Claude Rossman. The Tigers then load the bases, but Overall strikes out Charley O'Leary to end the inning.

O'Leary, still miffed over his rally-killing strikeout, uncorks a wild throw on a Johnny Evers grounder leading off the next inning. After a rain delay, Wildfire Schulte walks, Joe Tinker bunts the runners to second and third, and Overall singles them both home. An epidemic of errors leads to three Cubs runs in the seventh.

October 12 - World Series Game 5
The Cubs take their first World Championship as Three Finger Brown fires a seven-hit, 2-0 shutout in front of just 7,370 fans at Bennett Park. Chicago scores the only run it needs in the first, as Jimmy Slagle walks, steals second, and scores on a single by Harry Steinfeldt. They score their second run in the next inning on an error, a single, a double steal, a walk, and a groundout.

Brown gets into trouble just once, in the fourth. Sam Crawford leads off the inning with a double. Brown fans Ty Cobb, but a single by Claude Rossman puts runners on the corners. Brown then retires Bill Coughlin on a foul out and Jimmy Archer on a fly to left. Joe Tinker catches a popup by pinch-hitter Boss Schmidt for the final out of the series.

WORTH NOTING - Three-Finger Brown gained his nickname thanks to two childhood incidents on his Indiana farm. In the first accident, he caught his index finger in a corn shredder and had to have it amputated above the knuckle. A couple of weeks later he broke his third and fourth fingers and they never grew straight.

At the height of his career, the corn shredder was a tourist attraction in his home town of Nyesville, Indiana.

1908

Principle Owner and President: Charles W. Murphy; **Manager:** Frank Chance; **Ballpark:** West Side Park; **Attendance:** 665,325; **Finish:** First (99-55); **Recap:** The Cubs take their third straight flag but this time it's not a cakewalk. Chicago struggles with Pittsburgh and New York for most of the season, with the turning point coming on September 23rd at the Polo Grounds when Johnny Evers turns what should be a game-winning single by Fred Merkle into a game-ending force-out. The play, forever referred to as the Merkle Boner, turns out to be crucial to the pennant race as the game is ordered replayed on October 8 and is won by the Cubs for the pennant.

That the Cubs finished in the first division at all is largely due to the pitching staff, since no member of the lineup drives in more than 68 runs.

P	Player	R	HR	RBI	SB	AVE
1B	Frank Chance	65	2	55	27	.272
2B	Johnny Evers	83	0	37	36	.300
SS	Joe Tinker	67	6	68	30	.266
3B	Harry Steinfeldt	63	1	62	12	.241
RF	Wildfire Schulte	42	1	43	15	.236
CF	Jimmy Slagle	38	0	26	17	.222
LF	Jimmy Sheckard	54	2	22	18	.231
C	Johnny Kling	51	4	59	16	.276
UT	Solly Hoffman	55	2	42	15	.243
UT	Del Howard	42	1	26	11	.279
C	Pat Moran	12	0	12	6	.260
UT	Heinie Zimmerman	17	0	9	2	.292
OF	Kid Durbin	3	0	0	0	.250

T	Pitcher	W-L	SV	SO	SH	ERA
R	Mordecai Brown	29-9	5	123	9	1.47
R	Ed Reulbach	24-7	1	133	7	2.02
R	Orval Overall	15-11	4	167	4	1.92
L	Jack Pfiester	12-10	0	117	3	2.00
R	Chick Fraser	11-9	2	66	2	2.26

April 22 - The Cubs defeat the Reds 7-3 on Opening Day at West Side Park.

May 12 - Orval Overall is beaten for the

first time in 14 games, since August 11, 1907, by the Phillies 6-2.

August 27 - The Cubs complete a three-game sweep of the Giants in New York to move within one-half game of the league lead. Electric bulletin boards show the action in Chicago.

September 4 - With Pittsburgh and Chicago tied 0-0 in the bottom of the 10th at Forbes Field with two outs and the bases loaded, Pirates right fielder Owen Wilson singles to center, scoring left fielder Fred Clarke with the winning run. Pittsburgh's Doc Gill, on at first base, turns and runs to the dugout before touching second base. Johnny Evers calls for the ball from center fielder Jimmy Slagle, touches second, and declares that the run doesn't count since Gill has been forced out. The umpire, Hank O'Day, has left the field; the Cubs will protest the game to National League president Harry Pulliam but be denied. Evers will try this tactic in a more important game later in the month.

September22 - The Cubs sweep a doubleheader at the Polo Grounds, 4-3 and 2-1, tying the Giants for the league lead.

September 23 - In the most controversial game of the year - if not in history - Three Finger Brown and the Giants' Christy Mathewson battle to a 1-1 tie in the ninth. With New York's Harry McCormick on third base and Fred Merkle on first base, shortstop Al Bridwell singles, scoring McCormick. Merkle, seeing the winning run cross the plate, stops short of second base and heads for the dugout. Johnny Evers finds a ball (whether or not it's the game ball is unknown to this day) and touches second base as the crowd descends upon the field. Hank O'Day, again finding himself in the center of the controversy, declares that he didn't see the play, but that evening rules the game a tie.

WORTH NOTING - In 1908, Ed Reulbach beat the Dodgers a record nine times.

September24 - National League President Harry Pulliam upholds O'Day's decision and declares the previous day's game a tie. The Cubs immediately demand that the game be forfeited to them since the crowd had ran onto the field, preventing play from continuing.

Meanwhile, the Cubs beat the Giants 5-4 to take a one-game lead.

September 26 - Ed Reulbach caps a wild week for the Cubs by tossing a pair of complete game shutouts over Brooklyn, beating them 5-0 and 2-0 in less than three hours. Reulbach will compile 44 consecutive scoreless innings, a record until New York's Carl Hubbell hurls 46 in 1933.

October 4 - The Cubs beat the third-place Pirates 5-2 before 30,247, the largest West Side Park crowd ever.

October 5 - The National League directors rule that the September 23 Giants-Cubs game must be replayed on October 8, two days after NLpresident Harry Pulliam rejects the idea of calling in Fred Merkle for an interview.

October 8 - The Cubs whip Christy Mathewson and the Giants 4-2 in the replay of the September 23 game, handing the Cubs the pennant. Mathewson later admits to having "nothing on the ball."

October 10 - World Series Game 1
The Series begins in front of 10,812 fans at rainy Bennett Park. Ed Reulbach and Ed

WORTH NOTING- The Cubs' World Series opponents in 1908 are the Detroit Tigers, managed by **Hughie Jennings**. The Tigers finish with a 90-63 (.588) record, leading the American League in runs (647), hits (1347), doubles (199), and average (.263).

P	PLAYER	R	HR	RBI	SB	BA
1B	Claude Rossman	45	2	71	8	.294
2B	Red Downs	29	1	35	2	.221
SS	Germany Schaefer	96	3	52	40	.259
3B	Bill Coughlin	32	0	23	10	.215
RF	Ty Cobb	88	4	108	39	.324
CF	Sam Crawford	102	7	80	15	.311
LF	Matty McIntyre	105	0	28	20	.295
C	Boss Schmidt	45	1	38	5	.265

T	PITCHER	W	L	SV	SH	ERA
R	Ed Summers	24	12	1	5	1.64
R	Bill Donovan	18	7	0	6	2.07
R	George Mullin	17	12	1	1	3.09
R	Ed Willett	15	9	1	2	2.28
L	Ed Killian	12	10	1	0	2.98

Killian make the start for their respective teams, but neither is around at the end when Killian is knocked out in the third and Reulbach in the seventh in a 10-6 Chicago victory.

The Cubs score four in the third off Killian on a double, three singles, a walk, and an error. The Tigers rally back with three in the seventh off Reulbach and then take the lead in the eighth with two off Orval Overall and Three Finger Brown.

Behind 6-5 in the ninth, the Cubs tag Ed Summers for five runs, going ahead on a two-run, bases-loaded single by Solly Hoffman. Brown retires Ty Cobb with two men on in the bottom of the ninth to end the game.

WORTH QUOTING - "My favorite umpire is a dead one."

-Johnny Evers

October 11 - World Series Game 2

Just over 17,000 fans show up at West Side Grounds as team president Charles Murphy decides to quintuple ticket prices - pocketing much of the take - but the Cubs rally for a 6-1 win behind Orval Overall.

Both teams are held scoreless until the eighth, when Chicago explodes for six runs off Wild Bill Donovan on a Solly Hoffman double, a home run (the first World Series homer in Cubs history) by Joe Tinker, a Johnny Kling double, a triple by Wildfire Schulte,a and a wild pitch. The Bengals touch Overall for a run in the ninth but the game ends on a Tinker-to-Evers-to-Chance double play.

October 12 - World Series Game 3

The Tigers take their only series win when they erase a 3-1 Cubs lead with five runs in the sixth and two more in the eighth. Ty Cobb, who has four hits on the day, then rubs it in when, after singling in the ninth, steals second and third with a five-run Detroit lead. He's thrown out trying to steal home.

October 13 - World Series Game 4

Mordecai Brown extends his string of World Series shutout innings to 20 when he hurls a 3-0 shutout at Bennett Park, giving the Cubs a three-games-to-one lead. Run scoring singles by Harry Steinfeldt and Solly Hoffman in the third account for the game's only tallies.

A Tigers threat in the sixth is snuffed. The first two batters single to put runners on first and second but Brown pounces on a Ty Cobb bunt attempt and throws out the runner at third. Johnny Kling then picks Sam Crawford off second and Brown ends the inning by striking out Claude Rossman.

October 14 - World Series Game 5

Orval Overall, who would be the Series' MVP were there to be one, tosses a three-hit shutout, in front of the smallest World Series crowd in history (6,210). The Cubs score the only run they need on consecutive singles in the first by Johnny Evers, Wildfire Schulte and Frank Chance. An RBI double by Evers in the fifth gives Overall an insurance run.

Orvie gets into trouble only once, in the first, by walking Matty McIntyre and allowing a one-out single to Sam Crawford. Overall then fans Ty Cobb but Johnny Kling drops a called third strike, allowing Claude Rossman to reach first, loading the bases. Overall then fans Germany Schaefer - the fourth strikeout of the inning - to end the frame. He gets the Tigers 1-2-3 in the ninth on groundouts to give the Cubbies their second straight World Championship. Once again, Boss Schmidt tallies the final out, becoming the only man in history to make the last out in two consecutive World Series.

Joe Tinker and Johnny Evers

1909

Principle Owner and President: Charles W. Murphy; **Manager:** Frank Chance; **Ballpark:** West Side Park; **Attendance:** 633,480; **Finish:** Second (104-49); **Recap:** At the end of last year's World Series, Johnny Kling announced his retirement to become a professional pool player. Though Kling wasn't much of a threat in the batters box, his presence behind the plate gave the Cubs pitching staff confidence enough that many feel that his removal from the lineup costs the team a fourth straight pennant in 1909. With the team batting .245, it is once again the pitching that keeps the Cubs in hot pursuit of the pennant-winning Pirates. Three Finger Brown and Orval Overall combine for 47 wins and Ed Reulbach rides a 14-game winning streak to a 19-110 record. Overall leads the league in strikeouts (205), the only Cub to reach 200 until Ferguson Jenkins in 1967.

P	Player	R	HR	RBI	SB	AVE
1B	Frank Chance	53	0	46	29	.272
2B	Johnny Evers	88	1	24	28	.263
SS	Joe Tinker	56	4	57	23	.256
3B	Harry Steinfeldt	73	2	59	22	.252
RF	Wildfire Schulte	57	4	60	23	.264
CF	Solly Hoffman	60	2	58	20	.285
LF	Jimmy Sheckard	81	1	43	15	.255
C	Jimmy Archer	31	1	30	5	.230
C	Pat Moran	18	1	23	2	.220
IF	Del Howard	25	1	24	6	.197
IF	Heinie Zimmerman	23	0	21	7	.273
T	**Pitcher**	**W-L**	**SV**	**SO**	**SH**	**ERA**
R	Mordecai Brown	27-9	7	172	8	1.31
R	Orval Overall	20-11	3	205	9	1.42
R	Ed Reulbach	19-10	0	105	6	1.78
L	Jack Pfiester	17-6	0	73	5	2.42
L	Rube Kroh	9-4	0	51	2	1.65

January 11 - Owner Charles Murphy announces a $10,000 bonus to his players for winning the World Series.

February 4 - Former Chicago star John Clarkson dies at age 47 in Belmont, Massachusetts. Clarkson won 326 games

WORTH NOTING - A poem entitled "Baseball's Sad Lexicon", written by Franklin P. Adams, a Giants fan and sportswriter for the New York Evening Mail, first appeared in 1910.

These are the saddest of possible words—
Tinker to Evers to Chance
Trio of bear cubs and fleeter than birds
Tinker to Evers to Chance
Thoughtlessly pricking our gonfalon bubble,
Words that are weighty with nothing but trouble—
Tinker to Evers to Chance

in the 19th century.

March 28 - Lon Warneke is born in Mt. Ida, Arkansas.

April 9 - Claude Passeau is born in Waynesboro, Mississippi.

April 14 - It's another season-opening win as the Cubs beat the Cardinals 3-1.

May 2 - Pittsburgh star Honus Wagner steals second, third, and home in the first inning of a game with the Cubs. It's the fourth time Wagner has pulled off the trick, a National League record.

August 10 - Ed Reulbach beats the Dodgers 8-1 for his 14th straight win.

August 14 - The Giants snap Reulbach's 14-game winning streak, 5-2. It's the second 14-game streak of his career.

August 23 - The Cubs steal home three times in a win vs. Boston. Johnny Evers and Del Howard do it in the first, Solly Hoffman in the second.

September 16 - Christy Mathewson beats Three Finger Brown 3-1 in Chicago. President William Howard Taft attends the game.

December 6 - Stan Hack is born in Sacramento, California.

1910

Principle Owner and President: Charles W. Murphy; **Manager:** Frank Chance; **Ballpark:** West Side Park; **Attendance:** 526,152; **Finish:** First (104-50); **Recap:** After tanking it as a pool professional, Johnny Kling returns to the lineup and, not coincidentally, Chicago wins its fourth pennant in five years. With Three Finger Brown and rookie King Cole leading the way, the Cubs compile 104 wins. Wildfire Schulte and Solly Hoffman lead a rejuvenated offense. In September, however, Johnny Evers breaks his leg, ending his season. The weakened Cubs lose the World Series to Connie Mack's Philadelphia Athletics in five games.

P	Player	R	HR	RBI	SB	AVE
1B	Frank Chance	54	0	36	16	.298
2B	Johnny Evers	87	0	28	28	.263
SS	Joe Tinker	48	3	69	20	.288
3B	Harry Steinfeldt	70	2	58	10	.252
RF	Wildfire Schulte	93	10	68	22	.301
CF	Solly Hoffman	83	3	86	29	.325
LF	Jimmy Sheckard	82	5	51	22	.256
C	Johnny Kling	31	2	32	3	.269
UT	Heinie Zimmerman	35	3	38	7	.284
UT	Jimmy Archer	36	2	41	6	.259
OF	Ginger Beaumont	30	2	22	4	.267
UT	John Kane	11	1	12	2	.242
UT	Tom Needham	9	0	10	1	.184

T	Pitcher	W-L	SV	SO	SH	ERA
R	Mordecai Brown	25-13	7	143	6	1.80
R	King Cole	20-4	1	114	4	1.80
R	Harry McIntire	13-9	0	65	2	3.07
R	Orval Overall	12-6	1	92	4	2.66
R	Ed Reulbach	12-8	0	55	1	3.12

January 16 - Dizzy Dean is born in Lucas, Arkansas.

April 1 - The Cubs reinstate catcher Johnny Kling, who played for a semipro team in Chicago last year while holding out for a bigger contract for the Cubs. Kling agrees to a $700 fine and is required to play at his 1908 salary, $4,500.

April 27 - The Cubs nip the Pirates 1-0 on Opening Day at West Side Park.

June 22 - John Tener, who pitched for Chicago in 1888-89, wins the Republican nomination for Governor in Pennsylvania. He will be elected and serve as National League President at the same time.

June 28 - Joe Tinker steals home twice during an 11-1 win over Cincinnati.

July 31 - Rookie King Cole hurls a seven-inning no-hitter, beating St. Louis 4-0.

October 1 - The Cubs receive a damaging blow as Johnny Evers breaks his ankle sliding home in Cincinnati. Evers will not be available in the World Series.

October 17 - World Series Game 1
Chief Bender tosses a three-hitter to beat the Cubs 4-1 in front of 26,891 at Shibe Park. Orval Overall allows three runs over three innings, taking the loss. Harry McIntire pitches five innings of one-hit relief, allowing just an unearned run in the eighth. The Cubs push across their only run off Bender in the ninth when Johnny Kling singles home Joe Tinker. Wildfire Schulte is caught stealing twice.

October 18 - World Series Game 2
The Athletics bomb Three Finger Brown, ending his World Series scoreless streak at 24 2/3 innings, and the Cubs 9-3 to go up two games to none. Four doubles off Brown in the seventh lead to six runs. The Cubs strand 14 runners in the game, losing to Jack Coombs.

October 20 - World Series Game 3
Despite a return to West Side Grounds, the Cubs lose to Jack Coombs again, 12-5 as Ed Reulbach only lasts two innings and Harry McIntire is bombed for five in the third. Frank Chance becomes the first manager ejected from a World Series game when umpire Tom Connolly runs him for protesting Danny Murphy's home run off a sign over the right field bleachers in the inning, arguing that it should be ruled a ground-rule double.

WORTH NOTING- The Cubs' World Series opponents in 1910 are the Philadelphia Athletics, managed by **Connie Mack**. The Athletics finish with a 102-48 (.680) record, leading the American League in hits (1376), doubles (194), triples (106), batting average (.266, shutouts (24) and ERA(1.78).

P	PLAYER	R	HR	RBI	SB	BA
1B	Harry Davis	61	1	41	17	.248
2B	Eddie Collins	81	3	81	81	.322
SS	Jack Barry	64	3	60	14	.259
3B	Frank Baker	83	2	74	21	.283
RF	Danny Murphy	70	4	64	18	.300
CF	Rube Oldring	79	4	57	17	.308
LF	Topsy Hartsel	45	0	22	11	.221
C	Jack Lapp	18	0	17	0	.234

T	PITCHER	W	L	SV	SH	ERA
R	Jack Coombs	31	9	2	13	1.30
R	Chief Bender	23	5	1	3	1.58
R	Cy Morgan	18	12	0	3	1.55
L	Eddie Plank	16	10	2	1	2.02
L	Harry Krause	6	6	0	2	2.89

WORTH NOTING - From 1906-1910, the Cubs posted the highest winning percentage for a five-year period. They won 530 and lost only 235, for a winning percentage of .692.

Wildfire Schulte

October 22 - World Series Game 4
The Cubs avoid a sweep as they rally in the ninth for a run that ties the game and win it in the 10th. Down 3-2 in the bottom of the last frame, Wildfire Schulte doubles off Chief Bender and Frank Chance triples him home. The Cubs muff a chance to win the game when, with the winning run on third, Heinie Zimmerman pops out and Harry Steinfeldt fouls out.

Jimmy Archer opens the 10th with a double and scores the game-winner on a single by Jimmy Sheckard.

October 23 - World Series Game 5
Three Finger Brown, who tossed two scoreless innings the day before, keeps the Cubs in the game, 2-1, until the seventh, when the Athletics score five runs on four hits, two walks, and a wild pitch to win 7-2. Wildfire Schulte is again caught stealing twice, making him the only player caught stealing two times in two games of the same World Series.

1911

Principle Owner and President: Charles W. Murphy; **Manager:** Frank Chance; **Ballpark:** West Side Park; **Attendance:** 576,000; **Finish:** Second (92-62); **Recap:** The aging Cubs finish second, 7 1/2 games behind the Giants. Before the end of the season, Johnny Kling and Harry Steinfeldt are traded off and the team is forced to endure a nervous breakdown by Johnny Evers and the retiring of 29-year-old Orval Overall. After the season, the team receives a couple more crippling blows when Jim Doyle, who replaced Steinfeldt at third, dies of an appendicitis attack and Frank Chance, who takes himself out of the line-up in July because of severe headaches, is diagnosed with a blood clot in his brain from having been beaned so many times.

Wildfire Schulte takes advantage of a new, more tightly-wound official ball and leads the National League in home runs (21) and RBI (147) and becomes the first player to have more than 20 doubles (30), triples (21) and homers in one season. Schulte easily wins the National League's first MVP award, edging New York's Christy Mathewson.

P	PLAYER	R	HR	RBI	SB	AVE
1B	Vic Saier	42	1	37	11	.259
2B	Heinie Zimmerman	80	9	85	23	.307
SS	Joe Tinker	61	4	69	30	.278
3B	Jim Doyle	69	5	62	19	.282
RF	Wildfire Schulte	105	21	147	23	.300
CF	Solly Hoffman	66	2	70	30	.252
LF	Jimmy Sheckard	121	4	50	32	.276
C	Jimmy Archer	41	4	41	5	.253
OF	Wilbur Good	27	2	21	10	.269
IF	Dave Shean	17	0	15	4	.193
IF	Johnny Evers	29	0	7	6	.226
C	Peaches Graham	6	0	8	2	.239
IF	Frank Chance	23	1	17	9	.241

T	Pitcher	W-L	SV	SO	SH	ERA
R	Mordecai Brown	21-11	13	129	0	2.80
R	King Cole	18-7	0	101	2	3.13
R	Ed Reulbach	16-9	0	79	2	2.96
R	Lew Richie	15-11	1	78	4	2.31
R	Harry McIntire	11-7	0	56	1	4.11

April 12 - The Cardinals and Cubs tie 3-3 on Opening Day at West Side Park.

May 29 - The Pennsylvania Railroad sets a speed record while carrying the Cubs from Columbus, Ohio to Pittsburgh, covering the 191 miles in 215 minutes. The Cubs beat the Pirates 4-1.

May 30 - The Cubs drop from first place to third by losing a twinbill in Pittsburgh.

June 3 - Wildfire Schulte smacks a grand slam to beat the Giants. Schulte will hit four grand slams this year, a major league record until Babe Ruth ties it in 1919 and Ernie Banks tops it in 1955. The four Schulte hits this year will be his only grand slams over an 11-year career.

June 10 - The Cubbies trade catcher Johnny Kling, pitchers Hank Griffin and Orlie Weaver, and outfielder Al Kaiser to the Braves for catcher Peaches Graham, outfielder Bill Collins and pitcher Cliff Curtis.

June 11 - Heinie Zimmerman drives in nine runs with two homers, a triple and a single in a 20-2 crushing of Boston.

June 28 - Joe Tinker becomes the first player ever to steal home twice in a game during the Cubs' 11-1 win over Cincinnati.

July 1 - Manager Frank Chance leaves today's game with a headache. A blood clot in the brain will be discovered, effectively ending Chance's playing career.

July 20 - Wildfire Schulte hits for the cycle in a 4-3 victory over the Phillies.

August 5 - Angered over what he terms Joe Tinker's "indifferent play," Chance fines the shortstop $150.

October 1 - Jimmy Sheckard sets a major league record for walks with his 147th in a loss to the Giants. The record will hold until Dodger Eddie Stanky draws 148 in 1945.

1912

Principle Owner and President: Charles W. Murphy; **Manager:** Frank Chance; **Ballpark:** West Side Park; **Attendance:** 514,000; **Finish:** Third (91-59); **Recap:** Johnny Evers, who sat out most of 1911 with a nervous breakdown, enjoys a breakout year, batting .341, 65 points higher than his career average. Heinie Zimmerman just misses the Triple Crown and leads the NL in hits (207), average (.372), doubles (41), home runs (14) and slugging (.571). Spitballing rookie Larry Cheney spearheads the pitching staff, checking in with a 26-10 record.

After the season, Charles Murphy fires manager Frank Chance and finds himself in a public relations mess. To appease public outcry, he hires Evers as his new manager. Joe Tinker, who has feuded with Evers for years over the taxicab argument, demands a trade and is accommodated in an eight-player deal with Cincinnati.

P	Player	R	HR	RBI	SB	AVE
1B	Vic Saier	74	2	61	11	.288
2B	Johnny Evers	73	1	63	16	.341
SS	Joe Tinker	80	0	75	25	.282
3B	Heinie Zimmerman	95	14	99	23	.372
RF	Wildfire Schulte	90	13	64	17	.264
CF	Tommy Leach	50	2	32	14	.242
LF	Jimmy Sheckard	85	3	47	15	.245
C	Jimmy Archer	35	5	58	7	.283

P	PLAYER	R	HR	RBI	SB	AVE
OF	Ward Miller	45	0	22	11	.307
IF	Red Downs	9	1	14	5	.263
OF	Wilbur Good	7	0	1	3	.143
UT	Solly Hoffman	28	0	18	5	.282
C	Tom Needham	12	0	10	3	.178

T	PITCHER	W-L	SV	SO	SH	ERA
R	Larry Cheney	26-10	0	140	4	2.85
R	Lew Richie	16-8	0	69	4	2.95
R	Jimmy Lavender	16-13	3	109	3	3.03
R	Ed Reulbach	10+6	4	75	0	3.78
L	Lefty Leifield	7-2	0	23	1	2.41

February 1 - Third baseman Jim Doyle, who hit .282 for the Cubs last season, dies of complications during an appendicitis operation. Doyle's replacement, Heinie Zimmerman, will win the batting title.

April 12 - Frank Chance starts at first base for the last time; marking the final game in which the Tinker-Evers-Chance double play combination plays together. Vic Saier will replace Chance.

April 20 - Jimmy Sheckard almost commits a boner when he knocks a game winning home run and heads for the dugout before touching second. Sheckard's teammates yell at him to complete the circuit, which he does. The Cubs win their home opener 5-4. The manager of the Reds is Hank O'Day, who officiated the ill-fated Merkle Boner game in 1908.

July 8 - Rookie Jimmy Lavender and the Cubs stop New York lefty Rube Marquard's record 19-game winning streak, 7-2 in Chicago.

August 12 - Cubs owner Charles Murphy stirs up a hornet's nest by implying that the Cardinals and other clubs are going easy on John McGraw's Giants. Phillies owner Horace Fogel, who some assert is a puppet for Murphy, echoes the accusation, charging National League umpires with favoritism. Fogel's unfortunate comments will lead to his expulsion from baseball.

September 28 - After an operation for a blood clot in his brain, Frank Chance is released. He'll manage the Yankees for the next two seasons.

October 2 - Cubs catcher Dick Cotter bats out of turn in a game against Pittsburgh. Pirates manager Fred Clarke doesn't catch the error until after the game is over, but his protest will be upheld by National League President Thomas J. Lynch.

October 6 - Heinie Zimmerman's 0-for-3 performance today gives him just two hits over the last week, but it's good enough to finish at .372, the league's best.

October 24 - The Cubs name Johnny Evers manager.

December 11 - The Cubs trade shortstop Joe Tinker, catcher Harry Chapman, and pitcher Grover Lowdermilk to the Reds for pitcher Bert Humphries, infielders Red Corriden and Art Phelan, and outfielders Mike Mitchell and Pete Knisely. Tinker will be named Cincinnati's manager.

1913

Principle Owner and President: Charles Murphy; **Manager:** Johnny Evers; **Ballpark:** West Side Park; **Attendance:** 419,000; **Finish:** Third (88-65); **Recap:** It's obvious why Chicago sportswriters nickname manager Johnny Evers "The Crab" as he spends a third-place 1913 campaign fighting with his players, some of them during games on the field. It is no surprise when Evers is fired at the end of the season in favor of former umpire Hank O'Day. What *is* a surprise is the handling of Evers's departure. After Evers is sacked as manager, team president Charles

Murphy declares that he is working on a deal to send the second baseman to the Boston Braves. Evers responds by threatening to jump to the new Federal League's Chicago Whales. National League president John Tener then summons Murphy to a meeting in Cincinnati, where he calls him on the carpet for causing the potential loss of an NL star to the outlaw FL, recalls a few of his other administrative blunders, and asks that he resign. Under an agreement, Cubs owner Charles Taft buys out the stock Murphy has in the club for half a million dollars and installs Charles Thomas as club president. As for Evers, he's traded to Boston anyway, helping the Miracle Braves win the 1914 pennant.

P	PLAYER	R	HR	RBI	SB	AVE
1B	Vic Saier	93	14	92	26	.288
2B	Johnny Evers	81	3	49	11	.284
SS	Al Bridwell	35	1	37	12	.240
3B	Heinie Zimmerman	69	9	95	18	.313
RF	Wildfire Schulte	85	9	68	21	.279
CF	Tommy Leach	99	6	37	21	.289
LF	Mike Mitchell	37	4	35	15	.259
C	Jimmy Archer	38	2	44	4	.267
IF	Art Phelan	41	2	35	8	.251
OF	Ward Miller	23	1	16	13	.236
C	Roger Bresnahan	20	1	21	7	.230
OF	Wilbur Good	11	1	12	5	.253

T	PITCHER	W-L	SV	SO	SH	ERA
R	Larry Cheney	21-14	11	136	2	2.57
R	Bert Humphries	16-4	1	61	2	2.69
L	George Pearce	13-5	0	73	3	2.32
R	Jimmy Lavendar	10-14	2	91	0	3.66
R	Charlie Smith	7-9	0	47	1	2.55

January 10 - The Cubs release Three Finger Brown. He'll be picked up by the Reds, going 11-12 with a 2.91 ERA this year.

April 12 - The Cardinals spoil Opening Day in Chicago, beating the Cubs 5-3.

June 16 - The Cubs snap Grover Cleveland Alexander's 10-game winning streak, beating him 13-3.

June 19 - Wilbur Good hits the first pinch-hit homer in Cubs history. It'll be Good's only home run this season.

June 30 - One ball is used for the entire game in a 9-6 Cincinnati victory over Chicago.

August 18 - The Cubs collect a record nine straight hits in the ninth off Philadephia's Erskine Mayer, scoring six times to win 10-4.

August 19 - The Cubs collect nine straight hits again, this time off the Phillies'Grover Alexander, in a 9-4 victory.

September 14 - Larry Cheney allows 14 hits in a 7-0 whitewashing of the Giants, setting a major league record for hits allowed during a shutout.

1914

Principle Owner and President: Charles Thomas; **Manager:** Hank O'Day; **Ballpark:** West Side Park; **Attendance:** 202,516; **Finish:** Fourth (78-76); **Recap:** The Federal League will last only two years but the presence of three teams in Chicago cut the Cubs' attendance in half. Despite the emergence of Hippo Vaughn as the club's greatest lefthander, and another 20-win season from Larry Cheney, the Cubs drop to fourth.

P	PLAYER	R	HR	RBI	SB	AVE
1B	Vic Saier	87	18	72	19	.240
2B	Bill Sweeney	45	1	38	18	.218
SS	Red Corriden	42	3	29	13	.230
3B	Heinie Zimmerman	75	4	87	17	.296
RF	Wilbur Good	70	2	43	31	.272
CF	Tommy Leach	80	7	46	16	.263
LF	Wildfire Schulte	54	5	61	16	.241
C	Roger Bresnahan	42	0	24	14	.278
C	Jimmy Archer	17	0	19	1	.258
OF	Cy Williams	12	0	5	0	.202
UT	Jimmy Johnston	9	1	8	3	.228
OF	Pete Knisely	5	0	5	0	.130

WORTH NOTING - Johnny Evers is the only man to have managed both the Cubs and the White Sox.

T	PITCHER	W-L	SV	SO	SH	ERA
L	Hippo Vaughn	21-13	1	165	4	2.05
R	Larry Cheney	20-18	5	157	6	2.55
R	Jimmy Lavender	11-11	0	87	2	3.07
R	Bert Humphries	10-11	0	62	2	2.68
L	George Pearce	8-152	1	78	0	3.51

February 9 - Former Reds manager Hank O'Day, also a former umpire, is signed to manage the Cubs. Johnny Evers refuses to remain with the team as a player and is dealt to the Boston Braves.

February 21 - Charles Murphy sells the Cubs to Charles P.Taft of Cincinnati, Ohio.

April 22 - The Reds beat the Cubs 4-3 on Opening Day at West Side Park.

April 23 - The Federal League's Chicago Whales defeat the Kansas City Packers in the first game ever played at Weeghman Park, the ballpark that will eventually become Wrigley Field.

November 18 - The Cubs sign catcher Roger Bresnahan as their new manager.

December 11 - Bill Nicholson is born in Chestertown, Maryland.

1915

Principle Owner and President: Charles Thomas; **Manager:** Roger Bresnahan; **Ballpark:** West Side Park; **Attendance:** 217,058; **Finish:** Fourth (73-80); **Recap:** New manager Roger Bresnahan presides over the club's first losing season in 12 years, and is shown the door at season's end. Hippo Vaughn enjoys another solid season but Larry Cheney dips to 8-9 and is traded to the Dodgers before the year's out.

P	PLAYER	R	HR	RBI	SB	AVE
1B	Vic Saier	74	11	64	29	.264
2B	Heinie Zimmerman	65	3	62	19	.265
SS	Bobby Fisher	70	5	53	9	.287
3B	Art Phelan	41	3	35	12	.219
RF	Wilbur Good	66	2	27	19	.253
CF	Cy Williams	59	13	64	15	.257
LF	Wildfire Schulte	66	12	62	19	.249
C	Jimmy Archer	21	1	27	5	.243
P	**PLAYER**	**R**	**HR**	**RBI**	**SB**	**AVE**
C	Roger Bresnahan	19	1	19	19	.204
IF	Polly McLarry	16	1	12	2	.197
UT	Pete Knisely	12	0	17	1	.246
UT	Red Murray	20	0	11	6	.299
IF	Alex McCarthy	4	1	6	2	.264

T	PITCHER	W-L	SV	SO	SH	ERA
L	Hippo Vaughn	20-12	1	148	4	2.87
L	George Pearce	13-9	0	96	2	3.32
R	Jimmy Lavender	10-16	4	117	1	2.58
R	Larry Cheney	8-9	0	68	2	3.57
R	Bert Humphries	8-13	3	45	4	2.30

April 15 - It's an Opening Day victory as the Cubs beat the Cardinals 7-2 at West Side Park.

June 17 - George "Zip" Zabel relieves the Cubs' starter with two outs in the first inning and goes on to hurl 18-plus innings for a 4-3, 19-inning victory. It's the longest relief appearance ever.

June 24 - The Cubs erase a 13-10 defecit in the bottom of the ninth to beat the Cardinals 14-13 when Heinie Zimmerman slices a two-run double to tie it and steals home to win it.

July 17 - The Cubs, tied with Philadelphia for the National League lead, beat Phillies ace Grover Alexander 4-0, snapping the pitcher's 9-game winning streak.

August 18 - Wilbur Good steals second, third and home in the sixth inning of a 9-0 Cubs drubbing of Boston. Good is the first Cub to steal all three bases in one inning.

August 30 - The Cubs trade Larry Cheney, a three-time 20-game winner, to Brooklyn for outfielder Joe Schultz. Cheney is 8-9 at the time.

August 31 - Jimmy Lavender hurls a 2-0 no-hitter over John McGraw's Giants. Only two runners reach base in what is Lavender's only shutout of the season.

September 10 - Cubs legend and sporting goods tycoon Albert Goodwill Spalding dies at the age of 65 in Point Loma, California.

1916

Principle Owner and President: Charles Weeghman; **Manager:** Joe Tinker; **Ballpark:** Cubs Park; **Attendance:** 453,685; **Finish:** Fifth (67-86); **Recap:** The Cubs find themselves with a new owner and a new ballpark in 1916, taking the edge off a disastrous sixth-place finish. Charles Taft sells the franchise to a group headed by Charles Weeghman, owner of the now-defunct Federal League's Chicago Whales. Weeghman, whose group also includes fish wholesaler William Walker and chewing gum tycoon William Wrigley, pulls the Cubs out of West Side Park and installs them in the Whales' two-year-old Weeghman Park, which he renames Cubs Park (and will be re-renamed Wrigley Field in 1926). Weeghman names Whales manager Joe Tinker, the former shortstop, as the Cubs'new skipper. Tinker pilots the team to a 67-86 record and is fired after the season. The Cubs lead the league with 286 errors, 89 of them at the shortstop position, led by Eddie Mulligan's 40 in 58 games. Mulligan doesn't help himself with a light-weight .153 batting average; his replacement, Chuck Wortman, commits 32 miscues and bats .201. Heinie Zimmerman and Wildfire Schulte, the last links to Cubs greatness, are traded to Pittsburgh and New York by the end of the year.

P	Player	R	HR	RBI	SB	AVE
1B	Vic Saier	60	7	50	20	.253
2B	Otto Knabe	17	0	7	3	.276
SS	Chuck Wortman	17	2	16	4	.201
3B	Heinie Zimmerman	54	6	64	15	.291
RF	Max Flack	65	3	20	24	.258
CF	Cy Williams	55	12	66	6	.279
LF	Les Mann	46	2	29	11	.272
C	Jimmy Archer	11	1	30	3	.220

P	Player	R	HR	RBI	SB	AVE
UT	Rollie Zeider	29	1	22	9	.235
OF	Wildfire Schulte	31	5	27	9	.296
C	Bill Fischer	15	1	14	2	.196
IF	Eddie Mulligan	13	0	9	1	.153
OF	Joe Kelly	18	2	15	10	.254

T	Pitcher	W-L	SV	SO	SH	ERA
L	Hippo Vaughn	17-15	1	144	4	2.20
L	Gene Packard	10-6	5	36	2	2.79
R	Jimmy Lavendar	10-14	2	91	4	2.82
R	Claude Hendrix	8-16	2	117	3	2.68
R	Tom Seaton	6-6	1	45	0	3.27

January 5 - Charles H. Weeghman, owner of the now-defunct Federal League's Chicago Whales, purchases the Cubs for $500,000 and names Joe Tinker the team's new manager.

April 20 - The Cubs beat the Reds 7-6 in 11 innings in the first game at what will eventually become Wrigley Field.

April 29 - Weeghman declares that all foul balls hit into the stands at his ballpark may be kept by the fans. The policy will soon be adopted throughout baseball.

June 28 - Bill Fischer sets an NL record, since tied, by catching 27 innings in today's doubleheader. The Pirates sweep both games by a score of 3-2.

July 18 - The Cubs forfeit a game when Hippo Vaughn refuses to pitch because he believes that catcher Jimmy Archer's signs are being stolen by the Dodgers. Umpire

Bill "Lord" Byron calls the game in the 10th inning.

July 19 - Phil Cavarretta is born in Chicago.

September 4 - Three Finger Brown, back with the Cubs for one more season, closes out his career by locking horns with Christy Mathewson, who is also pitching his final game. Former Giant Mathewson, now the Reds'manager, beats Brown 10-8 in the only game he does not pitch in a New York uniform. Brown, 2-3 in his final season, has won 12 of the pair's 25 duels.

Vic Saier hits his fifth career homer off Matty, a three-run shot. Saier's five homers are the most Mathewson has given to any player.

1917

Principle Owner and President: Charles Weeghman; **Manager:** Fred Mitchell; **Ballpark:** Cubs Park; **Attendance:** 360,218; **Finish:** Fifth (74-80); **Recap:** The Cubs' sixth manager in six years is Fred Mitchell, who will break the revolving-door pattern by remaining at the helm for four years. The club wins seven more games than the year before but finishes fifth again.

P	Player	R	HR	RBI	SB	AVE
1B	Fred Merkle	65	3	57	13	.266
2B	Larry Doyle	48	6	61	5	.254
SS	Chuck Wortman	24	0	9	6	.174
3B	Charlie Deal	46	0	47	10	.254
RF	Max Flack	65	0	21	17	.248
CF	Cy Williams	53	5	42	8	.241
LF	Les Mann	63	1	44	14	.273
C	Art Wilson	17	2	25	6	.213
UT	Harry Wolter	44	0	28	7	.249
UT	Rollie Zeider	36	0	27	17	.243
C	Rowdy Elliott	18	0	28	4	.251
IF	Pete Kilduff	23	0	15	11	.277
C	Pickles Dillhoefer	3	0	8	1	.126

T	Pitcher	W-L	SV	SO	SH	ERA
L	Hippo Vaughn	23-13	0	195	5	2.01
R	Phil Douglas	14-20	1	151	5	2.55
R	Claude Hendrix	10-12	1	81	1	2.60
R	Vic Aldridge	6-6	2	44	1	3.11
R	Tom Seaton	5-4	1	27	1	2.52

April 11 - The Cubs take a season-opening 5-3 victory over the Pirates at Cubs Park.

May 2 - The Cubs'Hippo Vaughn and the Reds' Fred Toney hook up in a game for the ages. At the end of nine innings, both hurlers have no-hitters. With one out in the top of the 10th and runners on second and third, Cincinnati's Jim Thorpe, the former Olympian, chops a grounder in front of the mound. Vaughn picks the ball up and throws home, but catcher Art Wilson freezes; the ball hits him in the chest and the runner, shortstop Larry Kopf, slides in safe for the only run of the game. Toney sets the Cubs down in order in their half of the frame to record the fourth 10-inning no-hitter in major league history.

December 11 - The Cubs send righthander Mike Prendergast, catcher Pickles Dillhoefer and $55,000 to the Phillies for future Hall of Famer Grover Cleveland Alexander and catcher "Reindeer" Bill Killefer. Alexander won 30 games for the Phils this season.

1918

Principle Owner and President: Charles Weeghman; **Manager:** Fred Mitchell; **Ballpark:** Cubs Park; **Attendance:** 337,256; **Finish:** First (84-45); **Recap:** Though the war effort claims many major leaguers, the Cubs are one of the least affected. The acquisition of Lefty Tyler from Boston prior to the season turns out to be pivotal as the Cubs return to the top of the league standings for the first time in eight years. Together with 20-win seasons from Hippo Vaughn (who wins the pitching Triple Crown and also leads the league in

Cubs Park (Wrigley Field) in 1916

shutouts) and Claude Hendrix, Tyler's 19 victories more than compensate for a lack of offense.

P	PLAYER	R	HR	RBI	SB	AVE
1B	Fred Merkle	55	3	65	21	.297
2B	Rollie Zeider	31	0	26	16	.223
SS	Charlie Hollocher	72	2	38	26	.316
3B	Charlie Deal	43	2	34	11	.239
RF	Max Flack	74	4	41	17	.257
CF	Dode Paskert	69	3	59	20	.286
LF	Les Mann	69	2	55	21	.288
C	Bill Killefer	30	0	22	5	.233
UT	Turner Barber	11	0	10	3	.236
C	Bob O'Farrell	9	1	14	0	.283
IF	Pete Kilduff	7	0	13	1	.204
IF	Charlie Pick	13	0	12	7	.326
UT	Bill McCabe	9	0	5	2	.178

T	PITCHER	W-L	SV	SO	SH	ERA
L	Hippo Vaughn	22-10	0	148	8	1.74
R	Claude Hendrix	20-7	0	86	3	2.78
L	Lefty Tyler	19-8	1	102	8	2.01
R	Phil Douglas	10-9	2	51	2	2.12
R	Speed Martin	5-2	1	16	1	1.83

April 24 - The Cubs shut out the Cardinals 2-0 on Opening Day at Cubs Park.

April 30 - The Cubs take a hit as new ace Grover Alexander joins the Army after receiving his draft notice on April 18th.

July 17 - Lefty Tyler duels Philadelphia's Milt Watson for 21 innings, winning 2-1.

September 5 - World Series Game 1
Because of the shortened 126-game schedule, the World Series begins in Chicago, on the earliest date in history. Boston left-hander Babe Ruth slams the door on the anemic Cubs offense, limiting them to six hits in a 1-0 shutout. Ruth strands three Cubs on third during the shutout and works out of a bases-loaded jam in the second by striking out Charlie Pick.

The Red Sox score their only run off Hippo Vaughn in the fourth on a walk and two singles.

During the seventh-inning stretch, a major league tradition is born when a band plays "The Star Spangled Banner."

WORTH NOTING- The Cubs' World Series opponents in 1918 are the Boston Red Sox, managed by **Ed Barrow**. The Bosox finish with a 75-51 (.595) record, leading the American League in complete games (105) and shutouts (25).

P	PLAYER	R	HR	RBI	SB	BA
1B	Stuffy McInnis	40	0	56	10	.272
2B	Dave Shean	58	0	34	11	.264
SS	Everett Scott	40	0	43	11	.221
3B	Fred Thomas	19	1	11	4	.257
Rf	Harry Hooper	81	1	44	24	.289
CF	Amos Strunk	50	0	35	20	.257
LF	Babe Ruth	50	11	66	6	.300
C	Sam Agnew	11	0	6	0	.166

T	PITCHER	W	L	SV	SH	ERA
R	Carl Mays	21	13	0	8	2.21
R	Sad Sam Jones	16	5	0	5	2.25
R	Joe Bush	15	15	2	7	2.11
L	Babe Ruth	13	7	0	1	2.22
L	Dutch Leonard	8	6	0	3	2.71

September 6 - World Series Game 2
The Cubs take game two as they score three runs in the second off Bullet Joe Bush and Lefty Tyler limits the Sox to six hits. Chicago scores on a walk, single, double by Bill Killefer and a two-run single by Tyler. Boston scores their lone run in the ninth on consecutive triples by Amos Strunk and George Whiteman.

September 7 - World Series Game 3
Hippo Vaughn is the hard-luck loser once again as submariner Carl Mays holds the Cubs to one run, on a fifth-inning double by Charlie Pick and single by Bill Killefer, in a 2-1 seven-hitter. The Red Sox score two runs in the fourth on a hit batsman, two singles and an error by Vaughn. The Sox are robbed of a third run when right fielder Max Flack guns down a runner at the plate.

The game ends in thrilling fashion. With two outs and no one on in the ninth, Pick beats out an infield single and steals second. Boston catcher Wally Schang then commits a passed ball and Pick streaks for third. Schang scoops up the ball but his throw gets by third baseman Fred Thomas. Pick heads for home, but Thomas recovers the ball and throws him out.

WORTH NOTING - The Cubs' pitching staff in 1916 lost 10 games by a score of 1-0, a major league record.

September 9 - World Series Game 4
Babe Ruth wins his second game of the series 3-2, extending his record World Series scoreless innings streak to 29 2/3 (broken by Whitey Ford in 1961) before the Cubs rally for two in the eighth. Ruth is helped out by Max Flack, who is picked off twice - a major league first.

Ruth, batting sixth, drives in Boston's first two runs on a fourth-inning triple off starter Phil Douglas. In the eighth, the Cubs tie the game on a walk, a single by pinch-hitter Claude Hendrix, a wild pitch, a ground ball and a single by Les Mann. The Red Sox push across the winning run in the bottom of the frame on an error.

The ninth produces another nail-biter. Ruth gives up a single and a walk to put the first two runners on and Joe Bush relieves him. Bush wriggles out of trouble on a force play and 6-4-3 twin-killing.

September 10 - World Series Game 5
Players from both the Cubs and Red Sox threaten to strike Game 5 unless they are guaranteed $2,500 each for the winners and $1,000 for the losers. When told they would appear greedy while the nation is at war, they back off. The players will not be punished for their action but will not receive World Series rings this year.

The Cubs beat the Red Sox behind Hippo Vaughn and rookie shortstop Charlie Hollocher's three hits.

September 11 - World Series Game 6 The Red Sox take the trophy as Carl Mays tosses a three-hitter to win 2-1. Boston scores two runs in the third without a hit as Lefty Tyler walks Mays and second baseman Dave Shean and Max Flack drops a fly ball. The Cubs answer with a run in the fourth but Les Mann is picked off first by catcher Wally Schang. The Cubs don't reach scoring position again.

October 7 - Frank Baumholtz is born in Midvale, Ohio.

1919

Principle Owner and President: Fred Mitchell / William Veeck, Sr.; **Manager:** Fred Mitchell; **Ballpark:** Cubs Park; **Attendance:** 424,430; **Finish:** Third (75-65); **Recap:** The 1919 season is again reduced, this time to 140 games, because baseball owners are uncertain about the popularity of the national game after the end of the first World War. In fact, attendance is up all over, and the Cubs draw nearly 100,000 more fans than last year despite the shortened schedule and a third-place finish. Grover Cleveland Alexander returns from the war shell-shocked and alcoholic, but he manages a 16-win season, leading the league in ERA (1.72) and shutouts (9), complimenting Hippo Vaughn's 21 wins and NL-leading 141 strikeouts. The Cubs staff posts a collective 2.21 ERA, leading the league for the ninth time since 1901.

The team also sees another change in administration, with William Wrigley accumulating enough shares to pressure Charles Weeghman's ouster as president, replacing him with Bill Veeck, Sr.

P	Player	R	HR	RBI	SB	AVE
1B	Fred Merkle	52	3	62	20	.267
2B	Charlie Pick	27	0	18	17	.242
SS	Charlie Hollocher	51	3	26	16	.270
3B	Charlie Deal	37	2	52	11	.289
RF	Max Flack	71	6	35	18	.294
CF	Dode Paskert	21	2	29	7	.196
LF	Les Mann	31	1	22	12	.227
C	Bill Killefer	17	0	22	5	.286
UT	Lee Magee	36	1	17	14	.292
OF	Turner Barber	26	0	21	7	.313
IF	Buck Herzog	15	0	17	12	.275
C	Bob O'Farrell	11	0	9	2	.216
IF	Fred Lear	8	1	11	2	.224

T	Pitcher	W-L	SV	SO	SH	ERA
L	Hippo Vaughn	21-14	1	141	4	1.79
R	Grover Alexander	16-11	1	121	9	1.72
R	Phil Douglas	10-6	0	63	4	2.00
R	Claude Hendrix	10-14	0	69	2	2.62
R	Speed Martin	8-8	2	54	2	2.47

April 24 - The Cubs are victorious on Opening Day, beating the Pirates 5-1 in Chicago.

July 6 - Sportswriter Bill Veeck, Sr. replaces Fred Mitchell as club president. Mitchell will remain manager.

August 14 - The Cubs split a doubleheader with the Dodgers, losing the opener 2-0 in just one hour and 10 minutes and winning the nightcap in one hour and seven minutes.

September 21 - The Cubbies continue to set marks for efficiency, beating the Braves 3-0 in 58 minutes. On the same day, the Dodgers will beat the Reds 3-1 in 55 minutes. One week later the Giants will set the record by beating the Phillies 6-1 in 51 minutes.

1920

Principle Owner and President: William Veeck, Sr.; **Manager:** Fred Mitchell; **Ballpark:** Cubs Park; **Attendance:** 480,783; **Finish:** Fifth (75-79); **Recap:**

Claude Hendrix

The scandal-rocked Cubs drop to fifth despite an outstanding year by Grover Cleveland Alexander, who wins the pitching Triple Crown. His 1.91 ERAis the only one under 2.00 in either league this season.

In August, Claude Hendrix is yanked from a game by manager Fred Mitchell because of a rumor that he accepted money to throw a game to the Phillies, precipitating an investigation. After the probe, Hendrix is banned from baseball. Worse yet, the investigation into the Chicago-Philadelphia game will ultimately lead to the unraveling of the Black Sox scandal in last year's World Series.

P	Player	R	HR	RBI	SB	AVE
1B	Fred Merkle	33	3	38	3	.285
2B	Zeb Terry	56	0	52	12	.280
SS	Charlie Hollocher	53	0	22	20	.319
3B	Charlie Deal	48	3	39	5	.240
RF	Max Flack	85	4	49	13	.302
CF	Dode Paskert	57	5	71	16	.279
LF	Dave Robertson	68	10	75	17	.300
C	Bob O'Farrell	29	3	19	1	.248
UT	Turner Barber	27	0	50	5	.265
IF	Buck Herzog	39	0	19	8	.193
UT	Babe Twonbly	25	2	14	5	.235
C	Bill Killefer	16	0	16	2	.220

T	Pitcher	W-L	SV	SO	SH	ERA
R	Grover Alexander	27-14	5	173	7	1.91
L	Hippo Vuaghn	19-16	0	131	4	254
L	Lefty Tyler	11-12	0	57	2	3.31
R	Claude Hendrix	9-12	0	72	0	3.57
R	Speed Martin	4-15	2	44	0	4.83

April 22 - The Cubs defeat the Reds 4-3 on Opening Day at Cubs Park.

May 20 - During Grover Alexander's 6-0 shutout of the Phillies, policemen disguised as soldiers, farmers and bootblacks raid the stands at Cubs Park, arresting 24 fans for gambling.

May 31 - Alexander wins his own game in the bottom of the tenth with a homer to beat the Reds 3-2. It's Ol' Pete's 11th straight victory.

June 9 - Lee Magee, who sued the Cubs in February for allegedly releasing him without just cause, loses his suit in court. While on the witness stand, Magee admitted to having bet on a ballgame in 1918 while a member of the Reds.

October - Shaken by the ongoing Black Sox scandal, club owners begin a series of reform meetings. Albert Lasker, a Cubs shareholder, proposes a three-man board of non-baseball men. Among the names mentioned for the board are former president William Howard Taft, General George Pershing, General Leonard Wood, ex-treasury secretary William McAdoo, Senator Hiram Johnson, and Chicago Judge Kenesaw Mountain Landis.

In November, the owners will appoint Landis chairman of the three-man board. Landis will accept, but only as sole commissioner with absolute authority over the game. The owners will reluctantly agree; Landis will remain a judge for a few more years while at the same time drawing a $50,000 salary.

WORTH NOTING - Righthander Grover Cleveland Alexander was the first Cub elected to the Hall of Fame, in 1938.

1921

Principle Owner and President: William Veeck, Sr.; **Manager:** Johnny Evers / Bill Killefer; **Ballpark:** Cubs Park; **Attendance:** 410,107; **Finish:** Seventh (64-89); **Recap:** Club president Bill Veeck makes the same mistake that Charles Murphy did in 1913 bringing in Johnny Evers as manager. Evers'short tenure is marked with constant conflict with his players, with Hippo Vaughn quitting baseball in July after a particularly bitter argument. Evers is replaced by backup catcher Bill Killefer in August. The majors'new lively ball has an effect on the Cubs' lineup, as four players bat .300 or better and the team finishes with a then-record .292 average.

P	PLAYER	R	HR	RBI	SB	AVE
1B	Ray Grimes	91	6	79	5	.321
2B	Zeb Terry	59	2	45	1	.275
SS	Charlie Hollocher	71	3	37	5	.289
3B	Charlie Deal	52	3	66	3	.289
RF	Max Flack	80	6	37	17	.301
CF	George Michael	54	0	43	17	.310
LF	Turner Barber	73	1	54	5	.314
C	Bob O'Farrell	32	4	32	2	.250
P	PLAYER	R	HR	RBI	SB	AVE
UT	John Kelleher	31	4	47	2	.309
OF	Babe Twombly	22	1	18	4	.377
OF	John Sullivan	28	4	41	3	.329
C	Tom Daly	12	0	22	1	.238
C	Bill Killefer	11	0	16	3	.323

T	PITCHER	W-L	SV	SO	SH	ERA
R	Grover Alexander	15-13	1	77	3	3.39
R	Virgil Cheeves	11-12	0	39	1	4.64
R	Speed Martin	11-15	1	86	1	4.36
R	Buck Freeman	9-10	3	42	0	4.12
L	Lefty York	5-9	1	57	1	4.73

February 25 - Andy Pafko is born in Boyceville, Wisconsin.

April 13 - The Cubs win their season opener, beating the Cardinals 5-2 at home.

August 7 - The seventh-place Cubs replace manager Johnny Evers with Bill Killefer. In today's game, a 7-2 loss to the Giants, New York third baseman Frankie Frisch is knocked out by a ground ball that bounces up and hits him in the head.

August 30 - The Cubs turn a triple play but still lose to the Giants, 5-3.

September 21 - Grover Alexander beats his former teammate, Eppa Rixey, now with the Reds, 7-0.

1922

Principle Owner and President: William Veeck, Sr.; **Manager:** Bill Killefer; **Ballpark:** Cubs Park; **Attendance:** 542,283; **Finish:** Fifth (80-74); **Recap:** The Cubs begin spending spring training at William Wrigley's Catalina Island facility off the California coast. They'll remain there until 1952. The club hits at a higher clip than the previous year, but the rest of the league hits the pitching staff even harder, producing another fifth-place finish. Five players bat .300 or better, and Charlie Hollocher turns in a career year, fanning just five times in 592 official at bats.

P	PLAYER	R	HR	RBI	SB	AVE
1B	Ray Grimes	99	14	99	7	.354
2B	Zeb Terry	56	0	67	2	.286
SS	Charlie Hollocher	90	3	69	19	.340
3B	Marty Krug	67	4	60	7	.276
RF	Barney Friberg	51	0	23	8	.311
CF	Jigger Statz	77	1	34	16	.297
LF	Hack Miller	61	12	78	3	.352
C	Bob O'Farrell	68	4	60	5	.324

Grover Cleveland Alexander

P	PLAYER	R	HR	RBI	SB	AVE
UT	Turner Barber	35	0	29	7	.310
OF	Cliff Heathcote	37	1	34	5	.280
OF	Marty Callaghan	31	0	20	2	257
IF	John Kelleher	23	0	20	5	.259
OF	George Maisel	9	0	6	1	.190

T	PITCHER	W-L	SV	SO	SH	ERA
R	Grover Alexander	16-13	1	48	1	3.62
R	Vic Aldridge	16-15	0	66	2	3.52
R	Virgil Cheeves	12-11	2	40	1	4.09
R	George Stueland	9-4	0	44	0	5.81
R	Tiny Osborne	9-5	3	81	1	4.50

January 18 - The Cubs purchase pitcher Vic Aldridge and outfielder Jigger Statz from the minor-league Los Angeles Angels for eight players and cash.

April 14 - Cap Anson dies in Marshalltown, Iowa at the age of 70.

April 20 - The Cubs beat the Reds 3-1 on Opening Day in Chicago.

April 27 - Ray Grimes smacks a two-run homer in the sixth inning onto Waveland Avenue to tie the game 4-4, then ropes a two-run single in the seventh to beat the Cardinals 6-4.

May 30 - Between games of a Memorial Day doubleheader, the Cubs and Cardinals swap outfielders Max Flack and Cliff Heathcote. Flack, who lives near Cubs Park, learns of the trade after going home for lunch. The players trade uniforms and play against each other's former team in the nightcap. The Cubs sweep, 4-1 and 3-1.

In the nightcap, shortstop Charlie Hollocher strikes out for the first time this year. He will fan only five times in 1922.

July 18 - Ray Grimes, who has missed 10 days with an injury, returns to the lineup and collects a home run, double and two singles in a 6-3 Cubs win vs. Philadelphia.

July 21 - Grimes provides the only run with a double in a 1-0 Cubs victory over Brooklyn. Grover Cleveland Alexander is the winner. Grimes now has RBIs in 15 straight games.

July 23 - Grimes homers in Chicago's 4-1 win over the Dodgers, giving him an RBI in 17 straight games, a major league record. The streak will be snapped on the 25th vs. Boston.

August 13 - The Cubs hammer the Cardinals 16-5, led by Charlie Hollocher's three triples.

August 25 - It's as poorly a pitched game as has been seen since the turn of the century as the Cubs beat the Phillies 26-23 in a game that features 51 hits, 23 walks and 10 errors. The Phillies leave the bases loaded in the ninth to end the game.

Outfielder Marty Callaghan comes to the plate three times (a major league record) during a 14-run Cubs fourth that opens up a 25-6 lead. Callaghan gets two hits and fans once.

Hack Miller swats two three-run homers - the first hitting the center field scoreboard.

Records are set for total runs (49) and hits, most players scoring runs (Philadelphia with 13), and most plate appearances (Philadelphia with 66). Cliff Heathcote sets a record by reaching base seven times in a nine-inning game.

1923

Principle Owner and President: William Veeck, Sr.; **Manager:** Bill Killefer; **Ballpark:** Cubs Park; **Attendance:** 703,705; **Finish:** Fourth (83-71); **Recap:** Bill Killefer's boys finish fourth this season, and the Cubs set a new club record for attendance. A couple of injuries keep the Cubs from finishing higher - a slipped disc in June that ends Ray Grimes's season and shortstop Charlie Hollocher's regular disappearance from the lineup with mysterious stomach ailments. Grover Cleveland Alexander is again the big winner on the club's staff, posting 22 wins and walking just 30 men in 305 innings. The Cubs set a new team record with 90 home runs, 20 of them by left fielder Hack Miller.

P	Player	R	HR	RBI	SB	AVE
1B	Ray Grimes	32	2	36	5	.329
2B	George Grantham	81	8	70	43	.281
SS	Sparky Adams	40	4	35	20	.289
3B	Barney Friberg	91	12	88	13	.318
CF	Jigger Statz	110	10	70	29	.319
LF	Hack Miller	74	20	88	6	.301
C	Bob O'Farrell	73	12	84	10	.319
C	Gabby Hartnett	28	8	39	4	.268
IF	Charlie Hollocher	46	1	28	9	.342
IF	John Kelleher	27	6	21	2	.306
OF	Marty Callaghan	18	0	14	2	.225
IF	Allen Elliott	21	2	29	3	.250

WORTH NOTING - Grover Cleveland "Pete" Alexander's life was portrayed in the 1952 movie, *The Winning Season*, with Ronald Reagan playing the Hall of Fame pitcher. The was no mention of Ol'Pete's drinking habits in the picture.

T	Pitcher	W-L	SV	SO	SH	ERA
R	Grover Alexander	22-12	2	72	3	3.19
R	Vic Aldridge	16-9	0	64	2	3.48
R	Tony Kaufmann	14-10	3	72	2	3.10
R	Vic Keen	12-8	1	46	0	3.00
R	Tiny Osborne	8-15	1	69	1	4.55

April 17 - A record Opening Day crowd of 33,000 turn out for the Cubs'dedication of their newly remodeled ballpark. The Pirates triumph, 3-2.

April 20 - The Cubs hit six homers to beat the Pirates 12-11. Gabby Hartnett's solo blast in the ninth wins the game. Chicago will hit 90 homers this year, more than double their team total of 42 in 1922.

May 17 - Grover Alexander issues his first walk in 52 innings this year in a 7-4 win over Philadelphia. Alex walks three in the game.

July 23 - The Cubs score nine runs in the top of the 12th inning to beat the Pirates 12-3.

September 15 - Despite the presence of baseball commissioner Kenesaw Mountain Landis at the game, angry fans in Chicago pelt umpire Charlie Moran with bottles after a call at second base. Play is held up for 15 minutes until order is restored. The Giants beat the Cubs 10-6; New York manager John McGraw has to be escorted from the park by police.

1924

Principle Owner and President: William Veeck, Sr.; **Manager:** Bill Killefer; **Ballpark:** Cubs Park; **Attendance:** 716,922; **Finish:** Fifth (81-72); **Recap:** The Cubs finish fifth in 1924 but set an attendance record for the second year in a row. An early-season injury to catcher Bob O'Farrell leads to the installment of rookie Gabby Hartnett behind the plate. Hartnett bats just under .300 and will become a fixture there through the next decade.

P	Player	R	HR	RBI	SB	AVE
1B	Harvey Cotter	39	4	33	3	.261
2B	George Grantham	85	12	60	21	.316
SS	Sparky Adams	66	1	27	15	.280
3B	Barney Friberg	67	5	82	19	.279
RF	Cliff Heathcote	66	0	30	26	.309
CF	Jigger Statz	69	3	49	13	.277
LF	Denver Grigsby	58	3	48	10	.299
C	Gabby Hartnett	56	16	67	10	.299
IF	Charlie Hollocher	28	2	21	4	.245
C	Bob O'Farrell	25	3	28	2	.240
UT	Otto Vogel	28	1	24	4	.267
IF	Bob Barrett	12	5	21	1	.241
OF	Hack Miller	17	4	25	1	.336

T	Pitcher	W-L	SV	SO	SH	ERA
R	Tony Kaufmann	16-11	0	79	3	4.02
R	Vic Aldridge	15-12	0	74	0	3.50
R	Vic Keen	15-14	3	75	0	3.79
R	Grover Alexander	12-5	0	33	0	3.04
R	Elmer Jacobs	11-12	1	50	1	3.74

April 23 - The Cubs batter the Cardinals 12-1 on Opening Day at Cubs Park.

June 13 - The Cubs beat the Braves 5-1 to put them briefly atop the National League.

July 11 - Harvey "Lee" Cotter makes a record 21 putouts and one assist in a game vs. Brooklyn.

August 1 - Dazzy Vance of the Dodgers fans seven Cubs in a row during a 4-0 shutout.

September 12 - Outfielder Hack Miller smacks a pinch-homer in the eighth to tie a game with the Phillies 6-6. The Cubs win 10-8.

September 20 - Grover Alexander earns his 300th career victory, stopping the Giants 7-3 in 12 innings at the Polo Grounds.

September 24 - Former Cubs star player and manager Frank Chance, who resigned as White Sox manager in February, dies of a prolonged illness.

October 1 - The Cubs beat the White Sox 10-7 in a City Series game, with the game being broadcast over the radio - a first in Chicago. Sen Kaney calls the game. The Cubs will begin regular season broadcasts in 1925.

October 27 - The Cubs trade pitcher Vic Aldridge and first basemen Al Niehaus and George Granthan to the Pirates for rookie first baseman Charlie Grimm, shortstop Rabbit Maranville, and pitcher Wilbur Cooper. Grimm will star for the Cubs for 11 seasons, eventually becoming player-manager. Maranville, a future Hall of Famer, will also become a player-manager.

1925

Principle Owner and President: William Veeck, Sr.; **Manager:** Bill Killefer / Rabbit Maranville / George Gibson; **Ballpark:** Cubs Park; **Attendance:** 622,610; **Finish:** Eighth (68-86); **Recap:** Halfway through the 1925 season, the seventh-place Cubs fire manager Bill Killefer in favor of shortstop Rabbit Maranville.

Not surprisingly, the Cubs finish in the cellar for the first time in their history.

P	Player	R	HR	RBI	SB	AVE
1B	Charlie Grimm	73	10	76	4	.306
2B	Sparky Adams	95	2	48	26	.287
SS	Rabbit Maranville	37	0	23	6	.233
3B	Howard Freigau	77	8	71	10	.307
RF	Cliff Heathcote	57	5	39	15	.263
CF	Mandy Brooks	55	14	72	10	.281
LF	Art Jahn	30	0	37	2	.301
C	Gabby Hartnett	61	24	67	1	.289
OF	Tommy Griffith	38	7	27	2	.285
UT	Mike Gonzalez	26	3	18	2	.264
OF	Butch Weis	16	2	25	2	.267
IF	Pinky Pittinger	21	0	15	5	.312
OF	Denver Grigsby	20	0	20	1	.255

T	Pitcher	W-L	SV	SO	SH	ERA
R	Grover Alexander	15-11	0	63	1	3.39
R	Tony Kaufmann	13-13	2	49	2	4.50
L	Wilbur Cooper	12-14	0	41	0	4.29
R	Sheriff Blake	10-18	2	93	0	4.87
L	Percy Jones	6-6	0	60	1	4.65

March 15 - Rabbit Maranville breaks his leg sliding home during an exhibition game in Los Angeles. Maranville will be out until mid-season.

April 5 - Quin Ryan calls the first regular-season Cubs radio broadcast, from the grandstand roof at Cubs Park for WGN. Grover Cleveland Alexander beats the Pirates 8-2, adding a single, double and homer, on Opening Day.

July 7 - The Cubs, buried in seventh place, replace manager Bill Killefer with shortstop Rabbit Maranville.

July 20 - Dazzy Vance fans 17 Cubs in a 4-3 Dodger victory.

September 22 - The Cubs beat Brooklyn 3-2 in 12 innings; Dodgers starter Burleigh Grimes hits into two double plays and a triple play.

October 7 - Grover Alexander and the White Sox' Ted Blankenship battle for 19 innings in the cold opener of the annual Chicago City Series.

The game is called for darkness, tied 2-2. The Cubs will win four of the five games to win the series.

October 12 - Rabbit Maranville is fired as manager; Joe McCarthy, manager of the minor league Louisville club, is named to succeed him.

November 9 - The Cubs waive Maranville to the Dodgers.

1926

Principle Owner and President: William Veeck, Sr.; **Manager:** Joe McCarthy; **Ballpark:** Cubs Park; **Attendance:** 885,063; **Finish:** Fourth (82-72); **Recap:** Breaking with the club's tradition of player-managers, Bill Veeck reaches into the minor leagues and hires Joe McCarthy, skipper of the Triple-A American Association's Louisville team.

McCarthy uses his valuable minor league experience to acquire AA outfielders Riggs Stephenson and Hack Wilson. Stephenson launches a long career with a .338 average and Wilson leads the team with 109 RBIs, 27 more than anyone else on the club.

P	Player	R	HR	RBI	SB	AVE
1B	Charlie Grimm	58	8	82	3	.277
2B	Sparky Adams	95	0	39	27	.309
SS	Jimmy Cooney	52	1	47	11	.251
3B	Howard Freigau	51	3	51	6	.270
RF	Cliff Heathcote	98	10	53	18	.276
CF	Hack Wilson	97	<u>21</u>	109	10	.321
LF	Riggs Stephenson	40	3	44	2	.338
C	Gabby Hartnett	35	8	41	0	.275
C	Mike Gonzalez	24	1	23	3	.249
UT	Pete Scott	34	3	34	3	.286
OF	Joe Kelly	16	0	32	0	.335

T	Pitcher	W-L	SV	SO	SH	ERA
R	Charlie Root	18-<u>17</u>	2	127	2	2.82
R	Guy Bush	13-9	2	32	2	2.87
L	Percy Jones	12-7	2	80	2	3.09
R	Sheriff Blake	11-12	1	95	4	3.59
R	Tony Kaufmann	9-7	2	52	1	3.02

April 22 - The Cubs and Reds tie 5-5 on Opening Day in Chicago.

May 2 - The Cubs come from behind to win for the fourth straight time, beating the Cardinals 6-5.

May 8 - Grover Cleveland Alexander picks up his last win in a Cubs uniform, beating the Giants 6-4.

May 22 - Alexander is given the keys to a Lincoln automobile, a gift from the fans, before a game at Cubs Park against the Braves. Boston then pummels Alexander to win 7-1.

Alex will be left behind when the Cubs end their homestand.

May 23 - Hack Wilson, acquired from New York over the winter, smacks a fifth-inning homer off the scoreboard in left field in a 14-8 win over the Braves. The scoreboard will eventually be moved to a spot above the bleachers in center field.

Later that night, Wilson and a few friends are arrested for drinking beer, violating the Prohibition Act.

June 22 - The Cubs waive the 39-year-old Alexander. Ol'Pete is 3-3 with a 3.46 ERA at the time of the trade but battles with alcohol off the field lead to numerous encounters with rookie manager Joe McCarthy. Alex will go 9-7 down the stretch for the Cardinals, helping them win their first NLpennant.

June 26 - Alexander gains revenge against his old team, hurling a 5-0 four-hitter for the Cardinals at Sportsman's Park.

September 2 - Ol' Pete shuts out his old team again, 2-0 in the first game of a twin-bill at Cubs Park. The Cardinals will take the second game, too, 9-1.

1927

Principle Owner and President: William Veeck, Sr.; **Manager:** Joe McCarthy; **Ballpark:** Wrigley Field; **Attendance:** 1,159,168; **Finish:** Fourth (85-68); **Recap:** Thanks to the heavy hitting of Hack Wilson and Riggs Stephenson, more than one million fans go through the newly-doubledecked Wrigley Field turnstiles in 1927, and watch their young club turn in a fourth-place finish, 8 1/2 games behind Pittsburgh.

Riggs Stephenson leads the NLin doubles (46). Charlie Root gets MVPconsideration with a league-leading 26 victories.

P	PLAYER	R	HR	RBI	SB	AVE
1B	Charlie Grimm	68	2	74	3	.311
2B	Clyde Beck	44	2	44	0	.258
SS	Woody English	46	1	28	1	.290
3B	Sparky Adams	100	0	49	26	.292
RF	Earl Webb	58	14	52	3	.301
CF	Hack Wilson	119	30	129	13	.318
LF	Riggs Stephenson	101	7	82	8	.344
C	Gabby Hartnett	56	10	80	2	.294
OF	Cliff Heathcote	28	2	25	6	.294
OF	Pete Scott	28	0	21	1	.314
UT	Eddie Pick	23	2	15	0	.171
C	Mike Gonzalez	15	1	15	1	.241
IF	Chuck Tolson	6	2	17	0	.296

T	PITCHER	W-L	SV	SO	SH	ERA
R	Charlie Root	26-15	2	145	4	3.76
R	Sheriff Blake	13-14	0	64	2	3.29
R	Hal Carlson	12-8	0	27	2	3.18
R	Guy Bush	10-10	2	62	1	3.03
L	Percy Jones	7-8	0	37	1	4.06

April 12 - The Cubs beat the World-Champion Cardinals 10-1 on Opening Day at Wrigley Field.

April 28 - Chicago humiliates Pittsburgh with a 17-hit, eight-walk 16-4 win.

May 1 - Chuck Tolson comes off the bench to hit the first pinch-hit grand slam in Cubs history, giving Chicago a seventh-inning lead at Pittsburgh. Charlie Root, who will lead the NL with 26 wins this year, walks the bases loaded and gives up a game-winning single to Paul Waner in the ninth as the Pirates come from behind to win 7-6.

May 8 - Chicago leaves no runners on base but loses to New York 5-4.

May 14 - Guy Bush goes the distance in an 18-inning, 7-2 victory over•the Braves. Sparky Adams collects four hits for Chicago.

May 17 - The Cubs win another marathon in Boston as Charlie Grimm singles home Hack Wilson with the winning run in the 22nd inning for a 4-3 victory. Bob Osborne gets the win with 14 runless relief innings. The Cubs and Braves have now combined for 40 innings over their last two games, a major league record.

May 20 - During a 7-5 Cubs victory, angry Ebbets Field fans react to a disputed call by umpire Pete McGlaughlin by showering the field with bottles.

May 21 - The Cubs move into uncharted territory - first place - by pushing across nine runs in the ninth inning for an 11-6 win in the nightcap of a twinbill in Brooklyn. Ebbets Field fans interrupt the game again, this time over a call by umpire Frank Wilson.

May 30 - Shortstop Jimmy Cooney turns a rare unassisted triple play vs. Pittsburgh in the opening game of a Memorial Day doubleheader. Cooney catches a liner off the bat of Paul Waner, steps on second to retire Lloyd Waner, and tags Clyde Barnhart. The Cubs win 7-6, snapping an 11-game Pirates winning streak. The Bucs take the second game 6-5.

May 31 - The Pirates score nine runs in the last four innings to beat the Cubs 10-9. Pittsburgh now occupies first place.

WORTH NOTING - Guy Bush was signed out of the minor Cotton States League for $1,200 and a jug of whiskey.

June 7 - The Cubs trade Jimmy Cooney and Tony Kaufmann to the Phillies for pitcher Hal Carlson. Carlson will go 12-8 down the stretch.

June 16 - The red-hot Cubs win their 12th straight game. Hal Carlson picks up the victory.

June 17 - Chicago's winning streak is snapped by Philadelphia, 12-2. The Phillies will win again tomorrow, 7-2.

June 19 - The now-ice-cold Cubs drop a twinbill to St. Louis, 6-5 and 12-3.

June 22 - Chicago, now in third place, loses to the Cardinals 11-5. Pete Alexander is the winner, pitching out of turn at his own request.

July 7 - The up-and-down Cubs beat the Pirates on Charlie Root's one-hitter, vaulting into first place once again.

July 19 - The Cubs spoil John McGraw day at the Polo Grounds with an 8-5 win. McGraw is celebrating his 25th year at the Giants' helm.

September 25 - Chicago cements itself into third place, dropping a doubleheader to pennant-winning Pittsburgh.

September 26 - The Cubs report an attendance of 1,159,000 after playing their final home game. It's the first time Chicago has drawn a million or more fans.

Charlie Grimm

November 28 - Chicago trades Sparky Adams and outfielder Pete Scott to the Pirates for outfielder Kiki Cuyler. Cuyler, a .310 hitter in 1927, did not play in the World Series due to a feud with Pittsburgh manager Donie Bush.

1928

Principle Owner and President: William Veeck, Sr.; **Manager:** Joe McCarthy; **Ballpark:** Wrigley Field; **Attendance:** 1,143,740; **Finish:** Third (91-63); **Recap:** With the addition of Pittsburgh outfielder Kiki Cuyler, the Cubs stay in the pennant race before fading in September and finishing third, just four games behind St. Louis.

The Cubs are driven by what is probably the greatest outfield in their history - Cuyler, who bats a disappointing .285, Hack Wilson, who socks a league-leading 31 homers, and Riggs Stephenson, who bats .324 and drives in 90 runs.

P	Player	R	HR	RBI	SB	AVE
1B	Charlie Grimm	93	10	85	9	.323
2B	Freddie Maquire	67	1	41	6	.279
SS	Woody English	68	2	34	4	.299
3B	Clyde Beck	72	3	52	3	.257
RF	Kiki Cuyler	92	17	79	37	.285
CF	Hack Wilson	89	31	120	4	.313
LF	Riggs Stephenson	75	8	90	8	.324
C	Gabby Hartnett	61	14	57	3	.302
OF	Cliff Heathcote	26	3	18	6	.285
IF	Johnny Butler	17	0	16	2	.270
OF	Earl Webb	22	3	23	0	.250
C	Mike Gonzalez	12	1	21	2	.272
IF	Norm McMillan	11	1	12	0	.220

T	Pitcher	W-L	SV	SO	SH	ERA
R	Pat Malone	18-13	2	155	2	2.83
R	Sheriff Blake	17-11	1	78	4	2.46
R	Guy Bush	15-6	2	61	2	3.84
R	Charlie Root	14-18	2	122	1	3.57
L	Art Nehf	13-7	0	40	2	2.64

April 11 - The Cubs lose 5-1 on Opening Day to the Reds at Crosley Field.

April 18 - Things go no better in the home opener at Wrigley Field, with the Cubs losing to Cincinnati 9-6. The reported attendance of 46,000 is an Opening Day record.

May 15 - The Cubs hit into six double plays against the Giants at Wrigley but triumph 10-7.

May 19 - The first-place Cubbies win their 13th in a row, 3-2 over the Braves. Winning pitcher Charlie Root drives in the go-ahead run with a sacrifice fly. Hack Wilson adds a homer.

September 1 - Sheriff Blake holds the Reds to one hit in a 1-0 victory, allowing just a fifth-inning double by George Kelly.

September 15 - The Cubs keep their hold on second place by splitting a doubleheader with the Braves, winning the nightcap 6-1 behind Guy Bush.

September17 - Braves reliever Ray Boggs beans three Cubs and hurls a wild pitch in the ninth inning during a 15-5 Chicago victory.

September 18 - The Cubs and Braves combine for a National League-record eight double plays in an 8-3 Chicago win.

September 27 - It's crunch time as just three games separate the Cardinals, Cubs and Giants. Chicago beats New York, behind St. Louis by just half a game, in game one of a twinbill by a score of 3-2. The game's highlight is a controversial play at the plate in the sixth inning, when Giants catcher Shanty Hogan chops a ball back to pitcher Art Nehf, who throws to third to get the runner. But Andy Reese, the runner, bowls over catcher Gabby Hartnett, who is standing between third and home. Hartnett grabs Reese to keep but falling, and Clyde Beck tags Reese out. Enraged Giants manager John McGraw protests, but umpire Bill Klem insists that Reese is out.

The Giants win the nightcap 2-0, but the damage is done; St. Louis will win the pennant tomorrow. Chicago is eliminated with the loss.

November7 - The Cubs put the final piece of their 1929 pennant-winning team together by acquiring star second baseman Rogers Hornsby from the financially-strapped Braves for $200,000, infielder Fred Maguire, catcher Lou Legett and pitchers Harry Seibold, Percy Jones and Bruce Cunningham.

1929

Principle Owner and President: William Veeck, Sr.; **Manager:** Joe McCarthy; **Ballpark:** Wrigley Field; **Attendance:** 1,485,166; **Finish:** First (98-54); **Recap:** With Rogers Hornsby and Hack Wilson leading the way, the Cubs capture their first pennant in 11 years. Kiki Cuyler paces the NL with 43 steals, Pat Malone leads the leauge with 22 wins, and Charlie Root goes 19-6. The Cubs hit .303 as a team (second to the Phillies'.309) and attendance shoots to nearly 1.5 million, a new club record that will stand for 40 years.

Joe McCarthy

The Cubs take over first place midway through the sequent and never relinquish, finishing 10 1/2 games ahead of Pittsburgh.

P	PLAYER	R	HR	RBI	SB	AVE
1B	Charlie Grimm	66	10	91	3	.298
2B	Rogers Hornsby	156	39	149	2	.380
SS	Woody English	131	1	52	13	.276
3B	Norm McMillan	77	5	55	13	.271
RF	Kiki Cuyler	111	15	102	43	.360
CF	Hack Wilson	135	39	159	3	.345
LF	Riggs Stephenson	91	17	110	10	.362
C	Zack Taylor	29	1	31	0	.274
OF	Cliff Heathcote	45	2	31	9	.313
C	Mike Gonzalez	15	0	18	1	.240
IF	Clyde Beck	28	0	9	3	.211
OF	Johnny Moore	13	2	8	0	.286
IF	Chuck Tolson	13	1	19	0	.257

Hack Wilson

T	Pitcher	W-L	SV	SO	SH	ERA
R	Pat Malone	<u>22</u>-10	2	<u>166</u>	<u>5</u>	3.57
R	Charlie Root	19-6	5	124	4	3.47
R	Guy Bush	18-7	<u>8</u>	82	2	3.65
R	Sheriff Blake	14-13	1	70	1	4.29
R	Hal Carlson	11-5	2	35	2	5.14

April 16 - The Cubs best their Opening Day attendance record as a reported 50,000 are on hand to watch them lost to the Pirates 4-3.

April 21 - Guy Bush shuts down the Cardinals 4-0 before 45,000 at Wrigley. New second sacker Rogers Hornsby goes 4-for-4 with two doubles.

April 22 - The Cubs whitewash the Cardinals for the second day in a row, beating them 3-0 behind Pat Malone. Grover Alexander is the loser.

May 4 - The Cubs sweep a doubleheader from the Phillies. Pat Malone hurls a 16-0 shutout in the opener, contributing three singles and two RBI. Chicago takes the second game by a score of 9-7.

July 3 - The Cubs and Reds turn nine double plays, tying a major league mark set in 1925, during a 7-5 Chicago win in the first of two at Wrigley. It's the seventh win in a row for the Cubs, who regain the league lead.

Chicago completes a sweep of the twin-bill with a 10-5 win in the nightcap. During the game Hack Wilson is ejected for jumping into the Cincinnati dugout to pick a fight with pitcher Ray Kolp, who has been heckling him. Later that evening, as the two teams are waiting to board a train at Union Station, Wilson decks Reds pitcher Pete Donahue.

July 24 - The Cubs beat the Giants 8-7 at Wrigley Field, giving them a nine-game winning streak and a half-game NL lead. Chicago will win its next eight contests, opening the lead to 4 1/2 games.

August 3 - Though the Cubs post an official complaint about the ragged shirt sleeve on Brooklyn ace Dazzy Vance's pitching arm, a trick used by the Dazzler to distract the batter, they pound him to win 12-2. A rule will eventually be passed enforcing the diamond dress code.

August 6 - More than 29,000 women (and 11,000 men) show up for a Ladies Day game at Wrigley to watch their Cubbies lose to Brooklyn 5-4. Chicago's five-game winning streak is snapped.

WORTH QUOTING - "You have to improve your club even if it means letting your own brother go."

-Joe McCarthy

August 8 - Rogers Hornsby smacks his 24th homer of the year in the fourth inning to give the Cubs a 1-0 triumph over the Reds at Wrigley. Charlie Root scatters seven hits for the shutout.

August 9 - Guy Bush wins his 11th straight, a 12-6 decision over the Phillies in Philadelphia.

August 12 - Bush's winning streak is snapped as he comes in as a reliever and loses 4-2 at Boston. Bush now has a 16-2 record. The Cubs retain their eight-game lead over second-place Pittsburgh.

August 21 - First baseman Charlie Grimm suffers a hand injury during a 9-2 win over New York, sidelining him for the rest of the regular season. He will return to the lineup for the World Series.

August 23 - The Cubs purchase the contract of righthander Lon Warneke, from Alexandria of the Cotton State League, for $100. The Arkansas Hummingbird will win 100 games over six seasons for the Cubs, making the All-Star team three times.

August 26 - A bizarre grand slam off the bat of third baseman Norm McMillan gives the Cubs a 9-5 victory over the Reds at Wrigley Field. In the eighth inning with the bases loaded, McMillan hits a liner down the left field line. Cincinnati left fielder Evar Swanson, who is shaded toward center field, sees the ball bounce off a gutter in foul territory and disappear. As Swanson and the Reds search frantically for the ball, McMillan circles the bases for an inside-the-park grand slam. After the game, Cubs reliever Ken Penner discovers the ball inside the sleeve of his jacket.

August 27 - The Cubbies open up the National League's biggest lead since 1906, 14 1/2 games, when they beat the Reds 4-1. Rogers Hornsby's four hits back a six-hitter by Sheriff Blake.

WORTH NOTING - Gabby Hartnett sat out most of the 1929 season with what was diagnosed as a "dead arm," which forced manager Joe McCarthy to bench him in favor of Zach Taylor. Doctors could not offer any explanation for Hartnett's sudden inability to throw the ball but his mother insisted that it was a psychological thing, relating to his wife's pregnancy.

Sure enough, Hartnett returned next season, after his child was born over the winter, and became one of the best fielding catchers in major league history.

August 30 - The Cubs are pasted by the Pirates 15-0. It's Pittsburgh's fourth win in three days over Chicago.

September 2 - William Wrigley watches 81,000 fans go through his turnstiles for a doubleheader sweep of the Cardinals. A crowd of 38,000 watches the Cubbies win 11-7 in a rare morning game and 43,000 watch their team win 12-10 in the afternoon game. Rogers Hornsby belts two homers and Hack Wilson adds one.

September 18 - The Cubs clinch the runaway pennant despite losing 7-3 to the Giants; Boston beats the second-place Pirates 5-4 in the first of a twinbill at Forbes Field.

October 1 - Chicago defeats Cincinnati 3-2 before just 500 fans at Crosley Field.

October 6 - The Cubs lose their regular season closer at Wrigley 8-3 to Pittsburgh but announce a season attendance figure of 1,485,000 - a mark they will not surpass until 1969.

WORTH NOTING- The Cubs' World Series opponents in 1929 are the Philadelphia Athletics, managed by **Connie Mack**. The Athletics finish with a 104-46 (.693) record, leading the American League in saves (24), strikeouts (573) and ERA (3.44).

P	PLAYER	R	HR	RBI	SB	BA
1B	Jimmie Foxx	123	33	117	9	.354
2B	Max Bishop	102	3	36	1	.232
SS	Joe Boley	36	2	47	1	.251
3B	Sammy Hale	51	1	40	6	.277
Rf	Bing Miller	84	8	93	24	.335
CF	Mule Haas	115	16	82	0	.313
LF	Al Simmons	114	34	157	4	.365
C	Mickey Cochrane	113	7	95	7	.331

T	PITCHER	W	L	SV	SH	ERA
R	George Earnshaw	24	8	1	2	3.28
L	Lefty Grove	20	6	4	2	2.82
L	Rube Wahlberg	18	11	4	3	3.59
R	Eddie Rommel	12	2	4	0	2.84
R	Bill Shores	11	6	7	1	3.59

October 8 - Game One @ Chicago
Submarining veteran Howard Ehmke, reportedly washed up and who sat out the last month at the behest of Philadelphia manager Connie Mack, is the surprise starter in Game 1. Ehmke's slow stuff throws the Cubs off balance and he turns in a 3-1 win, scattering eight hits. Chicago pushes across its only tally in the ninth on a two-base error and RBI single by Riggs Stephenson. Charlie Grimm singles to put the tying run on but Ehmke retires pinch-hitter Footsie Blair on a ground ball and fans Chick Tolson.

October 9 - Game Two @ Chicago
Another 50,000 jam Wrigley Field for Game 2, and again they're disappointed. The Athletics roll to a 9-3 win behind George Earnshaw. The Cubs fight back from a 6-0 deficit, cutting the lead to 6-3, but manager Connie Mack summons Lefty Grove from the bullpen, who hurls four shutout innings for the save.

October 11 - Game Three @ Philadelphia
The Cubs score their only victory of the Series as Guy Bush beats George Earnshaw 3-1, pitching out of several jams. The Cubs score all of their runs in the sixth, on an RBI single by Rogers Hornsby and a two-run hit by Kiki Cuyler.

October12 - Game Four@ Philadelphia
The Athletics turn a laugher into a victory by scoring 10 runs in the seventh to erase an 8-0 deficit and hold on to win 10-8. A two-run homer in the fourth by Charlie Grimm starts the scoring for Chicago. The Cubs add five more runs in the sixth on five hits and a single and add another in the seventh. But in the bottom of the frame, the Athletics explode against starter Sheriff Blake and three relievers, helped in part by Hack Wilson's bumbling of two fly balls he claims are lost in the sun - one for a three-run, game-tying homer. Lefty Grove hurls two innings of hitless relief to notch his second save of the series.

October 14 - Game Five @ Philadelphia
The shell-shocked Cubs lose a 3-2 squeaker to Rube Wahlberg in the fifth and final game of the series. Chicago again takes the lead, 2-0 on singles by Charlie Grimm and Zack Taylor in the fourth. Pat Malone cruises into the ninth, holding on to a 2-0 lead. But with one out, Malone gives up a single to Max Bishop and a game-tying homer to Mule Haas. With two outs, Malone gives up a double to Al Simmons and, after an intentional walk to Jimmie Foxx, Bing Miller lines a series-winning double.

1930

Principle Owner and President: William Veeck, Sr.; **Manager:** Joe McCarthy / Rogers Hornsby; **Ballpark:** Wrigley Field; **Attendance:** 1,463,624; **Finish:** Second (90-64); **Recap:** The Cubs bash the ball at

1929 World Series action at Shibe Park

a record pace, led by Hack Wilson's NL-best 56 homers and jaw-dropping 191 RBIs, but the Cubs wind up two games short of St. Louis in the pennant race.

Throughout the year, reports surface that Joe McCarthy is on his way out as pilot, partly because of the manager's testy reply last October after owner William Wrigley criticized the team's World Series performance, and partly because the team has a proven winner, Rogers Hornsby, waiting in the wings. In fact, McCarthy *does* leave the Cubs before the end of the season, but ending up with the Yankees. Hornsby, indeed, takes over the club.

P	PLAYER	R	HR	RBI	SB	AVE
1B	Charlie Grimm	58	6	66	1	.289
2B	Footsie Blair	97	6	59	9	.273
SS	Woody English	152	14	59	3	.335
3B	Les Bell	35	5	47	1	.278
RF	Kiki Cuyler	155	13	134	37	.355
CF	Hack Wilson	146	56	191	3	.356
LF	Riggs Stephenson	56	5	68	2	.367
C	Gabby Hartnett	84	37	122	0	.339

P	PLAYER	R	HR	RBI	SB	AVE
IF	Clyde Beck	32	6	34	2	.213
OF	Danny Taylor	43	2	37	6	.283
OF	Cliff Heathcote	30	9	18	4	.260
P	Guy Bush	7	0	7	0	.282

T	PITCHER	W-L	SV	SO	SH	ERA
R	Pat Malone	20-9	4	142	2	3.94
R	Charlie Root	16-14	3	124	4	4.34
R	Guy Bush	15-10	3	75	0	6.20
L	Bud Teachout	11-4	0	59	0	4.06
R	Bob Osborn	10-6	1	42	0	4.96

January 8 - Veteran hurler Art Nehf, who went 8-5 in 1929 for the Cubs, announces his retirement. Nehf won 184 games over his 15-year career, reaching the World Series five times - once with the Cubs and

WORTH QUOTING - "Yes. If you drink liquor, you won't have worms."

-Hack Wilson, after manager Joe McCarthy tries to teach him a lesson on the evils of drink by dropping a worm in a glass of gin and asking him if he had learned anything

Kiki Cuyler

four times with the Giants.

January 20 - Hack Wilson is challenged to a boxing match by White Sox first baseman Art Shires, a part-time professional boxer. Baseball Commissioner Landis blocks the fight and bans boxing for all baseball players. Shire has fought several suspected bouts that has resulted in his being suspended by the boxing commissions of 32 states.

April 15 - The Cubs spoil Opening Day at Sportsman's Park, defeating the Cardinals 9-8.

April 22 - The Cards return the favor, beating Chicago 8-3 at the Wrigley Field opener.

May 12 - The Cubs belt six home runs off Giants starter Larry Benton, but lose 14-12. The Cubbies are losing 14-0 until the bottom of the seventh, when they tally five runs on four straight homers, tying the major league record.

May 28 - Tragedy strikes the Cubs as reliever Hal Carlson, aged 38, dies suddenly of a stomach ulcer hemorrhage. The previous evening he had been complaining of severe stomach pain while sitting with teammates in the lobby of Chicago's Carlos Hotel. Before today's game he calls the Cubs'trainer complaining of great pain but dies before the ambulance reaches his home. The 14-year veteran was 4-2 for the season.

May 30 - Rogers Hornsby breaks his ankle sliding into third base in the first game of a doubleheader at St. Louis. Hornsby will miss most of the season. The Cubs sweep the Cardinals 2-0 and 9-3 to move into third place.

June 23 - Hack Wilson hits for the cycle in a 21-8 pounding of Philadelphia.

June 25 - Gabby Hartnett tallies four hits, including two home runs, and knocks in seven runs in a 13-12 win over the Phils.

June 27 - More than 51,000 fans turn up for a Ladies Day contest with the Dodgers at Wrigley Field. The Cubs win 7-5 on Kiki Cuyler's 10th-inning homer.

June 30 - The Cubs move into first place with a 10-3 victory over New York.

July 24 - The Cubs beat the Phillies 19-15 in one of the highest-scoring games in team history. Chicago takes a 13-3 lead after two innings but the Phils chip away, scoring seven in an exciting eighth inning in which umpire Bill Klem ejects Chuck Klein, don Hurst and pinch-hitter Fresco Thompson. Thirty of the game's 34 hits are singles.

July 26 - Hack Wilson smacks three homers and Gabby Hartnett and pitcher Pat Malone add two in a 16-2 drubbing of pitching-challenged Philadelphia.

July 27 - Cincinnati reliever Ken Ash is brought in to face Charlie Grimm in the seventh with two runners on, tosses one pitch, and gets a triple play. Ash is lifted for a pinch-hitter but receives credit for the 6-5 victory, his last in the majors.

August 10 - The Cubs take two from Boston before 45,000 fans at Wrigley to move to within a game of the surprising first-place Dodgers. Hack Wilson enjoys his second three-homer game of the year, and Charlie Root tosses a three-hit shutout in a 6-0 opening win. The Cubs take game two 11-1 behind Pat Malone's five-hitter.

August 11 - The Cubs leapfrog the Dodgers into first, beating the Braves 4-3 in 10 innings.

August 12 - More than 40,000 fans jam Wrigley to watch the Cubs and Dodgers clash. Dazzy Vance strands 16 Chicago baserunners but enters the 11th inning tied 2-2, only to lose on a game-winning single by Riggs Stephenson. Brooklyn loads the bases in the eighth, ninth and tenth innings but fails to score.

August 13 - The Dodgers whip the Cubs 15-5, pulling to within a game of first place.

August 14 - Pat Malone beats Brooklyn 5-1, pushing them back to two games back.

August 16 - The Cubs beat the Phils 10-9 in the opener of a doublehader. Down 8-1, Philadelphia scores eight runs in the seventh to take a brief 9-8 lead, but a home run by Gabby Hartnett wins the game for Chicago. Hack Wilson smacks his 41st homer.

A two-run homer by Woody English in the ninth ties the nightcap 3-3, which is called for darkness.

WORTH NOTING - Woody English collected 200 hits and 100 walks in 1930, one of only nine major leaguers to have reached both marks in the same season. The others include Ty Cobb, Jimmie Foxx, Lou Gehrig, Hack Wilson, Stan Musial and Wade Boggs.

August 18 - Wilson collects his 42nd homer and English scores five runs in a 17-3 pummeling of the Phillies.

August 19 - Wilson continues his record-setting pace, delivering his 43rd homer in the first of two at Baker Bowl. The drive ties Phillies outfielder Chuck Klein's National League record set last year. Klein, in right field, waves to Wilson as he circles the bases. Philadelphia wins 9-8. Game two ends a 6-6 tie after 16 innings.

August 24 - The Cubs load the bases with two outs in the ninth of a tie game in New York. With the count 0-and-2, Danny Taylor, the runner on third, streaks home; a surprised Giants reliever Joe Heving uncorks a wild pitch and Taylor crosses the plate. The Cubs hold on to win 3-2. New York third baseman Freddie Lindstrom's 24-game hitting streak is snapped.

August 26 - Hack Wilson, on his way to 191 RBI, drives in four to lead the Cubs to a 7-5 triumph over the Pirates. Wilson, an average fielder on a good day, allows a Lloyd Waner line drive to skip by in the outfield for an inside-the-park home run, and vows to atone for his mistake. In his next at-bat he hits his 44th home run,

The Greatest Cubs

A list of the 70 greatest Cubs of all time, including 18th-century players. The list comprises Hall of Fame enshrinees, near-misses and notables who have not yet qualified. League leaders are underlined. • Indicates All-Star selection.

Grover Cleveland Alexander (P)

Notes: One of the greatest pitchers in the history of the game, Alexander piled up 373 National League victories, tying him with Christy Mathewson for best all-time. An accident while in military uniform during WWI rendered Alexander deaf in one ear and prone to epileptic seizures. A dependence on alcohol cost him many more victories, especially towards the end of his career. Alexander's post-baseball life was even more tragic; he even worked for a while at a Times Square flea circus. He died penniless in St. Paul, Nebraska in 1950. Alex was immortalized in a motion picture called *The Winning Season*, starring Ronald Reagan. He was elected to the Hall of Fame in 1938. **Numbers:** With the Philadelphia Phillies, led the National League in wins (28), complete games (31), shutouts (7), and innings pitched (367) in 1911; in innings pitched in 1912 (310.1); in shutouts (9) in 1913; in wins (27), complete games (32), innings pitched (355), and strikeouts (214) in 1914; in wins (31), winning percentage (.756), complete games (36), shutouts (12), innings pitched (376.1), strikeouts (241), and ERA (1.22) in 1915; in wins (33), complete games (38), shutouts (16), innings pitched (389), strikeouts (167) and ERA(1.55) in 1916; and in wins (30), complete games (34), shutouts (8), innings pitched (388), striketouts (200), and ERA(1.83) in 1917. Won 94 games in three-year span (1915-1917).

YEAR	W	L	G	GS	CG	SH	SV	IP	H	HR	BB	SO	ERA	PCT
1918	2	1	3	3	3	0	0	252	286	10	33	77	3.39	.667
1919	16	11	30	27	20	9	1	235	180	3	38	121	1.72	.593
1920	27	14	46	40	33	7	5	363.1	335	8	69	173	1.91	.659
1921	15	13	31	30	21	3	1	252	286	10	33	77	3.39	.536
1922	16	13	33	31	20	1	1	245.2	283	8	34	48	3.63	.552
1923	22	12	39	36	26	3	2	305	308	17	30	72	3.19	.647
1924	12	5	21	20	12	0	0	169.1	183	9	25	33	3.03	.706
1925	15	11	32	30	20	1	0	236	270	14	29	63	3.39	.577
1926	3	3	7	7	4	0	0	52	55	0	7	12	3.46	.500
TOT	**128**	**83**	**242**	**224**	**159**	**24**	**10**	**1884**	**1919**	**79**	**268**	**614**	**2.84**	**.607**

Cap Anson (1B/C) Manager, 1879-1897

Notes: Greatest hitter of the 19th century. Probably the greatest manager as well. As a skipper, Anson was militarily strict and efficient, winning five pennants. As a player, Anson won three batting championships, was the first major leaguer to record 3,000 hits, and finished with a lifetime average of .329. Anson was a legendary racist; he refused to let his club take the field against clubs that included such black players as Moses Fleetwood Walker and George Stovey. In his memoir, he referred to African-American team mascot Clarence Duval as a "chocolate-covered coon." He was elected to the Hall of Fame in 1939. **Numbers:** Led NLin on-base percentage in 1881 (.442), 1888 (.400), and 1890 (.443) and in fielding percentage in 1877

(.883), 1880 (.978), 1881 (.975), 1888 (.986) and 1889 (.982); led National Association in doubles in 1871 (11) and in on-base percentage in 1872 (.455). Elected to Hall of Fame, 1939.

YEAR	G	AB	R	H	2B	3B	HR	RBI	BB	SO	SB	BA	SLG
1876	66	309	63	110	9	7	2	59	12	8	-	.356	.450
1877	59	255	52	86	19	1	0	32	9	3	-	.337	.420
1878	60	261	55	89	12	2	0	40	13	1	-	.341	.402
1879	51	227	40	72	20	1	0	34	2	2	-	.317	.414
1880	86	356	54	120	24	1	1	74	14	12	-	.337	.419
1881	84	343	67	137	21	7	1	82	26	4	-	.399	.510
1882	82	348	69	126	29	8	1	83	20	7	-	.362	.500
1883	98	413	70	127	36	5	0	68	18	9	-	.308	.419
1884	112	475	108	159	30	3	21	102	29	13	-	.335	.543
1885	112	464	100	144	35	7	7	108	34	13	-	.310	.461
1886	125	504	117	187	35	11	10	147	55	19	29	.371	.544
1887	122	472	107	164	33	13	7	102	60	18	27	.347	.517
1888	134	515	101	177	20	12	12	84	47	24	28	.344	.499
1889	134	518	100	161	32	7	7	117	86	19	27	.311	.440
1890	139	504	95	157	14	5	7	107	113	23	29	.312	.401
1891	136	540	81	157	24	8	8	120	75	29	17	.291	.409
1892	146	559	62	152	25	9	1	74	67	30	13	.272	.354
1893	103	398	70	125	24	2	0	91	68	12	13	.314	.384
1894	83	340	82	132	28	4	5	99	40	15	17	.388	.538
1895	122	474	87	159	23	6	2	91	55	23	12	.314	.384
1896	108	402	72	133	18	2	2	90	49	10	24	.331	.400
1897	114	424	67	121	17	3	3	75	60	-	11	.285	.361
TOT	**2276**	**9108**	**1719**	**3000**	**528**	**124**	**96**	**1715**	**952**	**294**	**247**	**.329**	**.446**

Ernie Banks (SS/1B)

Notes: Known as "Mr. Cub" for his hometown enthusiasm, Banks shares a unique bond with the city of Chicago because he holds the record for most games (2,528) without ever appearing in the postseason. First played professional baseball with the Negro League's Kansas City Monarchs. Scouted by Buck O'Neil, Banks and Gene Baker arrived in Chicago in 1953 as the club's first black players. In 13 seasons, he hit at least 20 homers, reached 40 five times and drove in 100 or more runs eight times. His five grand slams in 1955 are a major league record. From 1955 to 1960, Banks hit more home runs than anyone in the majors, including Mickey Mantle, Hank Aaron and Willie Mays. Banks was the first player to be elected the National League's Most Valuable Player in successive seasons (1958 and 1959). He also established records for most homers in a season by a shortstop (47 in 1958) and for fewest errors in a season by ashortstop (12 in 1959). In the middle of his career, Banks transferred to first baseto accommodate his slowing reflexes. Banks was voted the greatest player in franchise history but was pushed aside when the Chicago Tribune bought the club from the Wrigley Family because of the organization's desire to become less identified with the losing teams of the 1950s and 60s. He was elected to the Hall of Fame in 1977. **Numbers:** Led NL in fielding percentage in 1955 (.972), 1959 (.985), 1960 (.977) and 1969 (.997).

YEAR	G	AB	R	H	2B	3B	HR	RBI	BB	SO	SB	BA	SLG
1953	10	35	3	11	1	1	2	6	4	5	0	.314	.571
1954	154	593	70	163	19	7	19	79	40	50	6	.275	.427
1955•	154	596	98	176	29	9	44	117	45	72	9	.295	.596
1956•	139	538	82	160	25	8	28	85	52	62	6	.297	.530
1957•	156	194	113	169	34	6	43	102	70	85	8	.285	.579
1958•	154	617	119	193	23	11	47	129	52	87	4	.313	.614
1959•	155	589	97	179	25	6	45	143	64	72	2	.304	.596
1960•	156	597	94	162	32	7	41	117	71	69	1	.271	.554
1961•	138	511	75	142	22	4	29	80	54	75	1	.278	.507
1962•	154	610	87	164	20	6	37	104	30	71	5	.269	.503
1963	130	432	41	98	20	1	18	64	39	73	0	.227	.403
1964	157	591	67	156	29	6	23	95	36	84	1	.264	.450
1965•	163	612	79	162	25	3	28	106	55	64	3	.265	.453
1966	141	511	52	139	23	7	15	75	29	59	0	.272	.432
1967•	151	573	68	158	26	4	23	95	27	93	2	.276	.455
1968	150	552	71	136	27	0	32	83	27	67	2	.246	.469
1969•	155	565	60	143	19	2	23	106	42	101	0	.253	.416
1970	72	222	25	56	6	2	12	44	20	33	0	.252	.459
1971	39	83	4	16	2	0	3	6	6	14	0	.193	.325
TOT	**2528**	**9421**	**1305**	**2583**	**407**	**90**	**512**	**1636**	**763**	**1236**	**50**	**.274**	**.500**

Glenn Beckert (2B)

Notes: Beckert was the Cubs' regular second baseman for nine seasons, a reliable contact hitter and Gold Glover (1968). Earned the nickname "Bruno" for his habit of knocking down teammates in pursuit of pop-ups. Was the most difficult batter to strike out in the National League five times, fanning only 20 times in 643 at-bats in 1968.

YEAR	G	AB	R	H	2B	3B	HR	RBI	BB	SO	SB	BA	SLG
1965	154	614	73	147	21	3	3	30	28	52	6	.239	.298
1966	153	656	73	188	23	7	1	59	26	36	10	.287	.348
1967	146	597	91	167	32	3	5	40	30	25	10	.280	.369
1968	155	643	98	189	28	4	4	37	31	20	8	.294	.369
1969•	131	543	69	158	22	1	1	37	24	24	6	.291	.341
1970•	143	591	99	170	15	6	3	36	32	22	4	.288	.349
1971•	131	530	80	1881	18	5	2	42	24	24	3	.342	.406
1972•	120	474	51	128	22	2	3	43	23	17	2	.270	.344
1973	114	372	38	95	13	0	0	29	30	15	0	.255	.290
TOT	**1247**	**5020**	**672**	**1423**	**194**	**31**	**22**	**353**	**248**	**235**	**49**	**.283**	**.348**

Mordecai "Three-Finger" Brown (P)

Notes: Brown was called "Three-Finger" due to two childhood accidents on his Indiana farm. In the first incident, he caught his index finger in a corn shredder and had to have the finger amputated; a couple of weeks later, he broke his third and fourth fingers, and they never grew straight. The deformity became an asset when Brown noticed he could snap off an ungodly curveball, leading to six straight years (1906-1911) of registering at least 20 wins, with a career-high of 29 in 1908. In 1906,

Brown compiled a major league-record 1.06 ERA; his 14-year career ERAof 2.06 is third all-time behind Ed Walsh (1.82) and Addie Joss (1.89). Brown was the anchor of the great "Tinker-Evers-Chance" dynasty; four of his five World Series victories were shutouts. Brown's battles with New York Giant ace Christy Mathewson were legendary, and never failed to provide a sellout. He faced Matty for the final time in 1916, each with 12 victories. Mathewson beat Brown in what turned out to be each pitcher's final National League start. Brown managed the Federal League's St. Louis club in 1914. He was elected to the Hall of Fame in 1949.

YEAR	W	L	G	GS	CG	SH	SV	IP	H	HR	BB	SO	ERA	PCT
1904	15	10	26	23	21	4	1	212.1	155	1	50	81	1.86	.600
1905	18	12	30	24	24	4	0	249	2119	3	44	89	2.17	.600
1906	26	6	36	32	27	9	3	277.1	198	1	61	144	1.04	.813
1907	20	6	34	27	20	6	3	233	180	2	40	107	1.39	.769
1908	29	9	44	31	27	9	5	312.1	214	1	49	123	1.47	.763
1909	27	9	50	34	32	8	7	342.2	246	1	53	172	1.31	.750
1910	25	14	46	31	27	6	7	295.1	256	3	64	143	1.86	.641
1911	21	11	53	27	21	0	13	270	267	5	55	129	2.80	.656
1912	5	6	15	8	5	2	0	88.2	92	2	20	34	2.64	.455
TOT	**188**	**83**	**346**	**241**	**206**	**48**	**39**	**2329**	**1879**	**19**	**445**	**1043**	**1.80**	**.694**

Bill Buckner (1B/OF)

Notes: Buckner's outstanding 22-year career has been forever marred by booting a Mookie Wilson grounder in the 1986 World Series while with the Boston Red Sox. With the Cubs, he was a consistent hitter, winning the batting title in 1980 and batting .300 or better between 1977-84. Buckner set a major league record for assists in a season (184) in 1985.

YEAR	G	AB	R	H	2B	3B	HR	RBI	BB	SO	SB	BA	SLG
1977	122	426	40	121	27	0	11	60	21	23	7	.284	.425
1978	117	446	47	144	26	1	5	74	18	17	7	.323	.419
1979	149	591	72	168	34	7	14	66	30	28	9	.284	.437
1980	145	578	69	187	41	3	10	68	30	18	1	.324	.457
1981•	106	421	45	131	35	3	10	75	26	16	5	.311	.480
1982	161	657	93	201	34	5	15	105	36	26	15	.306	.441
1983	153	626	79	175	38	6	16	66	25	30	12	.280	.436
1984	21	43	3	9	0	0	0	2	1	1	0	.209	.209
TOT	**974**	**3788**	**449**	**1136**	**235**	**25**	**81**	**516**	**187**	**159**	**56**	**.300**	**.439**

Tom Burns (SS)

Notes: Part of the club's "Stonewall Infield" of the 1880s that included first baseman Cap Anson, second baseman Fred Pfeffer, and third baseman Ned Williamson, shortstop Burns drove in at least 65 runs six times. On September 6, 1883, Burns collected two doubles and a home run for Chicago in an 18-run seventh inning of a 26-6 pounding of the Detroit Wolverines. It is regarded as the greatest individual offensive inning in major league history.

YEAR	G	AB	R	H	2B	3B	HR	RBI	BB	SO	SB	BA	SLG
1880	85	333	47	103	17	3	0	43	12	23	-	.309	.378
1881	84	342	41	95	20	3	4	42	14	22	-	.278	.389
1882	84	355	55	88	23	6	0	48	15	28	-	.248	.346
1883	97	405	69	119	37	7	2	67	13	31	-	.294	.435
1884	83	343	54	84	14	2	7	44	13	50	-	.245	.359
1885	111	445	82	121	23	9	7	71	16	48	-	.272	.411
1886	112	445	64	123	18	10	3	65	14	40	15	.276	.382
1887	115	424	57	112	20	10	3	60	34	32	32	.264	.380
1888	134	483	60	115	12	6	3	700	26	49	34	.238	.306
1889	136	525	64	127	27	6	4	66	32	57	18	.242	.339
1890	139	538	86	149	17	6	5	86	57	45	44	.277	.359
1891	59	243	36	55	8	1	1	17	21	21	18	.226	.280
TOT	**1239**	**4881**	**715**	**1291**	**235**	**69**	**40**	**567**	**267**	**446**	**161**	**.264**	**.365**

Guy Bush (P)

Notes: Signed by the Cubs out of the Cotton States League for $1,200 and a jug of whiskey, Bush won 152 games for Chicago over 12 seasons. Bush was a reliable swingman, starting 308 games and relieving in 234. Bush was traded to Pittsburgh in 1935, giving up the last two homers of Babe Ruth's career.

YEAR	W	L	G	GS	CG	SH	SV	IP	H	HR	BB	SO	ERA	PCT
1923	0	0	1	0	0	0	0	1	1	0	0	2	0.00	-
1924	2	5	16	8	4	0	0	80.2	91	7	24	36	4.02	.286
1925	6	13	42	15	5	0	4	182	213	15	52	76	4.30	.316
1926	13	9	35	15	7	2	2	157.1	149	3	42	32	2.86	.591
1927	10	10	36	22	9	1	2	193.1	177	3	79	62	3.03	.500
1928	15	6	42	24	9	2	2	204.1	229	10	86	61	3.83	.714
1929	18	7	50	29	18	2	8	270.2	277	16	107	82	3.66	.720
1930	15	10	46	25	11	0	3	225	291	22	86	75	6.20	.600
1931	16	8	39	24	14	1	2	180.1	190	9	66	54	4.49	.667
1932	19	11	40	30	15	1	0	238.2	262	13	70	73	3.21	.633
1933	20	12	41	32	20	4	2	259	261	9	68	84	2.75	.625
1934	18	10	40	27	15	1	2	209.1	213	15	54	75	3.83	.643
TOT	**152**	**101**	**428**	**252**	**127**	**14**	**27**	**2201**	**2354**	**122**	**734**	**712**	**3.81**	**.601**

Phil Cavaretta (1B/OF)

Notes: Cavarretta grew up in Chicago and was a lefthanded pitcher for Lane Tech in the Windy City when he signed a professional contract with Peoria. He was 18 when he was brought up by the Cubs in September, 1934, homering in his first start. He became the Cubs' regular second baseman at the age of 19. Exempt from military service because of an ear problem, Cavarretta enjoyed his best years during World War II. He hit .321 and tied for the league lead (with Stan Musial) with 197 hits in 1944. In that year's All-Star Game, he reached base five times, an All-Star record. Cavarretta was the Cubs' player-manager from 1951-1953. He was fired by Phil Wrigley when for being too honest: in spring training of 1954, Wrigley asked him for an honest assessment of the team; Cavarretta's reply earned him the pink slip for being "defeatist." **Numbers:** Also led the National League in on-base percentage in

1945 (.449) and in pinch hits in 1951 (12). Voted the National League Most Valuable Player (1945).

YEAR	G	AB	R	H	2B	3B	HR	RBI	BB	SO	SB	BA	SLG
1934	7	21	5	8	0	1	1	6	2	3	1	.381	.619
1935	146	589	85	162	28	12	8	82	39	61	4	.275	.404
1936	124	458	55	125	18	1	9	56	17	36	8	.273	.376
1937	106	329	43	94	18	7	5	56	32	35	7	.286	.429
1938	92	268	29	64	11	4	1	28	14	27	4	.239	.321
1939	22	55	4	15	3	1	0	0	4	3	2	.273	.364
1940	65	193	34	54	11	4	2	22	31	18	3	.280	.409
1941	107	346	46	99	18	4	6	40	53	28	2	.286	.413
1942	136	482	59	130	28	4	3	54	71	42	7	.270	.363
1943	143	530	93	154	27	9	8	73	75	42	3	.291	.421
1944•	152	614	106	<u>197</u>	35	15	5	82	67	42	4	.321	.451
1945	132	498	94	177	34	10	6	97	81	34	5	<u>.355</u>	.500
1946•	139	510	89	150	28	10	8	78	88	54	2	.294	.435
1947•	127	459	56	144	22	5	2	63	58	35	2	.314	.397
1948	111	334	41	93	16	5	3	40	35	29	4	.278	.383
1949	105	360	46	106	22	4	8	49	45	31	2	.294	.444
1950	82	256	49	70	11	1	10	31	40	31	1	.273	.441
1951	89	206	24	64	7	1	6	28	27	28	0	.311	.442
1952	41	63	7	15	1	1	1	8	9	3	0	.238	.333
1953	27	21	3	6	3	0	0	3	6	3	0	.286	.429
TOT	**1953**	**6592**	**968**	**1927**	**341**	**99**	**92**	**896**	**794**	**545**	**61**	**.292**	**.416**

Frank Chance (1B/C)

Notes: The leader of the great Tinker-Evers-Chance teams in the early part of the century, Chance was that rare breed of first baseman who could consistently steal bases. A lifetime .297 hitter, Chance was dubbed "The Peerless Leader" as he led the Cubs to pennants in 1906-1908 and in 1910. Sometimes known as "Husk," the first baseman's hearing declined over the years due to numerous beanings, resulting in a high-pitched whine that became quite annoying to his teammates, as well as to opponents. Like most managers of the era, Chance was allowed to make his own trades and personnel decisions, and his acquisitions of outfielder Jimmy Sheckard from the Dodgers and Harry Steinfeld from the Reds proved crucial to the team's early dynasty. A battle with Charles Murphy over the owner's cost-cutting led to his release in 1913; he signed with the Yankees for $40,000. Health problems forced him to quit as Yanks manager in 1914 and he returned home to California, where he became part owner and manager of the Pacific Coast League's Los Angeles Angels. He returned to major league baseball in 1923 to manage the Red Sox, but finished in the cellar due to owner Harry Frazee's fire sale of stars. Chance then signed to manage the White Sox in 1924 but his health worsened and he died that September. He finished with a 946-648 (.593) lifetime record as a major league manager. He was elected to the Hall of Fame in 1646. **Numbers:** Also led National League in on-base percentage in 1905 (.450).

YEAR	G	AB	R	H	2B	3B	HR	RBI	BB	SO	SB	BA	SLG
1898	53	147	32	41	4	3	1	14	7	-	7	.279	.367
1899	64	192	37	55	6	2	1	22	15	-	10	.286	.354
1900	56	149	26	44	9	3	0	13	15	-	8	.295	.396
1901	69	241	38	67	12	4	0	36	29	-	27	.278	.361
1902	75	240	39	69	9	4	1	31	35	-	27	.287	.371
1903	125	441	83	144	24	10	2	81	78	-	67	.327	.440
1904	124	451	89	140	16	10	6	49	36	-	42	.310	.430
1905	118	392	92	124	16	12	2	70	78	-	38	.316	.434
1906	136	474	103	151	24	10	3	71	70		57	.319	.430
1907	111	382	58	112	19	2	1	49	51	-	35	.293	.361
1908	129	452	65	123	27	4	2	55	37	-	27	.272	.363
1909	93	324	53	88	16	4	0	46	30	-	29	.272	.346
1910	88	295	54	88	12	8	0	36	37	15	16	.298	.393
1911	31	88	23	21	6	3	1	177	25	13	9	.239	.406
1912	2	5	2	1	0	0	0	0	3	0	1	.200	.200
TOT	**1274**	**4269**	**795**	**1266**	**200**	**79**	**20**	**590**	**546**	**28**	**404**	**.297**	**.394**

John Clarkson (P)
Notes: In the day of the two-man rotation, there were few pitchers better than righthander Clarkson. One of the first of the overhand pitchers, he won 53 games for the White Stockings in 1885, second only in major league history to Old Hoss Radbourne's 60 in 1884. Traded to Boston in 1888, Clarkson compiled 49 victories a year later. He was elected to the Hall of Fame in 1963. **Numbers:** With the Boston Beaneaters, led the National League in wins (49), winning percentage (.721), games (73), complete games (68), shutouts (8), innings pitched (620), strikeouts (284) and ERA(2.73) in 1889.

YEAR	W	L	G	GS	CG	SH	SV	IP	H	HR	BB	SO	ERA	PCT
1884	10	3	14	13	12	0	0	118	94	10	25	102	2.14	.769
1885	53	16	70	70	68	10	0	623	497	21	97	308	1.85	.768
1886	36	17	55	55	50	3	0	466.2	419	20	86	313	2.41	.679
1887	38	21	60	59	56	2	0	523	513	20	92	237	3.08	.644
TOT	**152**	**101**	**428**	**252**	**127**	**14**	**27**	**2201**	**2354**	**122**	**734**	**712**	**3.81**	**.601**

Larry Corcoran (P)
Notes: In his first five seasons (1880-84), Corcoran won 170 games and became the first pitcher to throw three no-hitters. He won 43 games as a rookie and won at least 27 games each season with the White Stockings. He teamed with Fred Goldsmith in 1880 to form the first major league rotation with two 20-game winners. Between 1880 and 1884, the combo gave Chicago 277 wins, the most of any rotation before 1887, when the major league schedule increased to 140 games. Corcoran was also the first pitcher to use signals with his catchers; he would shift the large wad of tobacco he invariably had in his mouth from one cheek to the other to signal a curve. His .663 winning percentage is ranked eighth all-time. After 1884, Corcoran's numbers slipped consistently due to overwork, dissipation, and Bright's disease. He died in New Jersey at the age of 32.

YEAR	W	L	G	GS	CG	SH	SV	IP	H	HR	BB	SO	ERA	PCT
1880	43	14	63	60	57	4	2	536.1	404	6	99	268	1.95	.754
1881	31	14	45	44	43	4	0	396.2	380	10	78	150	2.31	.689
1882	27	12	39	39	38	3	0	355.2	281	5	63	170	1.95	.692
1883	34	20	56	53	51	3	0	473.2	483	7	82	216	2.49	.630
1884	35	23	60	59	57	7	0	516.2	473	35	116	272	2.40	.603
1885	5	2	7	7	6	1	0	59.1	63	2	24	10	3.64	.714
TOT	**136**	**57**	**199**	**197**	**186**	**15**	**0**	**1731**	**1523**	**65**	**300**	**960**	**2.39**	**.705**

Kiki Cuyler (OF)

Notes: Cuyler was traded from Pittsburgh to the Cubs after a year-long confrontation with manager Donie Bush in 1927. Cuyler, a star for the pennant-winning Pirates, went on to play a major role in the team's pennants in 1929 and 1932. Cuyler's real name was Hazen Shirley Cuyler, picking up the nickname "Kiki" while playing for Nashville in the Southern Association in 1923. Called "Cuy" by his teammates, fans heard the players shout for him to take the ball on a pop fly, with both the shortstop and second baseman shouting "Cuy" at the same time. Cuyler was a coach with the Boston Red Sox in 1950 when he dropped dead at the age of 50. He was elected to the Hall of Fame in 1968. **Numbers:** With the Pittsburgh Pirates, led the National League in runs in 1925 (144) and 1926 (113), and in triples in 1925 (26).

YEAR	G	AB	R	H	2B	3B	HR	RBI	BB	SO	SB	BA	SLG
1928	133	499	92	142	25	9	17	79	51	61	37	.285	.473
1929	139	509	111	183	29	7	15	102	66	56	43	.360	.532
1930	156	642	155	228	50	17	13	134	72	49	37	.355	.547
1931	154	613	110	202	37	12	9	88	72	54	13	.330	.473
1932	110	446	58	130	19	9	10	77	29	43	9	.291	.442
1933	70	262	37	83	13	3	5	35	21	29	4	.317	.447
1934•	142	559	80	189	42	8	6	69	31	62	15	.338	.474
1935	45	157	22	42	5	1	4	18	10	16	3	.268	.389
TOT	**949**	**3687**	**665**	**1199**	**220**	**66**	**79**	**602**	**352**	**370**	**161**	**.325**	**.485**

Bill Dahlen (SS)

Notes: Dahlen was a hard-hitting shortstop for Chicago from 1891-1898, hitting .350 twice, driving in 100 runs twice, and compiling the longest hitting streak in franchise history (42 games in 1884). A slick fielder, Dahlen owns the National League record for career assists (7,500).

YEAR	G	AB	R	H	2B	3B	HR	RBI	BB	SO	SB	BA	SLG
1891	135	549	114	143	18	13	9	76	67	60	21	.260	.390
1892	143	581	114	169	23	19	5	58	45	56	60	.291	.422
1893	116	485	113	146	28	15	5	64	58	30	31	.301	.452
1894	121	502	149	179	32	14	15	107	76	33	42	.357	.566
1895	129	516	106	131	19	10	7	62	61	51	38	.254	.370
1896	125	474	137	167	30	19	9	74	64	36	51	.352	.553
1897	75	276	67	80	18	8	6	40	43	-	15	.290	.478
1898	142	521	96	151	35	8	1	79	58	-	27	.290	.393
TOT	**986**	**3904**	**896**	**1166**	**203**	**106**	**57**	**560**	**472**	**266**	**27**	**.299**	**.449**

Abner Dalrymple (OF)

Notes: The leadoff hitter and left fielder for Cap Anson's pennant-winners in the 1880s, Dalrymple sometimes kept an extra ball in his jersey, to be pulled out on suitable occasions. On a foggy day in 1880, he stole a home run from Boston's Ezra Sutton by backing up against the fence and pulling the ball out of his shirt just as the game ball soared out of the park; Sutton was called out by the umpire. That year, Dalrymple also led the National League in "total bases run," an official category in 1880, with 501. In 1884, Dalrymple benefitted from a 200-foot right field fence to compile 22 homers for a White Stockings team that hit a 140 for the season, a record that stood until the 1927 Yankees hit 158. Dalrymple hit four doubles in one game on July 3, 1883, tying him with many others for the major league record.

YEAR	G	AB	R	H	2B	3B	HR	RBI	BB	SO	SB	BA	SLG
1879	71	333	47	97	25	1	0	23	4	29	-	.291	.372
1880	86	382	91	126	25	12	0	36	3	18	-	.330	.458
1881	82	362	72	117	22	4	1	37	15	22	-	.323	.414
1882	84	397	96	117	25	11	1	36	14	18	-	.295	.421
1883	80	363	78	108	24	4	2	37	11	29	-	.298	.402
1884	111	521	111	161	18	9	22	69	14	39	-	.309	.505
1885	113	492	109	135	27	12	11	61	46	42	-	.274	.445
1886	82	331	62	77	7	12	3	26	33	44	16	.233	.353
TOT	**709**	**3181**	**666**	**938**	**173**	**65**	**40**	**216**	**14**	**241**	**16**	**.295**	**.428**

Jody Davis (C)

Notes: The lead-footed Davis was a fine defensive catcher for the Cubs from 1981-1987. He hit at least 17 homers five years in a row and played in two All-Star games. He was traded to the Braves in 1988 when Damon Berryhill began to blossom as a receiver and hitter. Davis starred in the 1984 NLCS, collecting seven hits in five games and hitting homers in Games 4 and 5. He won a Gold Glove in 1986.

YEAR	G	AB	R	H	2B	3B	HR	RBI	BB	SO	SB	BA	SLG
1981	56	180	14	46	5	1	4	21	21	28	0	.256	.361
1982	130	418	41	109	20	2	12	52	36	92	0	.261	.404
1983	151	510	56	138	31	2	24	84	33	93	0	.271	.480
1984•	150	523	55	134	25	2	19	94	47	99	5	.256	.421
1985	142	482	47	112	30	0	17	58	48	83	1	.232	.400
1986•	148	528	61	132	27	2	21	74	41	110	0	.250	.428
1987	125	428	57	106	12	2	19	51	52	91	1	.248	.418
1988	88	249	19	57	9	0	6	33	29	51	0	.229	.337
TOT	**990**	**3318**	**350**	**834**	**158**	**11**	**122**	**467**	**307**	**647**	**7**	**.251**	**.416**

Andre Dawson (OF)

Notes: An All-Star with the Montreal Expos, Dawson signed a blank contract with the Cubs in 1987 because of his desire to play in the Friendly Confines. Getting a below-market salary of $500,000, Dawson went on to become the National League's Most Valuable Player that season, the first time a player has won the award while playing for a last-place team. A fan favorite in Chicago, he is one of just three major leaguers (with Willie Mays and Barry Bonds) to compile 400 homers and 300 stolen bases. **Numbers:** With the Montreal Expos, led the National League in hits in 1983 (189). Voted the National League Most Valuable Player (1987).

YEAR	G	AB	R	H	2B	3B	HR	RBI	BB	SO	SB	BA	SLG
1987•	153	621	90	178	24	2	49	137	32	103	11	.287	.568
1988•	157	591	78	179	31	8	24	79	37	73	12	.303	.504
1989•	118	416	62	105	18	6	21	77	35	62	8	.252	.476
1990•	147	529	72	164	28	5	27	100	42	65	16	.310	.535
1991•	149	563	69	153	21	4	31	104	22	80	4	.272	.488
1992	143	542	60	150	27	2	22	90	30	70	6	.277	.456
TOT	**867**	**3262**	**431**	**929**	**149**	**27**	**174**	**587**	**198**	**453**	**57**	**.285**	**.507**

Shawon Dunston (SS)

Notes: Dunston was the first pick in the 1982 June Amateur Draft after batting .790 as a senior at Thomas Jefferson High in Brooklyn. The club's starting shortstop by 1985, Dunston had speed, a cannon arm, and not-bad power. In 1986, he led National League shortstops in putouts, assists, double plays, errors, and homers.

YEAR	G	AB	R	H	2B	3B	HR	RBI	BB	SO	SB	BA	SLG
1985	74	250	40	65	12	4	4	18	19	42	11	.260	.388
1986	150	581	66	145	37	3	17	68	21	114	13	.250	.411
1987	95	346	40	85	18	3	5	22	10	68	12	.246	.358
1988•	155	575	69	143	23	6	9	56	16	108	30	.249	.357
1989	138	471	52	131	20	6	9	60	30	86	19	.278	.403
1990•	146	545	73	143	22	8	17	66	15	87	25	.262	.426
1991	142	492	59	128	22	7	12	50	23	64	21	.260	.407
1992	18	73	8	23	3	1	0	2	3	13	2	.315	.384
1993	7	10	3	4	2	0	0	2	0	1	0	.315	.384
1994	88	331	38	92	19	0	11	35	16	48	3	.278	.435
1995	127	477	58	141	30	6	14	69	10	75	10	.296	.472
1995	114	419	57	119	18	4	9	41	8	64	29	.284	.411
TOT	**1254**	**4570**	**563**	**1219**	**225**	**48**	**107**	**489**	**171**	**770**	**175**	**.267**	**.407**

Leon Durham (1B/OF)

Notes: Durham was traded to the Cubs with third baseman Ken Reitz from the Cardinals for Bruce Sutter in 1980. Although St. Louis probably got the best of that deal, Bull finished third in the 1982 batting race and became the organization's first 20-homer, 20-steal player since 1911, when Wildfire Schulte did it. He played outfield for the Cubs until replacing Bill Buckner at first base in 1984. Although he hit 20 or more homers in five of his seven full seasons with Chicago, he never really fulfilled expectations. He was traded to the Cincinnati Reds in 1988 but spent most of the season in drug rehab. He made a comeback with the Cardinals in 1989, mostly as a pinch-hitter and defensive replacement, but was suspended again for drug use. He became a member of Cubs lore in 1984 when he let a ground ball off the bat of Tim Flannery go through his legs in Game 5 of the NLCS, allowing the tying run to score in an eventual 6-3 Padres win.

YEAR	G	AB	R	H	2B	3B	HR	RBI	BB	SO	SB	BA	SLG
1981	87	328	42	95	14	6	10	35	27	53	25	.290	.460
1982•	148	539	84	168	33	7	22	90	66	77	28	.312	.521
1983•	100	337	58	87	18	8	12	55	66	83	12	.258	.466
1984	137	473	86	1322	30	4	23	96	69	86	16	.279	.505
1985	153	542	58	153	32	2	21	75	64	99	7	.282	.465
1986	141	484	66	127	18	7	20	65	67	98	8	.262	.452
1987	131	439	70	120	22	1	27	63	51	92	2	.273	.513
1988	24	73	10	16	6	1	3	6	9	20	0	.219	.452
TOT	**921**	**3215**	**474**	**898**	**173**	**36**	**138**	**485**	**419**	**608**	**98**	**.279**	**.484**

Johnny Evers (2B)

Notes: Known as The Crab for his gruff disposition, Evers has poet Franklin P. Adams, more than anyone else, to thank for his induction into the Hall of Fame. Evers was a hustling infielder and slap hitter who stole 36 bases or more during the club's 1906-08 dynasty, Evers'inclusion in Adams poem "Baseball's Sad Lexicon," referring to the Tinkers-Evers-Chance double play combination, led to his Hall of Fame nod in 1946. With the Cubs, Evers hit .300 twice, including a soaring .341 mark in 1912, but saved his best work for the World Series, contributing significantly to the two World Championships in 1907 and 1908 and hitting .438 for the Miracle Braves in the 1914 Series. Never a friendly sort, Evers'argument with double play partner Joe Tinker in 1905 over a taxicab mixup led to the two refusing to speak to each other for 33 years. In 1911, Evers suffered a nervous breakdown but returned to be named manager Frank Chance's successor in 1913. Evers' firing by Charles Murphy after the season cost the owner his ballclub; the second baseman threatened to join the new Federal League, which was enough for National League President John Tener to force Murphy out for risking the loss of one of the league's biggest stars. In 1921, new owner Bill Veeck, Sr. brought Evers back to manage the Cubs again, but it ended even more quickly than before after Evers had numberous run-ins with his players (one of them, five-time 20 game-winner Hippo Vaughn, was so demoralized by Evers that he retired). **Numbers:** Led the National League in on-base percentage in 1912 (.431) and in fielding percentage while with Boston in 1914 (.976). Voted the National League Most Valuable Player (1914).

YEAR	G	AB	R	H	2B	3B	HR	RBI	BB	SO	SB	BA	SLG
1902	26	90	7	20	0	0	0	2	3	-	1	.222	.222
1903	124	464	70	136	27	7	0	52	19	-	25	.293	.381
1904	152	532	49	141	14	7	0	47	28	-	26	.265	.318
1905	99	340	44	94	11	2	1	37	27	-	19	.276	.329
1906	154	533	65	136	17	6	1	51	36	-	49	.255	.315
1907	151	508	66	127	18	4	2	51	38	-	46	.250	.313
1908	126	416	83	125	19	6	0	37	66	-	36	.300	.375
1909	127	463	88	122	19	6	1	24	73	-	28	.263	.337
1910	125	433	87	114	11	7	0	28	108	18	28	.263	.321
1911	46	155	29	35	4	3	0	7	34	10	6	.226	.290
1912	143	478	73	163	23	11	1	63	74	18	16	.341	.441
1913	136	446	81	127	20	5	3	49	50	14	11	.285	.372
TOT	**1408**	**4855**	**742**	**1339**	**183**	**64**	**9**	**448**	**556**	**60**	**291**	**.276**	**.345**

George Gore (OF)

Notes: Gore was a .301 hitter in 14 seasons, leading the league in 1880 with a .360 mark. The White Stockings'center fielder during the glorious 1880s, Gore's hitting prowess was second to his patience at the plate; in 1886, he became the first player with 100 or more walks, with each of his 102 free passes falling under the seven-ball rules of the day. Called "Piano Legs" for his bulging calf muscles, Gore was signed by Cap Anson after playing for a semipro New England team in an exhibition game against the White Stockings. When Chicago lost the postseason championship to the St. Louis Brown in 1886, Anson accused Gore of playing under the influence and traded him to the New York Giants. Gore, Billy Hamilton, and Harry Stovey are the only players (with 4,000 at-bats or more) with more runs scored than games (1,327 runs in 1,310 games).

YEAR	G	AB	R	H	2B	3B	HR	RBI	BB	SO	SB	BA	SLG
1879	63	266	43	70	17	4	0	32	8	30	-	.263	.357
1880	77	322	70	116	23	2	2	47	21	10	-	.360	.463
1881	73	309	86	92	18	9	1	44	27	23	-	.298	.424
1882	84	367	99	117	15	7	3	51	29	19	-	.319	.422
1883	92	392	105	131	30	9	2	52	27	13	-	.334	.472
1884	103	422	104	134	18	4	5	34	61	26	-	.318	.415
1885	109	441	115	138	21	13	5	57	68	25	-	.313	.454
1886	118	444	150	135	20	12	6	63	102	30	23	.304	.444
TOT	**719**	**2963**	**772**	**933**	**162**	**60**	**24**	**288**	**343**	**176**	**23**	**.315**	**.434**

Mark Grace (1B)

Notes: A contact hitter to the extreme, Grace batted .303 over 16 years with a high of .331 in 1996. The first baseman never struck out more than 56 times in a season but never hit more than 17 home runs either. He led the National League in doubles (51) in 1995, the only time he finished first in any category. In 1989 he led the Cubs with 8 RBIs and a .647 batting average during the National League Championship Series vs. the San Francisco Giants. After a bitter contract dispute in 2000, he joined the Arizona Diamondbacks the next year and appeared in his only World Series.

YEAR	G	AB	R	H	2B	3B	HR	RBI	BB	SO	SB	BA	SLG
1988	134	486	65	144	23	4	7	57	60	43	3	.296	.403
1989	142	510	74	160	28	3	13	79	80	42	14	.314	.457
1990	157	589	72	182	32	1	9	82	59	54	15	.309	.413
1991	160	619	87	169	28	5	8	58	70	53	3	.273	.373
1992	158	603	72	185	37	5	9	79	72	36	6	.307	.430
1993•	155	594	86	193	39	4	14	98	71	32	8	.325	.475
1994	106	403	55	120	23	3	6	44	48	41	0	.298	.414
1995•	143	552	97	180	51	3	16	92	65	46	6	.326	.516
1996	142	547	88	181	39	1	9	75	62	41	2	.331	.455
1997•	151	555	87	177	32	5	13	78	88	45	2	.319	.465
1998	158	595	92	184	39	3	17	89	93	56	4	.309	.471
1999	161	593	107	183	44	5	16	91	83	44	3	.309	.481
2000	143	510	75	143	41	1	11	82	95	28	1	.280	.429
TOT	**1910**	**7156**	**1057**	**2101**	**456**	**43**	**148**	**1004**	**946**	**561**	**67**	**.305**	**.444**

Clark Griffith (P)

Notes: Righthander Griffith was signed by Cap Anson after posting a 30-18 record for the Pacific Coast League's Oakland Oaks in 1893. Called "The Old Fox" for his six-pitch arsenal, including a screwball (which he claimed to have invented), Griffith claimed it was bad luck to pitch a shutout, and avoided doing so until 1897. After a stellar career with the Colts in which he won 21 or more games six straight years, Griffith jumped to the new American League's Chicago White Sox and in 1901 posted a seventh 20-win season. Griffith moved on to the New York Highlanders (later called the Yankees) in 1903 as manager, guiding them to a couple of second-place finishes, and finally ended up with the Washington Senators, becoming the club's owner in 1919. He held the post until his death in 1955 at age 85. He was elected to the Hall of Fame in 1946. **Numbers:** While with the Chicago White Sox, led the American League in winning percentage (.774) and shutouts (5) in 1901.

YEAR	W	L	G	GS	CG	SH	SV	IP	H	HR	BB	SO	ERA	PCT
1893	1	2	4	2	2	0	0	19.2	24	1	5	9	5.03	.333
1894	21	14	36	30	28	0	0	261.1	328	12	85	71	4.92	.600
1895	26	14	42	41	39	0	0	353	434	11	91	79	3.93	.650
1896	23	11	36	35	35	0	0	317.2	370	3	70	81	3.54	.676
1897	21	18	41	38	38	1	1	343.2	410	3	86	102	3.72	.538
1898	24	10	38	38	36	4	0	325.2	305	1	64	97	1.88	.706
1899	22	14	38	38	35	0	0	319.2	329	5	65	73	2.79	.611
1900	14	13	30	30	27	4	0	248	245	6	51	61	3.05	.519
TOT	**152**	**96**	**265**	**253**	**240**	**9**	**1**	**2189**	**2445**	**42**	**517**	**573**	**3.40**	**.613**

Charlie Grimm (1B)

Notes: Grimm was a slick-fielding first baseman for the Pittsburgh Pirates until owner Barney Dreyfuss, tired of Grimm's after-hours antics with teammate Rabbit Maranville, traded him to the Cubs. After a few years of batting at or around .300, Grimm was chosen as Roger Hornsby's replacement as manager in 1932, guiding the club to its second World Series in three seasons. After a couple of years of butting heads with owner Phil Wrigley, Grimm retired in 1938. Jolly Cholly manned the broadcast mic until 1944, when he was asked to take over as manager once again. He was the club's skipper when they made their last World Series appearance in 1945. In 1949, Wrigley decided that Grimm and general manager Jim Gallagher had the wrong jobs, so he put Grimm in charge of baseball operations, demoted Gallagher to a less meaningful post, and hired Frankie Frisch as manager. But after a few months, Grimm announced he had had enough of the organization's politics and resigned to help Bill Veeck, Jr. run the American Association's Milwaukee Brewers. In 1960, Grimm was asked to pilot the Cubs for a third time but lasted just over a month, traded back to the broadcast booth for Lou Boudreau. Grimm was named to manage the club a fourth time, joining Wrigley's College of Coaches the following year, but never actually rotated into the dugout. After his death in 1983, Grimm's ashes were scattered over Wrigley Field. **Numbers:** Also led the National League in fielding percentage in 1928 (.993), 1930 (.995), 1931 (.993), and 1933 (.996). With the Pittsburgh Pirates, led the National League in fielding percentage in 1920 (.995), 1923 (.995), and 1924 (.995).

YEAR	G	AB	R	H	2B	3B	HR	RBI	BB	SO	SB	BA	SLG
1925	141	519	73	159	29	5	10	76	38	25	4	.306	.439
1926	147	524	58	145	30	6	8	82	49	28	3	.277	.403
1927	147	543	68	169	29	6	2	74	45	21	3	.311	.398
1928	147	547	67	161	25	5	5	62	39	20	7	.294	.386
1929	120	463	66	138	28	3	10	91	42	25	3	.298	.436
1930	114	429	58	124	27	2	6	66	41	26	1	.289	.403
1931	146	531	65	176	33	11	4	66	53	29	1	.331	.458
1932	149	570	66	175	42	2	7	80	35	22	2	.307	.425
1933	107	384	38	95	15	2	3	37	23	15	1	.247	.320
1934	75	267	24	79	8	1	5	47	16	12	1	.296	.390
1935	2	8	0	0	0	0	0	0	0	1	0	.000	.000
1936	39	132	13	33	4	0	1	16	5	8	0	.250	.303
TOT	**1334**	**4917**	**596**	**1454**	**270**	**43**	**61**	**697**	**386**	**229**	**26**	**.296**	**.405**

Stan Hack (3B)

Notes: Hack was one of the most popular Cubs of his era. After batting .352 his first year in pro ball, at Sacramento, Hack was signed to a Cubs contract by Bill Veeck, Sr, who traveled to California to sign him in person. The slap-hitting Hack became the club's regular third baseman by 1934, and became a fan favorite for his good looks as much as for his play on the diamond. He twice led the National League in fielding and assists, and five times in putouts. In 1935, vendors in the Wrigley bleachers sold "Smile With Stan" mirrors, which the bleacherites used to reflect the sun into the eyes of opposing batters. Hack retired in 1943, mostly because he couldn't get along with manager Jimmy Wilson, but returned in 1944 when Wilson was fired. He retired for good in 1947, tying the record for most years (16) as a National League third baseman. He managed the Cubs from 1954-1956, never finishing higher than sixth. **Numbers:** Also led the National League in fielding percentage in 1942 (.965) and 1945 (.975).

YEAR	G	AB	R	H	2B	3B	HR	RBI	BB	SO	SB	BA	SLG
1932	72	178	32	42	5	6	2	19	17	16	5	.236	.365
1933	20	60	10	21	3	1	1	2	8	3	4	.350	.483
1934	111	402	54	116	16	6	1	21	45	42	11	.289	.366
1935	124	427	75	133	23	9	4	64	65	17	14	.311	.436
1936	149	561	102	167	27	4	6	78	89	39	17	.298	.392
1937	154	582	106	173	27	6	2	63	83	42	16	.297	.375
1938•	152	609	109	195	34	11	4	67	94	39	16	.320	.432
1939•	156	641	112	191	28	6	8	56	65	35	17	.298	.398
1940	149	603	101	191	38	6	8	40	75	24	21	.317	.439
1941•	151	586	111	186	33	5	7	45	99	40	10	.317	.427
1942	140	553	91	166	36	3	6	39	94	40	9	.300	.409
1943•	144	533	78	154	24	4	3	35	82	27	5	.289	.366
1944	98	383	65	108	16	1	3	32	53	21	5	.282	.352
1945	150	597	110	193	29	7	2	43	99	30	12	.323	.405
1946	92	323	55	92	13	4	0	26	83	32	3	.285	.350
1947	76	240	28	65	11	2	0	12	41	19	0	.271	.333
TOT	**1938**	**7278**	**1239**	**2193**	**363**	**81**	**57**	**642**	**1092**	**466**	**165**	**.301**	**.397**

Bill Hands (P)

Notes: A member of the Big Three (with Fergie Jenkins and Ken Holtzman) pitching staff of the late '60s and early '70s, Hanks was as bad in the batter's box as he was good on the mound. A .078 career hitter, Hands struck out 14 straight times in 1968, a major league record. After going 18-15 in 1970, back ailments began to limit his effectiveness. He was traded to Minnesota in 1973, retiring in 1975.

YEAR	W	L	G	GS	CG	SH	SV	IP	H	HR	BB	SO	ERA	PCT
1966	8	13	41	26	0	0	2	159	168	17	59	93	4.58	.381
1967	7	8	49	11	3	1	6	150	134	9	48	84	2.46	.497
1968	16	10	38	34	11	4	0	258.2	221	26	36	148	2.89	.615
1969	20	14	41	41	18	3	0	300	268	21	73	181	2.49	.588
1970	18	15	39	38	12	2	1	265	278	20	76	170	3.70	.545
1971	12	18	36	35	14	1	0	242.1	248	27	50	128	3.42	.400
1972	11	8	32	28	6	3	0	189	168	12	47	96	3.00	.579
TOT	**92**	**86**	**276**	**213**	**64**	**14**	**9**	**1564**	**1485**	**144**	**389**	**900**	**3.18**	**.517**

Gabby Hartnett (OF)

Notes: Known as "Old Tomato Face" for his large, pink noggin, Hartnett rivaled the Yanks'Bill Dickey as the greatest catcher of the 1930s. Signed by the Cubs in 1921, he became Chicago's starting catcher by 1924 and hit 24 homers in 1925 despite leading the league in strikeouts with 77. In the spring of 1929, Hartnett developed a dead arm. Nothing helped until after his pregnant wife delivered their first child on December 4; within two weeks Hartnett's arm soreness had disappeared. The next year he had his best offensive season, batting .339 with career highs of 37 homers and 122 RBIs. In 1931, Hartnett created a controversy when he was photographed with Cubs fan Al Capone, leading to NLpresident John Heydler's ruling that forbid players to socialize with fans before a game. Hartnett's most memorable highlight was his "Homer In The Gloamin'" shot on September 28, 1938, that sealed the pennant for Chicago. Defensively, Hartnett had few equals in major league history, leading the National League in putouts four times, assists six times, and fielding average six times. He managed the ballclub from 1938-1940, then skippered in the minors until 1946, when he retired from baseball and opened a bowling alley in Lincolnwood, Illinois. **Numbers:** Led the National League in fielding percentage in 1928 (.989), 1930 (.989), 1934 (.996), 1936 (.991), 1937 (.996) and 1938 (.995). Voted the National League Most Valuable Player (1935).

YEAR	G	AB	R	H	2B	3B	HR	RBI	BB	SO	SB	BA	SLG
1922	31	72	4	14	1	1	0	4	6	8	1	.194	.236
1923	85	231	28	62	12	2	8	39	25	22	4	.268	.442
1924	111	354	56	106	17	7	16	67	39	37	10	.299	.523
1925	117	398	61	115	28	3	24	67	36	77	1	.289	.555
1926	93	284	35	78	25	3	8	41	32	37	0	.275	.468
1927	127	449	56	132	32	5	10	80	44	42	2	.294	.454
1928	120	388	61	117	26	9	14	57	65	32	3	.302	.523
1929	25	22	2	6	2	1	1	9	5	5	1	.273	.591
1930	141	508	84	172	31	3	37	122	55	62	0	.339	.630
1931	116	380	53	107	32	1	8	70	52	48	3	.282	.434

1932	121	406	52	110	25	3	12	52	51	59	0	.271	.436
1933•	140	490	55	135	21	4	16	88	37	51	1	.276	.433
1934•	130	438	58	131	21	1	22	90	37	46	0	.299	.502
1935•	116	416	67	142	32	6	13	91	41	46	1	.344	.545
1936•	121	424	49	130	25	6	7	64	30	36	0	.307	.443
1937•	110	356	47	126	21	6	12	82	43	19	0	.354	.548
1938•	88	299	40	82	19	1	10	59	48	17	1	.274	.445
1939	97	306	36	85	18	2	12	59	37	32	0	.278	.467
1940	37	64	3	17	3	0	1	12	8	7	0	.266	.359
TOT	**1926**	**6282**	**847**	**1867**	**391**	**64**	**231**	**1153**	**691**	**683**	**28**	**.297**	**.490**

Billy Herman (2B)

Notes: Herman's career got off to an inauspicious start, when, facing Si Johnson of the Reds in his first major league at-bat on August 29, 1931, he hit a foul ball that hit the plate and bounced back to knock him out. For the rest of the 1930s and early 1940s, however, Herman was the best second baseman in the National League, batting more than .300 eight times and scoring at least 100 runs five times. He tied the National League record for most years leading the league in putouts (seven) and led the NLin assists three times and fielding average three times. He appeared in 10 All-Star games, batting .433 (13 for 30) overall. After a slow start in 1941, Herman was dealt to the Brooklyn Dodgers for two has-beens and $60,000. He later managed the Pirates and Red Sox. He was elected to the Hall of Fame in 1975. **Numbers:** Also led the National League in fielding percentage in 1935(.964), 1936 (.975), and 1938 (.981).

YEAR	G	AB	R	H	2B	3B	HR	RBI	BB	SO	SB	BA	SLG
1931	25	98	14	32	7	0	0	16	13	6	2	.327	.398
1932	154	656	102	206	42	7	1	51	40	33	14	.314	.404
1933	153	619	82	173	35	2	0	44	45	34	5	.279	.342
1934•	113	456	79	138	21	6	3	42	34	31	6	.303	.395
1935•	154	666	113	227	57	6	7	83	42	29	6	.341	.476
1936•	153	632	101	211	57	7	5	93	59	30	5	.334	.470
1937•	138	564	106	189	35	11	8	65	56	22	2	.335	.479
1938•	152	624	86	173	34	7	1	56	59	31	3	.277	.359
1939•	156	623	111	191	34	18	7	70	66	31	9	.307	.453
1940•	135	558	77	163	24	4	5	57	47	30	1	.292	.376
1941•	11	36	4	7	0	1	0	0	9	5	0	.194	.250
TOT	**1344**	**5532**	**875**	**1710**	**346**	**69**	**37**	**577**	**470**	**282**	**53**	**.309**	**.417**

Ken Holtzman (P)

Notes: After defeating Sandy Koufax 2-1 as a 20-year-old rookie in 1966, Holtzman was labelled "The New Koufax," a moniker that both he, and Koufax, rejected. A member of Chicago's "Big Three" pitching staff (with Fergie Jenkins and Bill Hands) of the late '60s and early '70s, Holtzman tossed two no-hitters and was a steady starter for a decade. The outspoken southpaw was a constant pain in manager Leo Durocher's backside, and Holtzman was traded to Oakland after the 1971 season, where he helped the A's win three consecutive World Championships in 1972-74. He briefly returned to the Cubs in 1978, after spending most of the season in Yankee manager Billy Martin's doghouse, before retiring in 1979.

YEAR	W	L	G	GS	CG	SH	SV	IP	H	HR	BB	SO	ERA	PCT
1965	0	0	3	0	0	0	0	4	2	1	3	3	2.25	-
1966	11	16	34	33	9	0	0	220.2	194	27	68	171	3.79	.407
1967	9	0	12	12	3	0	0	92.2	76	11	44	62	2.53	1.000
1968	11	14	34	32	6	3	1	215	201	17	76	151	3.35	.440
1969	17	13	39	39	12	6	0	261.1	248	18	93	176	3.58	.567
1970	17	11	39	38	15	1	0	287.2	271	30	94	202	3.38	.607
1971	9	15	30	29	9	3	0	195	213	18	64	143	4.48	.375
1978	1	0	5	3	0	0	0	17.2	21	2	9	3	4.08	1.000
1979	6	9	23	20	3	2	0	117.2	133	15	53	44	4.59	.400
TOT	**80**	**81**	**237**	**209**	**57**	**15**	**3**	**1427**	**1399**	**139**	**530**	**988**	**3.81**	**.497**

Rogers Hornsby (2B)

Notes: Hornsby was the greatest righthanded batter of all time. Although he was a legendary grump, Hornsby never argued with umpires and was never thrown out of a game. He also never drank, smoked, or went to movies (for fear of ruining his eyesight); his only vice, other than the dog track, was ice cream. There are no doubts about his numbers. Hornsby won two Triple Crowns, he reached the .300 level 17 times, and his average between the years of 1921 and 1925 exceeded .400. After scrapping with both Branch Rickey in St. Louis and John McGraw in New York, The Rajah was traded to the Boston Braves before the Cubs bought him for $200,000 in 1928. He won his second MVPaward in 1929, and was named the club's manager in 1930. As Chicago's skipper he won few public relations points for so ridiculing slugger Hack Wilson for his drinking habits, the outfielder stopped hitting just a year after setting the major league record with 191 RBIs and was shipped off to the Cardinals. After Cubs owner William Wrigley died in 1932, Hornsby found he had few supporters, and an enemy in Wrigley's son Phil, and was bounced after the season. In fact, Hornsby had so alienated his players that they refused to vote any of the 1932 World Series shares to him. Hornsby returned to St. Louis to manage the Browns until 1937, then managed in the minors for the next 15 seasons. He spent the last years of his life as a batting coach, working for the Cubs in 1958 and 1959. His last position in the majors was as a coach for the expansion Mets in 1962. He was elected to the Hall of Fame in 1942. **Numbers:** With the St. Louis Cardinals, led the National League in triples (17) and slugging percentage (.484) in 1917; hits (218), doubles (44), RBIs (94), batting average (.370) and slugging percentage (.559) in 1920; runs (131), hits (235), doubles (44), triples (18), RBIs, (126), batting average (.397) and slugging percentage (.639) in 1921; runs (141), hits (250), doubles (46), home runs (42), RBIs (152), batting average (.401), slugging percentage (.722) and fielding percentage (.967) in 1922; batting average (.384) and slugging percentage (.627) in 1923; runs (121), hits (227), doubles (43), walks (89), batting average (.424) and slugging percentage (.696) in 1924; and home runs (39), RBIs (143), batting average (.403), and slugging percentage (.756) in 1925. With the New York Giants, led the National League in runs (133), and walks (86) in 1927. With the Boston Braves, led the National League in walks (107), batting average (.387), and slugging percentage (.632). Voted the National League Most Valuable Player (1925, 1929).

YEAR	G	AB	R	H	2B	3B	HR	RBI	BB	SO	SB	BA	SLG
1929	156	602	156	229	47	8	39	149	87	65	2	.380	.679
1930	42	104	15	32	5	1	2	18	12	12	0	.308	.433
1931	100	357	64	118	37	1	16	90	56	23	1	.331	.574
1932	19	58	10	13	2	0	1	7	10	4	0	.224	.310
TOT	**317**	**1121**	**245**	**392**	**91**	**10**	**58**	**264**	**165**	**104**	**3**	**.350**	**.604**

Randy Hundley (C)

Notes: Hundley came to the Cubs from San Francisco via a trade that also included pitcher Bill Hands. From 1966-69, Hundley caught nearly every game on the schedule, and set the major league recrod with 160 games behind the plate in 1968. He also became the first major league receiver to catch 150 or more games for three consecutive years (1967-69). He won a Gold Glove in 1967, committing just four errors for a National League record. Unfortunately, the overwork that Hundley suffered shortened his career and his numbers began to slip after 1969. Hundley's son, Todd, set the major league home run record for catchers with 41 in 1996 while playing for the New York Mets. **Numbers:** Led the National League in fielding percentage in 1972 (.995).

YEAR	G	AB	R	H	2B	3B	HR	RBI	BB	SO	SB	BA	SLG
1966	149	526	50	124	22	3	19	63	35	113	1	.239	.397
1967	152	539	68	144	23	3	14	60	44	75	2	.267	.403
1968	160	553	41	125	18	4	7	65	39	69	1	.226	.311
1969•	151	522	67	133	15	1	18	64	61	90	2	.255	.391
1970	73	250	13	61	5	0	7	36	16	52	0	.244	.348
1971	9	21	1	7	1	0	0	2	0	2	0	.333	.381
1972	114	357	23	78	12	0	5	30	22	62	1	.218	.294
1973	124	368	35	83	11	1	10	43	30	51	5	.226	.342
1976	13	18	3	3	2	0	0	1	1	4	0	.167	.278
1977	2	4	0	0	0	0	0	0	0	1	0	.000	.000
TOT	**947**	**3158**	**301**	**758**	**111**	**12**	**80**	**364**	**248**	**519**	**12**	**.240**	**.360**

Bill Hutchison (P)

Notes: Pitching for mediocre Chicago clubs in the 1890s, Wild Bill led National League hurlers three straight years in wins, complete games, and innings pitched despite pitching in the same league as Cy Young, Amos Rusie, and Kid Gleason.

YEAR	W	L	G	GS	CG	SH	SV	IP	H	HR	BB	SO	ERA	PCT
1889	16	17	37	36	33	3	0	318	306	11	117	136	3.54	.485
1890	42	25	71	66	65	5	2	603	505	20	199	289	2.70	.627
1891	44	19	66	58	56	4	1	561	508	26	178	261	2.81	.698
1892	36	36	75	70	67	5	1	622	571	11	190	314	2.76	.500
1893	16	24	44	40	38	2	0	348.1	420	9	156	80	4.75	.400
1894	14	16	36	34	28	0	0	277.2	373	9	140	59	6.06	.467
1895	13	21	38	35	30	2	0	291	371	13	129	85	4.73	.382
TOT	**182**	**158**	**367**	**339**	**317**	**21**	**3**	**3026**	**3055**	**99**	**1106**	**1226**	**3.56**	**.535**

Ferguson Jenkins (P)

Notes: Jenkins is the winningest pitcher (284 victories) who never appeared in the postseason. From 1967 to 1972, Jenkins won at least 20 games every year even though he played in hitting-friendly Wrigley Field. In 1971 he won the Cy Young Award for his 24 victories while walking just 37 batters while striking out 263. In the 1967 All-Star Game, Jenkins equaled Carl Hubbell's 1934 strikeout performance, fanning six in three innings, but gave up a sixth-inning homer to Brooks Robinson. After failing to win 20 games in 1973 the Cubs traded Jenkins to the Rangers for third baseman Bill Madlock. After stints with Texas and Boston, Jenkins returned to the Cubs in 1982 and led the club in innings pitched and ERA. In 1980 he was stopped by a Canadian customs official for carrying marijuana, and was suspended by commissioner Bowie Kuhn. He was elected to the Hall of Fame in 1991. **Numbers:** With the Texas Rangers, led the AL in victories (25) and complete games (29) in 1974.

YEAR	W	L	G	GS	CG	SH	SV	IP	H	HR	BB	SO	ERA	PCT
1966	6	8	60	12	2	1	5	182	147	24	51	148	3.31	.429
1967•	20	13	38	38	20	3	0	289.1	230	30	83	236	2.80	.606
1968	20	185	40	40	20	3	0	308	255	26	65	260	2.63	.571
1969	21	15	43	42	23	7	1	311.1	284	27	71	273	3.21	.583
1970	22	16	40	39	24	3	0	313	265	30	60	274	3.39	.579
1971•	24	13	39	39	30	3	0	325	304	29	37	263	2.77	.649
1972•	20	12	36	36	23	5	0	289.1	253	32	62	184	3.20	.625
1973	14	16	38	38	7	2	0	271	267	35	57	170	3.89	.467
1982	14	15	34	34	4	1	0	217.1	221	19	68	134	3.15	.483
1983	6	9	33	29	1	1	0	167.1	176	19	46	96	4.30	.400
TOT	**167**	**132**	**401**	**347**	**154**	**29**	**6**	**2672**	**2402**	**271**	**600**	**2038**	**3.21**	**.559**

King Kelly (C/OF)

Notes: Mike "King" Kelly was the most celebrated baseball player of the 19th century. Beginning his career with the Cincinnati Reds in 1878, he was quickly titled the King of Baseball. He joined Cap Anson's White Stockings in 1880 and led the club to a string of five National League pennants. The legendary King won two batting titles and played every position well. Kelly, whose popularity in Chicago has been matched only by Ernie Banks, was also a problem child for Anson, once taking a day off so that he could "sweat off some excess weight," only to be found at a local racetrack. His baserunning thrilled the crowd, spawning a hit song, "Slide, Kelly, Slide." Kelly was colorful both on and off the field, always dressing in the finest tailored clothes. His face graced billboards across the country. In 1887, team president Al Spalding, tired of Kelly's annual salary demands, sold the star to Boston for $10,000 - a staggering sum at the time. Many Chicago fans were so upset they boycotted the team for years, unless Boston was in town. Overall, Kelly hit .300 or better eight times, and led his teams to eight titles. When his skills began to diminish, he drifted around the minor leagues, managing clubs in Allentown in the Penn League and Yonkers in the Eastern League. After his retirement, he opened a saloon in New York. He died of pneumonia on his way to Boston to appear at the Palace Theater in 1894. He was elected to the Hall of Fame in 1945. **Numbers:** Also led the National League in on-base percentage in 1884 (.414) and 1886 (.483). With the Boston Beaneaters, led the National League in doubles in 1889 (41).

YEAR	G	AB	R	H	2B	3B	HR	RBI	BB	SO	SB	BA	SLG
1878	60	237	29	67	7	1	0	27	7	7	-	.283	.321
1879	77	345	78	120	20	12	2	47	8	14	-	.348	.493
1880	84	344	72	100	17	9	1	60	12	22	-	.291	.401
1881	82	353	84	114	27	3	2	55	16	14	-	.323	.433
1882	84	377	81	115	37	4	1	55	10	27	-	.305	.432
1883	98	428	92	109	28	10	3	61	16	35	-	.255	.388
1884	108	452	120	160	28	5	13	95	46	24	-	.354	.524
1885	107	438	124	126	24	7	9	75	46	24	-	.288	.436
1886	118	451	155	175	32	11	4	79	83	33	53	.388	.534
TOT	**681**	**2873**	**728**	**899**	**193**	**49**	**33**	**323**	**229**	**179**	**53**	**.313**	**.449**

Don Kessinger (SS)

Notes: Kessinger rounded out the Cubs' All-Star infield with Ernie Banks, Glenn Beckert and Ron Santo. Kessinger, signed for a $25,000 bonus out of the University of Mississippi, led the National League in errors his rookie year, but quickly established himself as an outstanding shortstop. He had a 54-game errorless streak in 1969, a then-record for shortstops. Kessinger didn't have much power but was a reliable contact hitter. On July 17, 1970 he went 6-for-6 in a 10-inning contest. He was player-manager for the White Sox in 1979. **Numbers:** Led the National League in fielding percentage in 1969 (.976).

YEAR	G	AB	R	H	2B	3B	HR	RBI	BB	SO	SB	BA	SLG
1964	4	12	1	2	0	0	0	0	0	1	0	.167	.167
1965	106	309	19	62	4	3	0	14	20	44	1	.201	.233
1966	150	533	50	146	8	2	1	43	26	46	13	.274	.302
1967	145	580	61	134	10	7	0	42	33	80	6	.231	.272
1968•	160	655	63	157	14	7	1	32	38	86	9	.240	.287
1969•	158	664	109	181	38	6	4	53	61	70	11	.273	.366
1970•	154	631	100	168	21	14	1	39	66	59	12	.266	.349
1971•	155	6177	77	159	18	6	2	38	52	54	15	.258	.316
1972•	149	577	77	158	20	6	1	39	67	44	8	.274	.334
1973	160	577	52	151	22	3	0	43	57	44	6	.262	.310
1974•	153	599	83	155	20	7	1	42	62	54	7	.259	.321
1975	154	601	77	146	26	10	0	46	68	47	4	.243	.319
TOT	**1938**	**7278**	**1239**	**2193**	**363**	**81**	**57**	**642**	**1092**	**466**	**165**	**.301**	**.397**

Bill Lange (OF)

Notes: Lange was described by *Sporting News* founder Al Spink as "Ty Cobb enlarged," mixing speed, batting skill and baserunning. He was an outstanding baserunner with a .330 lifetime batting average but consitently gave manager Cap Anson fits for his high-life, Gay Nineties living. Lange, one of the most popular of the Chicago players, set the Cubs season batting record of .389 in 1895. The righthanded center fielder's defensive play was legendary; he is said to have once crashed through a wooden fence making a catch. In 1897, Lange held out so he could attend the Jim Corbett-Bob Fitzsimmons heavyweight boxing match in Carson City, Nevada. Lange quit baseball in 1899 to marry a woman whose father would not allow a ballplayer in the family.

YEAR	G	AB	R	H	2B	3B	HR	RBI	BB	SO	SB	BA	SLG
1893	117	469	92	132	8	7	8	88	52	20	47	.281	.380
1894	111	442	84	145	16	9	6	90	56	18	65	.328	.446
1895	123	478	120	186	27	16	10	98	55	24	67	.389	.575
1896	122	469	114	153	21	16	4	92	65	24	84	.326	.465
1897	118	479	119	163	24	14	5	83	48	-	73	.340	.480
1898	113	442	79	141	16	11	5	69	36	-	22	.319	.439
1899	107	416	81	135	21	7	1	58	38	-	41	.325	.416
TOT	**811**	**3195**	**689**	**1055**	**133**	**80**	**39**	**578**	**350**	**86**	**399**	**.330**	**.459**

Bill Lee (P)

Notes: Big Bill, uncle of the Red Sox'flaky namesake of the 1970s, was a 6-foot 3-inch Louisiana native who had a high leg kick and a dazzling fastball. Buried in the Cardinals'farm system for four years, Lee was sold to the Cubs in 1934. He shut out the Philadelphia Phillies in his first major league start. Lee's best season was 1938, leading the Cubs to a World Series with 22 wins and nine shutouts. During one stretch he pitched 32 straight scoreless innings and gave up just one run over 47 frames. When his eyes began to fail in 1940, his numbers began to slide because he had trouble picking up the catcher's signals. He rebounded to 13-13 in 1942 thanks to a new pair of eyeglasses, but bounced around the National League after 1943. After retiring, he underwent surgery for detatched retinas and eventually went blind.

YEAR	W	L	G	GS	CG	SH	SV	IP	H	HR	BB	SO	ERA	PCT
1934	13	14	35	29	16	4	1	214.1	218	9	74	104	3.40	.481
1935	20	6	39	32	18	3	1	252	241	11	84	100	2.96	.769
1936	18	11	43	33	20	4	1	258.2	238	14	93	102	3.31	.621
1937	14	15	42	34	17	2	3	272.1	289	14	73	108	3.54	.483
1938•	22	9	44	37	19	9	2	291	281	18	74	121	2.66	.710
1939•	19	15	37	36	20	1	0	282.1	295	18	85	105	3.44	.559
1940	9	17	37	30	9	1	0	211.1	246	12	70	70	5.03	.346
1941	8	14	28	22	12	0	1	167.1	179	6	43	62	3.76	.364
1942	13	13	32	30	18	1	0	219.2	221	4	67	75	3.85	.500
1943	3	7	13	12	4	0	0	78.1	83	4	27	18	3.56	.300
TOT	**139**	**123**	**364**	**297**	**153**	**25**	**9**	**2270**	**2317**	**110**	**704**	**874**	**3.51**	**.531**

Greg Maddux (P)

Notes: The greatest pitcher of the 1990s, Maddux had a rough start with the Cubs, going 6-14 in his rookie season. His rebound was remarkable, howeve: he was 15-3 by the All-Star break in 1988. After leading the National League with 20 victories and winning a Cy Young Award in 1992, Maddux was snubbed by the Tribune Company while seeking a long-term contract and signed with the Atlanta Braves. He then became the first pitcher to win the Cy Young in three consecutive seasons. **Numbers:** With the Atlanta Braves, led the National League in wins in 1994 (16) and 1995 (19), in winning percentage in 1995 (.905) and 1997 (.826), in complete games in 1993 (8), 1994 (10), and 1995 (10), in innings pitched in 1993 (267), 1994 (202) and 1995 (209.2), and in ERA in 1993 (2.36), 1994 (1.56), 1995 (1.63) and 1998 (2.22).

YEAR	W	L	G	GS	CG	SH	SV	IP	H	HR	BB	SO	ERA	PCT
1986	2	4	6	5	1	0	0	31	44	3	11	20	5.52	.333
1987	6	14	30	27	1	1	0	155.1	181	17	74	101	5.61	.300
1988	18	8	34	34	9	3	0	249	230	13	81	140	3.18	.692
1989	19	12	35	35	7	1	0	238.1	222	13	82	135	2.95	.613
1990	15	15	35	35	8	2	0	237	242	11	71	144	3.46	.500
1991	15	11	37	37	7	2	0	263	232	18	66	198	3.35	.577
1992•	20	11	35	35	9	4	0	268	201	7	70	199	2.18	.645
TOT	**95**	**75**	**212**	**208**	**42**	**13**	**0**	**1442**	**1352**	**82**	**455**	**937**	**3.35**	**.559**

Bill Madlock (3B)

Notes: Mad Dog won four batting titles, two with the Cubs and two with the Pittsburgh Pirates. He came to the Cubs in the trade that sent Fergie Jenkins to the Texas Rangers. Replacing Ron Santo at third base, the righthanded spray hitter hit .313 in 1974, the highest average for the position since 1945. After three years, Madlock was dealt to San Francisco for Bobby Murcer and Steve Otiveros. His departure was not necessarily an unhappy one, as he was sometimes portrayed as "moody" by his teammates and routinely took a day off against tougher pitchers in order to keep his average up. **Numbers:** With the Pittsburgh Pirates, led the National League in batting average in 1981 (.341) and 1983 (.323).

YEAR	G	AB	R	H	2B	3B	HR	RBI	BB	SO	SB	BA	SLG
1974	128	453	65	142	21	5	9	54	42	39	11	.313	.442
1975•	130	514	77	182	29	7	7	64	42	34	9	.354	.479
1976	142	514	68	174	36	1	15	84	56	27	15	.339	.500
TOT	**400**	**1481**	**210**	**498**	**86**	**13**	**31**	**202**	**140**	**124**	**35**	**.336**	**.475**

Pat Malone (P)

Notes: Malone lost his first seven decisions in his rookie season before rebounding to win 18 games. A year later, the righthander led the Cubs to a World Series with a 22 wins, the first of two straight years he led the National League in victories. A penchant for the nightlife probably shortened his career, and after four years of sliding numbers he was traded to the Cardinals for catcher Ken O'Dea. He ended with the New York Yankees, going 12-4 out of the bullpen in 1936 and leading the American League in relief wins with eight and saves with nine. Always a good hitter, Malone hit four homers in 1930 while batting .248. **Numbers:** With the New York Yankees, led the American League in saves in 1936 (9).

YEAR	W	L	G	GS	CG	SH	SV	IP	H	HR	BB	SO	ERA	PCT
1928	18	13	42	25	16	2	2	250.2	218	15	99	155	2.84	.581
1929	22	10	40	30	19	5	2	267	283	12	102	166	3.57	.688
1930	20	9	45	35	22	1	4	271.2	290	14	96	142	3.94	.690
1931	16	9	36	30	12	2	0	228.1	229	9	88	112	3.90	.640
1932	15	17	37	33	17	2	0	237	222	13	78	120	3.38	.469
1933	10	14	31	26	13	2	0	186.1	186	10	59	72	3.91	.417
1934	14	7	34	21	8	1	0	191	200	14	55	111	3.53	.667
TOT	**115**	**79**	**265**	**200**	**107**	**16**	**8**	**1632**	**1628**	**87**	**577**	**878**	**2.18**	**.593**

Rick Monday (OF)

Notes: Monday was the first player selected in the first June Amateur Draft, held in 1965. He signed with the Oakland (then Kansas City) A's for a $104,000 bonus. He came to the Cubs in 1971 in the trade that sent Ken Holtzman to Oakland. Although Monday hit 241 lifetime home runs, he reached the 20 mark only three times and never drove in more than 77 runs, even in 1976, when he launched 32 homers. A free swinger, he struck out at least 10 times in eight seasons. He was sent to Los Angeles in the blockbuster 1977 deal that brought Bill Buckner and Ivan DeJesus to Chicago. His greatest moment came on April 25, 1976, when he stopped a pair of demonstrators from setting the American flag on fire in the outfield at Dodger Stadium. **Numbers:** Led the National League in fielding percentage in 1972 (.996).

YEAR	G	AB	R	H	2B	3B	HR	RBI	BB	SO	SB	BA	SLG
1972	138	434	68	108	22	5	11	42	78	102	12	.249	.399
1973	149	554	93	148	24	5	26	56	92	124	5	.267	.469
1974	142	538	84	158	19	7	20	58	70	94	7	.294	.467
1975	136	491	89	131	29	4	17	60	83	95	8	.267	.446
1976	137	534	107	145	20	5	32	77	60	125	5	.272	.507
TOT	**947**	**3158**	**301**	**758**	**111**	**12**	**80**	**364**	**248**	**519**	**12**	**.240**	**.360**

Keith Moreland (C/OF/3B)

Notes: A catcher, third baseman and outfielder, Moreland was more valued for his offense. He was traded to Chicago in 1981 after a couple of part-time seasons in Philadelphia. Moreland led the Cubs in batting in 1983 with a .302 average and peaked in 1985, when he drove in 106 runs. In 1987 he moved back to third base to replace the slowing Ron Cey, and struggled defensively, but hit 27 homers. Moreland was traded to the San Diego Padres for Goose Gossage in 1988.

YEAR	G	AB	R	H	2B	3B	HR	RBI	BB	SO	SB	BA	SLG
1982	138	476	50	124	17	2	15	68	46	71	0	.261	.399
1983	154	533	76	161	30	3	16	70	68	73	0	.302	.460
1984	140	495	59	138	17	3	16	80	34	71	1	.279	.422
1985	161	587	74	180	30	3	14	106	68	58	12	.307	.440
1986	156	586	72	159	30	0	12	79	53	48	3	.271	.384
1987	153	563	63	150	29	1	27	88	39	66	3	.266	.465
TOT	**902**	**3240**	**394**	**912**	**153**	**12**	**100**	**491**	**308**	**387**	**19**	**.281**	**.429**

Bill Nicholson (OF)

Notes: Called "Swish" for his mammoth swing, Nicholson was a steady power hitter whose best years were during World War II. He was one of only two players in history (with Mike Schmidt) to lead the league in both homers and RBIs in consecutive seasons (1943-44). Nicholson's power-hitting feats were legendary; he once hit a ball that barely missed the Wrigley Field scoreboard and hit four consecutive homers in a July 23, 1944 doubleheader at the Polo Grounds in New York. He was also one of the toughest players to double up - he hit into double plays just once every 90.7 at-bats. Nicholson's production began to wane after 1944 due to eyesight problems. He was traded to the Phillies in 1948 for Harry Walker. **Numbers:** Also led the National League in fielding percentage in 1947 (.990).

YEAR	G	AB	R	H	2B	3B	HR	RBI	BB	SO	SB	BA	SLG
1939	58	220	37	65	12	5	5	38	20	29	0	.295	.464
1940•	135	491	78	146	27	7	25	98	50	67	2	.297	.534
1941•	147	532	74	135	26	1	26	98	82	91	1	.254	.453
1942	152	588	83	173	22	11	21	78	76	80	8	.294	.476
1943•	154	608	95	188	30	9	29	128	71	86	4	.309	.531
1944•	156	582	116	167	35	8	33	122	93	71	3	.287	.545
1945	151	559	82	136	28	4	13	88	92	73	4	.243	.377
1946	105	296	36	65	13	2	8	41	44	44	1	.220	.358
1947	148	487	69	119	28	1	26	75	87	83	1	.244	.466
1948	143	494	68	129	24	5	19	67	81	60	2	.261	.445
TOT	**1349**	**4827**	**738**	**1313**	**245**	**53**	**205**	**833**	**696**	**684**	**26**	**.272**	**.472**

Orval Overall (P)
Notes: Overall's career lasted just seven seasons but he was outstanding, posting a lifetime ERA of 2.24, eighth-best all-time. He was traded to the Cubs in July 1906 from Cincinnati, and provided the missing piece that drove the club to its first of three straight pennants. He was 23-8 the next season, tying Christy Mathewson for the National League lead in shutouts. He developed a sore arm in 1910 and retired, but tried a comeback in 1913 before quitting for good.

YEAR	W	L	G	GS	CG	SH	SV	IP	H	HR	BB	SO	ERA	PCT
1906	12	3	18	14	13	2	1	144	116	1	51	94	1.88	.800
1907	23	7	36	30	26	8	3	268.1	201	3	69	141	1.68	.767
1908	15	11	37	27	16	4	4	225	165	3	78	167	1.92	.577
1909	20	11	38	32	23	9	3	285	204	1	80	205	1.42	.645
1910	12	6	23	21	11	4	1	144.2	106	2	54	92	2.68	.667
1913	4	5	11	9	6	1	0	68	73	1	26	30	3.31	.444
TOT	**86**	**44**	**162**	**133**	**95**	**28**	**9**	**1132**	**863**	**11**	**358**	**727**	**1.92**	**.662**

Andy Pafko (OF)
Notes: Pafko was a popular player in Chicago throughout the 1940s, a strong-armed outfielder who hit for average and power. Sometimes used at third base, he was called "Handy Andy" by manager Charlie Grimm. He was traded to Brooklyn in 1951, a move that was very unpopular in Chicago. **Numbers:** Led the National League in fielding percentage in 1945 (.995).

YEAR	G	AB	R	H	2B	3B	HR	RBI	BB	SO	SB	BA	SLG
1943	13	58	7	22	3	0	0	10	2	5	1	.379	.431
1944	128	469	47	126	16	2	6	62	28	23	2	.269	.350
1945	144	534	64	159	24	12	12	110	45	36	5	.298	.455
1946	65	234	18	66	6	4	3	39	27	15	4	.282	.380
1947•	129	513	68	155	25	7	13	66	31	39	4	.302	.454
1948•	142	548	82	171	30	2	26	101	50	50	3	.312	.516
1949•	144	519	79	146	29	2	18	69	63	33	4	.281	.449
1950•	146	514	95	156	24	8	36	92	69	32	4	.304	.591
1951	49	178	26	47	5	3	12	35	17	10	1	.264	.528
TOT	**960**	**3567**	**486**	**1048**	**162**	**40**	**126**	**575**	**332**	**243**	**28**	**.294**	**.468**

Claude Passeau (P)

Notes: Passeau was a hard-throwing righthander with a reputation for buzzing a batter's chin whenever he felt necessary. He was traded to Chicago from the Philadelphia Phillies in mid-1939 and won 20 games for them the following year. In game 3 of the World Series in 1945, Passeau hurled a one-hit shutout of the Detroit Tigers. **Numbers:** With the Philadelphia Phillies, led the National League in innings pitched in 1937 (292.1). With the Phillies and Cubs combined, led the National League in strikeouts in 1939 (137).

YEAR	W	L	G	GS	CG	SH	SV	IP	H	HR	BB	SO	ERA	PCT
1939	13	9	34	27	13	1	3	221	215	8	48	108	3.05	.591
1940	20	13	46	31	20	4	5	280.2	259	8	59	124	2.50	.606
1941•	14	14	34	30	20	3	0	231	262	10	52	80	3.35	.500
1942•	19	14	35	34	24	3	0	278.1	284	13	74	89	2.68	.576
1943•	15	12	35	31	18	1	1	257	245	10	66	93	2.91	.556
1944	15	9	34	27	18	2	3	227	234	8	50	89	2.89	.625
1945	17	9	34	27	19	5	1	227	205	4	59	98	2.46	.654
1946•	9	8	21	21	10	2	0	129.1	118	5	42	47	3.13	.529
1947	2	6	19	6	1	1	2	63.1	97	7	24	26	6.25	.250
TOT	**124**	**94**	**292**	**234**	**143**	**23**	**15**	**1915**	**1919**	**73**	**474**	**754**	**2.96**	**.569**

Fred Pfeffer (2B)

Notes: Pfeffer took advantage of the 180-foot left field fence at Lakefront Park in 1884, belting a staggering 25 homers (three other Chicago teammates had 20 or more). According to legend, Pfeffer was the first player to cut off a catcher's throw to second base during a steal attempt and cut down the runner at the plate. In 1894, Pfeffer joined Louisville manager Billie Barnie and several investors to try to establish a new American Association. The rival league died before a single game was played. He later served as baseball coach at Princeton University.

YEAR	G	AB	R	H	2B	3B	HR	RBI	BB	SO	SB	BA	SLG
1883	96	371	41	87	22	7	1	45	8	50	-	.235	.340
1884	112	467	105	135	10	10	25	101	25	47	-	.289	.514
1885	112	469	90	113	12	7	5	73	26	47	-	.241	.328
1886	118	474	88	125	17	8	7	95	36	46	30	.264	.378
1887	123	479	95	133	21	6	16	89	34	20	57	.278	.447
1888	135	517	90	129	22	10	8	57	32	38	64	.280	.377
1889	134	531	85	121	15	7	7	77	53	51	45	.228	.322
1891	137	498	93	123	12	9	7	77	79	60	40	.247	.349
1896	94	360	45	88	16	7	2	52	23	20	22	.244	.344
1897	32	114	10	23	0	1	0	11	12	-	5	.228	.246
TOT	**1093**	**4280**	**742**	**1080**	**147**	**71**	**79**	**532**	**328**	**379**	**263**	**.252**	**.375**

Ed Reulbach (P)

Notes: Reulbach was an almost forgotten piece of the great pitching staff during the team's dynastic years of 1906-08, overshadowed by the exploits of teammate Three Finger Brown, but he may have been even more effective during those years than Brown. He was the only pitcher to throw a doubleheader shutout, doing it against

Brooklyn on September 26, 1908. That year he beat the Dodgers an astonishing nine times. His 1906 hits-per-innings ration of 5.33 per nine innings is third-best in major league history, and his career ERA of 2.28 is 11th all-time. He was the first pitcher to hurl a one-hitter in World Series history (1906) and, not counting the year he spent with the Federal League, he allowed only 35 homers in 2,363 lifetime innings.

YEAR	W	L	G	GS	CG	SH	SV	IP	H	HR	BB	SO	ERA	PCT
1905	18	14	34	29	28	5	1	291.2	208	1	73	152	1.42	.563
1906	19	4	33	24	20	6	3	218	129	2	92	94	1.65	.826
1907	17	4	27	22	16	4	0	192	147	1	64	96	1.69	.810
1908	24	7	46	35	25	7	1	297.2	227	4	106	133	2.03	.774
1909	19	10	35	32	23	6	0	262.2	194	1	82	105	1.78	.655
1910	12	8	24	23	14	1	0	173.1	161	1	49	55	3.12	.600
1911	16	9	33	29	15	2	0	221.2	191	3	103	79	2.96	.640
1912	10	6	39	19	8	0	4	169	161	7	60	75	3.78	.625
1913	1	3	10	3	1	0	0	38.2	41	1	21	10	4.42	.250
TOT	**136**	**65**	**281**	**216**	**149**	**31**	**7**	**1865**	**1459**	**21**	**650**	**799**	**2.24**	**.677**

Rick Reuschel (P)
Notes: Big Daddy became one of the Cubs' all-time leaders in wins, games and strikeouts, winning 10 or more in each of his first nine seasons. Reuschel's brother, Paul, was a reliever for the Cubs from 1975-78; they became the first brothers to combine on a major league shutout, on August 21, 1975. Reuschel missed the 1982 season with a torn rotator cuff and spent the next two years rehabilitating. The Cubs gave up on him, but he rebounded with the Pittsburgh Pirates and ended up pitching in the 1989 World Series while with the San Francisco Giants.

YEAR	W	L	G	GS	CG	SH	SV	IP	H	HR	BB	SO	ERA	PCT
1972	10	8	21	18	5	4	0	129	127	3	29	87	2.93	.556
1973	14	15	36	36	7	3	0	237	244	15	62	168	3.00	.483
1974	13	12	41	38	8	2	0	240.2	262	18	83	160	4.30	.520
1975	11	17	38	37	6	0	1	234	244	17	67	155	3.73	.393
1976	14	12	38	37	9	2	1	260	260	17	64	146	3.46	.538
1977•	20	10	39	37	8	4	1	252	233	13	74	166	2.79	.667
1978	14	15	35	35	9	1	0	242.2	235	16	54	115	3.41	.483
1979	18	12	36	36	5	1	0	239	251	16	75	125	3.62	.600
1980	11	13	38	38	6	0	0	257	281	13	76	140	3.40	.458
1981	4	7	13	13	1	0	0	85.2	87	4	23	53	3.47	.364
1983	1	1	4	4	0	0	0	20.2	18	1	10	9	3.92	.500
1984	5	5	19	14	1	0	0	92.1	123	7	23	43	5.17	.500
TOT	**135**	**127**	**358**	**343**	**65**	**17**	**3**	**2291**	**2365**	**133**	**640**	**1367**	**3.50**	**.515**

Charlie Root (P)
Notes: Root was named the all-time greatest Cubs righthander in 1969 (apparently by fans who had never seen Three Finger Brown pitch). He won at least 10 games in ten different seasons, with a career-best 26-15 record in 1927. His name went down in the record books as the pitcher who gave up Babe Ruth's controversial "Called Shot" during the 1932 World Series.

YEAR	W	L	G	GS	CG	SH	SV	IP	H	HR	BB	SO	ERA	PCT
1926	18	17	42	32	21	2	2	271.1	267	10	62	127	2.82	.514
1927	26	15	48	36	21	4	2	309	296	16	117	145	3.76	.634
1928	14	18	40	30	13	1	2	237	214	15	73	122	3.57	.438
1929	19	6	43	31	19	4	5	272	286	12	83	124	3.47	.760
1930	16	14	37	30	15	4	3	220.1	247	17	63	124	4.33	.533
1931	17	14	39	31	19	3	2	251	240	7	71	131	3.48	.548
1932	15	10	39	23	11	0	3	216.1	211	10	55	96	3.58	.600
1933	15	10	35	30	20	2	0	242.1	232	14	61	86	2.60	.600
1934	4	7	34	9	2	0	0	117.2	141	8	53	46	4.28	.364
1935	15	8	38	18	11	1	2	201.1	193	15	47	94	3.08	.652
1936	3	6	33	4	0	0	1	73.2	81	3	20	32	4.15	.333
1937	13	5	43	15	5	0	5	178.2	173	18	32	74	3.38	.722
1938	8	7	44	11	5	0	8	160.2	163	10	30	70	2.86	.533
1939	8	8	35	16	8	0	4	167.1	189	11	34	65	4.03	.500
1940	2	4	36	8	1	0	1	112	118	9	33	50	3.86	.333
1941	8	7	19	15	6	0	0	106.2	133	8	37	46	5.40	.533
TOT	**201**	**160**	**632**	**341**	**177**	**21**	**40**	**3197.1**	**3252**	**187**	**889**	**1459**	**3.59**	**.557**

Jimmy Ryan (OF)

Notes: A power-hitter for Chicago during the last of the 19th century, Ryan's clubhouse needling of teammates and managers led to a near-strike by the Chicago players when manager Tom Burns named him team captain for the 1898 season, instead of player favorite Bill Lange. When Burns changed his mind and appointed Lange captain, it was the Chicago sportswriters'turn to whine, asserting that Burns had lost his authority over the players and had no business managing the Colts. He was fired a year later. Ryan's best season was in 1888, when he batted .332 with a league-leading 182 hits, 33 doubles and 16 homers. A lefty, he also won an NL-best three games as a relief pitcher that year.

YEAR	G	AB	R	H	2B	3B	HR	RBI	BB	SO	SB	BA	SLG
1885	3	13	2	6	1	0	0	2	1	1	-	.462	.538
1886	84	327	58	100	17	6	4	53	12	28	10	.306	.431
1887	126	508	117	145	23	10	11	74	53	19	50	.285	.435
1888	129	549	115	182	33	10	16	64	35	50	60	.332	.515
1889	135	576	140	177	31	14	17	72	70	62	45	.307	.498
1890	118	486	99	165	32	5	6	89	60	36	30	.340	.463
1891	118	505	110	140	22	15	9	66	53	38	27	.277	.434
1892	128	505	105	148	21	11	10	65	61	41	27	.293	.438
1893	83	341	82	102	21	7	3	30	59	25	8	.299	.428
1894	108	474	132	171	37	7	3	62	50	23	11	.361	.487
1895	108	438	83	139	22	8	6	49	48	22	18	.317	.445
1896	128	489	83	149	24	10	3	86	46	16	29	.305	.413
1897	136	520	103	156	33	17	5	85	50	-	27	.300	.458
1898	144	572	122	185	32	13	4	79	73	-	29	.323	.446
1899	125	525	91	158	20	10	3	68	43	-	9	.301	.394
1900	105	415	66	115	25	4	5	59	29	-	19	.277	.393
TOT	**1660**	**6757**	**1409**	**2073**	**362**	**142**	**99**	**914**	**683**	**325**	**57**	**.307**	**.446**

Ryne Sandberg (2B)

Notes: Long-time fan favorite Sandberg came to the Cubs as a throw-in in the trade that sent shortstop Ivan DeJesus to the Philadelphia Phillies. The Cubs moved him to third in 1982, and he set a team record for steals by a third baseman with 32, and a team rookie record for runs scored with 103. Moving to second base the next year, he won a Gold Glove in his first season at the position. In 1984 he won a Most Valuable Player Award and earned the first of 10 straight All-Star berths. That year he was just a triple and a homer short of being the first player to post 200 hits, 20 doubles, 20 triples, 20 homers and 20 steals in one seasaon. In 1985, Sandberg became the third player in history to hit 25 homers and steal 50 bases in one year. At the end of the 1989 season he broke Manny Trillo's record of 89 consecutive scoreless games at second base (with manager Don Zimmer playing him for only one inning in each of the last three games of the season). In June of 1994, Sandberg walked away from his $16 million contract, saying that he had "lost his competitive edge." It turned out that his troubles probably were caused by a bitter divorce proceeding. He returned in 1996 to hit 25 homers and drive in 92 runs, but retired for good after the 1997 season. **Numbers:** Also led the National League in fielding percentage in 1983 (.986), 1984 (.993), 1986 (.994) and 1991 (.995). Voted the National League Most Valuable Player (1984).

YEAR	G	AB	R	H	2B	3B	HR	RBI	BB	SO	SB	BA	SLG
1982	156	635	103	172	33	5	7	54	36	90	32	.271	.372
1983	158	633	94	165	25	4	8	48	51	79	37	.261	.351
1984•	156	636	114	200	36	19	19	84	52	101	32	.314	.520
1985•	153	609	113	186	31	6	26	83	57	97	54	.305	.504
1986•	154	627	68	178	28	5	14	76	46	79	34	.284	.411
1987•	132	523	81	154	25	2	16	59	59	79	21	.294	.442
1988•	155	618	77	163	23	8	19	69	54	91	25	.264	.419
1989•	157	606	104	176	25	5	30	76	59	85	15	.290	.497
1990•	155	615	116	188	30	3	40	100	50	84	25	.306	.559
1991•	158	585	104	170	32	2	26	100	87	89	22	.291	.485
1992•	158	612	100	186	32	8	26	87	68	73	17	.304	.510
1993•	117	456	67	141	20	0	9	45	37	62	9	.309	.412
1994	57	223	36	53	9	5	5	24	23	40	2	.238	.390
1996	150	554	85	135	28	4	25	92	54	116	12	.244	.444
1997	135	447	54	118	26	0	12	64	28	94	7	.264	.403
TOT	**2151**	**8379**	**1316**	**2385**	**403**	**76**	**282**	**1061**	**761**	**1259**	**344**	**.285**	**.452**

Ron Santo (3B)

Notes: A fine third baseman and clutch hitter for Chicago in the 1960s and 70s, Santo has replaced Ernie Banks as the fan favorite in recent years, partly due to his honest enthusiasm for the ballclub and partly due to his tragic battle with diabetes, endearing him to Chicago as the greatest sufferer of all long-suffering Cubs fans. Beginning in 1960, Santo spent 14 years as the club's regular third baseman, putting up numbers that rivaled Hall of Fame contemporaries such as Brooks Robinson, Orlando Cepeda, and Tony Perez - only to be forgotten by Cooperstown. Santo, emotional and sometimes temperamental, had his best season in 1964, when he hit .313 with 30 homers and 114 RBIs, and led the league with 13 triples. In 1966 Santo put together a 28-game hitting streak, and in 1967 he set a then-record with 393 assists. A five-time Gold Glover, Santo finished first among National League first baseman in putouts seven times, assists seven times, and double plays four times. Santo was saddled with his share of controversy: during the Cubs' 1969 battle for the pennant with the Mets, the third baseman publicly dressed down teammate Don Young for making a key error in a key game, and his sophomoric in-your-face heel-clicking after each Cubs victory may have given New York the inspiration they needed to roll over the National League in their September pennant run. Two years later, Santo had to be physically restrained from attacking Leo Durocher for the manager's false accusation that he had been prodding the Cubs to organize a Ron Santo Day at Wrigley Field. In 1974, Santo became the first player to exercise his 5-and-10 rights (five years with the same club, ten years in the majors) to veto a trade to the California Angels; he reluctantly accepted a trade to the cross-town White Sox instead. **Numbers:** Also led the National League in on-base percentage in 1964 (.401) and 1966 (.4174) and in fielding percentage in 1968 (.971).

YEAR	G	AB	R	H	2B	3B	HR	RBI	BB	SO	SB	BA	SLG
1960	95	347	44	87	24	2	9	44	31	44	0	.251	.409
1961	154	578	84	164	32	6	23	83	73	77	2	.284	.479
1962	162	604	44	137	20	4	17	83	65	94	4	.227	.358
1963•	162	630	79	187	29	6	25	99	42	92	6	.297	.481
1964•	161	592	94	185	33	13	30	114	86	96	3	.313	.564
1965•	164	608	88	173	30	4	33	101	88	109	3	.285	.510
1966•	155	561	93	175	21	8	30	94	95	78	4	.312	.538
1967	161	586	107	176	23	4	31	98	96	103	1	.300	.512
1968•	162	577	86	142	17	3	26	98	96	106	3	.246	.421
1969•	160	575	97	166	18	4	29	123	96	97	2	.289	.485
1970	154	555	83	148	30	4	26	114	92	108	2	.267	.476
1971•	154	555	77	148	22	1	21	88	79	95	4	.267	.423
1972•	133	464	68	140	25	5	17	74	69	75	1	.302	.487
1973•	149	536	65	143	29	2	20	77	63	97	1	.267	.440
TOT	**2126**	**7768**	**1109**	**2171**	**353**	**66**	**337**	**1290**	**1071**	**1271**	**35**	**.279**	**.472**

Hank Sauer (OF)

Notes: There was no doubt about Sauer's ability to pound the ball - what kept him out of the majors until the ripe old age of 31 was his speed, or lack of it. But he hit 35 homers for the Cincinnati Reds his rookie year in 1948, then was traded to the Cubs the next season when he started slowly. The friendly confines were just what Sauer needed; he slugged 11 homers in his first full month as a Cub, finishing with 27 and a .291 average. In 1952, Sauer was voted the National League's Most Valuable Player when he led the league in RBIs (121) and tied Ralph Kiner for home runs (37). A broken finger kept him out of the lineup for half of 1953, but he rebounded the next year to smack 41 more homers. Sauer was the first player to twice hit three home runs in one game off the same pitcher, doing it off the Philadelphia Phillies'Curt Simmons on August 28, 1950 and on June 11, 1952. Sauer finished his career with the Giants, hitting 26 homers in their last season at the Polo Grounds in 1958. Sauer's brother, Ed, also played for the Cubs, as well as the Cardinals and Braves, from 1943-49.

YEAR	G	AB	R	H	2B	3B	HR	RBI	BB	SO	SB	BA	SLG
1949	96	357	59	104	17	1	27	83	37	47	0	.291	.571
1950•	145	540	85	148	32	2	32	103	60	67	1	.274	.519
1951	141	525	77	138	19	4	30	89	45	77	2	.263	.486
1952•	141	567	89	153	31	3	37	121	77	92	1	.270	.531
1953	108	395	61	104	16	5	19	60	50	56	0	.263	.473
1954	142	520	98	150	18	1	41	103	70	68	2	.288	.563
1955	79	261	29	55	8	1	12	28	26	47	0	.211	.387
TOT	**862**	**3165**	**498**	**852**	**141**	**17**	**198**	**587**	**365**	**454**	**6**	**.269**	**.512**

Wildfire Schulte (OF)

Notes: Frank "Wildfire" Schulte was the greatest offensive player during the Cubs' glory years of 1906-11. Schulte, whose nickname was taken from his pet horse, is one of only two men in history (the other was Willie Mays in 1957) to tally more than 20 doubles, 20 triples, 20 homers, and 20 stolen bases in a single season, doing it in 1911. He also led the National League in RBIs (121) and homers (21), and was voted the National League's Most Valuable Player that season. He also hit four grand slams that year, the major league record until the Cubs'Ernie Banks hit five in 1955.

YEAR	G	AB	R	H	2B	3B	HR	RBI	BB	SO	SB	BA	SLG
1904	20	84	16	24	4	3	2	13	2	-	1	.286	.476
1905	123	493	67	135	15	14	1	47	32	-	16	.274	.367
1906	146	563	77	158	18	13	7	60	31	-	25	.281	.396
1907	97	342	44	98	14	7	2	32	22	-	7	.287	.386
1908	102	386	42	91	20	2	1	43	29	-	15	.236	.306
1910	151	559	93	168	29	15	10	68	39	57	22	.301	.460
1911	154	577	105	173	30	21	21	107	76	71	23	.300	.534
1912	139	553	90	146	27	11	12	64	53	70	17	.264	.418
1913	132	497	85	138	28	6	9	68	39	68	21	.278	.412
1914	137	465	54	112	22	7	5	61	39	55	16	.241	.351
1915	151	550	66	137	20	6	12	62	49	68	19	.249	.373
1916	72	230	31	68	11	1	5	27	20	35	9	.296	.417
TOT	**1563**	**5835**	**827**	**1590**	**254**	**117**	**92**	**712**	**455**	**421**	**214**	**.272**	**.403**

Jimmy Sheckard (OF)

Notes: With Wildfire Schulte and Jimmy Slagle, Sheckard rounded out the great outfield of the team's dynastic period of 1906-08. Sheckard, the team's left fielder, was one of just a few Pennsylvania Dutch to ever play major league baseball. His best years were in Brooklyn, batting .353 in 1901 and leading the National League with nine homers in 1903. Sheckard got into a little trouble before the 1906 World Series with the cross-town White Sox, boasting that he would bat .400 against the American Leaguers. Instead, Sheckard went 0-for-21 as the Sox upset the Cubs in six games. In 1911 he set a club record with 147 walks. **Numbers:** Also led the National League in on-base percentage in 1911 (.434). While with the Brooklyn Dodgers, led the National League in triples in 1901 (19), in home runs in 1903 (9), in stolen bases in 1903 (67), and in slugging percentage in 1901 (.534). While with the Baltimore Orioles (NL), led the National League in stolen bases in 1899 (77).

YEAR	G	AB	R	H	2B	3B	HR	RBI	BB	SO	SB	BA	SLG
1906	149	549	90	144	27	10	1	45	67	-	30	.262	.353
1907	143	484	76	129	23	1	1	36	76	-	31	.267	.324
1908	115	403	54	93	18	3	2	22	62	-	18	.231	.305
1909	148	525	81	134	29	5	1	43	72	-	15	.255	.335
1910	144	507	82	130	27	6	5	51	83	53	22	.256	.363
1911	156	539	121	149	26	11	4	50	147	58	32	.276	.388
1912	146	523	85	128	22	10	3	47	122	81	15	.245	.342
TOT	**1001**	**3530**	**589**	**907**	**172**	**46**	**17**	**294**	**629**	**192**	**163**	**.257**	**.346**

Lee Smith (P)

Notes: A six-foot six-inch mountain of a man, Smith had an intimidating glare and an even more intimidating fastball, which he used to post at least 29 saves each year from 1983 to 1988. Over an 18-year career he saved a record 478 games, 180 of them with the Cubs. Smith became the Cubs'closer in 1982 but was traded to the Red Sox for Al Nipper and Calvin Schiraldi in 1987 amid rumors that his gigantic frame was beginning to affect his knees. Boston traded Smith to the Cardinals in 1990, believing that the big guy's career was coming to an end; he responded with an NL-best 47 saves in 1991 and 43 in 1992. The Cardinals thought the same thing when they traded him to the Orioles in 1994; he lead the ALwith 33 saves that year.

YEAR	W	L	G	GS	CG	SH	SV	IP	H	HR	BB	SO	ERA	PCT
1980	2	0	18	0	0	0	0	21.2	21	0	14	17	2.91	1.000
1981	3	6	40	1	0	0	1	66.2	57	2	31	50	3.51	.333
1982	2	5	72	5	0	0	17	117	105	5	37	99	2.69	.286
1983•	4	10	66	0	0	0	29	103.1	70	5	41	91	1.65	.286
1984	9	7	69	0	0	0	33	101	98	6	35	86	3.65	.563
1985	7	4	65	0	0	0	33	97.2	87	9	32	112	3.04	.636
1986	9	9	66	0	0	0	31	90.1	69	7	42	93	3.09	.500
1987•	4	10	62	0	0	0	36	83.2	84	4	32	96	3.12	.286
TOT	**40**	**51**	**458**	**6**	**0**	**0**	**180**	**682**	**591**	**38**	**264**	**644**	**2.92**	**.440**

Sammy Sosa (OF)

Notes: The Cubs'most popular player of the 90s and early 2000s, Sosa is the greatest slugger in team history and one of the greatest in the history of the major leagues. A native of talent-rich San Pedro de Macoris, Dominican Republic, Sosa started his career as a skinny, speedy outfielder for the Texas Rangers and Chicago White Sox. Acquired by the Cubs after the 1991 season, Sosa bulked up in 1993 and became the first Cub to hit more than 30 homers and steal more than 30 bases. After pounding 36 homers in 1995, a broken wrist the next year ended Sosa's consecutive games streak at 304, and he sat out the remaining 38 games of the season. After signing a four-year contract extension in 1997, Sosa responded with 36 homers, 119 RBIs and 22 stolen bases. The right fielder became a bona fide superstar in 1998, when he and the St. Louis Cardinals' Mark McGwire launched an assault on Roger Maris's 37-year-old single season home run record; Sosa finished with 68 (to McGwire's 70) thanks in part to a stretch of 21 homers in 22 games midway into the season. Though Sosa fell short of the quest, his production helped to power the Cubs into the playoffs, for which he was voted the National League's Most Valuable Player. Sosa hit

63 homers the next season, again finishing second to McGwire's 65. In 2001, the slugger ripped another 64 homers, becoming the only major league player to post three 60-homer seasons.

YEAR	G	AB	R	H	2B	3B	HR	RBI	BB	SO	SB	BA	SLG
1992	67	262	41	68	7	2	8	25	19	63	15	.260	.393
1993	159	598	92	156	25	5	33	93	38	135	36	.261	.485
1994	105	426	59	128	17	6	25	70	258	92	22	.300	.545
1995•	144	564	89	151	17	3	36	119	58	134	34	.268	.500
1996	124	498	84	136	21	2	40	100	34	134	18	.273	.564
1997	162	642	90	161	31	4	36	119	45	174	22	.251	.480
1998•	159	643	134	198	20	0	66	158	73	171	18	.308	.647
1999•	162	625	114	180	24	2	63	141	78	171	7	.288	.367
2000•	156	604	106	193	38	1	50	138	91	168	7	.320	.634
2001•	160	577	146	189	34	5	64	160	116	153	0	.328	.737
2002•	150	556	122	160	19	2	49	108	103	144	2	.288	.594
2003	137	517	99	144	22	0	40	103	62	143	0	.279	.553
TOT	**1685**	**6512**	**1176**	**1864**	**275**	**32**	**510**	**1334**	**742**	**1682**	**181**	**.278**	**.546**

Harry Steinfeldt (3B)

Notes: Steinfeldt proved to be the missing link in the Cubs'pennant quest in 1906, traded from the Reds and rounding out the great infield of the Tinker-Evers-Chance dynasty. Steinfeldt put together his best season in 1906, batting .327 and handling the hot corner with unusual grace. Originally hoping for a theatrical career, Steinfeldt played so well in a baseball game put on by his touring troupe that he switched careers.

YEAR	G	AB	R	H	2B	3B	HR	RBI	BB	SO	SB	BA	SLG
1906	151	539	81	176	27	10	3	83	47	-	29	.327	.430
1907	152	542	52	144	25	5	1	70	37	-	19	.266	.336
1908	150	539	63	130	20	6	1	62	36	-	12	.241	.306
1909	151	528	73	133	27	6	2	59	57	-	22	.252	.337
1910	129	448	70	113	21	1	2	58	36	29	10	.252	.317
TOT	**733**	**2596**	**339**	**696**	**120**	**28**	**9**	**332**	**213**	**29**	**92**	**.268**	**.346**

Riggs Stephenson (OF)

Notes: Stephenson's .336 lifetime batting average is the highest among 20th-century players not to be elected to the Hall of Fame. Stephenson was poor defensively, primarily due to chronic shoulder ailments (which he incurred while playing football for the University of Alabama), but his bat kept him in the lineup. Traded to the Cubs from the Cleveland Indians in 1926, he led the National League with 46 doubles a year later, batting .344. In 1929, he combined with future Hall of Famers Kiki Cuyler and Hack Wilson to form the only outfield in MLhistory in which each player drove in 100 or more runs (Wilson had 159, Stephenson had 110 and Cuyler had 102). Arm and leg injuries forced his retirement in 1934, but he managed in the minor leagues until 1939.

YEAR	G	AB	R	H	2B	3B	HR	RBI	BB	SO	SB	BA	SLG
1926	82	281	40	95	18	3	3	44	31	16	2	.338	.456
1927	152	579	101	199	46	9	7	82	65	28	8	.344	.491
1928	137	512	75	166	36	9	8	90	68	29	8	.324	.477
1929	136	495	91	179	36	6	17	110	67	21	10	.362	.562
1930	109	341	56	125	21	1	5	68	32	20	2	.367	.478
1931	80	263	34	84	14	4	1	52	37	14	1	.319	.414
1932	147	583	86	189	49	4	4	85	54	27	3	.324	.443
1933	97	346	45	114	17	4	4	51	34	16	5	.329	.436
1934	38	74	5	16	0	0	0	7	7	5	0	.216	.216
TOT	**978**	**3474**	**533**	**1167**	**237**	**40**	**49**	**589**	**395**	**176**	**39**	**.336**	**.469**

Rick Sutcliffe (P)

Notes: In 1984, Sutcliffe became the only major league pitcher to win a Cy Young Award for a team he joined in medseason. He was traded to the Cubs from the Cleveland Indians on June 13 in exchange for outfielders Joe Carter and Mell Hall. The Independence, Missouri native went 16-1 down the stretch, becoming the Cubs' ace in their 1984 division title quest. A former National League Rookie of the Yar (1979), Sutcliffe won Chicago's pennant-clinching game that year and Game 1 of the NLCS, but lost the decisive fifth game. Injuries plagued Sutcliffe after that, but he rebounded to post 18 wins in 1987. **Numbers:** With the Cleveland Indians, led the American League in ERAin 1982 (2.96).

YEAR	W	L	G	GS	CG	SH	SV	IP	H	HR	BB	SO	ERA	PCT
1984	16	1	20	20	7	3	0	150.1	123	9	39	155	2.69	.941
1985	8	8	20	20	6	3	0	130	119	12	44	102	3.18	.500
1986	5	14	28	27	4	1	0	176.2	166	18	96	122	4.64	.263
1987•	18	10	34	34	6	1	0	237.1	223	24	106	174	3.68	.643
1988	13	14	32	32	12	2	0	226	232	18	70	144	3.86	.481
1989	16	11	35	34	5	1	0	229	202	18	69	153	3.66	.593
1990	0	2	5	5	0	0	0	21.1	25	2	12	7	5.91	.000
1991	6	5	19	18	0	0	0	96.2	96	4	45	52	4.10	.545
TOT	**82**	**65**	**193**	**190**	**40**	**11**	**0**	**1267**	**1186**	**105**	**481**	**909**	**3.74**	**.558**

Bruce Sutter (P)

Notes: Burly Bruce Sutter was the National League's prime reliever of the late 1970s and early 80s. Always a hard thrower, Sutter developed a split-fingered fastball with the help of Cub pitching coach Mike Roarke, giving him instant success as a closer. He saved 31 games and posted a minute 1.34 ERAin 1977 and earned a Cy Young Award with 37 saves in 1979. After that season, Sutter won a hefty arbitration case against the Cubs, who promptly packed him off to St. Louis rather than pay his salary. The move brought other National League owners down on the Cubs for failing to reach an agreement with Sutter prior to the arbitration hearing, because the award effectively recognized diamond stardom based upon performance rather than years of service. After several successful years with the Cardinals, Sutter signed a huge guaranteed contract with Ted Turner's Atlanta Braves - then promptly blew out his arm. **Numbers:** With the St. Louis Cardinals, led the National League in saves in 1981 (25), 1982 (36) and 1984 (45).

YEAR	W	L	G	GS	CG	SH	SV	IP	H	HR	BB	SO	ERA	PCT
1976	6	3	52	0	0	0	10	83.1	63	4	26	73	2.70	.667
1977	7	3	62	0	0	0	31	107.1	69	5	23	129	1.34	.700
1978	8	10	64	0	0	0	27	99	82	10	34	106	3.18	.444
1979	6	6	62	0	0	0	37	101.1	67	3	32	110	2.22	.500
1980	5	8	60	0	0	0	28	102.1	90	5	34	76	2.64	.385
TOT	**32**	**30**	**300**	**0**	**0**	**0**	**133**	**492**	**371**	**27**	**149**	**494**	**2.40**	**.516**

Jack Taylor (P)

Notes: From June 20, 1901, to August 9, 1906, Taylor compiled 188 consecutive complete games - probably the most unassailable record in baseball. Aside from the complete games, Taylor also finished another 15 games from the bullpen for a total of 1,727 innings without being removed from a game. One game was a 19-inning affair and one was 18 innings, and he once pitched both ends of a doubleheader during the streak. In 1904 Taylor became the center of controversy when he announced that he had accepted money to throw a game in the 1903 postseason city championship series against the White Sox. Additional allegations surfaced in 1904 that he had thrown a regulation game while with St. Louis. Both times he was exonerated by the National League.

YEAR	W	L	G	GS	CG	SH	SV	IP	H	HR	BB	SO	ERA	PCT
1898	5	0	5	5	5	0	0	41	32	0	10	11	2.20	1.000
1899	18	21	41	39	39	1	0	354.2	380	6	84	67	3.76	.462
1900	10	17	28	26	25	2	1	222.1	226	4	58	57	2.55	.370
1901	13	19	33	31	30	0	0	275.2	341	5	44	68	3.36	.406
1902	23	11	36	33	33	7	1	324.2	271	2	43	83	1.33	.676
1903	21	14	37	33	33	1	1	312.1	277	2	57	83	2.45	.600
1906	12	3	17	16	15	2	0	147.1	116	1	39	34	1.83	.800
1907	7	5	18	13	8	0	0	123	127	3	33	22	3.29	.583
TOT	**108**	**90**	**215**	**196**	**188**	**14**	**3**	**1801**	**1770**	**23**	**368**	**425**	**2.66**	**.545**

Joe Tinker (SS)

Notes: Tinker was probably the most physically gifted of the Tinkers-Evers-Chance double play combination. Unlike his partner Johnny Evers, tinker led the National League in double plays once, and also paced NLshortstops in fielding average four times and in assists twice. Tinker was an aggressive player on the diamond, but off the field he was quiet and reserved. He had superior speed, stealing an average of 28 bases a year for the Cubs. On July 28, 1910, he stole home twice in one game. Tinker endeared himself to the hearts of baseball fans, but rarely to team owners. He sat out the early part of the 1909 season, demanding a $1,000 raise in salary, before settling for a $200 increase. In 1912 he was traded to the Cincinnati Reds, becoming player-manager, and argued with owner Garry Hermann all year over money. Tired of Tinker's bellyaching, Hermann sold the shortstop to the Brooklyn Dodgers after the season. Tinker refused to report unless given $10,000 of the $25,000 sale price, an outrageous request at the time. Instead, Tinker joined the Federal League, taking over as player-manager for the Chicago Whales. He led the Whales to a second-place finish in 1914 and to a pennant win in 1915, the FL's last year. During the 1920s, Tinker scouted for the Cubs and managed in the minors before striking it rich in Florida real estate. He died of diabetes complications in Orlando at the age of 68. He was elected to the Hall of Fame in 1946. **Numbers:** After Led the National League in fielding percentage in 1906 (.944), 1908 (.958), 1909 (.940), and 1911 (.937).

YEAR	G	AB	R	H	2B	3B	HR	RBI	BB	SO	SB	BA	SLG
1902	131	494	55	129	19	5	2	54	26	-	27	.261	.332
1903	124	460	67	134	21	7	2	70	37	-	27	.291	.380
1904	141	488	55	108	12	13	3	41	29	-	41	.221	.318
1905	149	547	70	135	18	8	2	66	34	-	31	.247	.320
1906	148	523	75	122	18	4	1	64	43	-	30	.233	.289
1907	117	402	36	89	11	3	1	36	25	-	20	.221	.271
1908	157	548	67	146	22	14	6	68	32	-	30	.266	.391
1909	143	516	56	132	26	11	4	57	17	-	23	.256	.372
1910	134	473	48	136	25	9	3	69	24	35	20	.288	.397
1911	144	536	61	149	24	12	4	69	39	31	30	.278	.390
1912	142	550	80	155	24	7	0	75	38	21	25	.282	.351
TOT	**1538**	**5554**	**669**	**1444**	**219**	**93**	**28**	**670**	**345**	**88**	**304**	**.260**	**.348**

Hippo Vaughn (P)
Notes: Vaughn was nicknamed Hippo for obvious reasons - his 215-lb frame. Vaughn won 20 or more games in a season five times and 19 more one time. In the 1918 World Series he pitched three complete games, losing the opener 1-0 and the third game 2-1. On May 2, 1917, Vaughn held the Cincinnati Reds hitless for nine innings, but Cincy's Fred Toney held the Cubs hitless over the nine frames as well. In the 10th, Vaughn gave up a single to Larry Kopf, who eventually scored on a Jim Thorpe bunt, completing Toney's no-hitter. The game has been widely recognized as the greatest pitching duel of all-time.

YEAR	W	L	G	GS	CG	SH	SV	IP	H	HR	BB	SO	ERA	PCT
1913	5	1	7	6	5	2	0	56	37	0	27	36	1.45	.833
1914	21	13	42	35	23	4	1	293.2	236	1	109	165	2.05	.618
1915	20	12	41	34	18	4	1	269.2	240	4	77	148	2.87	.625
1916	17	15	44	35	21	4	1	294	269	4	67	144	2.20	.531
1917	23	13	41	38	27	5	0	295.2	255	3	91	195	2.01	.639
1918	22	10	35	33	27	8	0	290.1	216	4	76	148	1.74	.688
1919	21	14	38	37	25	4	1	306.2	264	3	62	141	1.79	.600
1920	19	16	40	38	24	4	0	301	301	8	81	131	2.54	.543
1921	3	11	17	14	7	0	0	109.1	153	8	31	30	6.01	.214
TOT	**151**	**105**	**305**	**270**	**177**	**35**	**4**	**2216**	**1971**	**35**	**621**	**1138**	**2.33**	**.590**

Lon Warneke (P)
Notes: Known as the Arkansas Hummingbird, Warneke is the only man to ever play and umpire in both a World Series and an All-Star Game. Warneke won 100 games during his first tour with the Cubs, but was traded to the St. Louis Cardinals in 1937. While with the Cards, he no-hit the Cincinnati Reds on August 30, 1941. In 1942, the Cubs bought him back for $75,000, but lost him to the military a year later. After World War II he joined the National League as an umpire.

YEAR	W	L	G	GS	CG	SH	SV	IP	H	HR	BB	SO	ERA	PCT
1930	0	0	1	0	0	0	0	1.1	2	0	5	0	33.75	-
1931	2	4	20	7	3	0	0	64.1	67	1	37	27	3.22	.333
1932	22	6	35	32	25	4	0	277	247	12	64	106	2.37	.786
1933•	18	13	36	34	26	4	1	287.1	262	8	75	133	2.00	.581
1934•	22	10	43	35	23	3	3	291.1	273	16	66	143	3.21	.688
1935	20	13	42	30	20	1	4	261.2	257	19	50	120	3.06	.606
1936•	16	13	40	29	13	4	1	240.1	246	10	76	113	3.45	.552
1942	5	7	15	12	8	1	2	99	97	2	21	28	2.27	.417
1943	4	5	21	10	4	0	0	88.1	82	3	18	30	3.16	.444
1945	0	1	9	1	0	0	0	14	16	0	1	6	3.86	.000
TOT	**109**	**72**	**262**	**190**	**122**	**17**	**11**	**1625**	**1549**	**71**	**413**	**706**	**2.84**	**.602**

Billy Williams (OF)

Notes: The difference between Billy Williams and teammate Ernie Banks, other than he hit left-handed, was that Williams eventually got himself out of Chicago and managed to play in a postseason series. Williams joined the Cubs for good in 1961 and ticked off thirteen straight seasons of 21 or more home runs, reaching a career high of 42 in 1972. He reached the .300 mark five times, comipled 200 hits three times, tallied 30 or more doubles seven years, scored 100 or more runs five times, drove in 100 or more runs three times and hit .292 over his Hall of Fame career. From 1963 to 1970 he appeared in a National League-record 1,117 consecutive games - a mark later surpassed by the Dodgers' Steve Garvey. In September of 1969, while most of manager Leo Durocher's regulars began to wilt from overwork, Williams hit .304 for the month. Though Williams never played in a World Series, he managed to get into the playoffs after being traded to Oakland in 1975; he went 0-for-8 as the A's were swept by the Boston Red Sox. Williams retired after batting .211 in 1976 and returned to the Cubs, where he has been an on-again, off-again batting coach. He was elected to the Hall of Fame in 1987.

YEAR	G	AB	R	H	2B	3B	HR	RBI	BB	SO	SB	BA	SLG
1959	18	33	0	5	0	1	0	2	1	7	0	.152	.212
1960	12	47	4	13	0	2	2	7	5	12	0	.277	.489
1961	146	529	75	147	20	7	25	86	45	70	6	.278	.484
1962•	159	618	94	184	22	8	22	91	70	72	9	.298	.466
1963	161	612	87	175	36	9	25	95	68	78	7	.286	.497
1964•	162	645	100	201	39	2	33	98	59	84	10	.312	.532
1965•	164	645	115	203	39	6	34	108	65	76	10	.315	.552
1966	162	648	100	179	23	5	29	91	69	61	6	.276	.461
1967	162	637	92	176	21	12	28	84	68	67	6	.278	.481
1968•	163	642	91	185	30	8	30	98	48	53	4	.288	.500
1969	163	642	103	188	33	10	21	95	59	70	3	.293	.474
1970	161	636	137	205	34	4	42	129	72	65	7	.322	.586
1971	157	594	86	179	27	5	28	93	77	44	7	.301	.505
1972•	150	574	95	191	34	6	37	122	62	59	3	.333	.606
1973•	156	576	72	166	22	2	20	86	76	72	4	.288	.438
1975	117	404	55	113	22	0	16	68	67	44	4	.280	.453
TOT	**2213**	**8479**	**1306**	**2510**	**402**	**87**	**392**	**1353**	**911**	**934**	**86**	**.296**	**.503**

Ned Williamson (SS/3B)

Notes: Shortstop Williamson was called "the best all-around ballplayer the country ever saw" by his manager, Cap Anson. In 1883, when the White Stockings took advantage of the short fences in right and left field, Williamson set a new National League record of 49 doubles, most of them on fly balls over the fence. In 1884, when such fly balls were ruled home runs, he swatted 25 of them (adding the two he hit on the road, he finished with 27 that year, the NL record until 1919). A fine fielder, Williamson led National League shortstops or third baseman in assists seven times, in double plays six times, in fielding percentage four times, and in putouts twice. **Numbers:** Also led the National League in fielding percentage in 1879 (.871), 1880 (.893), 1881 (.909), 1882 (.881), and 1885 (.892).

YEAR	G	AB	R	H	2B	3B	HR	RBI	BB	SO	SB	BA	SLG
1879	80	320	66	94	20	13	1	36	24	31	-	.294	.447
1880	75	311	65	78	20	2	0	31	15	26	-	.251	.328
1881	82	343	56	92	12	6	1	48	19	19	-	.268	.347
1882	83	348	66	98	27	4	3	60	27	21	-	.282	.408
1883	98	402	83	111	49	5	2	59	22	48	-	.276	.438
1884	107	417	84	116	18	8	27	84	42	56	-	.278	.554
1885	113	407	87	97	16	5	3	65	75	60	-	.238	.324
1886	121	430	69	93	17	8	6	58	80	71	13	.216	.335
1887	127	439	77	117	20	14	9	78	73	57	45	.267	.437
1888	132	452	75	113	9	14	8	73	65	71	25	.250	.385
1889	47	173	16	41	3	1	1	30	23	22	2	.237	.283
TOT	**1065**	**4042**	**744**	**1050**	**211**	**80**	**61**	**478**	**465**	**482**	**85**	**.260**	**.397**

Hack Wilson (C/OF)

Notes: Wilson's Hall of Fame induction is thanks mostly to his monumental output spanning just five years, from 1926-1930. Wilson, whose 195 pounds were stretched over a five-foot six-inch frame, had a gargantuan torso and mammoth biceps that tapered down to tiny legs and feet. He wore a size 18 collar - and size 6 shoe! Wilson's 56 homers in 1930 were a National League record until Mark McGwire and Sammy Sosa surpassed them in 1998; his 191 RBIs that same year have yet to be breeched. Wilson, whose name was Lewis, earned his nickname from a resemblance to Hack Miller, another Cubs outfielder who played from 1922-1925. The Cubs obtained Wilson by accident; originally a New York Giant, he slumped to .239 in 1925 after batting .294 in 1924 and was sent to the Minors. In the postseason draft, the Cubs found him unprotected and bought him for $5,000. Though Wilson was a mighty slugger, he was also one of the National League's best center fielders, leading the league with 400 putouts in 1927. From the start of his career, though, Wilson was hampered by alcohol problems. Manager Joe McCarthy found ways to motivate his slugger, but McCarthy's successor, Rogers Hornsby, did not, and continually berated the thin-skinned Wilson for his drinking. After his astonishing 1930 season, Wilson slumped horribly in 1931, batting .261 with 13 homers, and was traded to the St. Louis Cardinals, and from there to the Brooklyn Dodgers. By 1934 he was out of baseball. He was elected to the Hall of Fame in 1979.

YEAR	G	AB	R	H	2B	3B	HR	RBI	BB	SO	SB	BA	SLG
1926	142	529	97	170	36	8	21	106	69	61	10	.321	.539
1927	146	551	119	175	30	12	30	129	71	70	13	.318	.579
1928	145	520	89	163	32	9	31	120	77	94	4	.313	.588
1929	150	574	135	198	30	5	39	159	78	83	3	.345	.618
1930	155	585	146	208	35	6	56	190	105	84	3	.356	.723
1931	112	395	66	103	22	4	13	61	63	69	1	.261	.435
TOT	**850**	**3154**	**652**	**1017**	**185**	**44**	**190**	**768**	**463**	**461**	**34**	**.322**	**.590**

Heinie Zimmerman (3B)

Notes: Zimmerman is the only Triple Crown winner who is not in the Hall of Fame. He became the Cubs regular third baseman in 1912, leading the National League with 14 home runs, 103 RBIs, and a .372 average. Zimmerman was traded to the Giants in 1916. In 1919, he and teammate Hal Chase, the notorious first baseman, were suspended by the Giants for conspiring to throw ball games. During the investigation it emerged that the pair had offered outfielder Benny Kauff and pitcher Fred Toney $500 to join them in intentionally losing a game to the St. Louis Cardinals. Both were banned from baseball. **Numbers:** With the New York Giants, led the National Leauge in RBIs in 1916 (83) and 1917 (102).

YEAR	G	AB	R	H	2B	3B	HR	RBI	BB	SO	SB	BA	SLG
1907	5	9	0	2	1	0	0	1	0	-	0	.222	.233
1908	46	113	17	33	4	1	0	9	1	-	2	.292	.345
1909	65	183	23	50	9	2	0	21	3	-	7	.273	.344
1910	99	335	35	95	16	6	3	38	20	36	7	.284	.394
1911	143	535	80	164	22	17	9	85	25	50	23	.307	.462
1912	145	557	95	207	41	14	14	103	38	60	23	.372	.571
1913	127	447	69	140	28	12	9	95	41	40	18	.313	.490
1914	146	564	75	167	36	12	4	87	20	46	17	.296	.424
1915	139	520	65	138	28	11	3	62	21	33	19	.265	.379
1916	107	398	54	116	25	5	6	64	16	33	15	.291	.425
TOT	**906**	**3356**	**473**	**1027**	**196**	**77**	**48**	**530**	**181**	**298**	**122**	**.306**	**.453**

WORTH NOTING - In 1930, Hack Wilson and Gabby Hartnett combined for 93 homers, an NL record for most home runs by teammates until the Cardinals' Mark McGwire and Ray Lankford combined for 101 in 1998. Sammy Sosa and Henry Rodriguez combined for 97 that year also.

breaking Chuck Klein's National League record.

September 6 - Trailing the Pirates 12-8 after seven innings, the Cubs score four runs in the eighth and six more in the ninth for an 18-14 victory. Hack Wilson smacks his 47th homer at Forbes Field.

September 15 - Lefty O'Doul's pinch-hit home run beats the Cubs in the opener but Hack Wilson's 50th home runs helps Chicago earn a doubleheader split with a 6-4 nightcap victory in Philadelphia.

September 20 - Wilson collects his 176th RBI, surpassing Lou Gehrig's 1927 major league record, in a 3-2 loss to the Braves.

September 25 - Joe McCarthy, who has been feuding with owner William Wrigley all season, resigns as manager. Rogers Hornsby takes over as Cubs skipper.

September 26 - Hack Wilson launches two home runs, his 55th and 56th, to set a National League record that will stand until 1998. Pat Malone picks up his 20th victory as the Cubs beat the Reds 13-8 at Wrigley Field.

Chicago is eliminated, however, as St. Louis beats Pittsburgh to clinch the National League pennant.

September 28 - Wilson picks up the final two RBI of the season, finishing at a stunning published mark of 190 (the record will later be adjusted to 191). Wilson is the only player in history to drive in more than 150 runs in consecutive seasons. The Cubs beat the Reds 12-11.

October 10 - Wilson picks up the National League's MVP award. The Cubs give Wilson a bonus of $1,000.

November 10 - Baseball Commissioner Kenesaw Mountain Landis re-instates left-hander Hippo Vaughn, who left the Cubs in 1921 following a dispute with manager Johnny Evers. He will go to spring training next season at age 43 but will not make the team.

1931

Principle Owner and President: William Veeck, Sr.; **Manager:** Rogers Hornsby; **Ballpark:** Wrigley Field; **Attendance:** 1,086,422; **Finish:** Third (84-70); **Recap:** Rogers Hornsby's tenure as club manager is slightly longer than Johnny Evers's two earlier stints, but the similarities in style are unmistakable: regular, sharp criticism and constant bickering with his players.

In addition to his testiness, Hornsby's handling of the pitching staff illicits sharp criticism from players and Chicago beat writers to the extent that only the large sum of money the manager owes to William Wrigley saves him from losing his job.

P	PLAYER	R	HR	RBI	SB	AVE
1B	Charlie Grimm	65	4	66	1	.331
2B	Rogers Hornsby	64	16	90	1	.331
SS	Woody English	117	2	53	12	.319
3B	Les Bell	30	4	32	0	.282
RF	Kiki Cuyler	110	9	88	13	.330
CF	Hack Wilson	66	13	61	1	.261
LF	Riggs Stephenson	34	1	52	1	.319
C	Gabby Hartnett	53	8	70	3	.282

P	PLAYER	R	HR	RBI	SB	AVE
IF	Bill Jurges	34	0	23	2	.201
OF	Danny Teylor	48	5	41	4	.300
IF	Footsie Blair	31	3	29	1	.258
OF	Vince Barton	45	13	50	1	.238
C	Rollie Hemsley	28	3	31	4	.309

T	PITCHER	W-L	SV	SO	SH	ERA
R	Charlie Root	17-14	2	131	3	3.48
R	Guy Bush	16-8	2	54	1	4.50
R	Pat Malone	16-9	0	112	2	3.91
R	Bob Smith	15-12	2	63	2	3.23
L	Lee Sweetland	8-7	0	32	0	5.05

January 17 - Don Zimmer is born in Cincinnati, Ohio.

February 5 - Hack Wilson signs a new contract calling for $35,000 a season, making him the highest paid National Leaguer.

April 14 - The Cubs beat the Pirates 6-2 on Opening Day at Wrigley Field.

April 24 - Rogers Hornsby connects for three home runs and drives in eight runs to beat the Pirates 10-6 at Forbes Field.

May 2 - Hack Wilson delivers his first home run of the season in a 6-3 victory at Sportsman's Park in St. Louis. He will hit only 12 more and end up on the bench.

May 7 - The Cubs defeat the Reds 5-4 in 11 frames. Jakie May gets the decision in relief.

May 26 - Jim Frey is born in Cleveland, Ohio.

May 31 - The Cubs beat the Pirates for the fourth straight time, 5-0 despite an unassisted double play by Pittsburgh center fielder Adam Comorosky.

July 12 - With an overflow crowd ringing the Sportsman's Park outfield, balls hit into the crowd are declared doubles. The result is a record 23 two-baggers, with ten of them hit by the Cubs in a 17-13 Cardinals victory.

July 27 - Riggs Stephenson breaks his ankle during a 6-5 loss to the Phils at Chicago.

August 3 - Bob Smith shuts out the Reds 8-0, handing Cincinnati its fourth straight shutout - a National League record.

August 4 - The Reds finally score but are swept by the Cubs, 4-2 and 7-3, in a twin-bill at Wrigley.

August 29 - Rookie Billy Herman, in his first major league at-bat, fouls a pitch from the Reds' Si Johnson off the plate that bounces back and knocks him out. He's removed from the field on a stretcher. Herman will go on to a Hall of Fame career.

September5 - Hack Wilson, who has been benched by manager Rogers Hornsby for drinking and not hitting, is in the bullpen warming up pitchers when Hornsby decides to put pitcher Bud Teachout in left field during a 4-3 loss in Cincinnati.

On the train back to Chicago that evening, Pat Malone wanders by the dejected Wilson's berth and decides to egg the slumping slugger on; who picks a fight with a couple of beat writers. Wilson will be suspended for the rest of the season without pay by club president Bill Veeck, Sr. and Malone will be fined $500 for his part in the incident.

WORTH QUOTING - "Any ballplayer that don't sign autographs for little kids ain't an American. He's a communist."
-Rogers Hornsby

WORTH NOTING - In 1931, Gabby Hartnett created a controversy in Chicago by posing with mobster Al Capone for a picture before a game at Wrigley Field. Because of the scandal, NLpresident John Heydler rushed through a rule forbidding players from socializing with fans before a game.

September 13 - Hornsby bashes an 11th-inning pinch-grand slam to give the Cubs an 11-7 win over the Braves at Wrigley. It's the first extra-inning pinch-grand slam in major league history.

The Cubs take the nightcap of the doubleheader 8-1 behind Guy Bush's second one-hitter of the year.

December 11 - The Cubs trade Hack Wilson to the Cardinals for spitball veteran Burleigh Grimes. Grimes will post three losing seasons for the Cubs and retire.

1932

Principle Owner and President: William Veeck, Sr.; **Manager:** Rogers Hornsby / Charlie Grimm; **Ballpark:** Wrigley Field; **Attendance:** 974,688; **Finish:** First (90-64); **Recap:** Team owner William Wrigley dies in January at the age of 70, leaving control of the club to his son, Phil. Manager Rogers Hornsby's job is saved for a few weeks when the club gets off to a strong start but when the team slips in August, Wrigley fires the Rajah in favor of first baseman Charlie Grimm. Relieved to be free of the tenacious Hornsby, the club goes 37-18 the rest of the season, surpassing Pittsburgh and winning the pennant by four games.

P	PLAYER	R	HR	RBI	SB	AVE
1B	Charlie Grimm	66	7	80	2	.307
2B	Billy Herman	102	1	51	14	.314
SS	Billy Jurges	40	2	52	1	.253
SS	Woody English	70	3	47	5	.272
RF	Kiki Cuyler	58	10	77	9	.291
CF	Johnny Moore	59	13	64	4	.305
LF	Riggs Stephenson	86	4	85	3	.324
C	Gabby Hartnett	52	12	52	0	.271
IF	Stan Hack	32	2	19	5	.236
UT	Rollie Hemsley	27	4	20	2	.238
UT	Marv Gudat	15	1	15	0	.255
OF	Lance Richbourg	22	1	21	0	.257
OF	Vince Barton	19	3	15	0	.224

T	PITCHER	W-L	SV	SO	SH	ERA
R	Lon Warneke	22-6	0	106	4	2.37
R	Guy Bush	19-11	0	73	1	3.20
R	Charlie Root	15-10	3	96	0	3.58
R	Pat Malone	15-11	0	120	2	3.38
R	Burleigh Grimes	6-11	1	36	1	4.79

January 26 - Cubs owner William K. Wrigley dies at age 70 on Catalina Island, California.

His only son, Philip K. Wrigley, inherits the team, plus the minor-league Los Angeles Angels (PCL), promising not to interfere with operations chief William Veeck, Sr.

April 12 - The Cubs lose on Opening Day to Cincinnati 5-4 at Crosley Field.

April 20 - Chicago loses its home opener 7-2 to the Reds.

April 24 - Kiki Cuyler breaks his leg during a 12-3 victory vs. Pittsburgh. He'll be out until mid-season.

May 1 - Wild Bill Hallahan of St. Louis walks 10 but still beats Guy Bush and the Cubs 7-1.

July 6 - Shortstop Billy Jurges is shot twice, once in the shoulder, and once in the hand, in his Chicago hotel room by Violet Popovich Valli, his spurned girlfriend. Jurges, however, decides not to prosecute, and Valli's notoriety will land her a 22-week engagement to sing in local nightclubs. She will be billed as "*Violet (What I Did For Love) Valli - the Most Talked About Girl in Chicago*."

July 22 - Jurges returns to the lineup as the Cubs lose to the Pirates 3-1 at Forbes Field.

August 2 - After a 4-2 loss to Brooklyn at Ebbets Field, Rogers Hornsby is fired as manager amid charges by the Tribune that he has been fraudulently "borrowing" money from Cubs players to place bets for them at the track. First baseman Charlie Grimm is named to replace him.

August 11 - The Cubs take first place for the first time as rookie shortstop Arky Vaughn's error in the 10th inning gives them a victory over the Pirates.

August 13 - Rogers Hornsby is acquitted of fraud charges by Commissioner Landis but upholds the fine levied against him by the Cubs. The players demand refunds from the embittered future Hall of Famer.

August 14 - Cardinals rookie Dizzy Dean fans six Cubs in a row, winning 2-1.

August 17 - The Cubs beat the Braves 3-2 in 19 innings, the longest game of the year. Guy Bush is the winner in relief. He'll pick up another relief win tomorrow, 4-3.

August 23 - Chicago ties a major league record with just one assist in a 5-1 win over the Phillies.

August 31 - The Cubs rally with a run in the ninth inning and five more in the 10th for a 10-9 victory over the Giants. Kiki Cuyler goes 5-for-6 with a three-run homer to win it.

Rogers Hornsby

September 2 - The Cubs push their winning streak to 13 games as Kiki Cuyler's fifth home run in six days leads them to an 8-5 victory. Mark Koenig, who once started at shortstop for the Murderer's Row Yankees, adds a homer of his own.

September 3 - Dizzy Dean wins 3-0, snapping the Cubs' winning streak in the second game of a doubleheader. Chicago wins its 14th in a row in the opener, 5-4.

September 10 - Brooklyn outfielder Johnny Frederick rips a pinch-hit homer off Burleigh Grimes in the ninth to defeat the Cubs 4-3. It's Frederick's sixth pinch-homer of the year, a major league record.

September 20 - The Cubbies clinch the pennant with a 5-2 win over Pittsburgh, thanks to Kiki Cuyler's bases-loaded triple. Rookie Billy Herman collects his 200th hit of the season.

WORTH NOTING- The Cubs' World Series opponents in 1932 are the New York Yankees, managed by former Cubs skipper **Joe McCarthy**. The Yanks finish with a 107-47 (.695) record, leading the AL in runs (1002), bases on balls (766), shutouts (11), and ERA(3.98).

P	PLAYER	R	HR	RBI	SB	BA
1B	Lou Gehrig	138	34	151	4	.349
2B	Tony Lazzeri	79	15	113	11	.300
SS	Frankie Crosetti	47	5	57	3	.247
3B	Joe Sewell	95	11	68	0	.272
RF	Babe Ruth	120	41	137	2	.341
CF	Earle Combs	143	9	65	3	.321
LF	Ben Chapman	101	10	107	38	.299
C	Bill Dickey	66	15	84	2	.310

T	PITCHER	W	L	SV	SH	ERA
L	Lefty Gomez	14	7	1	1	4.21
R	Red Ruffing	18	7	2	3	3.09
R	Johnny Allen	17	4	4	3	3.70
R	George Pipgras	16	9	0	2	4.19
R	Wilcy Moore	2	0	4	0	2.52

September 21 - The Cubs vote to exclude former manager Rogers Hornsby from the pot of World Series shares. They also vote just a half share for Mark Koenig, who was picked up by the team early in the season and played well during the absence of Billy Jurges. The Yankees will heckle the Cubs mercilessly during the World Series over their stinginess toward their former shortstop.

September 22 - Hornsby appeals to Judge Landis over the Cubs'refusal to vote him a World Series share, arguing that he was an active player as well as manager for 2/3 of the season. Landis turns him down, declaring that the team can split the pie any way it wants.

September 28 - World Series Game 1
The Yankees take advantage of six walks by three Cubs pitchers and score 12 runs despite collecting only eight hits in a 12-6 victory at Yankee Stadium. Chicago strands 11runners in the game.

September 29 - World Series Game 2
The Cubs take an early 1-0 lead in the first on a double by Billy Herman and a sacrifice fly by Riggs Stephenson but the Yankees answer with two more in the bottom of the frame on RBI singles by Lou Gehrig and Bill Dickey. The Yanks score two more in the third off Lon Warneke and never look back, winning 5-2 behind Lefty Gomez.

October 1 - World Series Game 3
Babe Ruth calls - or doesn't call - his shot in the fifth inning of today's 7-5 Yankee victory at Wrigley Field. Ruth's three-run homer in the first puts New York up 3-0 but the Cubs battle back and tie the game 4-4 in the fourth. But Ruth, taunted all series by the Chicago bench, points either to the dugout or the center field stands - depending on who's asked, and puts Charlie Root's pitch over the center field fence. Lou Gehrig follows with another homer. Gabby Hartnett's homer leading off the ninth accounts for the Cubs' only score after that.

October 2 - World Series Game 4
The Yankees load the bases on the first four pitches thrown by starter Guy Bush but score only one run thanks to a running catch by Frank Demaree and the relief pitching of Lon Warneke, who finishes the inning without further damage. The Cubs bomb Yankees starter Johnny Allen in the bottom of the frame by scoring four runs, three on Demaree's homer. In the third, Warneke gives up a home run to Tony Lazzeri, and leaves the game with a 4-3 lead. But reliever Jakie May allows two runs in the sixth and four more in the seventh. The Yanks add four in the ninth and win the game and the series, 13-6.

November30 - The Cubs acquire slugging outfielder Babe Herman from the Reds for utility player Rollie Hemsley and three minor leaguers.

1933

Principle Owner and President: William Veeck, Sr.; **Manager:** Charlie Grimm; **Ballpark:** Wrigley Field; **Attendance:** 594,112; **Finish:** Third (86-68); **Recap:** The Cubs finish third in 1933, thanks in part to a broken ankle suffered by Kiki Cuyler that sidelines him for half the season. The Cubs suffer another front-office loss when Bill Veeck, Sr. dies, leaving the team presidency to William Walker, Charles Weeghman's original partner. Walker's tenure will last just a year, as the executive commits various trading blunders and engages in semi-regular shouting matches with the Cubs' popular manager, Charlie Grimm.

P	PLAYER	R	HR	RBI	SB	AVE
1B	Charlie Grimm	38	3	37	1	.247
2B	Billy Herman	82	0	44	5	.279
SS	Billy Jurges	49	5	50	3	.269
3B	Woody English	54	3	41	5	.261
RF	Babe Herman	77	16	93	6	.289
CF	Frank Demaree	68	6	51	4	.272
LF	Riggs Stephenson	45	4	51	5	.329
C	Gabby Hartnett	55	16	88	1	.276
IF	Mark Koenig	32	3	25	5	.284
OF	Kiki Cuyler	37	5	35	4	.317
UT	Harvey Hendrick	30	4	23	4	.291
C	Gilly Campbell	11	1	10	0	.281
P	Lon Warneke	9	2	13	0	.300

T	PITCHER	W-L	SV	SO	SH	ERA
R	Guy Bush	20-12	2	84	4	2.75
R	Lon Warneke	18-13	1	133	4	2.01
R	Charlie Root	15-10	0	86	2	2.60
R	Rud Tinning	13-6	1	59	3	3.19
R	Pat Malone	10-14	0	72	2	3.92

March 6 - Ted Abernathy is born in Stanley, North Carolina.

March 11 - During an exhibition game between the Cubs and Giants at Los Angeles, a small earthquake occurs. Terrified players huddle around second base until the shaking stops; no one at the ballpark is injured.

WORTH QUOTING - "It is an argument over nothing, and the fact that Ruth did not point to center field before his home run does not diminish in the least what he did. He did challenge the Cubs before 50,000 people, did indicate he was going to hit a home run and did hit a home run. What more could you ask?"

-Robert Creamer on Babe Ruth's alleged "called shot" during the 1932 World Series, in *Babe: The Legend Comes to Life*"

March 29 - Kiki Cuyler breaks his leg for the second year in a row in another spring training injury. He'll be out of the lineup until late June.

April 12 - The Cubs whitewash the Cardinals 3-0 on Opening Day at Wrigley.

May 2 - Gabby Hartnett supplies the offense with two homers and Lon Warneke supplies the defense in an 11-0 pasting of New York.

June 23 - The Cubs sweep a doubleheader from the Phillies, winning the first game on a pinch-grand slam by Harvey Hendrick, the second pinch-slam in history and second in three years for Chicago. The Cubs win the second game 3-1.

July 20 - Babe Herman drives in eight runs with a grand slam and two two-run homers

WORTH NOTING - Lon Warneke is the only man to both pitch and umpire in a World Series.

in a 10-1 victory over Philadelphia.

July 30 - Burleigh Grimes is released by the Cubs. Grimes, nine days short of his 40th birthday, is 3-6. He'll sign with the Cardinals.

August 22 - It's in the blood: Cubs president Bill Veeck, Sr. proposes a split season for major league baseball and a midsummer series of interleague games.

September 15 - The Giants win two over the Cubs, winning 5-1 and 4-0.

September 16 - The Giants sweep another pair from the second place Cubs, winning 2-1 and 6-3 and effectively putting the NL Champs out of the race. Carl Hubbell notches his 22nd win in game one.

September 23 - The Cubs hand Reds righthander Paul Derringer a stunning 27th loss, tying the major league record set by George Bell of the Dodgers in 1910. Gabby Hartnett hits a grand slam in the 7-1 win.

September 30 - Babe Herman hits for the cycle in a 12-2 bashing of Dizzy Dean and the Cardinals. It's the third time Herman's hit for the cycle.

October 7 - Cubs president William L. Veeck, Sr. dies suddenly of a heart attack. Veeck's son, Hall of Famer Bill Veeck, Jr. will come to work for the Cubs as a ticket taker to support the family.

November 21 - The Cubs purchase outfielder Chuck Klein from the Phils for $125,000 and Mark Koenig, Harvey Hendrick, and rookie lefty Ted Kleinhans. Klein is the only player to be traded after winning the Triple Crown the year before. He also led the NL in hits, slugging, and doubles.

1934

Principle Owner and President: William Walker; **Manager:** Charlie Grimm; **Ballpark:** Wrigley Field; **Attendance:** 707,525; **Finish:** Third (86-65); **Recap:** The Cubs finish third this season, led by Kiki Cuyler's .338 average and Lon Warneke's 22 wins. Line drive-hitting rookie third baseman Stan Hack makes his first appearance for the Cubs this year, as does first baseman Phil Cavarretta and righthander Bill Lee. The trio will be instrumental in the team's success for much of the next decade.

P	Player	R	HR	RBI	SB	AVE
1B	Charlie Grimm	24	5	47	1	.296
2B	Billy Herman	79	3	42	6	.303
SS	Billy Jurges	43	8	33	1	.246
3B	Stan Hack	54	1	21	11	.289
RF	Babe Herman	65	14	84	1	.304
CF	Kiki Cuyler	80	6	69	15	.338
LF	Chuck Klein	78	20	80	3	.301
C	Gabby Hartnett	58	22	90	0	.299
IF	Woody English	65	3	31	6	.278
UT	Tuck Stainback	47	2	46	7	.306
IF	Augie Galan	31	5	22	4	.260
IF	Don Hurst	13	3	12	0	.199
C	Babe Phelps	7	2	12	0	.286

T	Pitcher	W-L	SV	SO	SH	ERA
R	Lon Warneke	22-10	3	143	3	3.22
R	Guy Bush	18-10	2	75	1	3.83
R	Pat Malone	14-7	0	111	1	3.53
R	Bill Lee	13-14	1	104	4	3.41
R	Jim Weaver	11-9	0	98	1	3.91

January 10 - William Walker is named president of the Cubs.

April 12 - Lon Warneke takes a no-hitter into the ninth inning before giving up a single to Adam Comorosky as the Cubs whitewash the Reds 6-0 on Opening Day at Crosley Field.

April 22 - Warneke hurls his second consecutive one-hitter as the Cubs pummel the Cardinals 15-2. Dizzy Dean is the loser.

May 2 - The Cubs drop to second place as Heinie Mein out-pitches Lon Warneke to give the Pirates a 4-2 victory at Forbes Field.

May 7 - Bill Lee shuts out the hapless Phillies 2-0 in his first major league start.

May 15 - The Cubs pick up pitcher Jim Weaver off waivers from St. Louis. He'll win 11 games for Chicago this season.

May 17 - In his first game at Baker Bowl since winning the Triple Crown the year before, new Cub Chuck Klein launches two homers to lead Chicago to a 10-3 win over Philadelphia. Chicago pummels Philly pitching for 20 hits, led by rookie Dolph Camilli's four.

June 6 - The Cubs push across six runs in the 13th to beat the Cardinals 12-6 at Sportsman's Park. Frankie Frisch picks a fight with umpire Cy Rigler, who hits the St. Louis manager in the jaw with his mask. Both will be fined $100 apiece.

June 7 - Jim Weaver, whom the Cubs picked up a month ago from Newark for $12,500, hurls a 1-0 shutout over the Cardinals.

June 8 - After his Reds defeat the Cubs 4-3 at Crosley Field, Cincinnati president Larry MacPhail gets permission to move the final two games of the three-game set to Chicago to gain relief from a midwest heat wave. MacPhail flies the Reds to Chicago on two American Airlines cabin planes. The Reds travel by train and will lose tomorrow's game, 5-2. They'll avoid a sweep with a 7-4 victory in the final game.

June 11 - The Cubs pack slugging rookie Dolph Camilli to the Phillies for first baseman Don Hurst. Camilli will later be traded to the Dodgers, winning the MVP award in 1941. Hurst will bat .199 for the Cubs in this, his final season.

WORTH NOTING - Gabby Hartnett set a record for catchers by leading the league in fielding for four years in a row, 1934 to 1937. He also set a record by turning 163 double plays during his career.

June 20 - Charlie Root gives up seven runs in the third as the Giants beat the Cubs 12-7.

June 30 - Bill Lee collects his eighth straight win, beating the Pirates 4-2 at Pittsburgh. Before the game, a granite monument to former owner Barney Dreyfuss is revealed, highlighting the 25th anniversary celebration of Forbes Field.

July 2 - The Cardinals protest a 7-4 loss to the Cubs in a dispute over a delayed infield fly call by veteran umpire Bill Klem.

July 17 - Leading 3-1, Lon Warneke intentionally walks a batter to get to Giants pitcher Roy "Tarzan" Parmelee in the seventh. Parmelee hits a grand slam to win 5-3.

July 17 - National League president William Heydler upholds the Cardinals protest of the game on July 2, declaring that umpire Bill Klem waited too long to make the call. The game will be resumed from that point and be finished prior to a scheduled contest on July 31. Chicago will still win, 7-1.

October 23 - Phil Wrigley usurps Walter Walker as Cubs president, buying up more shares of team stock. He gives manager Charlie Grimm complete control of the team.

WORTH QUOTING - "We gotta look at that all season!"
-Gabby Hartnett, yelling to the American League dugout during the 1934 All-Star Game at the Polo Grounds, after Giants lefthander Carl Hubbell fans five future Hall of Famers in succession.

November21 - The Cubs obtain 16-game-winner Tex Carleton from the Cardinals for pitchers Dick Ward, Bud Tinning and cash. Carleton will win 11 games for the Cubbies in 1935.

November 22 - Chicago lands lefty Larry French and veteran third baseman Freddie Lindstrom from the Pirates for Guy Bush, Jim Weaver, and Babe Herman.

1935

Principle Owner and President: Phil Wrigley; **Manager:** Charlie Grimm; **Ballpark:** Wrigley Field; **Attendance:** 692,604; **Finish:** First (100-54); **Recap:** Thanks to 21 straight victories down the home stretch, the Cubs bring the pennant home to Chicago in 1935, storming past New York and the World Champion Cardinals. Manager Charlie Grimm gambles by benching himself in favor of Phil Cavaretta, who turns in an 82-RBI season. Other contributions come from MVP Gabby Hartnett, Billy Herman and left fielder Augie Galan, who leads the league with 22 steals and 133 runs scored.

P	Player	R	HR	RBI	SB	AVE
1B	Phil Cavarretta	85	8	82	4	.275
2B	Billy Herman	113	7	83	6	.341
SS	Billy Jurges	69	1	59	3	.241
3B	Stan Hack	75	4	64	14	.311
RF	Chuck Klein	71	21	73	4	.293
CF	Frank Demaree	60	2	66	6	.325
LF	Augie Galan	133	12	79	22	.314
C	Gabby Hartnett	67	13	91	1	.344
UT	Fred Lindstrom	49	3	62	1	.275
C	Ken O'Dea	30	6	38	0	.257
OF	Tuck Stainback	16	3	11	1	.255
OF	Kiki Cuyler	22	4	18	3	.268
IF	Woody English	11	2	8	1	.202

T	Pitcher	W-L	SV	SO	SH	ERA
R	Bill Lee	20-6	1	100	3	2.96
R	Lon Warneke	20-13	4	120	1	3.06
L	Larry French	17-10	2	90	4	2.96
R	Charlie Root	15-8	2	94	1	3.09
R	Roy Henshaw	13-5	1	53	3	3.27

April 16 - The Cubs nip the World Champion Cardinals 4-3 on Opening Day at Wrigley.

May 21 - Babe Ruth, playing out the string in Boston, launches one of just six home runs he'll hit this season, leading the Braves to a 4-1 win over Chicago. Tex Carleton is the victim.

June 12 - After manager Charlie Grimm blasts the team for their recent poor performance, the Cubs pummel the Phils 15-0. Phil Cavaretta leads the way with three hits, and Chuck Klein hits a three-run homer. Larry French is the winner.

June 15 - The Cubbies batter Brooklyn pitchers for 18 hits in a 9-4 win. Stan Hack goes 4-for-4; add in his three hits yesterday and he has seven straight safeties. Bill Lee gives up four earned runs for the victory.

June 25 - Led by Billy Herman's first-inning homer, the Cubs bury Carl Hubbell and the league-leading Giants 10-5.

July 3 - In a move to trim payroll, the Cubs release Kiki Cuyler. He'll sign with the Reds two days later.

August 21 - In a doubleheader at Baker Bowl, the Cubs score 12 runs in the sixth inning of a 19-5 nightcap win after losing the opener 13-12. Billy Herman ties a major league record by coming to bat 13 times in the twinbill, and Chuck Klein ties a major league mark by scoring eight runs in the two games.

September 2 - The Cubs split a pair with Cincinnati, putting them just 2 1/2 back of St. Louis. Lon Warneke beats Tony Freitas 3-1 in the opener; Bill Lee takes a 4-2 loss in the nightcap.

September 4 - Augie Galan rips two home runs, one a grand slam, as Larry French and the Cubs beat the Phillies 8-2 at Wrigley.

September 5 - Frank Demaree's 11th-inning single gives the Cubs a 3-2 win over the Phillies. Charlie Root is the winner.

September 6 - The Cubs make it three in a row vs. Philadelphia as Galan triples and scores the tying run in the eighth, then hits a leadoff homer in the 10th to win it.

September 7 - Chicago moves into second place, ahead of the Giants, as Bill Lee shuts out Philadelphia 4-0, sweeping the four-game set at Wrigley.

September 9 - After a Sunday rainout, the Cubs take a doubleheader from the Braves, 5-1 and 2-1, behind Larry French and Tex Carleton. Their sixth win in a row puts them a game out of first place.

September 10 - Freddie Lindstrom drives in a pair with a double and single as Chicago takes its seventh straight, 4-0 over Boston. Charlie Root hurls the shutout.

September 11 - Bill Lee coasts to a 15-3 victory over the Braves.

September 12 - The Cubs win their ninth in a row, 13-3 over the Dodgers. Augie

Chuck Klein

Galan leads the way with four hits and five RBIs.

September 13 - Friday the 13th brings luck for the Cubbies as Larry French shuts down Brooklyn 4-1. With St. Louis losing 13-10 to New York, Chicago is just percentage points behind the first-place Cards.

September 14 - The Cubs win a wild one, 18-14 over the Dodgers, for their 11th straight triumph. The Cubs, now in first place, use a reliever for the first time in 11 straight games.

September 16 - The Cubs beat the third-place Giants 8-3 behind Lon Warneke.

September 17 - New York starter Hal Schumacher, winning 2-1, leaves the game with a sore arm in the fifth and the Cubs rally against reliever Allyn Stout for a 5-3 win.

WORTH NOTING- The Cubs' World Series opponents in 1935 are the Detroit Tigers, managed by **Mickey Cochrane**. The Tigers finish with a 93-58 (.616) record, leading the American League in runs (919), average (.290), complete games (87), and shutouts (16).

P	PLAYER	R	HR	RBI	SB	BA
1B	Hank Greenberg	121	36	170	4	.328
2B	Charlie Gehringer	123	19	108	11	.330
SS	Billy Rogell	88	6	71	3	.275
3B	Marv Owen	52	2	71	1	.263
RF	Pete Fox	116	15	73	14	.321
CF	Jo-Jo White	82	2	32	19	.240
LF	Goose Goslin	88	9	109	5	.292
C	Mickey Cochrane	93	5	47	5	.319

T	PITCHER	W	L	SV	SH	ERA
R	Tommy Bridges	21	10	1	4	3.51
R	Schoolboy Rowe	19	13	3	6	3.68
R	Eldon Auker	18	7	0	2	3.83
R	General Crowder	16	10	0	2	4.26
L	Chief Hogsett	6	6	5	0	3.53

September 18 - The Cubs' 15th straight win is an easy one, 15-3 over the Giants before 30,000 fans at Wrigley.

September 19 - The Bruins whip New York ace Carl Hubbell, 6-1, sweeping the four-game set at Wrigley Field. Billy Herman has three hits. The Cubs' 16th win in a row is the most since the Dodgers won 15 in 1924.

September 22 - The Cubbies win their final home game of the season, 2-0 over Pittsburgh. Larry French is the victor.

WORTH NOTING - In 1935, Wrigley Field bleacher vendors made a small fortune by selling "Smile With Stan (Hack)" mirrors, which were then used to reflect the sun into the eyes of opposing batters.

Chicago's 18th straight win puts them three games over the Cardinals in the standings.

September 25 - It's showdown time in St. Louis as the defending-champion Cards host the Cubs. Lon Warneke allows just two hits as Chicago takes the opener 1-0, beating Paul Dean. Phil Cavaretta's homer onto the right field roof accounts for the game's only run. Rain will washout game two tomorrow.

September 27 - The Cubs clinch the National League pennant by beating Dizzy Dean and the Cards 6-2 in the first game of a twinbill. Chicago rocks Diz for 15 hits, four by Freddie Lindstrom. The Cubbies reach 100 wins with their 21st in a row, a 5-3 triumph for Roy Henshaw in the nightcap.

September28 - After winning 21 in a row, the Cubs finally lose, 7-5 to St. Louis. The win streak is baseball's longest without a tie since 1880.

September 29 - In a 2-1 loss to the Cards, left fielder Augie Galan plays in his 154th game of the year, ending the year without hitting into a double play - a major league record. He did, however, hit into a triple play in the 11th inning of an 8-4 loss to the Reds on April 21.

October 2 - World Series Game 1
The World Series gets off to a good start as Lon Warneke tosses a four-hit, 3-0 shutout at Navin Field in Detroit. The Cubs take a two-run lead in the first on a double by Augie Galan, a throwing error by starter Schoolboy Rowe, and a single by Gabby Hartnett. Frank Demaree homers in the ninth to cap the scoring.

October 3 - World Series Game 2
The Tigers reach Charlie Root for four runs in the first, sending him to the showers, and score three more in the fourth in an

8-3 win behind Tommy Bridges.

October 4 - World Series Game 3
Things look good for the Cubs as Detroit is severely weakened by the loss of slugger Hank Greenberg, who goes down with a broken wrist. The Cubs take a 3-1 lead into the top of the eighth inning but Bill Lee tires and allows four runs. The Cubs tie the game with two in the ninth, when Stan Hack, Chuck Klein, and Ken O'Dea single and Augie Galan drives Klein home with a sacrifice fly. But Freddie Lindstrom, subbing for Stan Hack at third base, commits an error that allows the winning run to score in the 11th and the Tigers take a two-games-to-one lead with a 6-5 win.

October 5 - World Series Game 4
Gabby Hartnett's homer in the second gives the Cubs an early 1-0 lead but the Tigers answer with a run in the top of the third and then fall behind 2-1 in the sixth on a dropped fly ball by Augie Galan and a throwing error by shortstop Billy Jurges. The Cubs rally with one out in the ninth but Stan Hack grounds into a game-ending double play.

October 6 - World Series Game 5
A Billy Herman triple and Chuck Klein homer give the Cubs a 2-0 lead in the third and Lon Warneke pitches five shutout innings in a 3-1 Cubs win, their first World Series victory at home in five contests. Bill Lee relieves Warneke in the sixth when the righthander suffers a hurt shoulder. The Bengals load the bases in the ninth but Lee gets Billy Rogell on a pop-up and Flea Clifton on a foul out.

October 7 - World Series Game 6
The Tigers take a tight 4-3 victory at home for their first World Championship. The two teams combine for 24 hits but strand 17 runners as Larry French and Tommy

Billy Herman

Bridge work out of trouble in nearly every frame. Billy Herman drives in all three Chicago runs with an RBI single in the third and a two-run homer in the fifth. The Tigers tie the game in the sixth and win it all in the ninth when Mickey Cochrane singles off Herman's glove with one out, moves to second on a groundout and scores on a bloop hit by Goose Goslin. The Cubs have a chance in the top of the frame when Stan Hack leads off with a triple. But Billy Jurges strikes out, French (batting for himself thanks to the ejection of the entire Chicago bench) taps a grounder back to the pitcher and Augie Galan flies out.

1936

Principle Owner and President: Phil Wrigley; **Manager:** Charlie Grimm; **Ballpark:** Wrigley Field; **Attendance:** 699,370; **Finish:** Second (87-67); **Recap:** Thanks to a 15-game winning streak in

June, the Cubs spend a month in first place, then give way to the Giants, the eventual pennant-winner. Charlie Grimm's boys finish tied with the Cardinals for second, five games back. The team is buoyed by the starting pitching, with Larry French and Bill Lee posting 18 wins apiece and Lon Warneke coming in at 16.

P	Player	R	HR	RBI	SB	AVE
1B	Phil Cavaretta	55	9	56	8	.273
3B	Billy Herman	101	5	93	5	.334
SS	Billy Jurges	51	1	42	4	.280
3B	Stan Hack	102	6	78	17	.298
RF	Frank Demaree	93	16	96	4	.350
CF	Augie Galan	74	8	81	16	.264
LF	Ethan Allen	47	3	39	12	.295
C	Gabby Hartnett	49	7	64	0	.307
C	Ken O'Dea	36	2	38	0	.307
OF	Johnny Gill	20	7	28	0	.253
IF	Woody English	33	0	20	1	.247

T	Pitcher	W-L	SV	SO	SH	ERA
L	Larry French	18-9	3	104	4	3.39
R	Bill Lee	18-11	1	102	4	3.30
R	Lon Warneke	16-13	1	113	4	3.45
R	Tex Carleton	14-10	1	88	4	3.65
R	Curt Davis	11-9	1	52	0	3.00

April 14 - Billy Herman leads the Cubs to a 12-7 Opening Day victory with three doubles and a homer over the Cardinals at Sportsman's Park.

April 17 - The Cubs lose their home opener to Cincinnati, 12-3.

May 28 - Cincinnati pitcher Al Hollingsworth drills a grand slam off Lon Warneke in the top of the second, giving himself a 4-0 lead, but surrenders seven runs in the bottom of the inning and takes an 11-5 loss.

June 21 - A 15-game Cubs winning streak is snapped by Brooklyn's Van Lingle Mungo, 6-4 at Ebbets Field.

June 28 - Larry French and Bill Lee combine for a twinbill twin-shutout, 3-0 and 6-0 over the Giants at the Polo Grounds. The Cubs take over first place.

July 7 - Four different Cubs score in a 4-3 National League win in the 1936 All-Star Game, held at Boston's National League Park. It's the NL's first All-Star win, having lost the previous three. Augie Galan hits a home run and Lon Warneke picks up the win in relief.

July 13 - Bill Lee beats New York's Carl Hubbell 1-0 and the Cubs regain first place. It's the last game Hubbell will lose this year.

July 25 - The Cubs pound the Phillies 17-4, pushing their NLlead to three games. Augie Galan and Ethan Allen homer, leading a 19-hit attack.

August 10 - The Cardinals beat the Cubs 7-3 at Sportsman's Park to take over first place. The game is interrupted by a fistfight between dueling pitchers - and former teammates - Tex Carleton and Dizzy Dean.

September 27 - At Sportsman's Park, Cards first baseman Johnny Mize is ejected in the seventh for arguing and is replaced by rookie Walter Alston. It's the future Hall of Fame manager's only major league appearance. Lon Warneke strikes him out in his only at-bat. Cubs win, 6-3.

October 8 - The Cubs trade Lon Warneke to the Cardinals for first baseman Ripper Collins and pitcher Roy Parmalee.

December 4 - The Cubs trade Woody English and reliever Roy Henshaw to the Dodgers for utility player Lonny Frey.

1937

Principle Owner and President: Phil Wrigley; **Manager:** Charlie Grimm;

Ballpark: Wrigley Field; **Attendance:** 895,020; **Finish:** Second (93-68); **Recap:** The Cubs come close again in 1937, leading the NLuntil early September, when the Giants slip by them. The club finishes second, three games back. The Cubs lead the league with a .287 team average, steered by Gabby Hartnett's .354, Billy Herman's .335 and Frank Demaree's .325. Bill Lee slips to 14-15, but Larry French and Tex Carleton post a couple of 16-win seasons.

P	PLAYER	R	HR	RBI	SB	AVE
1B	Ripper Collins	77	16	71	2	.274
2B	Billy Herman	106	8	65	2	.335
SS	Billy Jurges	53	1	65	2	.298
3B	Stan Hack	106	2	63	16	.297
RF	Frank Demaree	104	17	115	6	.324
CF	Joe Marty	41	5	44	3	.290
LF	Augie Galan	104	18	78	23	.252
C	Gabby Hartnett	47	12	82	0	.354
UT	Phil Cavaretta	43	5	56	7	.286
C	Ken O'Dea	31	4	32	1	.301
UT	Lonny Frey	33	1	22	6	.278
OF	Tuck Stainback	18	0	14	3	.231
UT	John Bottarini	3	1	7	0	.275

T	PITCHER	W-L	SV	SO	SH	ERA
R	Tex Carleton	16-8	0	105	4	3.16
L	Larry French	16-10	0	100	4	3.98
R	Bill Lee	14-15	3	108	2	3.54
R	Charlie Root	13-5	5	74	0	3.37
R	Curt Davis	10-5	1	32	0	4.06

April 6 - Phil Regan is born in Otsego, Michigan.

April 20 - The Cubs open the season with a 5-0 loss to Pittsburgh at Wrigley.

April 28 - During a 10-3 loss to Cincinnati, catcher Ernie "Schnozz" Lombardi lines a ball through the box that breaks Larry French's pitching hand.

May 4 - Ripper Collins, Joe Marty and John Bottarini hit homers in the eighth inning as the Cubs beat Philadelphia 14-7 at Baker Bowl.

WORTH QUOTING - "He came up again in the ninth. I was a little mad. I told my catcher, Tommy Padden, he was not good enough to hit my fastball. I came through with a fastball for strike one. I missed with the second. The next pitch I nodded to Tommy. I was going to throw the ball past Mr. Ruth. It was on the outside corner.

"As he went around third, Ruth gave me the hand sign meaning 'to hell with you.' He was better than me. He was the best that ever lived.

"That big joker hit it clear out of the ballpark for his third home run of the game. It was the longest homer I'd ever seen in baseball."

-Guy Bush, on giving up Babe Ruth's final home run, 1935

May 9 - New York's Carl Hubbell defeats Chicago 4-1 for his 20th straight win. King Carl matches the NL record, set by Rube Marquard, also a Giant, in 1911-12. Hubbell's streak will reach 24 before Brooklyn defeats him 10-3 on May 31.

June 25 - Augie Galan, a switch-hitter, becomes the first National Leaguer to hit home runs from both sides of the plate in a game, helping the Cubs thwack Brooklyn 11-2.

July 5 - Frank Demaree goes 6-for-8 in Chicago's 14-inning 13-12 victory over the Cardinals at Wrigley Field.

August 10 - Ripper Collins' season ends when he breaks his right ankle sliding into home plate during a 6-5 loss to Pittsburgh.

August 13 - Cincinnati second baseman Alex Kampouris is given a day in his honor by the Hellenic Societies of St. Louis, then commits three errors and fans twice in a 22-6 Cubs win. Backup catcher Ken O'Dea tallies four hits, four runs and four RBIs in the game.

1938

Principle Owner and President: Phil Wrigley; **Manager:** Charlie Grimm / Gabby Hartnett; **Ballpark:** Wrigley Field; **Attendance:** 951,640; **Finish:** First (89-63); **Recap:** When the club gets of to a slow start, manager Charlie Grimm is sacked, replaced by Gabby Hartnett. Under Hartnett, the team surges toward the top of the standings. On September 28, Hartnett smacks his ninth-inning game-winning "Homer in the Gloamin'" off Pittsburgh's Mace Adams which turns the tide for the Cubs and sends them to the World Series.

P	Player	R	HR	RBI	SB	AVE
1B	Ripper Collins	78	13	61	1	.267
2B	Billy Herman	86	1	56	3	.277
SS	Billy Jurges	53	1	47	3	.245
3B	Stan Hack	109	4	67	16	.320
RF	Frank Demaree	63	8	62	1	.273
CF	Carl Reynolds	59	3	677	9	.302
LF	Augie Galan	52	6	69	8	.286
C	Gabby Hartnett	40	10	59	1	.274
UT	Phil Cavaretta	29	1	28	4	.239
C	Ken O'Dea	22	3	33	1	.263
OF	Joe Marty	32	7	35	0	.243
UT	Tony Lazzeri	21	5	23	0	.267
UT	Bob Garbark	2	0	5	0	.259

T	Pitcher	W-L	SV	SO	SH	ERA
R	Bill Lee	22-9	2	121	9	2.66
R	Clay Bryant	19-11	2	135	3	3.10
R	Tex Carleton	10-9	0	80	0	5.41
L	Larry French	10-19	0	83	3	3.81
R	Charlie Root	8-7	8	70	0	2.85

April 16 - The Cubs acquire sore-armed St. Louis star Dizzy Dean for $200,000 and pitchers Curt Davis and Clyde Shoun. Dean suffered an injury when a line drive off the bat of Earl Averill in last summer's All-Star game struck him on the foot; coming back from the injury too soon, he changed his delivery to favor his leg and put added pressure on his shoulder. He'll win a few big games for the Cubs this season but his Hall of Fame career is virtually over.

WORTH QUOTING - "Baseball is too much of a sport to be a business and too much of a business to be a sport."
-Phil Wrigley

April 22 - The Cardinals defeat the home team 6-5 on Opening Day at Wrigley.

May 5 - The Cubbies push 12 runs across the plate in the eighth inning of a 21-2 bashing of Philadelphia. The Phillies' Hal Kelleher faces 16 batters and gives up all 12 runs in the inning, setting two single-inning NL records.

May 19 - Bill Lee tosses a five-hitter and scores the only run in a 1-0, 10-inning shutout of New York at the Polo Grounds.

May 23 - Lee pitches another gem, defeating the Braves 4-1 in Boston. The Braves score their run in the fourth; it'll be the only run Lee gives up in 47 innings dating back to May 19. He'll shut out the Pirates 5-0 on May 27, the Reds 3-0 on May 30, and the Braves 4-0 on June 3.

June 3 - Lee's third consecutive shutout puts the Cubs to within 1 1/2 games of the Giants. Lee will hurl four consecutive shutouts in September.

June 5 - The Cubs leap-frog the Giants into first place, defeating the Phils 7-1.

June 15 - Billy Williams is born in Whistler, Alabama.

July 20 - After sliding into third place, Phil Wrigley fires Charlie Grimm as manager, replacing him with catcher Gabby Hartnett.

September 22 - Bill Lee tosses his fourth straight shutout, tying the major league mark set by former Cubs Ed Reulbach

(1908) and Grover Cleveland Alexander (1911).

September 23 - The Cubs sweep a pair from Philadelphia to cut the Pirates' lead to two games.

September 27 - The season goes into the homestretch as the Cubs take on Pittsburgh at Wrigley with the Pirates 1 1/2 games on top. Dizzy Dean hurls eight shutout innings and Bill Lee finishes up in a 2-1 win.

September 28 - Gabby Hartnett's "homer in the gloamin'" against Pittsburgh's Mace Brown in the bottom of the ninth breaks a 5-5 tie and puts the Cubs in first place by a half game. The game was to be called for darkness after Hartnett's at-bat.

October 1 - A 10-2 victory over St. Louis at Sportsman's Park clinches the National League pennant for the Cubbies.

October 5 - World Series Game 1
Red Ruffing stifles the Chicago offense, scattering nine hits in a 3-1 Series-opening win at Wrigley. The Cubs blow a chance in the third, as Ripper Collins leads off the inning with a single and moves to second with two outs. Stan Hack lines an RBI single and moves to second on the throw home. Billy Herman singles again, but the over-aggressive Hack is thrown out at home plate by shortstop Frank Crosetti.

Unbeknownst to one another, double play legends Joe Tinker and Johnny Evers are invited to help broadcast the game over the radio - 33 games after the two had a falling out over a taxicab dispute. When they see each other, Tinker and Evers, who haven't spoke to each other since that day, hug and cry for some time before they are able to speak.

Gabby Hartnett's "Homer in the Gloamin'"

October 6 - World Series Game 2
The Wrigley curse haunts the Cubs again, as Stan Hack and Billy Jurges collide in the second inning on a routine grounder by Joe Gordon that rolls for a two-run double. The Cubs take a 3-2 lead on a two-run double by Joe Marty in the third, and Dizzy Dean holds the Yanks scoreless until the eighth, when Frankie Crosetti homers with a man on. Joe DiMaggio adds two more off Dean with a round-tripper in the ninth. The Yankees take a two-games-to-nothing lead with a 6-3 win.

October 8 - World Series Game 3
Back in New York, Clay Bryant holds the Yanks hitless until the bottom of the fifth, when Joe Gordon hits a two-out, two-run homer for a 2-1 New York lead. Gordon adds a two-run single in the sixth and the Yankees go on to win 5-2.

WORTH NOTING- The Cubs' World Series opponents in 1938 are the New York Yankees, managed by **Joe McCarthy**. The Yankees finish with a 99-53 (.651) record, leading the American League in runs (966), homers (174), stolen bases (91), and ERA(3.91).

P	PLAYER	R	HR	RBI	SB	BA
1B	Lou Gehrig	115	29	114	6	.295
2B	Joe Gordon	83	25	97	11	.255
SS	Frankie Crosetti	113	9	55	27	.263
3B	Red Rolfe	132	10	80	13	.311
RF	Tommy Henrich	109	22	91	6	.270
CF	Joe DiMaggio	129	32	140	6	.324
LF	George Selkirk	58	10	62	9	.254
C	Bill Dickey	84	27	115	3	.313

T	PITCHER	W	L	SV	SH	ERA
R	Red Ruffing	21	7	0	3	3.32
L	Lefty Gomez	18	12	0	4	3.35
R	Monte Pearson	16	7	0	1	3.97
R	Spud Chandler	14	5	0	2	4.03
R	Johnny Murphy	8	2	11	0	4.25

October 9 - World Series Game 4
The Cubs reach Red Ruffing for three runs this time, but the Yankees score eight off starter Bill Lee and five others to take the Series-ending fourth game, 8-3. Billy Herman grounds out to end the game, making the Yanks the first team to "three-peat."

December6 - The Cubs trade Billy Jurges, Frank Demaree, and Ken O'Dea to the Giants for shortstop Dick Bartell, catcher Gus Mancuso, and outfielder Hank Lieber in a blockbuster. Bartell, a Chicago native, will play just one season at Wrigley.

1939

Principle Owner and President: Phil Wrigley; **Manager:** Gabby Hartnett; **Ballpark:** Wrigley Field; **Attendance:** 726,663; **Finish:** Fourth (84-70); **Recap:** The Cubs slip to fourth in 1939, despite 19 wins from Bill Lee and a 24-homer season from center fielder Hank Leiber. Early in the season, the Cubs acquire righthander Claude Passeau from the Phillies for Joe Marty and pitchers Ray Harrell and Kirby Higbe. Passeau responds with a 13-win season and will anchor the rotation for six years.

P	PLAYER	R	HR	RBI	SB	AVE
1B	Rip Russell	55	9	79	2	.273
2B	Billy Herman	111	7	70	9	.307
SS	Dick Bartell	37	3	34	6	.238
3B	Stan Hack	112	8	56	17	.298
RF	Jim Gleeson	43	4	45	7	.223
CF	Hank Leiber	65	24	88	1	.310
LF	Augie Galan	104	6	71	8	.304
C	Gabby Hartnett	36	12	59	0	.278
OF	Carl Reynolds	33	4	44	5	.246
C	Gus Mancuso	17	2	17	0	.231
OF	Bill Nicholson	37	5	38	0	.295
IF	Bobby Mattick	16	0	23	1	.287
C	Bob Garbark	1	0	0	0	.143

T	PITCHER	W-L	SV	SO	SH	ERA
R	Bill Lee	19-15	0	105	1	3.45
L	Larry French	15-8	1	98	2	3.29
R	Claude Passeau	13-9	3	108	1	3.05
R	Vance Page	7-7	1	43	1	3.88
R	Dizzy Dean	6-4	0	27	2	3.38

April 2 - The Los Angeles Angels, the Cubs' AAA Pacific Coast League team, launch a record 19-game winning streak with a 7-2 victory over restaurateur Bob Cobb's Hollywood Stars.

April 24 - The Cubs defeat the Pirates 6-2 on Opening Day at Wrigley Field.

April 27 - The Reds score eight runs in the eighth to defeat the Cubs 11-3.

April 28 - The Cubs blow another one, this time in the ninth when Cincinnati's Ival Goodman launches a three-run homer for a 7-6 Reds win.

May 8 - Phil Cavaretta breaks his leg sliding into base during a 4-2 Cubs victory at the Polo Grounds. He'll be out until July 25 and will appear in just seven more games this year.

May 17 - The Cubs and Dodgers battle to a 19-inning, 9-9 tie at Wrigley.

May 29 - The Cubs trade Kirby Higbe, Joe Marty and Ray Harrell for Philadelphia righthander Claude Passeau. Passeau will win 20 games for the Cubbies next season.

May 30 - Larry French and Vance Page toss 6-0 and 2-0 shutouts as the Cubs take two from Cincinnati at Crosley Field.

June 12 - Former Cub Grover Cleveland Alexander is among the first inductees at the Baseball Hall of Fame at Cooperstown, New York. Alexander joins Babe Ruth, Ty Cobb, Honus Wagner, Walter Johnson, Nap Lajoie, George Sisler, Eddie Collins, Tris Speaker, Cy Young and Connie Mack in the Hall.

June 18 - Dizzy Dean looks like the Diz of old in a 1-0 shutout of Brooklyn. Gabby Hartnett's homer accounts for the only run.

September17 - A yellow-dyed ball is used in the first game of a Wrigley twinbill with Brooklyn. The Dodgers take both games, 10-4 and 3-2.

December 6 - The Cubs trade Dick Bartell to the Detroit Tigers for shortstop Billy Rogell. Rogell, who injured his arm playing handball in 1938, will bat just .136 for Chicago in his final season.

December8 - The Cubs acquire catcher Al Todd from the Dodgers for Gus Mancuso and rookie pitcher Newt Kimball.

1940

Principle Owner and President: Phil Wrigley; **Manager:** Gabby Hartnett; **Ballpark:** Wrigley Field; **Attendance:** 534,878; **Finish:** Fifth (75-79); **Recap:** The Cubs finish 25 1/2 games back in 1940, the first of four straight losing seasons. Their slip to fifth ends a string of 14 consecutive first-division finishes. Attendance drops to 534,878, the lowest turnout since 1921. Those who do darken Wrigley's doorstep are thrilled, at least, by the power exploits of outfielder Bill "Swish" Nicholson and the steady hitting of Stan Hack. Claude Passeau turns in his only 20-win season, going 20-13.

P	PLAYER	R	HR	RBI	SB	AVE
1B	Phil Cavaretta	34	2	22	3	.280
2B	Billy Herman	77	5	57	1	.292
SS	Bobby Mattick	30	0	33	5	.218
3B	Stan Hack	101	8	40	21	.317
RF	Bill Nicholson	78	25	98	2	.297
CF	Hank Leiber	68	17	86	1	.302
LF	Jim Gleeson	76	5	61	4	.313
C	Al Todd	31	6	42	1	.255
OF	Dom Dallessandro	33	1	36	4	.268
IF	Rip Russell	15	5	33	1	.247
UT	Augie Galan	33	3	22	9	.230
IF	Zeke Bonura	20	4	20	1	.264
C	Bob Collins	11	1	14	4	.208

T	PITCHER	W-L	SV	SO	SH	ERA
R	Claude Passeau	20-13	5	124	4	2.50
L	Larry French	14-14	2	107	3	3.29
L	Vern Olsen	13-9	0	71	4	2.97
R	Bill Lee	9-17	0	70	1	5.03
L	Ken Raffensberger	7-9	3	55	0	3.37

February 25 - Ron Santo is born in Seattle, Washington.

March 22 - Dick Ellsworth is born in Lusk, Wyoming.

April 19 - Bill Lee tosses an Opening Day shutout, blanking the Cards at Wrigley 5-0. It's his only shutout of the year.

Stan Hack

May 17 - A line drive off the bat of Hank Lieber strikes Stan Hack in the head during a 4-0 win at the Polo Grounds. Hack, who is on third base, suffers a concussion and is removed from the field on a stretcher. Claude Passeau tosses a two-hitter, both singles by the Giants' Joe Moore.

June 1 - During a 4-3 win over the Dodgers at Wrigley, rookie shortstop Pee Wee Reese, filling in for veteran Leo Durocher, is beaned by Chicago pitcher Jake Mooty.

June 3 - Future Hall of Famer Dizzy Dean is sent to Tulsa of the Texas League after clearing waivers. Dean has undergone dozens of treatments, including teeth extraction, but has not been able to rejuvenate his sore arm. The Cubs are hoping that the Texas sun will help. Dean will pitch fairly well but will be more valuable at the box office.

June 25 - The Cubs score five runs in the top of the 13th to beat the Dodgers 8-3 at Ebbets Field. Claude Passeau is the winner with four innings of relief.

August 15 - Passeau keeps rolling, hurling a five-hit 1-0 shutout over the Reds. Passeau, on his way to a 20-win season, doesn't allow a runner past first after the first inning.

August 17 - Stan Hack drills a single in the 13th to give the Cubs a 6-5 win over the Pirates. It's Hack's fourth hit of the game. Claude Passeau, the fifth Chicago pitcher of the game, gets the win.

August 21 - The Phils stun the Cubs with a 7-5 win as rookie pitcher Charlie Frye belts a two-run pinch homer to break the tie.

August 28 - The Cubs release dead-armed infielder Billy Rogell and recall Dizzy Dean from Tulsa.

November 17 - Jimmie Wilson, who managed the Phillies in the 1930s and was a backup catcher for the World Champion Reds this season, becomes the Cubs' new manager, replacing Gabby Hartnett.

December 4 - The Cubs trade shortstop Bobby Mattlick and outfielder Jim Gleeson to the Reds for shortstop Billy Myers. Myers will bounce from the majors to the minors next season. By 1942 he'll be out of baseball.

1941

Principle Owner and President: Phil Wrigley; **Manager:** Jimmie Wilson; **Ballpark:** Wrigley Field; **Attendance:** 545,159; **Finish:** Sixth (70-84); **Recap:** Wrigley appoints Chicago sportswriter Jim Gallagher his new general manager.

Gallagher's first move is not a popular one, sending Billy Herman to the Dodgers for infielder Johnny Hudson, outfielder Charlie Gilbert, and $65,000. It's the first of several deals between Gallagher and Brooklyn's Larry MacPhail. The lethargic Cubs finish sixth, led by Bill Nicholson's 26 homers and 98 RBIs and Stan Hack's league-leading 186 hits.

P	Player	R	HR	RBI	SB	AVE
1B	Babe Dahlgren	50	16	59	2	.281
2B	Lou Stringer	59	5	53	3	.246
SS	Bobby Sturgeon	45	0	25	5	.245
3B	Stan Hack	111	7	45	10	.317
RF	Bill Nicholson	74	26	98	1	.254
CF	Phil Cavaretta	46	6	40	2	.286
LF	Dom Dallessandro	73	6	85	3	.272
C	Clyde McCullough	41	9	53	5	.227
OF	Augie Galan	18	1	13	0	.208
OF	Lou Novikoff	22	5	24	0	.241
UT	Hank Leiber	20	7	25	0	.216
C	Bob Scheffing	9	1	20	2	.242
IF	Johnny Hudson	8	0	6	3	.202

T	Pitcher	W-L	SV	SO	SH	ERA
R	Claude Passeau	14-14	0	80	3	3.35
L	Vern Olsen	10-8	1	73	2	3.15
R	Charlie Root	8-7	0	46	0	5.38
R	Jake Mooty	8-9	4	45	1	3.35
R	Bill Lee	8-14	1	62	0	3.77

January 8 - Stan Hack is named to The Sporting News' 1940 Major League All-Star Team. Hack joins Hank Greenberg (LF), Joe DiMaggio (CF), Ted Williams (RF), Frank McCormick (1B), Joe Gordon (2B), Luke Appling (SS), Harry Danning (C), and Bob Feller, Bucky Walters, and Paul Derringer (P).

April 15 - Rookie Lou Stringer, starting at shortstop, makes four errors in his Major League debut but the Cubs win the season opener at Wrigley 7-4 behind Claude Passeau. Bill Nicholson's home run is the difference in the game.

April 26 - The Cubs again make baseball history, installing an organ at the ballpark. Roy Nelson debuts at the keyboard. The home team loses, however, 6-2 to the Cardinals.

May 6 - The Cubs trade slumping Billy Herman to the Dodgers for outfielder Charlie Gilbert, infielder Johnny Hudson, and $65,000. The veteran Herman is batting just .194 but will go 4-for-4 in his debut with Brooklyn. Lou Stringer will move to second base for Chicago.

May 7 - Bill Lee homers twice in an 11-2 rout of the Phillies at Baker Bowl. Lee also picks up the victory.

May 14 - Dizzy Dean is given his release. Ol' Diz pitched one inning this season, giving up three runs.

May 19 - Bill Lee, who seems to be having a better offensive year than on the mound, hits a grand slam off Hugh Casey in a nine-run second inning of a 14-1 win over Brooklyn at home. Dodgers skipper Leo Durocher protests the game, claiming that the mound at Wrigley is several inches over the 15-inch height limit; the umpires suggest that Casey pitch several inches in front of the rubber, but it doesn't help.

Durocher then protests the game a second time, claiming that the Cubs are over their 25-man limit. The National League finds that Chicago is, indeed, over its limit but since it didn't use every single player in today's game, the protest will be disallowed. The Cubs will be fined $500, however.

WORTH QUOTING - "All ballplayers want to wind up their careers with the Cubs, Giants or Yankees...they just can't help it."

-Dizzy Dean, 1939

WORTH NOTING - Outfielder Lou Novikoff's minor league slugging feats of the late 1930s never translated into the major leagues. Novikoff, ballyhooed as the next Babe Ruth, was unable to cope with major league pitching and had a neurotic fear of the ivy that grew along the Wrigley Field wall. His refusal to go after fly balls close to the fence cost the Cubs dearly and Novikoff eventually returned to the minors.

July 8 - Boston slugger Ted Williams homers off Claude Passeau to lead the American League to a 7-5 win in the All-Star Game at Detroit's Briggs Stadium.

August 27 - Charlie Root, having a miserable season at age 42, wins his 200th game using his arm and then his bat with a clutch single in the ninth inning to beat the Reds 6-4. Root goes the distance for the win.

1942

Principle Owner and President: Phil Wrigley; **Manager:** Jimmie Wilson; **Ballpark:** Wrigley Field; **Attendance:** 590,972; **Finish:** Sixth (70-84); **Recap:** The majors won't be hit hard by the war effort until after the 1942 season, but Cubs fans barely notice as the team finishes sixth again, 30 games behind St. Louis. Claude Passeau's 19-wins saves the team from a cellar finish, with Bill Lee dropping to 13-13 and the rest of the starting staff going 34-56.

P	PLAYER	R	HR	RBI	SB	AVE
1B	Phil Cavaretta	59	3	54	7	.270
2B	Lou Stringer	45	9	41	3	.236
SS	Lennie Merullo	53	2	37	14	.256
3B	Stan Hack	91	6	39	9	.300
RF	Bill Nicholson	83	21	78	8	.294
CF	Dom Dellessandro	30	4	43	4	.261
LF	Lou Novikoff	48	7	64	3	.300
C	Clyde McCullough	39	5	31	7	.282
UT	Rip Russell	32	8	41	0	.242
OF	Charlie Gilbert	18	0	7	1	.184
UT	Jimmie Foxx	25	3	19	1	.205
IF	Bobby Sturgeon	8	0	7	2	.247
C	Chico Hernandez	6	0	7	0	.229

T	PITCHER	W-L	SV	SO	SH	ERA
R	Claude Passeau	19-14	0	89	3	2.69
R	Bill Lee	13-13	0	75	1	3.85
R	Hi Bithorn	9-14	2	65	0	3.68
L	Vern Olsen	6-9	1	46	1	4.50
R	Bill Fleming	5-6	2	59	2	3.02

January 4 - Former Cub Rogers Hornsby is elected to the Baseball Hall of Fame. Frank Chance misses the cut.

January 15 - The Cubs, who had been preparing to install lights at Wrigley Field because of a wartime dropoff of day attendance, decide against it because of the military needs for the material.

April 17 - The Cubs defeat Cincinnati 3-2 on Opening Day at Wrigley.

May 12 - Rookie Ed Hanyzewski wins his only game of the year as the Cubs beat the Braves 9-8.

May 19 - The Cubs sell Babe Dahlgren to the Dodgers, a day after getting him back from the Browns. Chicago had sent him to St. Louis a week earlier on condition that he could still hit; after a couple of pinch-hitting appearances the Browns decided he could not.

May 24 - Satchel Paige beats the Dizzy Dean All-Stars, a collection of major league castaways, 3-1 at Wrigley Field before 29,000 fans. A week later Commissioner Landis will prohibit a scheduled July 4th game at Griffith Stadium because the matchup between Negro League and Major League veterans consistently outdraw MLgames.

June 1 - The Cubs pick up legendary slugger Jimmie Foxx on waivers from the Red Sox. Foxx, who hit 58 home runs for the Athletics in 1932, was batting .270 with five homers with Boston; he'll hit .205 for Chicago in a limited role.

Randy Hundley is born in Martinsville, Virginia.

July 26 - Clyde McCullough hits three homers but the Cubs lose 4-3 to the Phillies at Shibe Park.

August 9 - The Cubs win a wild one at Cincinnati, 10-8 in 18 innings. Chicago takes the lead in the ninth, 10th, and 12th innings but the Reds come back to tie it in every frame. Stan Hack leads the way with five hits and three runs. The Cubs strand 23 runners, the Reds strand 21 - a major league record until 1974. Each team uses six pitchers, also a major league record.

August 22 - Chicago turns a triple play in the top of the 11th and Bill Nicholson homers in the bottom of the inning to beat the Reds 5-4 at Wrigley.

August 23 - Claude Passeau and Lon Warneke toss a pair of 3-0 shutouts as the Cubs sweep a twinbill with the Reds.

September 13 - Shortstop Lennie Merullo makes a record four errors in the second inning of a 12-8 victory over the Braves.

1943

Principle Owner and President: Phil Wrigley; **Manager:** Jimmie Wilson; **Ballpark:** Wrigley Field; **Attendance:** 508,247; **Finish:** Fifth (74-79); **Recap:** Bill Nicholson leads the NLin both homers (29) and RBIs (128) for the first of two straight years but Cubs fans haven't much more to cheer about in 1943. The team does have a few bright spots this season, with rookie Eddie Stanky solidifying the second base position, coaxing 92 walks and scoring 92 runs despite batting .245, and Hi Bithorn putting together an 18-win season. Bithorn, Puerto Rico's first big-league baseball hero, posts a league-high seven shutouts. Rookie outfielder Andy Pafko, who will later become one of Chicago's most popular players, breaks into the lineup in September and hits .379.

Due to wartime travel restrictions, the Cubs are forced to abandon their spring training site of Catalina Island, California, for French Lick, Indiana.

WORTH NOTING - Rookie catcher Paul Gillespie hit a home run in his first major league at-bat in 1942 but only five more in 89 career games.

P	PLAYER	R	HR	RBI	SB	AVE
1B	Phil Cavaretta	93	8	73	3	.291
2B	Eddie Stanky	92	0	47	4	.245
SS	Lennie Merullo	37	1	25	7	.254
3B	Stan Hack	78	3	35	5	.289
RF	Bill Nicholson	95	29	128	4	.309
CF	Peanuts Lowrey	59	1	63	13	.292
LF	Ival Goodman	31	3	45	4	.320
C	Clyde McCullough	20	2	23	6	.237
OF	Dom Dallessandro	13	1	31	1	.222
OF	Lou Novikoff	22	0	28	0	.279
IF	Stu Martin	13	0	5	1	.220
C	Chico Hernandez	10	0	9	0	.270
UT	Mickey Livingston	11	4	16	1	.261

T	PITCHER	W-L	SV	SO	SH	ERA
R	Hi Bithorn	18-12	2	86	7	2.59
R	Claude Passeau	15-12	1	93	1	2.91
R	Paul Derringer	10-14	3	75	2	3.57
R	Hank Wyse	9-7	5	45	2	2.94
R	Ed Hanyzewski	8-7	0	55	0	2.56

February 2 - The Cubs announce they are returning to their old flannel jerseys after experimenting with vests worn over knit jerseys. The club makes the change because of cash savings rather than aesthetics.

Phil Cavarretta

February 20 - Cubs owner Phil Wrigley and Dodgers executive Branch Rickey found the All-American Girls Softball League, formed as a backup in case the government shuts down baseball during wartime. The league will later become the All-American Girls Baseball League, with a pitching distance of 40 feet and bases 68 feet apart. For now, the league will operate with clubs around the Chicago area.

April 22 - The Cubs take the season opener at Wrigley, 4-3 over the Pirates.

May 30 - Bill Nicholson hits the first Cubs homer in 32 games, a two-run shot during a 5-1 win over the Braves.

September 24 - The smallest crowd in Wrigley Field history, 314, watch rookie Andy Pafko drive in four runs with a double and a single in his major league debut as the Cubs beat the Phillies 7-4. The game is called in the fifth because of rain.

October 7 - Jose Cardenal is born in Matanzas, Cuba.

December13 - Ferguson Jenkins is born in Chatham, Ontario, Canada.

1944

Principle Owner and President: Phil Wrigley; **Manager:** Jimmie Wilson / Roy Johnson / Charlie Grimm; **Ballpark:** Wrigley Field; **Attendance:** 640,110; **Finish:** Fourth (75-79); **Recap:** When the Cubs open the season with a 13-game losing streak, manager Jimmie Wilson is fired in favor of Charlie Grimm, who has been managing at the team's American Association Milwaukee franchise. Grimm brings the Cubs in fourth, the highest spot in the standings since 1939. Bill Nicholson's 33 homers and 122 RBIs pace the NL, as does his 116 runs scored, and Phil Cavaretta breaks through with a .321 mark and 106 runs.

P	PLAYER	R	HR	RBI	SB	AVE
1B	Phil Cavaretta	106	5	82	4	.321
2B	Don Johnson	50	2	71	8	.278
SS	Lennie Merullo	20	1	16	3	.212
3B	Stan Hack	65	3	32	5	.282
RF	Bill Nicholson	116	33	122	3	.287
CF	Andy Pafko	47	6	62	2	.269
LF	Dom Dallessandro	53	8	74	1	.305
C	Dewey Williams	23	0	27	2	.240
IF	Roy Hughes	86	1	28	16	.287
OF	Lou Novikoff	15	3	19	1	.281
OF	Ival Goodman	24	1	16	0	.262
IF	Bill Schuster	14	1	14	4	.221
C	Bill Holm	10	0	6	1	.136

T	PITCHER	W-L	SV	SO	SH	ERA
R	Hank Wyse	16-15	1	86	3	3.15
R	Claude Passeau	15-9	3	89	2	2.89
L	Bob Chipman	9-9	2	41	1	3.49
R	Bill Fleming	9-10	0	42	1	3.13
R	Hy Vandenberg	7-4	2	54	0	3.64

April 20 - Rookie Mike Kosman, sent in to

pinch-run for Steve Mesner at third base, is thrown out at the plate in a 2-1 Cubs loss at Crosley Field. Kosman will never appear in another major league box score.

April 23 - The Cardinals spoil Opening Day at Wrigley Field, 4-0.

May 5 - After a 1-9 start, Jimmie Wilson is fired as Cubs manager. Roy Johnson will take over until the team finds a replacement.

May 7 - Charlie Grimm, skipper of the AA Milwaukee Brewers, is reinstated as Cubs manager. Casey Stengel is named manager in Milwaukee.

A 6-5 loss to the Pirates is the 12th in a row for Chicago, ruining Grimm's debut.

May 11 - After Grimm gives a four-leaf clover to starting pitcher Eddie Hanyzewski, the Cubs beat the Phils to snap their 13-game losing streak. Hanyzewski wears the lucky charm under his hat.

June 8 - The Cubs score three runs on one wild pitch by Pittsburgh rookie Cookie Cuccurullo and win 10-6 at Forbes Field.

The Cubs swap reserve infielder Eddie Stanky for Dodgers pitcher Bob Chipman.

July 11 - Phil Cavaretta sets an All-Star Game record by reaching base five straight times with a triple, single and three walks. The National League triumphs 7-1.

July 23 - After hitting four consecutive homers in a doubleheader with the Giants, Bill Nicholson is walked with the bases loaded in the seventh inning of game two. The Cubs lose the nightcap 12-10 after winning the opener 7-4. Nicholson has now hit six homers in 48 hours (including one on the 21st and one yesterday).

WORTH NOTING - In 1943, Phil Wrigley organized the All-American Girls Professional Baseball League due to the possibility of major league baseball being shut down during the war. Baseball was not shut down, but the women's league lasted until 1954. The AAGPBL included the Rockford Peaches, Chicago Colleens, Kalamazoo Lassies, Fort Wayne Daisies, Racine Belles, South Bend Blue Sox, and Grand Rapids Chicks. Former major leaguers Jimmie Foxx and Max Carey were among the team managers.

August 3 - Sixteen-year-old Tommy Brown plays shortstop for Brooklyn during a doubleheader sweep by the Cubs at Ebbets Field. He goes 1-for-8 with a double and scores a run.

September 26 - The Cubs pummel the Phillies 15-0 in Philadelphia. Hank Wyse tosses a four-hitter. Lou Novikoff hits his last major league homer.

December 21 - Cardinals shortstop Marty Marion, who hit just .267 for the World Champs, edges Bill Nicholson by one vote in NL MVPvoting.

1945

Principle Owner and President: Phil Wrigley; **Manager:** Charlie Grimm; **Ballpark:** Wrigley Field; **Attendance:** 1,036,386; **Finish:** First (96-56); **Recap:** The Cubs take the NL lead on July 8th for good, winning the pennant despite losing 16 of 22 games to the Cardinals. Phil Cavaretta's .355 season earns him an MVP

WORTH NOTING - Bill Nicholson is the last National Leaguer to hit more than half of his team's home runs (1943).

WORTH NOTING - Bill Nicholson is one of just two players in history to lead the NLin home runs and RBIs in two consecutive seasons (1943-44). Mike Schmidt is the other (1980-81).

nod, and Andy Pafko finishes right behind him, driving in 110 runs and batting .298. Hank Borowy, purchased from the Yankees for $97,000 in July, goes 11-2 down the stretch and Hank Wyse turns in 22 victories.

P	PLAYER	R	HR	RBI	SB	AVE
1B	Phil Cavaretta	94	6	97	5	.355
2B	Don Johnson	94	2	58	9	.302
SS	Lennie Merullo	40	2	37	7	.239
3B	Stan Hack	110	2	43	12	.323
RF	Bill Nicholson	82	13	88	4	.243
CF	Andy Pafko	64	12	110	5	.298
LF	Peanuts Lowrey	72	7	89	11	.283
C	Mickey Livingston	19	2	23	2	.254
UT	Paul Gillespie	12	3	25	2	.288
IF	Roy Hughes	34	0	8	6	.261
IF	Heinz Becker	25	2	27	0	.286
C	Dewey Williams	16	2	5	0	.280
T	**PITCHER**	**W-L**	**SV**	**SO**	**SH**	**ERA**
R	Hank Wyse	22-10	0	77	2	2.69
R	Claude Passeau	17-9	1	98	5	2.46
R	Paul Derringer	16-11	4	86	1	3.45
L	Ray Prim	13-8	2	88	2	2.40
R	Hank Borowy	11-2	1	47	1	2.14

January 10 - Frank Chance is snubbed once again in Hall of Fame voting. The Hall fails to induct anyone this year, not even pitching legends Ed Walsh or Rube Waddell, who also appear on the ballot.

March 5 - Because of wartime travel restrictions, the Cubs open spring training in Indiana.

WORTH NOTING - In 1945, Hank Borowy became the third pitcher this century to win 20 games in a season split between two major leagues.

April 17 - The Cubs defeat the defending champion Cards, 3-2 on Opening Day at Wrigley Field.

April 27 - The Cubs, enjoying first place for the first time in years, win their fifth straight, as Paul Derringer beats Pittsburgh 7-3.

April 28 - Hank Wyse takes a no-hitter into the eighth inning before giving up a single by Bill Salkeld in a 6-0 one-hitter over the Pirates.

July 3 - The Cubs' infield scores a record 16 runs in a 24-2 win over Boston at Braves Field. Phil Cavaretta, Don Johnson, and Stan Hack tally five apiece.

July 8 - The Cubs take the National League lead for good with a doubleheader sweep of the Phillies, 12-6 and 9-2.

July 12 - Hank Wyse snaps Tommy Holmes' 37-game hitting streak, a modern NL record at the time, in a 6-1 Cubs win over Boston.

July 27 - Chicago purchases pitcher Hank Borowy from the Yankees for $97,500. Borowy, who was 10-5 with the Yanks, was put on waivers to solve a roster problem. Borowy will go 11-2 for the Cubs down the stretch.

August 5 - The Cubs pummel Cincinnati pitching for 22 hits in a 12-5 win in the opener of a twinbill at Crosley Field. Chicago also takes the nightcap, 2-1 behind Claude Passeau. The Cubs have now won 17 of their last 18.

August 11 - Claude Passeau takes a no-hitter into the eighth before giving up a pair of singles, in an 8-0 victory at Braves Field.

August 12 - Phil Caverretta is sidelined for a month after colliding with Philadelphia baserunner Fred Daniels at first base. The Cubs sweep a doubleheader, 4-3 and 12-6.

August 15 - The Cubs continue their onslaught of wartime pitching, tallying 19 hits, including two homers by utility player Paul Gillespie, in a 20-6 romp over the Dodgers. Chicago scores eight runs in the fourth inning before a single out is recorded. Hank Borowy gets the win.

August 30 - Stan Hack singles for his 2,000th hit off Preacher Roe in the first inning of a 6-4 loss to Pittsburgh. Hack is the 82nd player in history to collect 2,000 hits.

September 29 - Hank Borowy pitches the Cubs to a NL-clinching 4-3 win over the Pirates in the first game of a twinbill.

October 3 - World Series Game 1
The Cubs and Tigers face each other for the fourth time in the World Series, with Chicago taking Game One 9-0, bombing Hal Newhouser for four runs in the first and three runs in the third. Bill Nicholson provides the big blow with a two-out triple in the first after Newhouser walks Andy Pafko to pitch to him. Hank Borowy hurls a six-hit shutout, stranding 10 runners.

October 4 - World Series Game 2
Swish Nicholson's two-out single provides the only scoring for the Cubs in a 4-1 loss to Virgil Trucks at Briggs Stadium. Veteran slugger Hank Greenberg, who has just returned from military duty, slams a three-run homer off Hank Wyse in the fifth.

October 5 - World Series Game 3
Claude Passeau tosses the second one-hitter in World Series history, beating the Tigers 3-0 in Detroit. First baseman Rudy York singles in the second for the Bengals' only safety. Passeau faces just 28 batters, one over the minimum, and retires the last 11 batters. Bill Nicholson knocks in his fifth run of the Series with a single in the fourth.

Bill "Swish"Nicholson

October 6 - World Series Game 4
The Cubs, who lead two games to one, return to Wrigley Field for Game 4. Once again, the Cubs find that Wrigley is a tough place to play during the World Series as Dizzy Trout scotches them on five hits in a

WORTH NOTING - Cub fan William Sianis, angry after Wrigley Field refuses to allow him to bring his billy goat into a 1945 World Series game, put a hex on the club. The team has not been in a World Series since. Sianis's Billy Goat Tavern was the model for a series of *Satuday Night Live* skits, notably featuring Chicago native George Wendt of *Cheers*.

WORTH NOTING- The Cubs' World Series opponents in 1945 are the Detroit Tigers, managed by **Steve O'Neill**. The Tigers finish with a 88-65 (.545) record, leading the American League in doubles (227) saves (16), and shutouts (19).

P	PLAYER	R	HR	RBI	SB	BA
1B	Rudy York	71	18	87	6	.264
2B	Eddie Mayo	71	10	54	7	.285
SS	Skeeter Webb	43	0	21	8	.199
3B	Bob Maier	58	1	34	7	.263
RF	Roy Cullenbine	80	18	93	2	277
CF	Doc Cramer	62	6	58	2	.275
LF	Jimmy Outlaw	56	0	34	6	.271
C	Bob Swift	19	0	24	1	.233

T	PITCHER	W	L	SV	SH	ERA
L	Hal Newhouser	25	9	2	8	1.81
R	Dizzy Trout	18	15	2	4	3.15
R	Al Benton	13	8	3	5	2.02
L	Stubby Overmire	9	9	4	0	3.89
R	George Caster	5	1	2	0	3.88

4-1 win. Ray Prim retires the first 10 batters before allowing a walk, two singles, and a double with one out. The Cubs score their only run in the sixth on an error by Rudy York.

October 7 - World Series Game 5
The Cubs lose the tenth of their last 11 World Series games at home as the Tigers roll, 8-4 behind Hal Newhouser. The Tigers erupt for four runs in the sixth off Hank Borowy and add two in the ninth when a line drive off the bat of Roy Cullenbine is lost in the Wrigley vines by Andy Pafko.

October 8 - World Series Game 6
The Cubs beat the Tigers 8-7 in 12 innings to tie the Series at three games apiece. At 3 1/2 hours, it's the longest World Series game ever played so far. Chicago scores four in the fourth on a pair of RBI singles by Stan Hack and Phil Cavarretta. Cruising along at 4-1, Claude Passeau tries to one-hand a shot up the middle and tears the nail on the middle finger of his pitching hand. He struggles through another inning before being lifted with a 5-2 lead with two outs in the seventh. Hank Wyse gives up another run before retiring the Tigers. The Cubs score two more in the bottom of the frame on a single and bases-loaded walk, making it 7-3. The Tigers rally with four in the eighth on a walk, double, error, single, sacrifice fly, and Hank Greenberg home run. Hank Borowy, in relief, holds the Tigers scoreless until the bottom of the 12th when a two-out Stan Hack double pushes across the winning run.

October 10 - World Series Game 7
The Tigers virtually end the series in the first inning, bombing Hank Borowy and Paul Derringer with five runs on three singles, two walks and a bases-clearing double by catcher Paul Richards. Detroit cruises to a 9-3 title-clinching victory. Hal Newhouser goes the distance for the win.

November 3 - Ken Holtzman is born in St. Louis, Missouri.

November 20 - Rick Monday is born in Batesville, Arkansas.

December 6 - Larry Bowa is born in Sacramento, California.

1946

Principle Owner and President: Phil Wrigley; **Manager:** Charlie Grimm; **Ballpark:** Wrigley Field; **Attendance:** 1,342,970; **Finish:** Third (82-71); **Recap:** The Cubs finish third, 14 1/2 games behind the Cardinals. It'll be 21 years before they finish even that high again. Claude Passeau stumbles to 9-8 and Hank Borowy slumps to 12-10.

P	PLAYER	R	HR	RBI	SB	AVE
1B	Eddie Waitkus	50	4	55	3	.304
2B	Don Johnson	37	1	19	6	.242
SS	Billy Jurges	26	0	17	3	.222
3B	Stan Hack	55	0	26	3	.285
RF	Phil Cavaretta	89	8	78	2	.294
CF	Peanuts Lowrey	75	4	54	10	.257
LF	Marv Rickert	44	7	47	3	.263
C	Clyde McCullough	38	4	34	2	.287
OF	Bill Nicholson	36	8	41	1	.220
IF	Bobby Sturgeon	26	1	21	0	.296
IF	Lou Stringer	26	3	19	0	.244
C	Mickey Livingston	14	2	20	0	.256
T	**PITCHER**	**W-L**	**SV**	**SO**	**SH**	**ERA**
R	Hank Wyse	14-12	1	52	2	2.69
R	Hank Borowy	12-10	0	95	1	3.76
L	Johnny Schmitz	11-11	2	135	2	2.61
R	Emil Kush	9-2	2	50	1	3.05
R	Paul Erickson	9-7	0	70	1	2.43

April 20 - The Cubs suffer an Opening Day loss, 2-0 to the visiting Cardinals. It's the first televised game in Cubs history, broadcasted by Whispering Joe Wilson of WBKB.

April 24 - Frank Chance is finally elected to the Hall of Fame. Joining him in the Hall, controversially, are legendary double-play teammates Joe Tinker and Johnny Evers (who, despite their legendary status, combined for just 56 double plays scored 6-4-3 or 4-6-3).

May 5 - The Cubs score 11 runs in the seventh, beating the Phils 13-1 at Wrigley. Hank Borowy becomes one of only three National League pitchers (all Cubs) to get two extra-base hits in the same inning, joining Fred Goldsmith (1883) and Adonis Terry (1895).

May 18 - The Cubs bomb the Giants 19-3 in the first of two at the Polo Grounds after losing the previous two dates to rain. Game two of the twinbill is washed out, too.

May 20 - Claude Passeau commits his first error since September 21, 1941, snapping his all-time record of 273 consecutive errorless chances. Most amazing is the fact that Passeau uses a small glove due to a gunshot wound he received on his fielding hand as a child. He beats Boston 6-4 today.

WORTH NOTING - Phil Cavarretta is the only Cub to hit grand slams in three different decades, doing it in 1936, 1945 and 1951.

May 22 - Ugliness occurs during a game at Ebbets Field, when Brooklyn's Eddie Stanky slides hard into shortstop Len Merullo with the score tied 1-1 in the 10th. Merullo decks Stanky, precipitating a bench-clearing brawl that ends with Claude Passeau ripping off manager Leo Durocher's jersey. The Dodgers win 2-1 in 13 innings.

May 23 - Lenny Merullo and Brooklyn's Dixie Walker get into a pre-game fistfight despite the presence of police on the field before a 2-1 Dodger win at Ebbets Field. The police have been placed along the dugouts of both clubs due to yesterday's brawl. Five players will be fined $650 for participating in the fight; Walker, Merullo and Cubs coach Red Smith will be suspended. During the game, both coach Augie Galan and Brooklyn skipper Leo Durocher will be ejected.

June 23 - Eddie Waitkus and Marv Rickert hit back-to-back inside-the-park home runs in the fourth inning of a 15-10 loss to the Giants.

September 15 - A game at Ebbets Field is postponed in the fifth inning due to a swarm of gnats that descends upon the field. The Cubs are losing 2-0 at the time.

Hank Borowy

1947

Principle Owner and President: Phil Wrigley; **Manager:** Charlie Grimm; **Ballpark:** Wrigley Field; **Attendance:** 1,364,039; **Finish:** Sixth (69-85); **Recap:** The Cubs plunge to sixth place, 25 games behind Jackie Robinson's Brooklyn Dodgers. The Cubs' .259 team average is the second-worst in the league, despite .300 seasons from Andy Pafko and Phil Cavarretta. The Cubs *do* manage to draw 1.3 million fans to Wrigley Field, however, a number they won't reach again until 1969.

P	PLAYER	R	HR	RBI	SB	AVE
1B	Eddie Waitkus	60	2	35	3	.262
2B	Don Johnson	33	3	26	2	.259
SS	Lennie Merullo	24	0	29	4	.241
3B	Peanuts Lowrey	56	5	37	2	.281
RF	Bill Nicholson	69	26	75	1	.244
CF	Andy Pafko	68	13	66	4	.302
LF	Phil Cavaretta	56	2	63	2	.314
C	Bob Scheffing	33	5	50	2	.264
IF	Bobby Sturgeon	16	0	21	0	.254
C	Clyde McCullough	25	3	30	1	.252
IF	Stan Hack	28	0	12	0	.271
UT	Mickey Rickert	7	2	15	0	.146
OF	Dom Dallessandro	18	1	14	0	.287

T	PITCHER	W-L	SV	SO	SH	ERA
L	Johnny Schmitz	13-18	4	97	3	3.22
R	Doyle Lade	11-10	0	62	1	3.95
R	Emil Kush	8-3	5	44	0	3.36
R	Hank Borowy	8-12	2	75	1	4.38
L	Bob Chipman	7-6	0	51	1	3.67

April 15 - The Pirates nip the Cubs 1-0 on Opening Day at Wrigley Field.

April 16 - The Cubs buy second baseman Lonnie Frey from the Reds but will sell him to the Yankees in June after he hits just .209 in 24 games.

April 20 - Bill Nicholson drives in six runs on two homers in a 7-4 win over the Cardinals.

May 11 - The Cubs take over first place by sweeping a pair from Cincinnati, 6-3 and 4-3.

May 18 - A crowd of 46,572, including many African-Americans, set the Wrigley attendance record for a game against Jackie Robinson and the Dodgers. Brooklyn beats the Cubs 4-2, handing Chicago its fifth straight loss. Robinson goes 0-for-4.

August 2 - Peanuts Lowrey and Eddie Waitkus collect five hits apiece in a 12-7 Cubs victory at Wrigley Field.

August 8 - Bill Nicholson belts an 11-inning solo homer to break up a 1-1 pitching duel between Johnny Schmitz and Cincinnati's Ewell Blackwell. Chicago turns a triple play in the seventh when shortstop Len Merullo grabs a line drive, steps on second and fires to first baseman Eddie Waitkus.

August 24 - In an 8-3 triumph over the Giants, Eddie Waitkus hits an inside-the-park grand slam, his record-setting third of the season.

August 25 - Billy Jurges, a Cub coach who was put on the active roster two days earlier, crushes a two-run homer in the 10th to provide the winning margin in a 9-7 decision over the Giants.

September8 - Pitcher Johnny Miller hits a game-winning grand slam to beat the Pirates 4-3. He does not go the required five innings to get the win, however.

1948

Principle Owner and President: Phil Wrigley; **Manager:** Charlie Grimm; **Ballpark:** Wrigley Field; **Attendance:** 1,237,792; **Finish:** Eighth (64-90); **Recap:** The Cubs finally bottom out in 1948, the first of two straight seasons in the cellar. Andy Pafko remains the team's biggest draw, bashing 26 homers and driving in 101 runs and Johnny Schmitz contributes 18 of the club's 64 wins.

P	PLAYER	R	HR	RBI	SB	AVE
1B	Eddie Waitkus	87	7	44	11	.295
2B	Hank Schenz	43	1	14	3	.261
SS	Roy Smalley	25	4	36	0	.216
3B	Andy Pafko	82	26	101	3	.312
RF	Bill Nicholson	68	19	67	2	.261
CF	Hal Jeffcoat	53	4	42	8	.279
LF	Peanuts Lowrey	47	2	54	2	.294
C	Bob Schefffing	23	5	45	0	.300
UT	Phil Cavaretta	41	3	40	4	.278
OF	Clarence Maddern	16	4	27	0	.252
C	Rube Walker	17	5	26	0	.275
C	Clyde McCullough	10	1	7	0	.209
IF	Emil Verban	37	1	16	4	.294

T	PITCHER	W-L	SV	SO	SH	ERA
L	Johnny Schmitz	18-13	1	100	2	2.64
R	Russ Meyer	10-10	0	89	3	3.65
R	Jess Dobernic	7-2	1	48	0	3.14
R	Doyle Lade	5-6	0	29	0	4.03
R	Ralph Hamner	5-9	0	53	0	4.70

WORTH NOTING - In 1946, Claude Passeau became the first - and only - Cubs pitcher to start an All-Star Game. He took the loss in a 12-0 ALwin at Fenway Park.

January 29 - The Cubs, as well as the Yankees and Phillies, are fined $500 each by Baseball Commissioner Happy Chandler for signing high school players.

February 15 - Ron Cey is born in Tacoma, Washington.

April 16 - Jack Brickhouse is at the mic for WGN-TV in Chicago's first baseball telecast, a 4-1 White Sox exhibition win over the Cubs at Wrigley Field.

April 23 - The Cards spoil the Cubs'home opener with a 1-0 win.

April 24 - Bill Nicholson crushes a pitch over the Wrigley Field scoreboard and onto Sheffield Avenue during a 6-2 win over the Cards. Allegedly, the ball bounces off a building and lands on the hood of a car.

May 2 - Rookie outfielder Hal Jeffcoat doubles twice in the Cubs' 7-run eighth inning of a 13-4 pounding of Cincinnati.

May 16 - After spotting the Reds to an 8-1 lead in the second, the Cubs rally back to win 13-11.

May 18 - The Cubs capitalize on four Phillie errors to win 3-2 behind Johnny Schmitz.

May 26 - Johnny Schmitz tallies his

WORTH NOTING - In 1948, pitcher Dutch McCall set the Cubs record with 13 consecutive losses.

WORTH NOTING - IN 1948, Andy Pafko became the first Cub to be voted into the starting lineup at the All-Star Game. Cubs lefty Johnny Schmitz took the loss in a 5-2 American League win at Sportsman's Park in St. Louis.

fourth win in a row, beating Brooklyn 4-1.

May 31 - Almost 47,000 pack Wrigley Field for a doubleheader with the Pirates. The Cubs win the opener, 4-3 and lose the nightcap, 4-2. Young Andy Pafko collects five hits on the day, including two homers.

July 18 - Another rousing crowd, 39,623, passes through the turnstiles at Wrigley for a twinbill with the lowly Phillies. With two outs and the bases loaded in the opener, rookie Robin Roberts plunks Phil Cavaretta and Andy Pafko with successive pitches to hand the Cubs a 3-2 win. In game two, Philadelphia collects 17 hits for a 6-4 victory.

August 11 - Johnny Schmitz goes 11 innings and scores the winning run on a double by Eddie Waitkus in a 4-2 win at Brooklyn.

August 26 - A near-riot holds up a game at Wrigley during the nightcap of a doubleheader sweep of the Braves. In the third inning, a drive off the bat of Phil Cavarretta is ruled a ground-rule double by umpire Jocko Conlan instead of an inside-the-park homer when Boston left fielder Jeff Heath pretends to lose the ball in the Wrigley ivy, though it is really at his feet. The fans shower the field with debris in protest. After calm is restored, Andy Pafko walks and Peanut Lowrey clears the bases with a triple. Conlan will later bawl out Chicago police for failing to act during the ugliness.

August 27 - Johnny Schmitz hurls a six-hit 1-0 shutout of the first-place Braves and scores the only run in the bottom of the ninth. The loss knocks Boston from the top of the standings.

August 31 - A crowd of 45,531 jam Wrigley Field to watch the last-place Cubs sweep the league-leading Dodgers, 3-0 and 7-2. Hank Borowy tosses a one-hitter in the opener, facing just 27 batters.

December 8 - The Cubs trade pitcher Cliff Chambers and catcher Clyde McCullough to the Pirates for second baseman Frankie Gustine and pitcher Cal McLish.

December 14 - The Cubs send Eddie Waitkus and Hank Borowy to the Phillies for pitchers Dutch Leonard and Monk Dubiel. Knuckleballer Leonard let the NL with 18 losses in 1948.

December 21 - Dave Kingman is born in Pendleton, Oregon.

1949

Principle Owner and President: Phil Wrigley; **Manager:** Charlie Grimm / Frankie Frisch; **Ballpark:** Wrigley Field; **Attendance:** 1,143,139; **Finish:** Eighth (61-93); **Recap:** The Cubs finish last again, with the lowest win total (61) since 1901. After fifty games the team fires manager Charlie Grimm, replacing him with former Gas House Gang skipper Frankie Frisch. Grimm is promoted to vice president.

P	PLAYER	R	HR	RBI	SB	AVE
1B	Herm Reich	43	3	34	4	.280
2B	Emil Verban	38	0	22	3	.289
SS	Roy Smalley	57	8	35	2	.245
3B	Frankie Gustine	29	4	27	3	.226
RF	Hal Jeffcoat	43	2	26	12	.245
CF	Andy Pafko	79	18	69	4	.281
LF	Hank Sauer	59	27	83	0	.291
C	Mickey Owen	15	2	18	1	.273

P	PLAYER	R	HR	RBI	SB	AVE
UT	Phil Cavaretta	46	8	49	2	.294
IF	Gene Mauch	15	1	7	3	.247
IF	Bob Ramazzotti	14	0	6	9	.179
OF	Hank Edwards	25	7	21	0	.290
OF	Frankie Baumholtz	15	1	15	2	.226

T	PITCHER	W-L	SV	SO	SH	ERA
L	Johnny Schmitz	11-13	3	75	3	4.35
R	Bob Rush	10-18	4	80	1	4.07
L	Bob Chipman	7-8	1	46	1	3.98
R	Dutch Leonard	7-16	0	83	1	4.15
R	Monk Dubiel	6-9	4	52	1	4.14

April 20 - The Cubs lose 1-0 yet again on Opening Day at Wrigley.

April 30 - Rocky Nelson hits the legendary "inside-the-glove" home run when center fielder Andy Pafko's diving catch of Nelson's liner in the ninth inning is ruled a trap by umpire Al Barlick and the Cardinals first baseman rounds the bases while Pafko argues.

May 15 - Dusty Baker is born in Riverside, California.

May 16 - The Cubs purchase second baseman Bob Ramazzotti from the Dodgers for infielder Harry Schenz and $25,000.

Rick Reuschel is born in Quincy, Illinois.

June 10 - Charlie Grimm is fired as Cubs manager. Giants coach Frankie Frisch, who managed the Gas House Gang Cardinals to a World Championship in 1934, is tapped to replace Jolly Cholly.

June 14 - Former Cub Eddie Waitkus, in town with the Phillies, is shot at Chicago's Edgewater Beach Hotel by an obsessed fan, 19-year-old Ruth Steinhagen. Although Waitkus is near-dead when he's found, he'll battle back and play next season. Steinhagen, who said she loved the first baseman from afar and was determined that nobody else would have him, will be placed in a mental hospital. The episode will be the inspiration for Bernard Malamud's novel *The Natural,* in which Roy Hobbs is shot by a woman he invites to his hotel room.

December 14 - The Cubs acquire Braves infielder Gene Mauch for pitcher Bill Voiselle and $35,000.

1950

Principle Owner and President: Phil Wrigley; **Manager:** Frankie Frisch; **Ballpark:** Wrigley Field; **Attendance:** 1,165,944; **Finish:** Seventh (64-89); **Recap:** Frankie Frisch's Gas House Gang style of managing doesn't improve things on the field much, as the Cubs finish seventh, 26 1/2 games out. The season is highlighted by the slugging of Hank Sauer and Andy Pafko, and by fighting within the new front office, chiefly between GM Jim Gallagher and new vice-president Charlie Grimm. Grimm, in fact, quits after six months. Frisch exploits his friendship with Phil Wrigley to persuade the owner to hire Wid Mathews away from the Dodgers and to demote Gallagher to business manager. Unfortunately, Mathews will prove to be even more of a bonehead than Gallagher, becoming a major mark for Brooklyn president Branch Rickey, who dupes him into a series of deals that produce disastrous results for Chicago.

P	PLAYER	R	HR	RBI	SB	AVE
1B	Preston Ward	31	6	33	3	.253
2B	Wayne Terwilliger	63	10	32	13	.242
SS	Roy Smalley	58	21	85	2	.230
3B	Bill Serena	27	4	29	1	.273
RF	Bob Borkowski	27	4	29	1	.273
CF	Andy Pafko	95	36	92	4	.304
LF	Hank Sauer	85	32	103	1	.274
C	Mickey Owen	22	2	21	2	.243

WORTH QUOTING - "We don't care who wins - as long as it's the Cubs."
-Cubs broadcaster Bert Wilson

P	PLAYER	R	HR	RBI	SB	AVE
UT	Phil Cavaretta	49	10	31	1	.273
C	Rube Walker	19	6	16	0	.230
OF	Hal Jeffcoat	19	1	10	3	.227
OF	Carmen Mauro	19	1	10	3	.227
IF	Bob Ramazzotti	19	1	6	3	.262

T	PITCHER	W-L	SV	SO	SH	ERA
R	Bob Rush	13-20	1	93	1	3.71
R	Frank Hiller	12-5	1	55	2	3.53
L	Johnny Schmitz	10-16	0	75	3	4.99
L	Paul Minner	8-13	4	99	1	4.12
R	Monk Dubiel	6-10	2	51	2	4.15

January 6 - Former manager Charlie Grimm signs a three-year contract for a record $90,000 to manage minor-league Dallas (Texas League).

January 12 - The Cubs acquire the Newark Bears, the Yankees' International League team, and announce that they will move the club to Springfield, Massachusetts. The Bears finished last in 1949.

April 21 - The Cubs blank the Cardinals 2-0 on Opening Day at Wrigley.

April 30 - Johnny Schmitz allows just four hits and at one point retires 20 batters in a row but loses to Harry Brecheen and the Cardinals 1-0.

May 18 - In the top of the sixth of a 10-4 loss at the Polo Grounds, Rube Walker hits a grand slam. In the bottom of the frame, the Giants' Monte Irvin also hits a grand slam, marking the first time players from each team have slammed in the same inning.

June 28 - Roy Smalley hits for the cycle during a 15-3 victory over the Cardinals.

July 2 - The Cubs pummel Cincinnati 16-0 at Crosley Field behind Monk Dubiel. Andy Pafko drives in five runs with a double, triple and home run, missing the cycle by just a single.

July 16 - The Cubs knock the Whiz Kid Phillies, the eventual pennant-winners, out of first place for the time being with a pair of victories at Wrigley. The Cubs lose Phil Cavarretta when Ken Johnson hits him with a pitch in game one, an 8-0 shutout behind Monk Dubiel. Hank Sauer takes over at first. Doyle Lade is the winner in game two, 10-3.

August 2 - Andy Pafko launches three home runs but the Cubs lose to the Giants 8-6.

August 28 - Hank Sauer launches three homers of his own, in consecutive at-bats off the Phillies' Curt Simmons. Sauer will hit three homers off Simmons again, in 1952. Knuckleballing reliever Dutch Leonard, making his only start of the year, is the winner 7-5.

September 2 - Phil Cavarretta breaks up Ewell Blackwell's no-hitter with a single to lead off the ninth as the Reds beat the Cubs 5-1.

September 16 - Reserve outfielder Ron Northey hits his third lifetime pinch-grand slam, setting a major league record, to give the Cubs a 9-7 win over the Dodgers despite Brooklyn outfielder Tommy Brown's three round-trippers.

1951

Principle Owner and President: Phil Wrigley; **Manager:** Frankie Frisch / Phil Cavaretta; **Ballpark:** Wrigley Field; **Attendance:** 894,415; **Finish:** Eighth

(62-92); **Recap:** Frankie Frisch is fired in July for making critical comments in the Chicago papers. Under new manager Phil Cavarretta, the Cubs finish last again, with only one pitcher, Bob Rush, winning in double digits. Hank Sauer's RBI production is drastically reduced without Andy Pafko's presence in the lineup.

P	PLAYER	R	HR	RBI	SB	AVE
1B	Chuck Connors	16	2	18	4	.239
2B	Eddie Miksis	48	3	35	11	.266
SS	Roy Smalley	24	8	31	0	.231
3B	Randy Jackson	78	16	76	14	.275
RF	Hal Jeffcoat	44	4	27	8	.273
CF	Frankie Baumholtz	62	2	50	5	.284
LF	Hank Sauer	77	30	89	2	.263
C	Smoky Burgess	21	2	20	2	.251
IF	Phil Cavaretta	24	6	28	0	.311
OF	Gene Hermanski	28	3	20	3	.281
IF	Bob Ramazzotti	13	1	15	0	.247
IF	Jack Cusick	16	2	16	2	.177
C	Mickey Owen	10	0	15	1	.184

T	PITCHER	W-L	SV	SO	SH	ERA
R	Bob Rush	11-12	2	129	2	3.84
L	Paul Minner	6-17	1	68	3	3.79
R	Frank Hiller	6-12	1	50	2	4.85
R	Cal McLish	4-10	0	46	1	4.44
R	Dutch Leonard	10-6	3	30	0	2.63

January 2 - Bill Madlock is born in Memphis, Tennessee.

April 17 - The Cubs are winners on Opening Day at Wrigley, 8-3 over the Cincinnati Reds. Rookie first baseman Dee Fondy rips a second-inning, bases-loaded triple in his first major league at bat. During the pregame ceremony, golfer Sam Snead tees off from home plate and hits a ball off the center field scoreboard.

April 25 - Two Cubs are thrown out at home in the fifth inning by Cincinnati right fielder Bob Usher, preserving a 4-3 Reds victory at Crosley Field.

May 20 - The Cubs sweep the Braves in a twinbill to climb within a game of the front-running Dodgers, 4-3 and 5-4. Dutch Leonard hurls two innings in each game to earn both victories.

June 15 - Prior to a game at Wrigley Field, Chicago and Brooklyn make a 4-for-4 trade. The Cubs send Andy Pafko, catcher Rube Walker, pitcher Johnny Schmitz, and infielder Wayne Terwilliger to the Dodgers for pitcher Joe Hatten, infielder Eddie Miksis, catcher Bruce Edwards, and outfielder Gene Hermanski. The deal will be called "the most barefaced swindle in years" by the New York Post; Cubs fans will soon agree.

Edwards drives in four runs for the Cubs today, three on a homer, off former teammate Carl Erskine in a 6-4 triumph. Pafko hits his 13th homer in a losing cause and will go down to injury, missing more than three weeks.

June 27 - Boyd Tepler, who pitched in the Cubs' farm system during the 1940s, brings suit against the team, owner Phil Wrigley, and Major League Baseball, contending that "negligent" coaching allowed him to continue with flaws in his pitching motion that resulted in arm damage and the end of his career.

June 28 - Frank Hiller hurls a one-hit shutout versus St. Louis, facing the minimum 27 batters. Enos Slaughter singles in the fifth but is erased in a double play. The Cubs score four in the ninth, one on a Jack Cusick steal of home, and win 8-0.

July 22 - With the Cubs now 10 games under .500 (35-45), Frankie Frisch is fired, relaced by veteran first baseman Phil Cavarretta. They'll go 27-47 the rest of the way; Cavarretta will hit .311 as a part-timer.

WORTH NOTING - Chuck Connors, who started at first base for the Cubs in 1951, was the most successful of the major leaguers who established a second career in Hollywood. Aside from his popular *The Rifleman* television series, he appeared in many motion pictures, including *The Big Country* and *Soylent Green*.

July 27 - The Cubs suffer their ninth straight loss at Wrigley, 2-0 to the Phillies.

July 29 - Cavarretta drives home three runs to lead the Cubs to victory in game one of a twinbill at Wrigley Field, 5-4 over the Phils. The win snaps the Cubs' 10-game home losing streak. Cavarretta pinch-hits in game two and hits a grand slam off Robin Roberts as the Cubs take the night-cap, 8-6.

August 1 - The Cubbies squeak by the Giants 3-2 in game one of a doubleheader. During the game, Eddie Miksis lines a ball to rookie center fielder Willie Mays, which caroms off his head for a double.

August 25 - Chicago takes a rain-shortened, eight-inning victory in Brooklyn 5-1. Player-manager Phil Cavarretta drives in four runs. Dodgers right fielder Carl Furillo has two outfield assists, bringing his league-leading total to 25.

August 26 - First baseman Chuck Connors, who will go on to fame as TV's "The Rifleman", hits his second - and last - major league homer, a three-run shot off Sal Maglie in the ninth, to tie a game at the Polo Grounds 4-4. The Giants' Wes Westrum answers in the bottom of the frame with a homer to win it 5-4.

September 17 - Gene Hermanski, the ex-Dodger, rips a pinch-homer off former teammate Clyde King to lead the Cubs to a 5-3 win over first-place Brooklyn. Reliever Turk Lown hits Dodger catcher Roy Campanella on the head with a pitch in the fifth; Campy is taken off the field by stretcher and will remain in a Chicago hospital overnight. He'll rejoin his team in St. Louis.

November18 - Chuck Connors, sold to the team's Los Angeles Angels PCL franchise in September, becomes the first player to oppose the Major League draft, preferring to stay in California. His notoriety will help land him a job in television.

1952

Principle Owner and President: Phil Wrigley; **Manager:** Phil Cavaretta; **Ballpark:** Wrigley Field; **Attendance:** 1,024,826; **Finish:** Fifth (77-77); **Recap:** Phil Cavarretta's 1952 Cubs improve to fifth place, and a .500 record, actually occupying the third spot in the standings after 1/3 of the season. But a nine-game losing streak brings the team back to reality and they settle 19 1/2 games out. The clubs benefit from an MVP season from Hank Sauer, who leads the NL with 37 homers and 121 RBIs, and a .325 season by Frankie Baumholtz. Bob Rush posts 17 victories for a pitching staff that finishes third with a 3.58 ERA.

P	PLAYER	R	HR	RBI	SB	AVE
1B	Dee Fondy	69	10	67	13	.300
2B	Eddie Miksis	44	2	19	4	.232
SS	Roy Smalley	36	5	30	0	.222
3B	Randy Jackson	44	9	34	6	.232
RF	Frankie Baumholtz	59	4	35	5	.325
CF	Hal Jeffcoat	29	4	30	7	.219
LF	Hank Sauer	89	37	121	1	.270
C	Toby Atwell	36	2	31	2	.290
IF	Bill Serena	49	15	61	1	.274
OF	Gene Hermanski	28	4	34	2	.255
OF	Bob Addis	38	1	20	4	.295
IF	Tommy Brown	24	3	24	1	.320

T	Pitcher	W-L	SV	SO	SH	ERA
R	Bob Rush	17-13	0	157	4	2.70
L	Paul Minner	14-9	0	61	2	3.73
R	Johnny Klippstein	9-14	3	110	2	4.43
R	Warren Hacker	15-9	1	84	5	2.58
R	Dutch Leonard	2-2	11	37	0	215

April 18 - The Cubs win their home opener, 5-4 over the Cardinals.

May 2 - Turk Lown takes a no-hitter into the ninth but then gives up three hits and loses to Brooklyn 3-1. The Cubs' only score is in the first inning on a double steal by Bob Addis and Frankie Baumholtz.

May 30 - The Cubs delight a Memorial Day crowd of 40,000 at Wrigley by sweeping a doubleheader with the Reds, 7-6 and 11-0. Bob Rush fires a two-hitter in the nightcap as the Cubs light up Bud Byerly and Joe Nuxhall for 15 hits. Rush stretches his scoreless innings streak to 29 frames.

June 11 - Hank Sauer rips three homers off Curt Simmons to account for all the scoring as the Cubs beat the Phillies 3-0.

June 14 - Warren Spahn of Boston ties Jim Whitney's National League record with 18 strikeouts versus the Cubs in a 15-inning 3-1 loss. Spahn's home run is accounts for the Braves' lone run.

June 19 - Carl Erskine of Brooklyn no-hits the Cubs, 5-0. Reliever Willard Ramsdell is the only baserunner, in the third.

June 29 - Down 8-2 with two outs in the ninth, the Cubs rally to push across seven runs to beat the Reds 9-8. Pinch-hitter Johnny Pramesa drives in the tying and lead runs on a single. It's the greatest two-out, ninth-inning rally in NL history.

July 8 - Bob Rush and Hank Sauer lead the Nationals to a 3-2 victory in the All-Star

Hank Sauer

Game at Philadelphia. Rush earns a save; Sauer hits a two-run blast in the fourth to deliver the deciding tally.

August 15 - The Cubs sign Phil Cavarretta to another year as pilot.

September 29 - In a publicity move, the Cardinals' Stan Musial takes the mound to pitch to Frankie Baumholtz, whom The Man has beaten in the NL batting race. Baumholtz, batting righthanded, reaches base on an error. Musial is then relieved. Although the Cardinals originally drafted Musial as a pitcher, this is his only Major League appearance on the mound. The Cubs win 3-0 behind Paul Minner.

November 9 - Jim Riggleman is born in Fort Dix, New Jersey.

November20 - Despite a fifth-place finish by the Cubs, Hank Sauer is voted the

Phil Wrigley

National League's Most Valuable Player.

1953

Principle Owner and President: Phil Wrigley; **Manager:** Phil Cavaretta; **Ballpark:** Wrigley Field; **Attendance:** 763,658; **Finish:** Seventh (65-89); **Recap:** General manager Wid Mathews, who is convinced that Hank Sauer's type of slugging will lead the Cubs to post-season success, spends most of the season searching for another power hitter, and finally comes away with Ralph Kiner from cash-strapped Pittsburgh for $150,000 and four marginal players. Kiner does manage to lead the team with 27 homers, and Sauer, third baseman Randy Jackson and shortstop Roy Smalley all hit 19, but the Cubs drop to seventh in the standings, 40 games behind Brooklyn.

P	PLAYER	R	HR	RBI	SB	AVE
1B	Dee Fondy	79	18	78	10	.309
2B	Eddie Miksis	61	8	39	13	.251
SS	Roy Smalley	61	19	66	8	.285
3B	Randy Jackson	61	19	66	8	.285
RF	Hank Sauer	61	19	60	0	.263
CF	Frankie Baumholtz	75	3	25	3	.306
LF	Ralph Kiner	73	28	87	1	.283
C	Clyde McCullough	21	6	23	0	.258
OF	Hal Jeffcoat	22	4	22	5	.235
IF	Bill Serena	30	10	52	0	.251
C	Joe Garagiola	21	1	21	0	.272
UT	Tommy Brown	19	2	13	1	.196
UT	Catfish Metkovich	19	2	12	2	.234

T	PITCHER	W-L	SV	SO	SH	ERA
R	Warren Hacker	12-19	2	106	0	4.38
R	Bob Rush	9-14	0	84	1	4.53
L	Paul Minner	12-15	1	64	2	4.21
R	Johnny Klippstein	10-11	6	113	0	4.82
R	Dutch Leonard	2-3	8	27	0	4.57

January 8 - Bruce Sutter is born in Lancaster, Pennsylvania.

January 21 - Former Cub Dizzy Dean is elected to the Hall of Fame.

April 14 - The Cubs open the season with a 3-2 victory over Cincinnati at Wrigley.

June 4 - The Cubs acquire slugger Ralph Kiner, along with catcher Joe Garagiola, lefty Howie Pollett, and outfielder Catfish Metkovich from the Pirates for catcher Toby Atwell, pitcher Bob Schultz, infielders George Freese and Preston Ward, outfielders Gene Hermanski and Bob Addis, and $150,000.

August 15 - Randy Jackson ties a National League record by grounding into three double plays in a 2-0 Cubs loss to Boston.

September 14 - Johnny Klippstein snaps Duke Snider's 27-game hitting streak at 27. The Cubs win 3-1.

September 17 - Cubs rookie Ernie Banks

goes 0-for-3 and makes an error in his rookie debut. Chicago loses to Philadelphia, 16-4.

September 20 - Banks hits his first major league homer, off Gerry Staley, in an 11-6 loss to the Cards.

November 30 - Catcher Carl Sawatski, batting .220 in 43 games, is sold to the White Sox.

1954

Principle Owner and President: Phil Wrigley; **Manager:** Stan Hack; **Ballpark:** Wrigley Field; **Attendance:** 748,183; **Finish:** Seventh (64-90); **Recap:** After the Cubs lose 15 of their first 20 spring training games, owner Phil Wrigley asks manager Phil Cavarretta for an honest assessment of the team. Cavarretta's answer gets him fired for being a "defeatist," and new manager Stan Hack proves him right, as the team slogs to another seventh-place finish, just ahead of the miserable Pirates. A 4-21 June does them in this season, a month that includes an 11-game losing streak. The Cubs finish third in the league with 159 homers, led by Hank Sauer's 41, Ralph Kiner's 22, and 19 apiece from Randy Jackson and rookie Ernie Banks.

The club draws moderately well thanks mostly to the excitement generated by Banks and Gene Baker, the first two African-American players ever to don a Cubs uniform.

P	Player	R	HR	RBI	SB	AVE
1B	Dee Fondy	77	9	49	20	.285
2B	Gene Baker	68	13	61	4	.275
SS	Ernie Banks	70	19	79	6	.275
3B	Randy Jackson	77	19	67	2	.273
RF	Hank Sauer	98	41	103	2	.288
CF	Dale Talbot	45	1	19	3	.241
LF	Ralph Kiner	88	22	73	2	.285
C	Joe Garagiola	16	5	21	0	.281
OF	Frankie Baumholtz	38	4	28	1	.297
C	Walker Cooper	21	7	32	0	.310
OF	Hal Rice	5	0	5	0	.153
IF	Steve Bilko	11	4	12	0	.239
C	Ed Tappe	5	0	4	0	.185

T	Pitcher	W-L	SV	SO	SH	ERA
R	Bob Rush	15-15	0	124	0	3.78
L	Paul Minner	11-11	1	79	0	3.96
R	Johnny Klippstein	4-11	1	69	0	5.29
L	Howie Pollet	8-10	0	79	0	3.96
R	Hal Jeffcoat	5-6	7	35	0	5.19

March 20 - With Ernie Banks waiting in the wings, the Cubs trade Roy Smalley to the Braves for pitcher Dave Cole.

March 29 - Phil Wrigley fires Phil Cavarretta for having a "defeatist attitude" after the manager gives him an honest assessment of the team's chances this year. Stan Hack replaces him. Cavarretta will be proven right: the Cubs will drop to seventh.

April 17 - It's a Wrigley opener to remember; the Cubs bomb the Cardinals 23-13 in an NL-record three hour and 43-minute game. The Cubs score 10 runs in the fifth; Randy Jackson has four hits, including a home run that hits the facade of an apartment building across Waveland Avenue.

April 30 - The Cubs purchase legendary minor league slugger Steve Bilko from the Cardinals for $12,500. They'll let him go at the end of the year. Bilko will then lead the Pacific Coast League in home runs for three straight years and win the PCL Triple Crown before returning to the majors with the expansion Los Angeles Angels.

May 2 - Hank Sauer hits three home runs in a doubleheader split with the Pirates. Sauer will hit 13 homers vs. Pittsburgh this year, tying a major league record for home runs against one team. In the nightcap the Cubs set a new National League mark by

WORTH QUOTING - "He has full authority (to buy players and make trades), but he always checks with me. I guess maybe if he didn't check with me, he might not have the authority."
-Phil Wrigley on GM Wid Matthews, quoted in *Baseball Digest*, 1953

homering in their 13th straight game.

July 10 - Bob Rush snaps Red Schoendienst's 28-game hitting streak in a 2-1 loss to the Cardinals.

September 2 - The Cubs lose to Brooklyn's Russ Meyer for the 16th consecutive time, dating back to 1950, 10-2 at Wrigley.

November 17 - Ralph Kiner is traded to Cleveland for outfielder Gale Wade, pitcher Sam Jones and $60,000.

1955

Principle Owner and President: Phil Wrigley; **Manager:** Stan Hack; **Ballpark:** Wrigley Field; **Attendance:** 875,800; **Finish:** Sixth (72-81); **Recap:** The Cubs in 1955 rise as high as third place by the All-Star break but finish sixth, 26 games behind the Brooklyn Dodgers. A 1-12 road trip in late July proves to be the turning point. An aging, injured Hank Sauer appears in just 79 games, batting .211, and Frankie Baumholtz plays his way out of the lineup. On the bright side, Ernie Banks puts together a 44-homer year, a record for a big league shortstop, belting five grand slams in the process.

WORTH NOTING - Hall of Famer Ernie Banks survived a jarring 18 managerial changes during his career.

P	PLAYER	R	HR	RBI	SB	AVE
1B	Dee Fondy	69	17	65	8	.265
2B	Gene Baker	82	11	52	9	.268
SS	Ernie Banks	98	44	117	9	.295
3B	Ramdy Jackson	73	21	70	0	.265
RF	Jim King	43	11	45	2	.256
CF	Eddie Miksis	52	9	41	3	.235
RF	Hank Sauer	29	12	28	0	.211
C	Harry Chiti	24	11	41	0	.231
OF	Frankie Baumholtz	23	1	27	0	.289
UT	Bob Speake	36	12	43	3	.218
OF	Lloyd Merriman	15	1	8	1	.214
OF	Jim Bolger	19	0	7	2	.206
C	Walker Cooper	11	7	15	0	.279

T	PITCHER	W-L	SV	SO	SH	ERA
R	Sam Jones	14-<u>20</u>	0	<u>198</u>	4	4.09
R	Bob Rush	13-11	0	130	3	3.50
R	Warren Hacker	11-15	3	80	0	4.27
L	Paul Minner	9-9	0	53	1	3.47
R	Hal Jeffcoat	8-6	6	32	0	2.94

March 19 - Pitcher Dave Cole is sold to the Phillies. "That's too bad," he says. "They're the only team I can beat." Cole was 3-8 in 14 starts for the Cubs in 1954.

March 20 - The Giants and Indians, last year's World Series teams, play an exhibition rematch at Wrigley Field. The Giants, who swept the Tribe in October, win again 7-3. Meanwhile, the Cubs, in Arizona, defeat their PCL farm team, the Los Angeles Angels, 7-0.

April 12 - The Cubs are big winners on Opening Day at Wrigley, defeating St. Louis 14-4.

April 16 - Three Cubs hit two home runs apiece, with Ernie Banks and Dee Fondy going back-to-back twice, in a 12-11 loss to the Cards.

April 17 - The Cards score 10 runs in the first in a 14-1 rout of the Cubs at Sportsman's Park.

May 11 - The Cubs roll five double plays

en route to a 10-8 win over the Dodgers. Ernie Banks hits a grand slam; he'll hit four more this season.

May 12 - Sam "Toothpick" Jones hurls a 4-0 no-hitter over Pittsburgh, striking out the final three batters after walking the bases loaded. It's the first no-hitter at Wrigley Field since 1917, and the first Major League no-hitter by an African-American.

Cubs broadcaster Harry Creighton jokes during a pre-game interview that he'll give Jones a gold toothpick if he pitched a no-hitter. Creighton will be true to his word.

May 21 - Warren Hacker takes a no-hitter into the ninth but gives up a home run to George Crowe in a 2-1 Cubs victory at Milwaukee.

May 30 - Rookie Bob Speake homers in both games of a twinbill in St. Louis, finishing the month of May with 10. The Cubs sweep the doubleheader 9-5 and 4-3 with Speake's homer the deciding factor in game two. Speake will hit just two more homers this year.

August 2 - Ernie Banks hits his fourth grand slam of the year in a 12-4 win over the Pirates, tying the major league record.

August 4 - Banks hits three homers in an 11-10 Wrigley triumph over Pittsburgh.

September 9 - Thirteen homers are hit in a doubleheader with the Dodgers at Wrigley. The Cubs win the opener 11-4 with Dee Fondy, Ernie Banks and Eddie Miksis homer in the first inning.

The Dodgers take the second game 16-9, with Fondy, Gene Baker, and Banks going deep in the eighth.

Ralph Kiner

September 19 - Mr. Cub hits his record-setting fifth grand slam of the season in a 6-5, 12-inning loss to the Cardinals.

November28 - Chicago trades pitcher Hal Jeffcoat to Cincinnati for catcher Hobie Landrith.

December 6 - The Cubs acquire Brooklyn third baseman Don Hoad and outfielder Walt Moryn for Randy Jackson.

December 9 - If you can't beat 'em, make 'em join you. The Cubs trade pitcher Don Elston and cash to the World Champion Dodgers for pitcher Russ Meyer. Meyer was 22-1 lifetime vs. Chicago.

Frankie Baumholtz is sold to the Phillies. He'll play 76 games next year without an extra-base hit, setting a National League record.

WORTH QUOTING - "The Chicago Cubs are like Rush Street - a lot of singles, but no action."

-Joe Garagiola

1956

Principle Owner and President: Phil Wrigley; **Manager:** Stan Hack; **Ballpark:** Wrigley Field; **Attendance:** 720,118; **Finish:** Eighth (60-94); **Recap:** After another last-place season, Phil Wrigley cleans house, firing manager Stan Hack, GM Wid Mathews, and business manager Jim Gallagher, hiring catcher Bob Scheffing as skipper, John Holland, president of the Cubs' minor-league Los Angeles Angels franchise as general manager, and the ever-present Charlie Grimm as vice president.

P	Player	R	HR	RBI	SB	AVE
1B	Dee Fondy	52	9	46	9	.269
2B	Gene Baker	65	12	57	4	.258
SS	Ernie Banks	82	28	85	6	.297
3B	Don Hoak	51	5	37	8	.215
RF	Walt Moryn	69	23	67	4	.285
CF	Pete Whisenant	37	11	46	8	.239
LF	Monte Irvin	44	15	50	1	.271
C	Hobie Landrith	22	4	32	0	.221
OF	Jim King	32	15	54	1	.249
UT	Eddie Miksis	54	9	27	4	.239
C	Harry Chiti	17	4	18	0	.212
IF	Frank Kellert	10	4	17	0	.186
OF	Solly Drake	29	2	15	9	.256

T	Pitcher	W-L	SV	SO	SH	ERA
R	Bob Rush	13-10	0	104	1	3.19
R	Sam Jones	9-14	0	176	2	3.90
R	Warren Hacker	3-13	0	65	0	4.66
R	Don Kaiser	4-9	0	74	1	3.60
R	Turk Lown	9-8	13	74	0	3.57

March 30 - The Cubs trade Hank Sauer to the Cardinals for outfielder Pete Whisenant and cash.

April 20 - The Cubs bomb the Reds 12-1 on Opening Day at Wrigley.

May 2 - Nearly the entire roster of both the Giants and Cubs appear in a 17-inning marathon won by the Giants 6-5 at Wrigley Field. Twenty-three Cubs and 25 Giants - a major league record - appear in the wild five-hour and 19-minute affair that includes 11 intentional walks, seven by Chicago. Don Hoak fans six times.

May 30 - Russ Meyer gives up three consecutive homers - to Eddie Mathews, Hank Aaron and Bobby Thomson - in the first inning of a twinbill opener then beans Billy Bruton with a pitch, igniting a bench-clearing brawl. Both Meyer and Bruton are ejected. Chicago comes back with three of their own in the bottom of the frame and holds on to win, 10-9.

The Braves take the nightcap 11-9; the two teams combine for a major league-record 15 round-trippers in the doubleheader.

May 31 - The Cubs and Braves continue to pummel each other, with Milwaukee taking a 15-8 decision. Paul Minner loses his 12th in a row vs. the Braves.

June 21 - Rick Sutcliffe is born in Independence, Missouri.

August 26 - Ernie Banks launches a Cubs-record 717 consecutive games played streak during a doubleheader with Pittsburgh. The Pirates take both games, 2-0 and 2-1.

November13 - The Cubs trade Don Hoak, Pete Whisenant, and pitcher Warren Hacker to the Reds for 36-year old pitcher Elmer Singleton, who was 18-8 for the PCL's Seattle team, and third baseman Ray Jablonski. Singleton, who last pitched in 1950 for Washington, will appear in just

28 games for the Cubs over the next three seasons.

December10 - The Cubs purchase catcher Charlie Silvera from the Yankees and trade pitchers Sam Jones and Jim Davis, infielder Eddie Miksis, and catcher Hobie Landrith to the Cardinals for catcher Ray Katt and pitchers Tom Poholsky and Jackie Collum.

1957

Principle Owner and President: Phil Wrigley; **Manager:** Bob Scheffing; **Ballpark:** Wrigley Field; **Attendance:** 670,629; **Finish:** Seventh (62-92); **Recap:** The 1957 Cubs are hard-hitting (147 homers) but slow of foot (28 stolen bases), just managing to escape the cellar. What pitching the club has is further depleted by the trade of Sam Jones to St. Louis for Tom Poholsky, who goes 1-7. Bob Rush sinks to 6-16 and is traded after the season. Ernie Banks finishes the season with 43 homers, one shy of the league lead.

P	PLAYER	R	HR	RBI	SB	AVE
1B	Dale Long	55	21	62	1	.305
2B	Bobby Morgan	43	5	27	5	.207
SS	Ernie Banks	113	43	102	8	.285
3B	Bobby Adams	21	1	10	0	.251
RF	Walt Moryn	76	19	88	0	.289
CF	Chuck Tanner	42	7	42	0	.286
LF	Lee Walls	42	6	33	5	.240
C	Cal Neeman	37	10	39	0	.258
UT	Bob Speake	65	16	50	5	.232
UT	Jim Bolger	28	5	29	0	.275
IF	Jerry Kindall	18	6	12	1	.160
OF	Bob Will	13	1	10	1	.223
IF	Jack Littrell	8	1	13	0	.190

T	PITCHER	W-L	SV	SO	SH	ERA
R	Moe Drabowsky	13-15	0	170	2	3.53
R	Dick Drott	15-11	0	170	3	3.58
R	Bob Rush	6-16	0	103	0	4.39
R	Don Elston	6-7	8	102	0	3.56
R	Turk Lown	5-7	12	51	0	3.77

April 16 - The Cubs loşe to the Milwaukee Braves 4-1 on Opening Day in Chicago.

April 24 - Moe Drabowsky, Jackie Collum and Jim Brosnan combine to walk nine Cincinnati Reds in the fifth inning, a National League record, of a 9-5 loss at Crosley Field.

May 1 - The Cubs acquire first baseman Dale Long and outfielder Lee Walls to Pittsburgh for first baseman Dee Fondy and second baseman Gene Baker.

May 24 - Rookie outfielder Frank Ernaga hits a solo home run in his first major league at-bat and follows with a triple in the fourth, collecting seven total bases in his first two plate appearances—both against Milwaukee ace Warren Spahn. Ernaga will hit just one more home run this season. The Cubs beat the Braves 5-1.

May 26 - Rookie hurler Dick Drott, 20, fans 15 Braves, including Hank Aaron and Billy Bruton three times, en route to a 7-5 triumph in game one of a twinbill at Wrigley. Drott's 15 wins this year will be the most for a Cubs rookie since Pat Malone won 18 in 1928. Chicago takes the nightcap, too, 5-4.

June 1 - The Cubs give up a team-record seven homers in a 22-2 loss to the Reds. The record will be tied on July 12, 1996, when the Cardinals pummel Steve Trachsel.

WORTH QUOTING - "Mr. Grand Slam Himself, Ernie Banks, is available for a limited number of selected talks and appearances at luncheons, dinners and Christmas parties during December and January."

-Ad in the *Chicago American*, 1955

Ernie Banks - Mr. Cub

June 2 - Moe Drabowsky ties a National League record by hitting four batters in the first game of a doubleheader at Crosley Field. The Reds beat the Cubs, 6-4 but Chicago wins the nightcap, 4-2.

June 6 - With the Dodgers ahead 1-0 due to an error by Cubs left fielder Bob Speake, who loses sight of a fly ball, a game at Ebbets Field is delayed because of fog. After an hour and 26 minutes the game is called, the first time in history because of weather conditions other than rain.

July 2 - Lee Walls hits for the cycle in an 8-6 loss to Cincinnati.

July 18 - Chuck Tanner and Ernie Banks each hit inside-the-park home runs as the Cubs clip Pittsburgh 6-5 at Forbes Field.

July 21 - While warming up in the late innings of a 5-4 Cubs win at Ebbets Field, reliever Jim Brosnan falls on the ground, injuring his Achilles tendon. He is helped off the field, leaving the game before throwing a single pitch.

July 31 - Leon Durham is born in Cincinnati, Ohio.

September 2 - The Cubs drop a pair to the Braves, 23-10 and 4-0. Milwaukee first baseman Frank Torre scores six runs in the first game, tying the major league record.

September 29 - Ernie Banks goes 5-for-5 as the Cubs beat the Cardinals 8-3 at Sportsman's Park.

December 4 - Lee Smith is born in Shreveport, Louisiana.

December 5 - The Cubs trade Bob Rush and two minor leaguers to the Braves for pitcher Taylor Phillips and catcher Sammy Taylor.

1958

Principle Owner and President: Phil Wrigley; **Manager:** Bob Scheffing; **Ballpark:** Wrigley Field; **Attendance:** 979,904; **Finish:** Fifth (72-82); **Recap:** Despite a lineup as prolific as any in baseball, the Cubs manage to finish only as high as fifth, 20 games behind Milwaukee. The team slugs a club-record 182 home runs, with five players hitting 20 or more, led by 47 from National League MVP Ernie Banks. The Cubs lead the league in that category for the first time since 1930.

Horrific pitching dooms Chicago this season, with no one reaching as many as 11 wins. Don Elston leads the NL in appearances (69).

P	PLAYER	R	HR	RBI	SB	AVE
1B	Dale Long	68	20	75	2	.271
2B	Tony Taylor	63	6	27	21	.235
SS	Ernie Banks	119	47	129	4	.313
3B	Al Dark	54	3	43	1	.295
RF	Lee Walls	80	24	72	4	.304
CF	Bobby Thomson	67	21	82	0	.283
LF	Walt Moryn	77	26	77	1	.264
C	Sammy Taylor	30	6	36	2	.289
OF	Jim Bolger	15	1	11	0	.225
IF	Johnny Goryl	27	4	14	0	.242
C	Cal Neeman	30	12	29	0	.259
OF	Chuck Tanner	10	4	17	1	.262

T	PITCHER	W-L	SV	SO	SH	ERA
R	Dick Drott	7-11	0	127	0	5.44
L	Taylor Phillips	7-10	1	102	1	4.76
R	Moe Drabowski	9-11	0	77	1	4.50
R	Glen Hobbie	10-6	2	91	1	3.75
R	Don Elston	9-8	10	84	0	2.88

April 18 - The Cubs beat the Cardinals 11-6 in the Wrigley opener.

April 24 - Lee Walls hits three homers, driving in eight runs, in a 15-1 win over the Dodgers.

May 2 - Trailing 7-0 after six innings, the Cubs rally to beat the Braves 8-7. Moose Moryn wins the game with a homer off Dick Littlefield in the ninth.

May 8 - This one hurts: the Reds score eight runs in the ninth at Wrigley Field to come from an 8-2 deficit to beat the Cubs 10-8. Catcher Smokey Burgess provides the winning run with a three-run homer.

May 13 - Stan Musial collects career hit number 3,000 with a pinch-double off Moe Drabowsky in a 5-3 Cardinals victory at Wrigley.

May 20 - The Cubs send reliever Jim Brosnan to the Cards for shortstop Alvin Dark.

May 30 - Walt Moryn hits three homers in the nightcap of a Wrigley Field twinbill vs. Brooklyn. Moryn goes back-to-back with Ernie Banks in the fourth inning and with Chuck Tanner in the seventh. His two-run shot in the ninth hands Sandy Koufax his first loss, 10-8. The Cubbies win the first game, too, 3-2, as Moryn scores the winning run.

WORTH NOTING - The 1958 Cubs are just the third NLteam to have five players with 20 or more home runs.

June 8 - Moe Drabowsky hurls a 4-0 one-hitter over the Pirates. Ted Kluszewski's broken bat single in the second is Pittsburgh's only safety.

July 1 - Second baseman Tony Taylor lines a ball down the third base line that lodges itself in a rain gutter in fair territory at Wrigley Field. Giants rookie outfielder Leon Wagner, fooled by Cubs relievers into thinking that the ball has bounced under a bullpen bench, frantically searches the pen while Taylor rounds the bases for an inside-the-park home run. Cubs win 9-5.

July 6 - The Cubs beat the Dodgers 6-2 on a combined one-hitter by Dick Drott and Don Elston. Junior Gilliam's seventh-inning single is the only Los Angeles hit.

September 9 - Jim Brosnan earns his first win over his old team as the Cardinals defeat the Cubs 8-7 at Sportsman's Park.

WORTH QUOTING - "When I shake hands with a boy and he has a good grip, that's one of the essentials. Then I pat him on the shoulder to see how muscular he is."

-GM Wid Mathews, explaining his method of assessing talent

WORTH QUOTING - "Banks to Baker to Addison Street."
-Jack Brickhouse on the Cubs' double play combination in 1954

Ernie Banks hits his first home run in St. Louis in two years.

September 21 - Left-handed first baseman Dale Long catches the ninth inning of a 2-1 loss to the Dodgers.

November 25 - Ernie Banks is named the National League's Most Valuable Player. Mr. Cub's 47 homers and 32 errors make him the only player in history to lead the league in both categories.

1959

Principle Owner and President: Phil Wrigley; **Manager:** Bob Scheffing; **Ballpark:** Wrigley Field; **Attendance:** 858,255; **Finish:** Fifth (74-80); **Recap:** The Cubs continue to slug the ball in 1959, and again manage to finish just fifth despite the tireless pitching of Don Elston and Bill Henry. Elston and Henry form the perfect righty-lefty platoon out of the bullpen, saving 13 and 12 games respectively and both tying for the NLlead in appearances (65). Phil Wrigley, again disappointed in the team's finish, fires manager Bob Scheffing in favor of Charlie Grimm, who returns to the team for a third time.

P	Player	R	HR	RBI	SB	AVE
1B	Dale Long	34	14	37	0	.236
2B	Tony Taylor	96	8	38	23	.280
SS	Ernie Banks	97	45	143	2	.304
3B	Al Dark	60	6	45	1	.264
RF	Lee Walls	43	8	33	0	.257
CF	George Altman	54	12	47	1	.245
LF	Bobby Thomson	55	11	52	1	.259
C	Sammy Taylor	41	13	43	1	.269

P	Player	R	HR	RBI	SB	AVE
OF	Walt Moryn	41	14	48	0	.234
UT	Jim Marshall	39	11	40	0	.252
UT	Earl Averill	22	10	34	0	.237
UT	Irv Noren	27	4	19	2	.321
C	Cal Neeman	7	3	9	0	.162

T	Pitcher	W-L	SV	SO	SH	ERA
R	Bob Anderson	12-13	0	113	1	4.14
R	Glen Hobbie	16-13	0	138	3	3.69
R	Dave Hillman	8-11	0	88	1	3.53
R	Moe Drabowsky	5-10	0	70	1	4.12
R	Don Elston	10-8	13	82	0	3.31
L	Bill Henry	9-8	12	115	0	2.69

April 11 - After being snowed out the day before, the Cubs defeat the Dodgers 6-1 in their home opener. Bob Anderson defeats Don Drysdale, who homers for the only Los Angeles run.

April 14 - Ernie Banks hits two two-run homers off Jack Sanford as the Cubs beat the Giants 5-2. Sanford won't forget and will bean Banks three times this year.

April 21 - Glen Hobbie loses a no-hitter in the seventh as Stan Musial doubles for the Cardinals'only safety in a 1-0 Cubs win.

May 10 - The Cubs and Cards split a doubleheader at Sportsman's Park. Chicago reliever Elmer Singleton defeats St. Louis reliever Lindy McDaniel 10-9 in the opener; McDaniel defeats Singleton 8-7 in the nightcap.

May 12 - Milwaukee's Lew Burdette takes a 3-2 lead into the ninth inning at Wrigley but gives up a game-tying homer to Walt Moryn, walks the bases loaded, and allows a grand slam to pinch-hitter EarlAverill for a 7-3 Cubs triumph.

June 30 - The famed "two-ball" game occurs at Wrigley Field. The Cards' Stan Musial draws a walk on a wild pitch from the Bob Anderson. When he sees the ball bounce toward the Chicago dugout, Musial takes off for second. Umpire Vic Delmore doesn't see Musial round the bag at first and flips another ball to catcher Sammy Taylor. Taylor fires the ball to second base. It skips by shortstop Ernie Banks into center field.

Meanwhile, third baseman Al Dark who has retrieved the wild pitch, spots Musial - looking confused - off the bag at second. Dark tosses the ball to Banks, who tags the first baseman. After a 10-minute meeting, Musial is ruled out.

The Cardinals initially file a protest but withdraw it after they win, 4-1. Delmore will be fired over the incident.

August 13 - The Cubs and Giants set a major league record for the longest nine-inning game to date, three hours and 50 minutes. Chicago pummels San Francisco 20-9, collecting 19 hits and five homers.

September 13 - Glen Hobbie snaps Ken Boyer's 29-game hitting streak and beats the Cardinals 8-0 on four hits.

September 18 - Ryne Sandberg is born in Spokane, Washington.

September 22 - The Cubs, in fifth place and playing for pride, suddenly become a factor in the NLpennant race as the season enters the home stretch. Chicago defeats San Francisco, just two games behind Los Angeles, 5-4 on a ninth-inning homer by George Altman.

September23 - Cal Neeman's 10th-inning home run gives the Cubs a 9-8 win, pushing the Giants to four games back. Saan Francisco will not recover, finishing third behind Los Angeles and Milwaukee.

September 26 - The Cubs defeat the Dodgers 12-2 at Wrigley, dropping Los Angeles into a first-place tie with Milwaukee. The Cubs chase Johnny Podres and collect 18 hits. The Braves and Dodgers will finish the season in a tie, with the Giants a close third. Los Angeles will win the best-of-three playoff.

WORTH NOTING - Ernie Banks' 143 RBIs in 1959 were 91 more than runner-up Bobby Thompson, the biggest gap ever between teammates.

September 28 - Cubs manager Bob Scheffing resigns and is replaced, once again, by Charlie Grimm.

November 4 - Ernie Banks wins his second straight National League MVP award. It's an all-Chicago MVP season as Nellie Fox, second baseman of the pennant-winning White Sox, nudges teammates Luis Aparicio and Early Wynn for the American League trophy.

November 21 - The Cubs send first baseman Jim Marshall to the Red Sox for first baseman Dick Gernert in the first-ever inter-league trade.

December 6 - The Cubs acquire outfielder Frank Thomas from the Reds for pitcher Bill Henry and outfielders Lee Walls and Lou Jackson.

1960

Principle Owner and President: Phil Wrigley; **Manager:** Charlie Grimm / Lou

WORTH QUOTING - "Every player should be accorded the privelege of at least one season with the Chicago Cubs. That's baseball as it should be played - in God's own sunshine. And that's really living."

-Al Dark, 1958

Boudreau; **Ballpark:** Wrigley Field; **Attendance:** 809,770; **Finish:** Seventh (60-94); **Recap:** Charlie Grimm, in his third go-round as Cubs skipper, lasts little more than a month into the season. Grimm steps down for "health reasons", switching jobs with broadcaster Lou Boudreau. In addition, Grimm is given a vice-presidency position, though his job description is a little vague. After bringing the team home in seventh place and then demanding a two-year contract extension, Boudreau goes back to the broadcast booth.

Although Ernie Banks slugs a league-leading 41 homers and drives home 117, the team bats a collective .243, the lowest mark since 1917, with no other Cub collecting more than 53 RBIs.

P	Player	R	HR	RBI	SB	AVE
1B	Ed Bouchee	33	5	44	2	.237
2B	Jerry Kindall	17	2	23	2	.240
SS	Ernie Banks	94	41	117	1	.271
3B	Ron Santo	44	9	44	0	.251
RF	Bob Will	58	6	53	1	.255
CF	Richie Ashburn	99	0	40	16	.291
LF	George Altman	50	13	51	4	.266
C	El Tappe	11	0	3	0	.233
UT	Frank Thomas	54	21	64	1	.238
UT	Don Zimmer	37	6	35	8	.258
C	Sammy Taylor	14	3	17	0	.207
C	Moe Thacker	5	0	6	1	.156

T	Pitcher	W-L	SV	SO	SH	ERA
R	Glen Hobbie	16-20	1	134	4	3.96
R	Bob Anderson	9-11	1	115	0	4.10
L	Dick Ellsworth	7-13	0	94	0	3.71
R	Don Elston	8-9	11	85	0	3.40

January 11 - The Cubs trade Al Dark, pitcher John Buzhardt and minor leaguer Jim Woods to the Phillies for Richie Ashburn.

April 5 - The Cubs peddle Dale Long to the Giants.

April 8 - The Cubs pick up third baseman Don Zimmer from the Dodgers for outfielder Lee Handley, infielder John Goryl, and minor league pitcher Ron Perranoski.

April 14 - In San Francisco's brand-new Candlestick Park, the Cubs beat the Giants 6-5 despite a late-inning boner by Moe Drabowsky. The reliever, warming up in the bullpen, fields a drive down the third base line by teammate Frank Thomas, thinking it's foul.

The ball is ruled fair, however, and Thomas is forced to stay at first base because of interference. Ernie Banks leads the Cubbie attack with a grand slam in the third.

April 16 - San Francisco's Sam Jones takes a no-hitter into the eighth until Walt Moryn spoils it with a pinch-home run. The Giants beat the Cubs 6-1.

April 22 - The Giants spoil Opening Day at Wrigley with a 10-8 victory.

April 24 - Umpire Ken Burkhart accidently counts a balk called against San Francisco's Billy Loes a ball and awards first base to George Altman - a "three-ball walk." Cubs win 9-4.

April 29 - Ernie Banks drills two home runs to break Gabby Hartnett's team record of 231 homers but the Cardinals pummel the Cubs 16-6. St. Louis's Stan Musial plays his 1,000th game at first base, becoming the first player ever to play 1,000 at two positions (he played 1,513 as an outfielder).

May 4 - With the Cubs off to a 6-11 start, Charlie Grimm is fired and replaced by Lou Boudreau, the team's broadcaster. Grimm takes Boudreau's spot in the WGN booth. Rookie Dick Ellsworth earns his first major league victory, 5-1 over the Pirates.

May 13 - Don Cardwell, who was traded to the Cubs two days ago, hurls a no-hitter over the Cardinals, beating them 4-0. Right fielder George Altman earns a save by making a leaping catch of a drive off the bat of Carl Sawatski.

June 14 - The Cubs sign high school star Danny Murphy to a record $130,000 contract. Murphy, who went 11-0 on the mound and hit .489 his senior year, will bat just .120 this year and drop to the minor leagues after three seasons. He'll return to the big leagues as a pitcher for the White Sox in 1969.

June 18 - Murphy makes his first major league start, as an outfielder in a 7-1 loss to the Reds at Crosley Field.

June 26 - Rookie Ron Santo makes his major league debut in a twinbill at Forbes Field, going 3-for-7 with five RBI as the Cubs sweep, 7-5 and 7-6.

August 4 - At Wrigley Field, Reds second baseman Billy Martin, believing that Jim Brewer is throwing at him, chucks his bat at the Cubs' lefty. Martin then charges the mound and decks Brewer, fracturing the orbital bone of his right eye. Both benches empty; Martin flattens Frank Thomas before being ejected. The Cubs win, 5-3, thanks to Ernie Banks'home run.

Brewer will require surgery and will be disabled for a month. Martin will be fined $500.

August 22 - Brewer and the Cubs sue Martin for $1,040,000. Brewer will settle out of court years later for $25,000.

September 18 - Don Zimmer, Ron Santo and George Altman all homer in the sixth inning of a 5-2 win over Los Angeles at Wrigley. Ernie Banks draws his 27th intentional walk of the year, a record.

Ron Santo

September25 - Glen Hobbie's 5-0 shutout vs. Cincinnati hands Pittsburgh its first pennant since 1927.

October 1 - The Cubs and Dodgers play for 14 innings at the Los Angeles Coliseum before Chicago pushes across a pair of unearned runs to win 10-8. Rookie Billy Williams hits his first major league homer during the four-hour and 54-minute marathon.

December 21 - Cubs owner Phil Wrigley announces his new college of coaches scheme, saying that there will be no official manager in 1961.

December 23 - Rip Collins is added to the college of coaches.

1961

Principle Owner and President: Phil Wrigley; **Manager:** Vedie Himsl / Harry Craft / El Tappe / Lou Klein; **Ballpark:** Wrigley Field; **Attendance:** 673,057; **Finish:** Seventh (64-90); **Recap:** Since 1959, Phil Wrigley has believed that there should be "relief managers" as well as "relief pitchers" and astounds the baseball world - and the city of Chicago - that he is installing a "college of coaches", rotating up to eight baseball men as managers, coaches and instructors, not only to the parent team, but throughout the minors. In addition, Wrigley announces that all of the organization's players are Cubs, and none are to be referred to as "major leaguers" or "minor leaguers." Named as members of the first college are Charlie Grimm, Ripper Collins, Harry Craft, Rube Walker, Goldie Holt, Bobby Adams, El Tappe, and Vedie Himsl. The strategy doesn't work, as the team trudges home in seventh place once again.

P	PLAYER	R	HR	RBI	SB	AVE
1B	Ed Bouchee	49	12	38	1	.248
2B	Don Zimmer	57	13	40	5	.252
SS	Ernie Banks	75	29	80	1	.278
3B	Ron Santo	84	23	83	2	.284
RF	George Altman	77	27	96	6	.303
CF	Al Heist	48	7	37	3	.255
LF	Billy Williams	75	25	86	6	.278
C	Dick Bertell	20	2	33	0	.273
OF	Richie Ashburn	49	0	19	7	.257
IF	Jerry Kindall	37	9	44	2	.242
C	Sammy Taylor	26	8	23	0	.238
UT	Bob Will	9	0	8	0	.257
UT	Andre Rodgers	27	6	23	1	.266

T	PITCHER	W-L	SV	SO	SH	ERA
R	Don Cardwell	15-14	0	156	3	3.82
L	Dick Ellsworth	10-11	0	91	1	3.85
R	Glen Hobbie	7-13	2	103	2	4.25
L	Jack Curtis	10-13	0	57	0	4.90
R	Don Elston	6-7	8	59	0	5.61

January 12 - Charlie Grimm and Verlon Walker are added to Phil Wrigley's college of coaches.

April 14 - The Cubs are 3-2 winners on Opening Day at Wrigley Field.

April 23 - Philadelphia's Art Mahaffey fans 17 in a 6-0 victory over the Cubs.

May 15 - Dick Ellsworth allows six runs in the first without retiring a batter in a 14-1 loss to the Giants.

May 23 - Ernie Banks debuts in left field, going 1-for-4 in a 2-1 10-inning loss to the Phillies.

May 28 - Banks hits a two-out grand slam in the bottom of the eighth to tie the Giants 4-4. San Francisco pulls out a 6-5 victory.

June 2 - Banks collects three run-scoring sacrifice flies, tying a major league record, in a 7-6 win vs. Cincinnati.

June 23 - Mr. Cub's consecutive games streak ends at 717 when he voluntarily sits out a game because of a sore knee. The streak began August 26, 1956. The Cubs beat the Braves 5-3 at Wrigley.

July 2 - Tony Taylor and Glen Hobbie - a pitcher - each hit two home runs in a 10-9 loss to the Cardinals.

August 4 - George Altman hits two homers off Sandy Koufax, the first time the Dodgers' lefty has been tagged twice, in a 4-2 Cubs triumph in Los Angeles. Bob Anderson is the winner.

August 11 - T he Cubs are the victims of Warren Spahn's 300th career victory, 2-1 at Milwaukee's County Stadium.

August 20 - The Cubs and Pirates play their third straight extra-inning game, a

National League record. Chicago wins two of the three, including this one, 1-0.

September 1 - Thirty-year old rookie Cuno Barragan hits a home run in his first major league at-bat. It will be his only homer in the big leagues. The Cubs lose 4-3 to the Giants.

September10 - Lou Brock debuts with the Cubs, collecting a hit, a run and a pair of errors in a 14-6 loss to the Phillies. Ken Hubbs also makes his big league debut, notching two safeties and two runs.

September 14 - The Cubs and Cardinals set a National League record by using 72 players in a doubleheader. St. Louis sweeps 8-7 and 6-5.

October 1 - The Cubs set another record, this time with the Dodgers, as the two clubs use 11 pinch-hitters in an 8-2 Los Angeles triumph. Chicago uses seven of the 11 pinch-hitters.

November30 - Billy Williams is voted the National League's Rookie of the Year.

December 8 - The Mets purchase Richie Ashburn from the Cubs for $50,000.

December 31 - Rick Aguilera is born in San Gabriel, California.

1962

Principle Owner and President: Phil Wrigley; **Manager:** El Tappe / Lou Klein / Charlie Metro; **Ballpark:** Wrigley Field; **Attendance:** 609,802; **Finish:** Ninth (59-103); **Recap:** For the second straight season, a Cub enjoys Rookie of the Year honors, as second baseman Ken Hubbs earns the honor (mostly because of his flashy fielding), just ahead of teammate Lou Brock. But there's little else to cheer about as the club drops to a worst-ever ninth place finish, losing 103 games in the process.

WORTH NOTING - In 1961, Cubs rookie Facundo Barragan hit a home run in his first major league at-bat, just the third NL player to do it (including Ed Morgan of the 1936 Cardinals and Dan Bankhead of the 1947 Dodgers) and never hit another.

P	PLAYER	R	HR	RBI	SB	AVE
1B	Ernie Banks	87	37	104	5	.269
2B	Ken Hubbs	90	5	49	3	.260
SS	Andre Rodgers	40	5	44	5	.278
3B	Ron Santo	44	17	83	4	.227
RF	George Altman	74	22	74	19	.318
CF	Lou Brock	73	9	35	16	.263
LF	Billy Williams	94	22	91	9	.298
C	Dick Bertell	19	2	18	0	.302
P	PLAYER	R	HR	RBI	SB	AVE
OF	Bob Will	6	2	15	0	.239
OF	Don Landrum	29	1	15	9	.282
C	Moe Thacker	8	0	9	0	.187
UT	Jim McKnight	6	0	5	0	.224
C	Cuno Barragan	11	0	12	0	201

T	PITCHER	W-L	SV	SO	SH	ERA
L	Dick Ellsworth	9-20	1	113	0	5.08
R	Bob Buhl	12-13	0	109	1	3.69
R	Cal Koonce	10-10	0	84	1	3.96
R	Don Cardwell	7-16	4	104	1	4.91
R	Don Elston	4-8	8	37	0	2.45

March 25 - Elvin Tappe is named this season's "head coach."

April 10 - The Cubs lose to the expansion Colt .45s 11-2 in Houston's inaugural game at mosquito-infested Colt Stadium. The Colts will sweep the three-game series.

April 13 - The Cubs suffer their fourth straight loss, 8-5 to the Cardinals on Opening Day at Wrigley. Chicago will run their record to 0-7 before beating Houston on April 18.

April 17 - Chicago uses five pitchers in the eighth inning of a 10-6 defeat to Pittsburgh, tying an NL record.

April 22 - The Cubbies, 1-9 going into today's doubleheader, sweep the undefeated Cardinals 11-5 and 5-1. Ernie Banks hits a three-run homer in the opener.

April 30 - The Cubs acquire Bob Buhl from the Braves for pitcher Jack Curtis. Buhl will win 51 games for Chicago over the next four seasons.

May 15 - Chicago's Barney Schultz ties a major league record held by Elroy Face by appearing in his ninth consecutive game. The Cubs lose to the lowly Mets, 6-5 in 13 innings.

May 20 - Lou Brock hits a grand slam in the second inning to give the Cubs a 6-4 win in the first of two at Philadelphia. Chicago wins the second game 11-2. Ken Hubbs collects eight singles in the twinbill.

May 25 - Ernie Banks is beaned by former teammate Moe Drabowski in a 2-1 loss to Cincinnati. Banks is taken from the field on a stretcher.

May 26 - Cal Koonce allows just two hits but loses to the Reds 2-1. Frank Robinson's fourth-inning double drives in both runs for Cincinnati.

WORTH NOTING - In 1962, the Cubs hired Buck O'Neill as the first African American coach in major league history. O'Neill, a first baseman and long-time manager of the Kansas City Monarchs, O'Neill had been scouting for the Cubs since 1956. Among his recommendations were Lou Brock and Ernie Banks. O'Neill found fame in the 1990s after appearing on several segments of Ken Burns' *Baseball* PBS documentary series.

May 29 - Ernie Banks, back in the lineup after three days, clouts three home runs and a double in an 11-9 loss to the Braves at Wrigley Field. The Cubs outhit Milwaukee 15-8 but an error by shortstop Andre Rodgers in the third leads to six unearned runs.

June 17 - Lou Brock becomes just the second player in major league history to reach the center-field bleachers at the Polo Grounds with a 470-foot home run in the first game of a Cubs doubleheader sweep of the Mets, 8-7 and 4-3. Milwaukee's Joe Adcock is the other major leaguer to reach the bleachers. Hank Aaron will do it tomorrow.

Also in the opener, Marvelous Marv Throneberry, the Mets' first baseman, triples but misses both first and second bases while running and is called out on an appeal.

July 13 - Cal Koonce hurls a 1-0 one-hitter over the Cincinnati Reds.

August 26 - Dick Ellsworth snaps Hank Aaron's 25-game hitting streak in a 4-1 win vs. Milwaukee. The Cubs lay down three sacrifice bunts in the sixth inning, tying a major league record.

September 5 - Ken Hubbs sets a pair of major league records, most consecutive games without an error (78) and most consecutive chances without an error (418) in a 4-1 loss to Cincinnati. Both streaks end in the fourth when Hubbs makes a throwing error.

September 19 - Randy Myers is born in Vancouver, Washington.

September 26 - The Cubs lose their 101st of the year, 5-3 to the Phillies. Only 903 fans see the game at Wrigley Field. Just

607 will watch tomorrow's 8-0 loss, also to Philadelphia.

September 28 - The Cubs beat the Mets, 3-2, before 595 hard-core fans.

September 29 - Dick Ellsworth loses his 20th game, 3-2 to the Mets, before 2,870 at the Wrig.

September 30 - The Cubs end the season on a high note with a 5-1 win vs. New York, turning a triple play in the process. The Met's loss is their 120th, a modern major league record.

October 17 - Pitchers Larry Jackson and Lindy McDaniel and catcher Jimmie Schaffer are acquired from the Cards for pitcher Don Cardwell, outfielder George Altman and catcher Moe Thacker.

November 14 - Bob Kennedy is signed as the eighth and final member of the coach college.

1963

Principle Owner and President: Phil Wrigley; **Manager:** Bob Kennedy; **Ballpark:** Wrigley Field; **Attendance:** 979,551; **Finish:** Seventh (82-80); **Recap:** The Cubs have a stunning reversal of fortune, improving to 82-80, their first over-.500 season since 1946. Part of the team's success is partly due to the abysmal play of the Pirates (74-88), Houston Colt .45s (66-96) and New York Mets (51-111) and is partly due to the timely hitting of Ron Santo and Billy Williams, and a phenomenal season by lefthander Dick Ellsworth. The team's .506 winning percentage is a major league record for a seventh-place club. Abandoning his "college of coaches" scheme, owner Phil Wrigley names Bob Kennedy "head coach."

Billy Williams

P	Player	R	HR	RBI	SB	AVE
1B	Ernie Banks	41	18	64	0	.227
2B	Ken Hubbs	54	8	47	8	.235
SS	Andre Rogers	51	5	33	5	.229
3B	Ron Santo	79	25	99	6	.297
RF	Lou Brock	79	9	37	24	.258
CF	Ellis Burton	45	12	41	6	.230
LF	Billy Williams	87	25	95	7	.286
C	Dick Bertell	15	2	14	0	.233
OF	Don Landrum	27	1	10	6	.242
UT	Merritt Ranew	18	3	15	1	.338
OF	Nelson Mathews	12	4	10	3	.155
C	Jimmy Schaffer	17	7	19	0	.239
UT	Steve Boros	9	3	7	0	.211

T	Pitcher	W-L	SV	SO	SH	ERA
L	Dick Ellsworth	22-10	0	185	4	2.10
R	Larry Jackson	14-18	0	153	4	2.55
R	Bob Buhl	11-14	0	108	0	3.38
R	Glen Hobbie	7-10	0	94	1	3.93
R	Lindy McDaniel	13-7	22	75	0	2.86

January 5 - Former Cub great Rogers Hornsby dies of a heart ailment at age 66.

January 10 - Retired Air Force Colonel Robert V. Whitlow is hired as the Cubs'

WORTH NOTING - Rookie Merritt Ranew hit .338 with 17 pinch-hits for the Cubs in 1963. But the next season, he went 3-for-33 and was traded to the Braves.

athletic director.

January 27 - The Hall of Fame Veterans Committee votes a plaque to John Clarkson, Chicago's greatest 19th century pitcher.

February 20 - Phil Wrigley scraps his college of coaches experiment, hiring Bob Kennedy as the club's full-time manager.

March 21 - Shawon Dunston is born in Brooklyn, New York.

April 9 - The Dodgers clip the Cubs 5-1 on Opening Day at Wrigley Field.

May 4 - Cubs baserunners induce a record six balks, including three in the third by Bob Shaw in a 7-5 victory over the Braves.

June 6 - Lindy McDaniel relieves with the bases loaded and one out in the 12th, picks off Giant Willie Mays at second and fans Ed Bailey, then wins the game in the bottom of the frame with a home run. The 3-2 win puts the Cubs in first place for the first time since May 1958.

June 9 - Ernie Banks slams two homers as the Cubs knock Dodger ace Sandy Koufax from the box with six runs in five and 2/3 innings, but the Dodgers take the game 11-8. Dick Ellsworth is the loser.

June 15 - Banks, who has 15 home runs to date, is diagnosed with sub-clinical mumps, a blood disease, and will hit just three more this season.

June 20 - Billy Williams rips two homers and a double, and Larry Jackson hurls a four-hitter to beat the Houston Colts 5-0.

July 28 - Dick Ellsworth fans 10, including Stan Musial three times, in a 5-1 Cubs victory versus St. Louis.

August 1 - Ellis Burton becomes the eighth player in history to homer from both sides of the plate in a 10-2 win over the Braves.

August 7 - Sandy Koufax and Dick Ellsworth battle to a 1-1 tie through 10 innings before each is removed. The eventually Dodgers eke out a 3-1 win.

August 8 - The Cubs hang on to beat the Dodgers 5-4 despite back-to-back pinch-homers by Frank Howard and Moose Skowron in the fifth. It's just the second time in history this has occurred.

August 31 - Ellis Burton poles a 2-out ninth-inning grand slam off reliever Hal Woodeshick to give the Cubs a 6-5 victory over Houston at Wrigley.

September 3 - Ron Santo commits three errors in an inning, tying the NL record, in a 16-3 loss to San Francisco.

September 28 - Dick Ellsworth notches his 22nd win, a 4-1 decision over the Braves in Milwaukee.

1964

Principle Owner and President: Phil Wrigley; **Manager:** Bob Kennedy; **Ballpark:** Wrigley Field; **Attendance:** 751,647; **Finish:** Eighth (76-86); **Recap:** The 1964 season begins tragically for the Cubs, as second baseman Ken Hubbs is killed in a plane crash near Provo, Utah, in February. Things don't improve much after that, as manager Bob Kennedy brings the club in eighth, 17 games behind St. Louis. Dick Ellsworth slumps to 14-18 but Larry Jackson wins 24 games, becoming the first Cub to lead the league since Bill Lee in 1939.

P	PLAYER	R	HR	RBI	SB	AVE
1B	Ernie Banks	67	23	95	1	.264
2B	Joey Amalfitano	51	4	27	2	.241
SS	Andre Rogers	50	12	46	5	.239
3B	Ron Santo	94	30	114	3	.313
RF	Len Gabrielson	22	5	23	9	.246
CF	Billy Cowan	52	19	50	12	.241
LF	Billy Williams	100	33	98	10	.312
C	Dick Bertell	29	4	35	2	.238
UT	Jimmy Stewart	59	3	33	10	.253
UT	Leo Burke	11	1	14	0	.262
C	Jimmie Schaffer	9	2	9	2	.205
OF	Doug Clemens	23	2	12	0	.279
OF	Lou Brock	30	2	14	10	.251

T	PITCHER	W-L	SV	SO	SH	ERA
R	Larry Jackson	24-11	0	148	3	3.14
L	Dick Ellsworth	14-18	0	148	1	3.75
R	Bob Buhl	15-14	0	107	3	3.83
R	Lew Burdette	9-9	0	40	2	4.88
R	Lindy McDaniel	1-7	15	71	0	3.88

February 15 - Ken Hubbs dies when his plane crashes in Provo, Utah while flying to Colton, California. Hubbs was 22.

April 17 - The Phillies win a wild Opening Day game at Wrigley 11-8. The two teams combine for five home runs in the fifth inning, three by Philadelphia and two by Chicago.

April 21 - The Pirates beat the Cubs 8-5 at Wrigley, with all runs being scored on home runs, tying an NLrecord. Home runs are hit by nine different players, tying the major league mark.

May 1 - The Cubs score 10 runs in the first inning in an 11-3 win vs. Houston. Billy Williams drives in five with a single and a grand slam in the inning, setting a club record. He adds a run-scoring double in the eighth.

June 2 - The Cubs trade Glen Hobbie to the Cardinals for pitcher Lew Burdette.

June 15 - They'll never live this one down: The Cubs trade Lou Brock, along with pitchers Jack Spring and Paul Toth, for pitchers Ernie Broglio and Bobby Shantz and outfielder Doug Clemens. Broglio, who won 18 games for the Cards in 1963, will go 3-5 for Chicago while Brock will lead St. Louis to a World Championship and go on to a Hall of Fame career.

June 28 - Mark Grace is born in Winston-Salem, North Carolina.

June 30 - Larry Jackson allows just one hit and drives in the game's only run with a single in a 1-0 win vs. the Reds. Cincinnati's starter, Joey Jay, gives up just two hits in the loss.

August 15 - Ernie Banks goes hitless on Ernie Banks Day in a 5-4 Cubs loss to Pittsburgh. Mayor Richard Daley is among the 26,000 fans at Wrigley to cheer Mr. Cub.

September13 - The Cardinals score in every inning vs. the Cubs at Wrigley, beating them 15-2.

1965

Principle Owner and President: Phil Wrigley; **Manager:** Bob Kennedy / Lou Klein; **Ballpark:** Wrigley Field; **Attendance:** 641,361; **Finish:** Eighth (72-90); **Recap:** The Cubs finish eighth again despite strong seasons from reliever Ted Abernathy, who leads the league in saves (31) and appearances (84) and Ernie Banks, Ron Santo and Billy Williams, who each drive in more than 100 runs. During the season, manager Bo Kennedy is fired and replaced by Lou Klein.

Career Batting Records

(Minimum Five Seasons with Chicago)

GAMES PLAYED

Player	Total
Ernie Banks	2,528
Cap Anson	2,276
Billy Williams	2,213
Ryne Sandberg	2,151
Ron Santo	2,126

RUNS SCORED

Player	Total
Cap Anson	1,719
Jimmy Ryan	1,409
Ryne Sandberg	1,316
Billy Williams	1,306
Ernie Banks	1,305

HITS

Player	Total
Cap Anson	3,000
Ernie Banks	2,583
Billy Williams	2,510
Ryne Sandberg	2,385
Stan Hack	2,193

BASES ON BALLS

Player	Total
Stan Hack	1,092
Ron Santo	1,071
Cap Anson	952
Billy Williams	911
Phil Cavarretta	794

DOUBLES

Player	Total
Cap Anson	528
Ernie Banks	407
Ryne Sandberg	403
Billy Williams	402
Gabby Hartnett	391

STOLEN BASES

Player	Total
Frank Chance	404
Ryne Sandberg	344
Joe Tinker	304
Johnny Evers	291
Wildfire Schulte	214

TRIPLES

Player	Total
Jimmy Ryan	142
Cap Anson	124
Wildfire Schulte	117
Bill Dahlen	106
Phil Cavarretta	99

BATTING AVERAGE

Player	Total
Rogers Hornsby	.350
Bill Madlock	.336
Riggs Stephenson	.336
Ray Grimes	.335
Bill Lange	.330

HOME RUNS

Player	Total
Ernie Banks	512
Sammy Sosa	510
Billy Williams	392
Ron Santo	337
Ryne Sandberg	282

SLUGGING

Player	Total
Rogers Hornsby	.604
Hack Wilson	.590
Dave Kingman	.569
Sammy Sosa	.526
Hank Sauer	.512

RUNS BATTED IN

Player	Total
Cap Anson	1,715
Ernie Banks	1,636
Billy Williams	1,353
Ron Santo	1,290
Gabby Hartnett	1,153

Career Pitching Records

(Minimum Five Seasons with Chicago)

VICTORIES

Player	Total
Charlie Root	201
Three Finger Brown	188
Bill Hutchison	182
Larry Corcoran	175
Ferguson Jenkins	167

STRIKEOUTS

Player	Total
Ferguson Jenkins	2,038
Charlie Root	1,432
Rick Reuschel	1,367
Bill Hutchison	1,226
Hippo Vaughn	1,138

WINNING PCT.

Player	Total
Al Spalding	.787
John Clarkson	.705
Three Finger Brown	.694
Ed Reulbach	.677
Larry Corcoran	.673

SHUTOUTS

Player	Total
Three Finger Brown	48
Hippo Vaughn	35
Ed Reulbach	31
Ferguson Jenkins	29
Orval Overall	28

APPEARANCES

Player	Total
Charlie Root	605
Lee Smith	458
Don Elston	449
Guy Bush	428
Fergie Jenkins	401

SAVES

Player	Total
Lee Smith	180
Bruce Sutter	133
Randy Myers	112
Phil Regan	60
Mitch Williams	52

ERA

Player	Total
Al Spalding	1.78
Three Finger Brown	1.80
Jack Pfiester	1.87
Orval Overall	1.92
Jack Weimer	2.15

BASES ON BALLS

Player	Total
Bill Hutchison	1,106
Charlie Root	871
Guy Bush	734
Bob Rush	725
Bill Lee	704

INNINGS PITCHED

Player	Total
Charlie Root	3,138
Bill Hutchison	3,026
Ferguson Jenkins	2,672
Larry Corcoran	2,338
Three Finger Brown	2,329

COMPLETE GAMES

Player	Total
Bill Hutchison	317
Larry Corcoran	252
Clark Griffith	240
Three Finger Brown	206
Jack Taylor	188

Season Batting Records

(Minimum 300 At-Bats)

RUNS SCORED

Player	Year	Total
Rogers Hornsby	1929	156
King Kelly	1886	155
Kiki Cuyler	1930	155
Woody English	1930	152
George Gore	1886	150

HITS

Player	Year	Total
Rogers Hornsby	1929	229
Kiki Cuyler	1930	228
Billy Herman	1935	227
Woody English	1930	214
Frank Demaree	1936	212

DOUBLES

Player	Year	Total
Billy Herman	1935	57
Billy Herman	1936	57
Mark Grace	1995	51
Kiki Cuyler	1930	50
Ned Williamson	1883	49

TRIPLES

Player	Year	Total
Wilfire Schulte	1911	21
Vic Saier	1913	21
Bill Dahlen	1892	19
Bill Dahlen	1896	19
Ryne Sandberg	1984	19

HOME RUNS

Player	Year	Total
Sammy Sosa	1998	66
Sammy Sosa	2001	64
Sammy Sosa	1999	63
Hack Wilson	1930	56
Sammy Sosa	2000	50

RUNS BATTED IN

Player	Year	Total
Hack Wilson	1930	191
Sammy Sosa	2001	160
Sammy Sosa	1998	158
Hack Wilson	1929	159
Rogers Hornsby	1929	149

BASES ON BALLS

Player	Year	Total
Jimmy Sheckard	1911	147
Jimmy Sheckard	1912	122
Richie Ashburn	1960	116
Sammy Sosa	2001	116
Cap Anson	1890	113

STOLEN BASES

Player	Year	Total
Frank Chance	1903	67
Billy Maloney	1905	59
Frank Chance	1906	57
Ryne Sandberg	1985	54
Johnny Evers	1906	49

BATTING AVERAGE

Player	Year	Total
Bill Lange	1895	.389
King Kelly	1886	.388
Rogers Hornsby	1929	.380
Heinie Zimmerman	1912	.372
Cap Anson	1886	.371

SLUGGING

Player	Year	Total
Sammy Sosa	2001	.737
Hack Wilson	1930	.723
Rogers Hornsby	1929	.679
Sammy Sosa	1998	.647
Sammy Sosa	1999	.635

Season Pitching Records

(Minimum 50 Innings Pitched)

VICTORIES (PRE-1900)

Player	Year	Total
John Clarkson	1885	53
Al Spalding	1876	47
Bill Hutchison	1891	44
Larry Corcoran	1880	43
Bill Hutchison	1890	42

VICTORIES (POST-1900)

Player	Year	Total
Three Finger Brown	1908	29
Three Finger Brown	1909	27
Grover Alexander	1920	27
Larry Cheney	1912	26
Charlie Root	1927	26

APPEARANCES

Player	Year	Total
Ted Abernathy	1965	84
Dick Tidrow	1980	84
Bill Campbell	1983	82
Rod Beck	1998	81
Bob Patterson	1996	79

COMPLETE GAMES

Player	Year	Total
John Clarkson	1885	68
Bill Hutchison	1892	67
Bill Hutchison	1890	65
John Clarkson	1887	56
Bill Hutchison	1891	56

EARNED RUN AVERAGE

Player	Year	Total
Three Finger Brown	1906	1.04
Jack Pfiester	1907	1.15
Carl Lundgren	1907	1.17
Three Finger Brown	1909	1.31
Jack Taylor	1902	1.33

STRIKEOUTS

Player	Year	Total
Bill Hutchison	1892	316
John Clarkson	1886	313
John Clarkson	1885	308
Bill Hutchison	1890	286
Ferguson Jenkins	1970	274

SHUTOUTS

Player	Year	Total
John Clarkson	1885	10
Three Finger Brown	1906	9
Three Finger Brown	1908	9
Orval Overall	1909	9
Grover Alexander	1919	9
Bill Lee	1938	9

SAVES

Player	Year	Total
Lee Smith	1991	47
Bruce Sutter	1984	45
Lee Smith	1992	43
Lee Smith	1993	43

(Three tied with 36)

WORTH NOTING - Ernie Banks played in a record 2,528 games without ever appearing in a World Series.

P	PLAYER	R	HR	RBI	SB	AVE
1B	Ernie Banks	79	28	106	3	.265
2B	Glenn Beckert	73	3	30	6	.239
SS	Don Kessinger	19	0	14	1	.201
3B	Ron Santo	88	33	101	3	.285
RF	Billy Williams	115	34	108	10	.315
CF	Don Landrum	60	6	34	14	.226
LF	Doug Clemens	36	4	26	5	.221
C	Vic Roznovsky	9	3	15	1	.221
UT	Jimmy Stewart	26	0	19	13	.223
UT	George Altman	24	4	23	3	.235
IF	Joey Amalfitano	13	0	8	2	.271
UT	Ed Bailey	13	5	23	0	.253
C	Chris Krug	16	5	24	0	.201

T	PITCHER	W-L	SV	SO	SH	ERA
R	Larry Jackson	14-21	0	131	4	3.85
L	Dick Ellsworth	14-15	1	130	0	3.81
R	Bob Buhl	13-11	0	92	0	4.40
R	Cal Koonce	7-9	0	88	1	3.69
R	Ted Abernathy	4-6	31	104	0	2.58

March 19 - Cubs broadcaster Jack Quinlan is killed during spring training in Arizona when his car hits a truck while he is returning from a golf outing.

April 12 - Bob Gibson and the Cardinals take a 5-1 lead in the first off Larry Jackson but the Cubs roar back and the game ends a 10-10 tie, called in the 11th inning for darkness, a Wrigley Opening Day first.

May 15 - Dick Ellsworth takes a no-hitter into the eighth before Al Farrara hits a pinch-hit three-run homer for a 3-1 Dodger victory.

May 23 - The Dodgers tally two runs off Bob Buhl in the first but they're the only runs the Cubs staff will earn over the next 15 innings; Chicago wins 3-2 in the 16th on a bases-loaded walk.

May 29 - Philadelphia's Dick Allen crushes a homer estimated at 529 feet over the center field roof at Connie Mack Stadium off Larry Jackson in the first inning of a 4-2 Phillies triumph.

July 22 - Backup catcher Ed Bailey drives in eight runs, including a grand slam, to help the Cubs beat the Phillies 10-6.

August 8 - The Cubs score six runs in the ninth to beat the Mets 14-10. Chicago's Chris Krug strikes out twice in the inning, the first Cub who's fanned twice in one inning.

September 2 - Ernie Banks hits his 400th career home run, a three-run shot off the Cardinals' Curt Simmons, in the third inning of a 5-3 Cubs win at Wrigley.

September9 - Chicago's Bob Hendley and Los Angeles' Sandy Koufax duel through four perfect innings before Dodger outfielder Lou Johnson walks in the fifth. After a sacrifice, Johnson steals third base and scores on a bad throw by catcher Chris Krug. Johnson later gets the game's only hit, a single in the seventh. Koufax hurls a perfect game, his fourth - and final - no-hitter. The Dodgers win 1-0; only one runner is left on base, a major league record. It's the second time this season a Chicago pitcher has tossed a one-hitter and lost.

September14 - Hendley and Koufax hook up again; the Cubs'pitcher allows four hits but wins this time, 2-1.

September 18 - Larry Jackson beats the Mets, 4-3. It's his 1th straight victory over New York.

September 23 - Jackson becomes the first pitcher since Murry Dickson of the 1951-52 Pirates to follow a 20-win season with a 20-loss season as he loses to the Phillies today, 7-4.

October3 - The Cubs turn their third triple play of the season, tying an MLrecord, but Pittsburgh wins 6-3 at Forbes Field. Ted Abernathy makes his record 84th appearance, taking the loss.

October25 - The legendary Leo "The Lip" Durocher becomes the Cubs'new manager, replacing Lou Klein.

December 2 - The Cubs trade pitcher Lindy McDaniel and outfielder Don Landrum to the Giants for catcher Randy Hundley and pitcher Bill Hands. Hundley and Hands will put together several fine seasons for Chicago.

1966

Principle Owner and President: Phil Wrigley; **Manager:** Leo Durocher; **Ballpark:** Wrigley Field; **Attendance:** 635,891; **Finish:** Tenth (59-103); **Recap:** New manager Leo Durocher sets the tone for his tenure as soon as his first press conference, when he informs the press and players - as well as Wrigley - that he will be referred to as manager, and manager only - not "coach". He then asserts himself in the front office, stopping the club's routine of trading away good, young players.

In spring training, Durocher insists that the Cubs are "not an eighth-place team," and they prove him right, finishing tenth.

P	Player	R	HR	RBI	SB	AVE
1B	Ernie Banks	52	15	75	0	.272
2B	Glenn Beckert	73	1	59	10	.287
SS	Don Kessinger	50	1	43	13	.274
3B	Ron Santo	93	30	94	4	.312
RF	Billy Williams	100	29	91	6	.276
CF	Adolfo Phillips	68	16	36	32	.262
LF	Byron Browne	46	16	51	3	.243
C	Randy Hundley	50	19	63	1	.236

WORTH NOTING - The Cubs turned three triple plays in 1965. Bill Faul was on the mound for all three.

P	Player	R	HR	RBI	SB	AVE
UT	George Altman	19	5	17	2	.222
UT	John Boccabella	22	6	25	0	.228
UT	Lee Thomas	15	1	9	0	.242
UT	Jimmy Stewart	4	0	4	1	.178
IF	Joey Amalfitano	8	0	3	0	.158

T	Pitcher	W-L	SV	SO	SH	ERA
L	Dick Ellsworth	8-22	0	144	0	3.98
L	Ken Holtzman	11-16	0	171	0	3.79
R	Bill Hands	8-13	2	93	0	4.58
R	Ferguson Jenkins	6-8	5	148	1	3.31
L	Bob Hendley	4-5	7	65	0	3.90

April 14 - Greg Maddux is born in San Angelo, Texas.

April 19 - The Giants edge the Cubs in a wind-blown slugfest, 11-10 on Opening Day at Wrigley.

April 21 - The Cubs, struggling at 1-7, swap pitchers Larry Jackson and Bob Buhl to the Phillies for Ferguson Jenkins, outfielder Adolfo Phillips and utility player John Hernstein. Jenkins, who went 2-1 for the Phillies last year, will go on to a Hall of Fame career.

April 23 - Jenkins pays dividends right away, hurling a 2-0 and shutout and hitting a home run to beat the Dodgers at Wrigley Field. Rookie Don Sutton is the loser.

May 19 - In the fifth inning, Randy Hundley triples off Houston's Dick Farrell and then steals home against reliever Gary Kroll. Cubs win 5-1.

May 28 - Ron Santo swats a 12th-inning, three-run homer to beat the Braves 8-5.

May 29 - Santo does it again, smacking a

Leo Durocher

10th-inning home run to beat Atlanta 3-2.

May 31 - Santo appears in his 364th consecutive game at third base, setting a National League record. The Cubs beat the Pirates 2-1 at Pittsburgh.

June 4 - Santo homers twice and singles, leading the Cubs to a 6-4 triumph over the Reds.

June 11 - Ernie Banks triples three times, tying a major league record, as Chicago beats the Astros 8-2 at the Astrodome.

June 26 - Ron Santo becomes the victim of on-field ugliness when a pitch by the Mets' Jack Fisher fractures his cheek. Before Santo came to bat, New York's Ron Hunt and Chicago's Adolfo Phillips had also been beaned. Santo will return to action in a week. His consecutive games played streak ends at 390, but his hitting streak, now at 27, continues.

WORTH QUOTING - "Fergie (Jenkins) had tremendous control. I could almost catch him with a pair of pliers."
-Randy Hundley

July 3 - Moises Alou is born in Haina, Dominican Republic.

July 4 - Santo returns to the lineup and sets a Cubs hitting streak record, 28, in the first game of a doubleheader. The streak is snapped in the nightcap. The Cubs and Pirates split the twinbill.

July 5 - Ernie Broglio, who the Cubs received as the centerpiece of a 1964 trade that sent future Hall of Famer Lou Brock to St. Louis, is released.

July 17 - Billy Williams hits for the cycle as the Cubs beat the Cardinals 7-2 behind rookie lefty Ken Holtzman.

July 19 - Cincinnati's Jim Maloney fans Cubs outfielder Byron Browne five times in a 3-2, 18-inning marathon. Browne will strike out three more times tomorrow to set a National League mark. He will lead the NL in strikeouts this year with 143.

August 11 - Randy Hundley hits for the cycle to lead the Cubs to a 9-8 win over Houston.

August 12 - Kenny Holtzman beats the Dodgers' Don Sutton 2-1. Chicago will beat the Los Angeles righthander again in two days, 12-10.

August 29 - Future Hall of Famer Robin Roberts, just acquired by the Cubs from Houston, beats the Braves 4-2 for the final victory of his career. Roberts has now beaten the Braves franchise in its three locations: Boston, Milwaukee and Atlanta.

September 21 - Just 440 turn out at Wrigley Field to watch Ken Holtzman beat the Cincinnati Reds 9-3.

September 25 - Holtzman beats Sandy Koufax 2-1 in a duel of Jewish pitchers. Holtzman holds the Dodgers hitless until the ninth.

December7 - The Cubs send veteran Dick Ellsworth to the Phillies for pitcher Ray Culp and cash.

1967

Principle Owner and President: Phil Wrigley; **Manager:** Leo Durocher; **Ballpark:** Wrigley Field; **Attendance:** 977,226; **Finish:** Third (87-74); **Recap:** Leo Durocher nearly pulls off a miracle in 1967, jumping from last place to finish third, 14 games behind St. Louis. Chicago actually ties the Cardinals for first on July 25, but a couple of long losing stretches eases them out of contention.

The team now features perhaps the game's best infield, with Ernie Banks (now at first base), and Ron Santo providing the power and Don Kessinger and Glenn Beckert the defense. Billy Williams enjoys another productive year and newcomers Adolfo Phillips (17 homers) and Randy Hundley (60 RBIs) contribute solid numbers. Hundley's .996 fielding average sets an NL record.

P	Player	R	HR	RBI	SB	AVE
1B	Ernie Banks	68	23	95	2	.276
2B	Glenn Beckert	91	5	40	10	.280
SS	Don Kessinger	61	0	42	6	.231
3B	Ron Santo	107	31	98	1	.300
RF	Ted Savage	40	5	33	7	.218
CF	Adolfo Phillips	66	17	70	24	.268
LF	Billy Williams	92	28	84	6	.278
C	Randy Hundley	68	14	60	2	.267

WORTH NOTING - Fergie Jenkins holds the all-time record for putouts by a pitcher (363).

P	Player	R	HR	RBI	SB	AVE
UT	Lee Thomas	16	2	23	1	.220
OF	Al Spangler	18	0	13	2	.254
UT	Clarence Jones	13	2	16	0	.252
IF	Paul Popovich	18	0	2	0	.214

T	Pitcher	W-L	SV	SO	SH	ERA
R	Ferguson Jenkins	20-13	0	236	3	2.80
R	Rich Nye	13-10	0	119	0	3.20
R	Joe Niekro	10-7	0	77	2	3.34
R	Ray Culp	8-11	0	111	1	3.88
R	Chuck Hartenstein	9-5	10	20	0	3.08

April 11 - The Cubs take an Opening Day victory, beating the Phils 4-2 at Wrigley.

April 18 - Outfielder Adolfo Phillips drops a fly ball that allows three Phillies to cross the plate but homers and triples to lead the Cubs to an 8-4 triumph.

May 10 - Phillips steals home in a 5-4 victory over the Giants.

May 20 - Phillips drives in six and Randy Hundley adds a grand slam as the Cubs pummel the Dodgers 20-3. Ken Holtzman improves to 5-0, just before leaving for a six-month tour of duty in the Army. Holtzman will occasionally pitch on weekend passes and finish 9-0, the first pitcher since Howie Krist went 10-0 in 1941 to win as many as nine in a season without a loss.

June 11 - Phillips hits three home runs in the second game to finish with four round-trippers in a Wrigley doubleheader with the Mets. The Cubs sweep the twinbill 5-3 and 18-10. There are 11 homers hit in the nightcap, setting an NL record for two teams in a nine-inning game. Phillips drives in eight

WORTH NOTING - Randy Hundley's fielding percentage of .996 in 1967 tied a club record. He commited just four errors.

runs and collects six hits for the day.

June 25 - Rookie Joe Niekro tosses a three-hitter and Ernie Banks swats two two-run homers off Bo Belinsky as the Cubs beat the Astros 8-0.

July 2 - For the first time in a long time, the Cubs own a piece of first place as they beat the Reds 4-1 behind Fergie Jenkins. Chicago has now won 17 of their last 19.

July 3 - Billy Williams, Ron Santo, and Randy Hundley connect for home runs in the top of the first inning and Rico Carty and Felipe Alou answer for the Braves in the bottom of the frame for a major league record five home runs by two teams in the first inning. Glenn Beckert adds a three-run shot later in the game to help the Cubs defeat Atlanta 12-6.

July 4 - In their first-ever matchup, Atlanta's Phil Niekro beats his brother Joe 8-3.

July 24 - The Cubs return to the top after suffering a seven-game losing streak, beating the first-place Cardinals 3-1.

September 4 - The Cubs beat Don Sutton 2-1 in 11 innings; the Dodger righthander is now 0-7 against them in his career.

September 11 - Houston uses an NL-record eight pitchers to defeat the Cubbies 11-10.

November 30 - The Cubs trade Ray Culp to the Red Sox for minor leaguer Rudy Schlesinger and cash. A washout in Chicago, Culp will go 16-6 with Boston.

1968

Principle Owner and President: Phil Wrigley; **Manager:** Leo Durocher; **Ballpark:** Wrigley Field; **Attendance:** 1,043,409; **Finish:** Third (84-78); **Recap:** The Cubs show flashes in 1968, winning 29 of 39 in July and August to jump from ninth place to third, but they don't have the depth or staying power to contend late in the season. Amid complaints that Leo Durocher is over-extending his starters, who play nearly every inning this year, several Cubs put together solid seasons including Billy Williams (98 RBIs), Ernie Banks (32 homers), Ron Santo (26 homers), and Fergie Jenkins (20-15). Righthander Phil Regan, obtained from the Dodgers in a mid-season trade, saves a league-leading 25 games and wins 10.

The Cubs lead the slugging-thin NL with 130 homers and finish first in fielding percentage (.981).

P	Player	R	HR	RBI	SB	AVE
1B	Ernie Banks	71	32	83	2	.246
2B	Glenn Beckert	<u>98</u>	4	37	8	.294
SS	Don Kessinger	63	1	32	9	.240
3B	Ron Santo	86	26	98	3	.246
RF	Jim Hickman	22	5	23	1	.223
CF	Adolfo Phillips	49	13	33	9	.241
LF	Billy Williams	91	30	98	4	.288
C	Randy Hundley	41	7	65	1	.226
OF	Al Spangler	21	2	18	0	.271
IF	Dick Nen	8	2	16	0	.181
OF	Lou Johnson	14	1	14	3	.244
UT	Jose Arcia	15	1	8	0	.190
UT	Willie Smith	13	5	25	0	.275

T	Pitcher	W-L	SV	SO	SH	ERA
R	Ferguson Jenkins	20-15	0	260	3	2.63
R	Bill Hands	16-10	34	148	4	2.88
L	Ken Holtzman	11-14	1	151	3	3.35
R	Joe Niekro	14-10	2	65	1	4.32
R	Phil Regan	10-5	<u>25</u>	60	0	2.20

March 23 - Cubs pitcher Jim Ellis goes to

his mouth intentionally on a 3-and-1 count to a batter, issuing a "Lip Pass" intentional walk. Cubs manager Leo Durocher, who ordered the act because of his opposition to the new major league rule preventing pitchers from going to their mouths while on the rubber, will be warned not to do it again or be fined. He'll ignore the threat and the rule will later be relaxed.

April 13 - The Cubs are losers on Opening Day at Wrigley, 8-5 to St. Louis.

April 23 - The Cubs trade outfielder Ted Savage and pitcher Jim Ellis to the Dodgers for pitcher Phil Regan and outfielder Jim Hickman. Regan will lead the NL in saves with 25 and win 10 games. Hicman will hit 21 homers during next year's pennant run.

May 16 - The Dodgers' Don Sutton holds the Cubs to one run, but loses to Rich Nye 1-0.

May 21 - Billy Williams plays in his 695th straight game, a record for outfielders, in a 6-5 win over Philadelphia.

June 20 - The Cubs are shutout for the fifth time in a row, 1-0. Fergie Jenkins, who takes today's loss, has allowed just one run in his last two starts but has just a loss and a no-decision to show for it.

June 21 - Chicago ends its scoreless streak at a major league-record 48 innings, beating the Reds 3-2 behind Joe Niekro.

July 7 - Phil Regan notches two wins in a doubleheader sweep over the Pirates, 5-4 and 4-3, the second time this season the Cubs'reliever has picked up two wins in a twinbill.

July 11 - Bill Hands beats the New York Mets 2-0 but strikes out in his 14th straight at-bat, setting a major league record.

July 28 - Ken Holtzman beats Don Sutton and the Dodgers 1-0. Sutton is now 0-10 against the Cubbies. Holtzie will beat him the next three times they face each other.

July 31 - Billy Williams, Ernie Banks, and Jim Hickman all homer in the fourth inning of a 6-1 defeat of Houston at Wrigley Field. Fergie Jenkins is the winner.

August 8 - The Cubs beat the Braves 4-0 behind Bill Hands and Phil Regan at Wrigley. In the ninth, home plate umpire Chris Pelekoudas, suspecting that Regan has been throwing a spitball, goes to the mound to inspect The Vulture's cap and glove. He finds nothing and the game is allowed to continue but Pelakoudas accuses Regan of throwing three illegal pitches and nullifies a fly out, a strikeout and changes a strike to a ball. In protest, Wrigley Field fans begin to toss garbage onto the field. Leo Durocher, Al Spangler and Randy Hundley get the heave-ho as well.

August 18 - Pelekoudas is at it again, this time in the first game of a Wrigley doubleheader with the Reds. In the opener, the umpire calls three illegal pitches against Regan, twice allowing a retired batter to hit again. Pete Rose singles in a second try. Again, however, Pelekoudas can't find any evidence on Regan, basing his calls on "the flight of the ball." The Cubs lose both games, 2-1 and 6-3, and protest to National

WORTH QUOTING - "One thing you learn as a Cubs fan: When you bought your ticket, you could bank on seeing the bottom of the ninth."

-Joe Garagiola

League president Warren Giles. Giles will order Pelekoudas to apologize to Regan and declares that umpires must have evidence before declaring illegal pitches. However, at this year's winter meetings, major league baseball will amend the spitball rule to allow umpires to call an illegal pitch based on the flight of a ball.

September 11 - Ferguson Jenkins suffers his record fifth 1-0 loss this season, this time to the Mets though allowing just two hits. Despite the losses, Jenkins will win 20 games for the second straight season. Fergie will tally 40 starts to do it, the most since Grover Cleveland Alexander's 40 in 1920.

September 21 - Cubs reliever Jophrey Brown makes his only major league appearance, during a 5-1 loss to the Pirates. His next appearance will be in the movie *Jurassic Park* (he is dragged into a cage and eaten by a raptor in the opening scene).

November12 - Sammy Sosa is born in San Pedro De Macoris, Dominican Republic.

1969

Principle Owner and President: Phil Wrigley; **Manager:** Leo Durocher; **Ballpark:** Wrigley Field; **Attendance:** 1,674,993; **Finish:** Second (92-70); **Recap:** The Cubs are largely expected to win the newly-created National League's Eastern Division, thanks to the league's best infield and a strong starting pitching staff. Instead, the club tires and finishes a disappointing second, holding first place for 155 games but winding up eight games behind the Miracle Mets.

P	Player	R	HR	RBI	SB	AVE
1B	Ernie Banks	60	23	106	0	.253
2B	Glenn Beckert	69	1	37	6	.291
SS	Don Kessinger	109	4	53	11	.273
3B	Ron Santo	97	29	123	1	.289
RF	Jim Hickman	38	21	54	2	.237
CF	Don Young	36	6	27	1	.239
LF	Billy Williams	103	21	95	3	.293
C	Randy Hundley	67	18	64	2	.255
UT	Willie Smith	21	9	25	1	.246
OF	Al Spangler	23	4	23	0	.211
UT	Paul Popovich	26	1	14	0	.312
IF	Nate Oliver	15	1	4	0	.159
UT	Jim Qualls	12	0	9	2	.250

T	Pitcher	W-L	SV	SO	SH	ERA
R	Ferguson Jenkins	21-15	1	273	7	3.21
R	Bill Hands	20-14	0	181	3	2.49
L	Ken Holtzman	17-13	0	176	6	3.59
R	Dick Selma	10-8	1	161	2	3.62
R	Phil Regan	12-6	17	56	0	3.70

January 11 - The Cubs re-acquire reliever Ted Abernathy from the Reds for minor leaguers Bill Plummer, Clarence Jones, and Ken Myette.

April 8 - The Cubs edge the Phillies 8-7 on Opening Day at Wrigley Field. With the Cubs trailing 6-5 in the bottom of the 11th, Willie Smith rips a pinch-homer with a runner on to win it. Ernie Banks homers twice in the game.

April 9 - Billy Williams tallies an ML-record four straight doubles in an 11-3 Cubs win over Philadelphia.

May 13 - Ernie Banks collects his 1,500th RBI, and six more, on two-three run homers and a double in a 19-0 Cubs pummeling of San Diego. The shutout margin ties the National League record. It's Chicago's third straight shutout; Dick Selma's three-hitter follows blankings by

WORTH QUOTING - "If any of my players don't take a drink now and then they'll be gone. You don't play this game on gingersnaps."

-Leo Durocher

Ferguson Jenkins and Ken Holtzman.

May 20 - The Cubs beat the Dodgers' Don Sutton yet again, 7-0. Chicago is now 10-0 vs. the righthander. Holtzman hurls the shutout.

June 15 - Don Kessinger sets an NL mark with his 54th consecutive errorless game to start a season, in a 7-6 loss to Cincinnati.

June 27 - Ken Holtzman retires the first 20 batters before St. Louis pushes across two runs in the seventh and one in the eighth to win 3-1.

June 29 - Billy Williams passes Stan Musial's NL record for consecutive games played with his 896th on Billy Williams day at Wrigley. The Cubs sweep the Cards 3-1 and 12-1.

July 8 - The Mets cut the Cubs' lead in the NL's Eastern Division to four games with a 4-3 win at Shea Stadium. Ron Santo publicly criticizes the play of Don Young after the game because of a couple of misplays by the center fielder. Fuming, Young skips the team bus and leaves the park early. Santo will apologize tomorrow but will be booed in his first game back at Wrigley.

July 10 - The Cubs score five runs in the fifth to beat the Mets 6-2, snapping New York's seven-game winning streak.

July 11 - He's been through this before: Fergie Jenkins suffers his fourth 1-0 loss of the year, this time to the streaking Mets.

July 14 - Billy Williams singles home the winning run in a 1-0 victory over Tom Seaver and the Mets, giving the Cubs a 5 1/2-game lead in the NLEast. Bill Hands is the winner. After the last out, Ron Santo jumps into the air and clicks his heels, an act that gives New York the incentive to rally the second half of the season.

Ken Holtzman

July 24 - Ken Holtzman beats Don Sutton for the third time this year, and fourth overall, in a 5-3 Cubs win vs. Los Angeles.

August 10 - Sutton snaps his 13-game losing streak versus Chicago with a 4-2 win at Los Angeles. Holtzman is the loser. Starting 0-13, Sutton will improve to 18-20 lifetime vs. Chicago.

August 19 - Holtzman hurls a 3-0 no-hitter over the Atlanta Braves. Holtzie completes the first no-no without a strikeout since Sad Sam Jones did for the Yankees on September 4, 1923.

August 27 - The Cubs lose the seventh of their last eight games, 6-3 to Cincinnati. Chicago is now just two games ahead of the Mets.

August 29 - A couple of spectacular catches by outfielder Oscar Gamble help Bill Hands and the Cubs to a 2-1 win over the Braves. The Cubbies are now 3 1/2 games in front.

September 5 - The Cubs lose 9-2 to the Pirates with all of Chicago's offense supplied by Billy Williams. The outfielder collects all four of Chicago's hits - two doubles and two homers. He sets an NLrecord for most hits in a game with no other hits, tying the major league mark set by the Yanks'Kid Elberfeld on August 1, 1903.

It's the first Pittsburgh win at Wrigley since July 5, 1968. They'll sweep the three-game series and reduce Chicago's lead to 2 1/2 games.

September 8 - The Mets whittle the Cubs' lead to a game and a half with a 3-2 win at Shea Stadium. Chicago has lost five in a row.

September 9 - The Mets hand the Cubs their sixth straight defeat, 3-2 behind Tom Seaver.

September 10 - A 6-2 loss to Philadelphia drops the Cubs to second place, one game behind New York. It's the first time in 155 games that Chicago has been out of first.

September 11 - With the Cubs ahead 1-0 and runners on first and second, pitcher Dick Selma unexpectedly throws to third base instead of home. The throw sails past Ron Santo and into left field; Philadelphia's Tony Taylor scores the tying run. The play, calculated to catch a runner off base, was tried during spring training but never during the season. The Phillies win, 4-3.

September 12 - The Cubs beat the Cardinals 5-1 to snap their eight-game winning streak, but drop to 2 1/2 games behind the Mets as New York sweeps Pittsburgh.

September 22 - The Cubs continue their nosedive, losing to the expansion Montreal Expos 7-3 to drop to six games out with six to play.

September 24 - The Cubs beat the Expos 6-3 but the Mets defeat the Cardinals 6-0 to take the pennant.

December 4 - Chicago sends outfielder Boots Day to the Cardinals for pitcher Rich Nye.

WORTH QUOTING - "CUB POWER!"
-Rallying cry of the 1969 Cubs

1970

Principle Owner and President: Phil Wrigley; **Manager:** Leo Durocher; **Ballpark:** Wrigley Field; **Attendance:** 1,642,705; **Finish:** Second (84-78); **Recap:** The Cubs come close again in 1970, thanks mostly to solid seasons by Jim Hickman and newcomer Johnny Callison, who hits 19 home runs. The Cubs hold the league lead for 64 straight days before stumbling in September. A 12-game losing streak in June probably costs them the pennant, which is won by Pittsburgh. The loss of Randy Hundley for half the season due to a knee injury is also costly.

In addition to batting .322, slugging 42 homers (second only to Cincinnati's Johnny Bench) and driving in 129 runs, Billy Williams leads the NL in hits (205) and runs (137).

P	PLAYER	R	HR	RBI	SB	AVE
1B	Ernie Banks	25	12	44	0	.252
2B	Glenn Beckert	99	3	36	4	.288
SS	Don Kessinger	100	1	39	12	.266
3B	Ron Santo	83	26	114	2	.267
RF	Johnny Callison	65	19	68	7	.264
CF	Jim Hickman	102	32	115	0	.315
LF	Billy Williams	137	42	129	7	.322
C	Randy Hundley	13	7	36	0	.244
OF	Cleo James	33	3	14	5	.210
UT	Willie Smith	15	5	24	2	.216
IF	Paul Popovich	22	4	20	0	.253
UT	Jack Hiatt	19	2	22	0	.242
UT	Joe Pepitone	38	12	44	0	.268

T	PITCHER	W-L	SV	SO	SH	ERA
R	Ferguson Jenkins	22-16	0	274	3	3.39
R	Bill Hands	18-15	1	170	2	3.70
L	Ken Holtzman	17-11	0	202	1	3.34
R	Milt Pappas	10-8	0	80	2	2.67
R	Phil Regan	5-9	12	31	0	4.74

February 27 - Lawrence Bankhead, a Chicago man who has been making threatening phone calls to Ernie Banks, is arrested by police.

April 14 - The Cubs beat the Phillies 5-4 on Opening Day in Chicago. The win launches an 11-game winning streak that vaults the team into first place. During the streak, however, the team loses Randy Hundley until July on a collision at home plate.

April 27 - The Cubs notch their 11th straight victory, a 1-0 squeaker over the Pirates. It's their longest winning streak since 1945. Joe Decker, with relief help in the ninth, is the winner. He'll win just two games all year.

April 30 - Billy Williams becomes the first National Leaguer to play in 1,000 consecutive games. The Cubs lose to the Braves, 9-2.

May 10 - Pete Rose rips a two-run homer off Fergie Jenkins in the ninth to give the Reds a 7-6 victory over the Cubs at Wrigley.

WORTH NOTING - After his retirement in 1977, Randy Hundley popularized the fantasy camp vacations for baseball fans.

May 12 - Ernie Banks hits his 500th career home run, the eighth major leaguer to reach the mark, off Pat Jarvis in a 4-3 Cubs victory over the Braves at Wrigley Field.

Frank Secory, an outfielder for the Cubs from 1942-46 is the home plate umpire, and he was one of the umpires in the 1953 game in which Banks hit his first homer.

June 4 - The Cubs pick up Rick Reuschel in the third round of the June baseball draft. Future Cub Dave Kingman is selected by the Giants in the first round.

June 20 - The Cubs beat the Cardinals 8-3 behind Bill Hands today, but will lose their next 12 straight, one shy of the club record set in 1944.

June 28 - The Pirates sweep the Cubs in a doubleheader 3-2 and 4-1 in the final games played at legendary Forbes Field in Pittsburgh.

July 6 - Ron Santo has a productive day in a Wrigley doubleheader. In the opener, the third baseman hits a two-run homer to give the Cubs a 3-2 win vs. Montreal; in the nightcap, he drives in eight runs on two homers and a bases-loaded walk in a 14-2

WORTH QUOTING - "When Leo (Durocher) touched his nose, it meant the hit-and-run was on. But there was a problem. He was always picking his nose."
-Herman Franks

Ferguson Jenkins

Chicago victory.

July 14 - Cubbie Jim Hickman drives home Pete Rose with a single to give the National League a 5-4 12-inning victory at the All-Star Game in Cincinnati. To score, Rose bowls over Cleveland catcher Ray Fosse, sending him to the hospital.

July 16 - A drive off the bat of Billy Williams that should have been a game-tying home run bounces of an Astrodome speaker and lands foul. Ken Holtzman gives up two hits and two unearned runs but is saddled with a 2-1 loss to the Astros.

July 20 - With the score tied 1-1 in the ninth, Holtzman walks Hank Aaron and Tommie Aaron, Hank's brother, homers to give the Braves a 3-1 victory in Atlanta.

July 23 - Milt Pappas hurls the only shutout versus Cincinnati this season, nipping them 1-0 at Wrigley.

July 24 - Ron Santo and Billy Williams drive in four runs apiece and Glenn Beckert scores four times as the Cubs roll over the Braves 11-1 behind Ken Holtzman.

July 29 - The Cubs purchase first baseman Joe Pepitone from the Astros. Pepitone, once a star prospect with the Yankees, will drive in 31 runs in his first 31 games with the Cubs.

August 19 - The Cubs manhandle the lowly Padres, 12-2 behind homers by Fergie Jenkins, Jim Hickman, Glenn Becker, Johnny Callison, Joe Pepitone and Billy Williams. Six of the Cubs'homers are solo shots and San Diego adds a solo homer; the seven solo home runs set an NL record.

August 22 - Ken Holtzman tosses a one-hit, 15-0 shutout versus the Giants. San Francisco's Gaylord Perry allows eight runs in 1 1/3 innings.

September 13 - The Cubs pull out a 3-2 win when Pittsburgh's Matty Alou drops a fly ball off the bat of Willie Smith that leads to two runs with two outs in the ninth. Chicago pulls to within a game of the Pirates and a half game of the Mets.

September 18 - Fergie Jenkins wins his 20th in game one of a twinbill with Montreal, 3-2. The Cubs win game two, also, 5-4.

September 24 - Ken Holtzman tosses a seven-hitter and the Cubs beat the Cards 7-1 to stay 2 1/2 behind the Pirates. The Cubs will lose their next two games, though, and the Pirates will clinch on September 27.

1971

Principle Owner and President: Phil Wrigley; **Manager:** Leo Durocher; **Ballpark:** Wrigley Field; **Attendance:** 1,653,007; **Finish:** Third (83-79); **Recap:** By 1971 increasing tensions between old-school skipper Leo Durocher and many of his players come to a head. An August confrontation between The Lip and Ron Santo results in the manager threatening to retire. Although some of the players applaud the decision, many warn that a Durocher exit under the circumstances would result in negative publicity for Santo. In the end, Durocher stays and the situation gets all the chillier when Phil Wrigley issues full support for his manager. The owner backs up his words by ridding the team of a few anti-Durocher players, such as Ken Holtzman, after the season.

1971 also marks the end of an era, as Ernie Banks plays his final season. By mid-season, Mr. Cub has been relegated to the bench, batting .193 and hitting just three home runs.

P	Player	R	HR	RBI	SB	AVE
1B	Joe Pepitone	50	16	61	1	.307
2B	Glenn Beckert	80	2	42	3	.342
SS	Don Kessinger	77	2	38	15	.258
3B	Ron Santo	77	21	88	4	.267
RF	Johnny Callison	27	8	38	2	.210
CF	Brock Davis	22	0	28	0	.256
LF	Billy Williams	86	28	93	7	.301
C	Chris Cannizzaro	18	5	23	0	.213
UT	Jim Hickman	50	19	60	0	.256
IF	Paul Popovich	24	4	28	0	.217
UT	Cleo James	25	2	13	6	.287
UT	J.C. Martin	13	2	17	1	.264
UT	Ferguson Jenkins	13	6	20	0	.243

T	Pitcher	W-L	SV	SO	SH	ERA
R	Ferguson Jenkins	24-13	0	263	3	2.77
R	Milt Pappas	17-14	0	99	5	3.52
R	Bill Hands	12-18	0	128	1	3.42
L	Ken Holtzman	9-15	0	143	3	4.48
R	Phil Regan	5-5	6	28	0	3.95

WORTH NOTING - Fergie Jenkins tied a major league record by losing five 1-0 games in 1968. In his career, Jenkins will lose 45 games by a 1-0 margin. Jenkins came within 16 wins of 300 for his career.

March 12 - Randy Hundley suffers a severely sprained right knee that will put him out of action in all but nine games this season.

April 6 - Billy Williams tags Bob Gibson for a game-winning homer in the 11th as the Cubs beat the Cardinals 2-1 on Opening Day in Chicago.

May 15 - Fergie Jenkins hits a two-run homer and tosses his seventh complete game in eight starts in a 6-4 win over the Padres.

June 3 - Ken Holtzman hurls his second no-hitter, beating the Reds 1-0. Holtzman also scores the only run, in the third inning. Gary Nolan is the hard-luck loser.

June 17 - Banjo-hitting Don Kessinger goes 6-for-6 in a 7-6 Cubs victory over the Cardinals at Wrigley. He's the first Cub to post six hits since Frank Demaree did it on July 5, 1937.

August 17 - Billy Williams collects his 2000th hit in a 5-4 loss to the Braves. (The same day, Pittsburgh's Bill Mazeroski tallies his 2,000th career safety.)

August 20 - Fergie Jenkins posts his 20th victory, beating Houston 3-2. The Cubs are

WORTH QUOTING - "The riches of the game are in the thrills, not the money."
-Ernie Banks, after hitting his 500th home run on May 12, 1970.

Randy Hundley

now just 1/2 game behind Pittsburgh.

August 23 - After a 4-3 loss to Houston, their second in a row, Leo Durocher accuses Ron Santo for slacking and the third baseman has to be restrained from throttling the manager. When the players square off with The Lip, Durocher declares that he's quitting after the season. He'll hang on until July of 1972, though.

August 24 - Ernie Banks hits his 512th, and final, home run in a 5-4 win vs. Cincinnati, sliding past Mel Ott into an eighth place tie with Eddie Mathews on the all-time list. The Cubs will lose their next 10 of 12 to drop from the race.

August 28 - The Braves beat Fergie Jenkins and the Cubs 4-3 on Ron Santo Day at Wrigley.

August 31 - The Cubs trade Bill McNulty to the Athletics for Frank Fernandez and Adrian Garrett.

September 1 - Fergie Jenkins drives in three runs with two homers and pitches the Cubs to a 5-2 win over Montreal.

September 3 - Cubs owner Phil Wrigley sponsors a newspaper ad in the Tribune accusing his players of mutiny against Leo Durocher. The end of the ad reads, "If we could only find more team players like Ernie Banks."

September 11 - Lefty Juan Pizarro pitches the Cubs to a 7-0 shutout of the Cardinals, aided by Paul Popovich's first major league grand slam.

September26 - Ernie Banks plays his final game, recording a first-inning single for his 2,583rd career hit, off the Phillies' Ken Reynolds. It's Mr. Cub's last hit. The Cubs lose 5-1 at Wrigley.

October 26 - Fergie Jenkins is voted the National League's Cy Young winner.

November 29 - The Cubs trade Ken Holtzman to the A's for outfielder Rick Monday.

December 1 - The Cubs sign the retired Ernie Banks as a coach.

1972

Principle Owner and President: Phil Wrigley; **Manager:** Leo Durocher / Whitey Lockman; **Ballpark:** Wrigley Field; **Attendance:** 1,299,163; **Finish:** Second (85-70); **Recap:** Despite Phil Wrigley's pro-Leo Durocher stance, the owner announces in June that the manager is "stepping aside" in favor of Whitey Lockman. Under Lockman, the team finishes with two more wins than the previous year, but still completes the season 11 games behind the Pirates.

Happily, the Cubs continue to turn out quality pitchers, with Burt Hooton (11-14) and Rick Reuschel (10-8) appearing in the rotation for the first time. Sadly, the team's offense is on the decline, as Jim Hickman, Randy Hundley and Ron Santo suffer season-long slumps. Billy Williams, however, enjoys another Williams-like season, leading the league in hitting (.333) and pacing the club with 37 homers and 122 RBIs (no other Cub drives in more than 74 runs).

P	PLAYER	R	HR	RBI	SB	AVE
1B	Jim Hickman	65	17	64	3	.272
2B	Glenn Beckert	51	3	43	2	.270
SS	Don Kessinger	77	1	39	8	.274
3B	Ron Santo	68	17	74	1	.302
RF	Jose Cardenal	96	17	70	25	.291
CF	Rick Monday	68	11	42	12	.249
LF	Billy Williams	95	37	122	3	.333
C	Randy Hundley	23	5	30	1	.218
UT	Carmen Fanzone	26	8	42	2	.225
IF	Joe Pepitone	23	8	21	1	.262
OF	Billy North	22	0	4	6	.181
IF	Paul Popovich	8	1	11	0	.194

T	PITCHER	W-L	SV	SO	SH	ERA
R	Ferguson Jenkins	20-12	0	184	5	3.21
R	Burt Hooton	11-14	0	132	3	2.81
R	Milt Pappas	17-7	0	80	3	2.77
R	Bill Hands	11-8	0	96	3	3.00
R	Jack Aker	6-6	17	36	0	2.96

January 19 - The Cubs trade Johnny Callison to the Yanks for Jack Aker.

April 15 - The Cubs are on the wrong side of a 4-2 decision vs. the Phillies on Opening Day in Chicago. Opening day is delayed for two weeks due to a players strike that began in spring training.

April 16 - Rookie Burt Hooton hurls a 4-0 no-hitter vs. Philadelphia in just his fourth major league start.

April 28 - Joe Pepitone, back in the lineup after a stomach ailment, hits two three-run homers in a 10-8 Cub victory over the Reds. The Cubs snap a nine-game losing streak.

May 3 - The Cubs crush the Braves 12-1 for the second day in a row. Jose Cardenal collects a double, triple and two singles.

May 16 - Rick Monday clouts three home runs and drives in five in an 8-1 win vs. Philadelphia. The Phils' Greg Luzinski smashes a 500-foot homer off the Liberty Bell in center field at Veterans Stadium.

June 20 - The Cubs score seven in the first off San Francisco starter Don Carrithers, punctuated by Randy Hundley's grand slam, in a 15-8 Cubs win. The Cubs win their seventh straight.

July 11 - Billy Williams goes 8-for-8 during a doubleheader split with Houston.

July 21 - Williams drives in six to lead the Cubs to an 11-3 win over the Astros, with four hits including a double and homer.

July 25 - Leo Durocher resigns as Cubs manager, succeeded by Whitey Lockman. Houston will hire Durocher in August.

July 27 - Fergie Jenkins hurls a 4-0 one-hitter over the Phillies in Lockman's first game as manager.

August 3 - Bill Hands tosses a one-hitter, beating the Expos 3-0.

August 18 - The Cubs trade outfielder Tommy Davis to the Orioles for catcher Ellie Hendricks.

August 26 - Ron Santo slams a three-run homer off San Francisco's Ron Bryant for his 2,000th career hit, in a 10-9 Cubs win at Wrigley Field. The homer also gives Santo his 1,200th RBI.

September 2 - Milt Pappas no-hits the Padres 8-0, taking a perfect game into the ninth when pinch-hitter Larry Stahl walks with two outs.

September 8 - Fergie Jenkins beats Philadelphia 4-3 to post his 20th victory, the sixth year in a row he's reached the mark.

September 16 - Glenn Beckert sets a major league record by stranding 12 runners but the Cubs beat the Mets anyway, 18-5. Chicago knocks Tom Seaver out of the box in just 2 2/3 innings. The Cubs collect 15 walks, with Ellie Hendricks setting an NLrecord with five free passes.

October 20 - The Cubs acquire future manager Tony LaRussa from the Braves for pitcher Tom Phoebus. LaRussa will play just one game, scoring the winning run as a pinch-runner in next year's season opener.

November 21 - The Cubs trade outfielder Billy North to the A's for pitcher Bob Locker.

1973

Principle Owner and President: Phil Wrigley; **Manager:** Whitey Lockman; **Ballpark:** Wrigley Field; **Attendance:** 1,351,705; **Finish:** Fifth (77-84); **Recap:** Although the Cubs finish a lackluster 77-84, they very nearly end up in the post-season thanks to a season-long slump by the Pirates and a more balanced Eastern Division. Going into the final week of the season, five of the six Eastern teams have a shot, with the Mets eventually winning at 82-79. Chicago, who is in first place at the All-Star break, finishes five games back.

P	PLAYER	R	HR	RBI	SB	AVE
1B	Jim Hickman	27	3	20	1	.244
2B	Glenn Beckert	38	0	29	0	.255
SS	Don Kessinger	52	0	43	6	.262
3B	Ron Santo	65	20	77	1	.267
RF	Jose Cardenal	80	11	68	19	.303
CF	Rick Monday	93	26	56	5	.267
LF	Billy Williams	72	20	86	4	.288
C	Randy Hundley	35	10	43	5	.226
OF	Gene Hiser	15	1	6	4	.174
IF	Paul Popovich	24	2	24	3	.236
UT	Carment Fanzone	22	6	22	1	.273
C	Ken Rudolph	12	2	17	1	.206
IF	Pat Bourque	11	7	20	1	.209

T	PITCHER	W-L	SV	SO	SH	ERA
R	Ferguson Jenkins	14-16	0	170	2	3.89
R	Rick Reuschel	14-15	0	168	3	3.00
R	Burt Hooton	14-17	0	134	2	3.68
R	Milt Pappas	7-12	0	48	1	4.28
R	Jack Aker	4-5	12	25	0	4.08

January 10 - The Cubs choose righthander Donnie Moore in the first round of the January baseball draft.

April 6 - The Cubs are 2-1 winners over Montreal on Opening Day at Wrigley.

May 8 - Bench coach Ernie Banks technically becomes the first African American manager when he takes over for Whitey Lockman after the Cubs'skipper is ejected during a 3-2 win over San Diego. Cubbie Bob Locker pitches his 500th game in relief, a major league record.

May 19 - A 26-game hitting streak by Glenn Beckert is snapped by Philadelphia's Ken Brett during a 3-0 Phillies victory.

The Cubs acquire rookie first baseman Andre Thornton from the Braves for Joe Pepitone. Thornton will put together a couple of decent seasons in Chicago before going on to stardom in Cleveland.

May 31 - The Cubs score 10 runs with two outs in the first inning, beating the Astros 16-8 at Wrigley.

June 9 - The Cincinnati Reds score seven runs in the ninth inning to turn a 4-1 defecit into an 8-4 win over the Cubs at Wrigley.

June 30 - The Mets trim the lead of the first-place Cubs to six games with a 2-1 victory behind Jon Matlack.

July 1 - The Mets and Cubs split a dramatic doubleheader in Chicago. New York takes the first game 6-5 but Randy Hundley smacks a three-run homer in the bottom of the ninth to give the Cubs a 6-5 triumph in the nightcap. Ron Santo collects seven hits in the twinbill.

July 6 - Fergie Jenkins earns his 13th straight victory over the Padres, beating them 8-5.

September 19 - Ron Santo and Billy Williams each hit their 20th home run in an 8-6 win vs. Montreal. It's Santo's 325th and Williams's 376th career homer; the teammates have played in more than 2,000 games together.

October 25 - The Cubs stun Chicago by trading away six-time 20-game winner Fergie Jenkins to the Texas Rangers for third baseman Bill Madlock and utility player Vic Harris. Jenkins is the first pitcher in history to be traded after leading his team in victories for seven straight seasons.

November 7 - The Cubs ship popular second baseman Glenn Beckert to the Padres for outfielder Jerry Morales.

December 4 - The Cubs continue to pack off their veteran stars, sending Ron Santo to the Angels for two pitchers. Santo, however, invokes the new five-and-10 rule and vetoes the deal. Santo will eventually agree to be traded to the crosstown White Sox for pitcher Steve Stone and three others.

WORTH QUOTING - "Aslump starts in your head and winds up in your stomach. You know that eventually it will happen, and you begin to worry about it. Then you know you're in one. And it makes you sick."

-Billy Williams, quote in *Insight*

1974

Principle Owner and President: Phil Wrigley; **Manager:** Whitey Lockman / Jim Marshall; **Ballpark:** Wrigley Field; **Attendance:** 1,015,378; **Finish:** Sixth (66-96); **Recap:** Though the club tanks in 1974, leading to the firing of manager Whitey Lockman, Cubs fans enjoy strong seasons from several young players acquired during the offseason, particularly by third baseman Bill Madlock, who arrived from Texas in the Fergie Jenkins trade. The Cubs nearly lose 100 games in their first rebuilding year, finishing ninth in batting (.251), 11th in pitching (4.28) and leading the NLin errors (199), the most by a Cubs team since 1950. Lockman returns to his old job as director of player development, replaced by third base coach Jim Marshall, the fourth ex-Cub first baseman to manage the team this century.

P	Player	R	HR	RBI	SB	AVE
1B	Billy Williams	55	16	68	4	.280
2B	Vic Harris	18	0	11	9	.195
SS	Don Kessinger	83	1	42	7	.259
3B	Bill Madlock	65	9	54	11	.313
RF	Jose Cardenal	75	13	72	23	.293
CF	Rick Monday	84	20	58	7	.294
LF	Jerry Morales	70	15	82	2	.273
C	Steve Swisher	21	5	27	0	.214

P	Player	R	HR	RBI	SB	AVE
UT	Andre Thornton	41	10	46	2	.261
UT	Chris Ward	8	1	15	0	.204
C	George Mitterwald	17	7	28	1	.251
UT	Carmen Fanzone	13	4	22	0	.190
IF	Dave Rosello	9	0	10	1	.303

T	Pitcher	W-L	SV	SO	SH	ERA
R	Rick Reuschel	13-12	0	160	2	4.29
R	Bill Bonham	11-22	1	191	2	3.85
R	Steve Stone	8-6	0	90	0	4.13
R	Burt Hooton	7-11	1	94	1	4.81
R	Oscar Zemora	3-9	10	38	0	3.11

March 23 - The Cubs trade Jim Hickman to the Cardinals for pitcher Scipio Spinks.

April 9 - The Cubs shut the Phillies out, 2-0, on Opening Day at Wrigley Field.

April 17 - Catcher George Mitterwald hits three home runs, one a grand slam, driving in eight runs of an 18-9 victory over the Pirates. Mitterwald adds a double; his 14 total bases is a team record.

April 24 - Bill Bonham walks George Foster with the bases loaded in the ninth to end a scoreless duel with Cincinnati's Jack Billingham.

July 24 - Whitey Lockman resigns as manager to become the Cubs' director of player development. Third base coach Jim Marshall replaces him.

July 31 - Bill Bonham fans four batters in the second inning, tying a major league record, but the Cubs lose to the Expos 7-4.

September 10 - Pinch-hitters Carmen Fanzone and Jim Tyrone homer against the Pirates, but Pittsburgh beats the Cubs anyway, 12-4.

October 23 - The Cubs trade the last of their veteran stars, Billy Williams, to the A's for second baseman Manny Trillo and pitchers Darold Knowles and Bob Locker.

1975

Principle Owner and President: Phil Wrigley; **Manager:** Jim Marshall; **Ballpark:** Wrigley Field; **Attendance:** 1,034,819; **Finish:** T-Fifth (75-87); **Recap:** The Cubs tie Montreal for last place in the Eastern Division, 17 1/2 games out. The team finishes fifth in batting (.259) and third in runs (712), led by third baseman Bill Madlock, who earns his first batting title with a .354 mark. The pitching, however, is woeful, with the Cubs finishing last in the NL in ERA (4.57). Ray Burris and Steve Stone are moderately successful, winning 15 and 12 games, respectively.

P	Player	R	HR	RBI	SB	AVE
1B	Andre Thornton	70	18	60	3	.293
2B	Manny Trillo	55	7	7	1	.248
SS	Don Kessinger	77	0	46	4	.243
3B	Bill Madlock	77	7	64	9	.354
RF	Jose Cardenal	85	9	68	34	.317
CF	Rick Monday	89	17	60	8	.267
LF	Jerry Morales	62	12	91	3	.270
C	Steve Swisher	20	1	22	1	.213
UT	Pete LaCock	30	6	30	0	.229
UT	George Mitterwald	19	5	26	0	.220
OF	Champ Summers	14	1	16	0	.231
UT	Rob Sperring	25	1	9	0	.208
C	Tim Hosley	22	6	20	1	.255

T	Pitcher	W-L	SV	SO	SH	ERA
R	Rick Reuschel	11-17	1	155	0	3.73
R	Bill Bonham	13-15	0	165	2	4.72
R	Ray Burris	15-10	0	108	2	4.12
R	Steve Stone	12-8	0	139	1	3.95
L	Darold Knowles	6-9	15	63	0	5.83

February 3 - Billy Herman is selected for the Hall of Fame by the Veterans Committee.

April 10 - The Pittsburgh Pirates are victorious, 8-4, on Opening Day in Chicago.

April 11 - The Cubs beat the Expos, 2-1, as Rick Monday scores from second base on a deep fly ball to right field in the ninth inning.

May 2 - The Cubs trade Burt Hooton to the Dodgers for pitchers Geoff Zahn and Eddie Solomon.

June 25 - Montreal scores 10 unearned runs to beat the hapless Cubs, 12-2.

July 6 - The Cubs and Pirates score in 14 or the game's 18 half-innings in an 18-12 Pittsburgh victory. Darold Knowles shuts out the Pirates in the top of the ninth to keep the Cubs from becoming the only team this century to be scored upon in every inning twice.

July 15 - Bill Madlock shares the MVP award with New York's Jon Matlack in a 6-3 National League victory in the All-Star Game at Milwaukee.

July 26 - Madlock goes 6-for-6 in a 9-8 loss to the Mets.

August 5 - Bill Bonham gives up a major league-record seven hits to the first seven Phillies he faces. He leaves the game without retiring a batter; his replacement immediately gives up another hit.

August 21 - Rick Reuschel and his brother, Paul, combine to shut out the Dodgers 7-0. It's the first time that brothers have teamed to toss a shutout. Paul relieves in the seventh because of a blister on Rick's finger.

August 23 - Champ Summers and Rick Monday hit a pair of pinch-home runs in a 14-12 loss to the Astros.

September 3 - Reserve first baseman Pete LaCock touches the Cardinals' Bob Gibson for a pinch-grand slam in an 11-6 Cubs victory at Busch Stadium. The blast ends Gibson's career.

WORTH QUOTING - "Marvin Miller should have been invited to throw out the first ball on opening day. After all, he helped throw out the first 86 games of the season."

-The *Sun-Times*' Irv Kupcinet on the head of the Major League Baseball Players Association, after the 1972 players' strike

September 9 - Bill Madlock is hit on the right thumb by Pittsburgh starter Bruce Kison, suffering a fracture, in a 6-5 Cubs win.

September 16 - Pittsburgh second baseman Rennie Stennett punctuates a lousy day at Wrigley, as he goes 7-for-7, tying an ML record, in a 22-0 skunking of the Cubs. It's the biggest shutout margin this century. Rick Reuschel takes the loss.

September 24 - Pinch-hitter Joe Wallis spoils a no-hit bid by New York's Tom Seaver with a two-out single in the ninth. The Cubs win the game in 11 innings, 1-0.

October 28 - New Cubs general manager Salty Saltwell trades Don Kessinger to the Cardinals for reliever Mike Garman and a minor leaguer.

1976

Principle Owner and President: Phil Wrigley; **Manager:** Jim Marshall; **Ballpark:** Wrigley Field; **Attendance:** 1,026,217; **Finish:** Fourth (75-87); **Recap:** The Cubs celebrate their centennial by improving to 75-87, good enough for fourth place. Bill Madlock enjoys his second straight batting crown with a .339 average (out-hitting Cincinnati's Ken

WORTH NOTING - Fergie Jenkins holds the major league record for most seasons leading the league in home runs (seven) as well as the National League record (five-1967, 1968, 1971, 1972, and 1973.

Griffey on the final day of the season) and Rick Monday contributes 32 home runs. The pitching improves, with Rick Reuschel bouncing back with 14 wins and a 3.46 ERA and Ray Burris providing another 15 victories.

The most significant addition to the team in years is rookie reliever Bruce Sutter, whose diving split-fingered fastball accounts for 10 saves and six wins in 52 appearances. Sutter fans 73 in 83 innings.

P	PLAYER	R	HR	RBI	SB	AVE
1B	Pete LaCock	34	8	28	1	.221
2B	Manny Trillo	42	4	59	17	.239
SS	Mick Kelleher	28	0	22	0	.228
3B	Bill Madlock	68	15	84	15	.339
RF	Jerry Morales	66	16	67	3	.274
CF	Rick Monday	107	32	77	5	.272
LF	Jose Cardenal	64	8	47	23	.299
C	Steve Swisher	25	5	42	2	.236
OF	Joe Wallis	51	5	21	3	.254
UT	George Mitterwald	19	5	28	1	.215
IF	Dave Rosello	27	1	11	1	.242
UT	Champ Summers	11	3	13	1	.206
UT	Larry Biittner	21	0	17	0	.245

T	PITCHER	W-L	SV	SO	SH	ERA
R	Rick Reuschel	14-12	1	146	2	3.46
R	Ray Burris	15-13	0	112	4	3.11
R	Bill Bonham	9-13	0	110	0	4.27
R	Steve Renko	8-11	0	112	1	3.87
R	Bruce Sutter	6-3	10	73	0	2.71

April 13 - The Cubs nip the Mets, 5-4, on Opening Day at Wrigley.

April 14 - Randy Hundley, back with the Cubs after being released by San Diego, ignites a three-run rally in the seventh with a pinch-double as Chicago takes a 6-5 win vs. New York. During the game, the Mets' Dave Kingman launches a home run that smacks a house 530 feet from home plate.

April 17 - The Phillies' Mike Schmidt launches four consecutive homers in an 18-16 Philadelphia triumph at Wrigley. The Phils overcome a 12-1 defecit to take the victory.

April 25 - Rick Monday becomes a national hero when he snatches an American flag from the hands of two fans who are about to set it on fire during a 5-4 loss at Dodger Stadium. The next day, the Illinois legislature will declare May 4 as Rick Monday Day.

May 2 - Jose Cardenal leads the Cubs to a 6-5, 14-inning victory over the Giants with a 6-for-7 day, including a double and a home run.

May 4 - Rick Monday is honored on Rick Monday Day at Wrigley with a copy of an Illinois Legislature proclamation and the flag he had rescued. Less than 5,000 are on hand to watch the Cubs lose to the Dodgers 9-6.

May 5 - The Cubs take advantage of a windy day in a 14-12 victory over Los Angeles.

May 17 - The Cubs send struggling slugger Andre Thornton to the Expos for pitcher Steve Renko and outfielder Larry Biittner. Thornton, batting just .200 at the time, will eventually land in Cleveland and put together a solid career.

June 8 - The Cubs acquire veteran hurler Joe Coleman from the Tigers for cash and a player to be named later.

August 11 - The Cubs take a 10-1 lead

after three innings, but the Reds storm back to win 13-10.

September 24 - Bill Madlock suffers bruises and a concussion when he is mugged in New York during a series with the Mets. The Cubs lose today, 4-3.

October 3 - Madlock collects four singles in an 11-1 win vs. Atlanta, giving him the National League batting crown. Mad Dog beats runner-up Ken Griffey of Cincinnati, .339 to .333.

November 24 - Bob Kennedy is named head of baseball operations. His first act is to fire Jim Marshall as manager and Salty Saltwell as GM. Herman Franks will be named the Cubs'new skipper.

December 8 - The Cubs acquire Greg Gross from the Royals for infielder Julio Gonzales. Chicago then trades first baseman Pete LaCock to the Mets for outfielder Jim Dwyer. LaCock will eventually end up in Kansas City.

1977

Principle Owner and President: Phil Wrigley; **Manager:** Herman Franks; **Ballpark:** Wrigley Field; **Attendance:** 1,439,834; **Finish:** Fourth (81-81); **Recap:** Herman Franks is tapped to be the Cubs' new manager in 1977, replacing Jim Marshall. Franks had led the San Francisco Giants to second place four years in a row in the late 60s and had served briefly as a coach for Leo Durocher after that.

An era comes to an end in April, when owner Phil Wrigley passes away at the age of 82. Ownership passes to Phil's son William, who almost immediately begins looking for buyers.

Bill Madlock takes his two batting titles to San Francisco before the season, traded (after demanding an exhorbitant $1 million over five years) for Bobby Murcer and third baseman Steve Ontiveros. A more productive transaction sends Rick Monday to the Dodgers for first baseman Bill Buckner and shortstop Ivan DeJesus.

Murcer hits 27 homers and Rick Reuschel posts 20 wins for the Cubs, who improve to an 81-81 mark. The ballclub actually leads the division for 69 days, until early August when a shoulder injury sends closer Bruce Sutter to the 21-day disabled list. Despite losing a month, Sutter posts 31 saves and seven victories, fanning 129 in 107 innings and recording a miniscule 1.35 ERA.

P	Player	R	HR	RBI	SB	AVE
1B	Bill Buckner	40	11	60	7	.284
2B	Manny Trillo	51	7	57	3	.280
SS	Ivan DeJesus	91	3	40	24	.266
3B	Steve Ontiveros	54	10	68	3	.299
RF	Bobby Murcer	90	27	89	16	.265
CF	Jerry Morales	56	11	69	0	.290
LF	Jose Cardenal	33	3	18	5	.239
C	George Mitterwald	40	9	43	3	.230
UT	Larry Biittner	74	12	62	2	.298
OF	Greg Gross	43	5	32	0	.322
OF	Gene Clines	27	3	41	1	.293
C	Steve Swisher	21	5	15	0	.190
IF	Mick Kelleher	14	0	11	0	.230

T	Pitcher	W-L	SV	SO	SH	ERA
R	Ray Burris	14-16	0	105	1	4.72
R	Rick Reuschel	20-10	1	166	4	2.79
R	Bill Bonham	10-13	0	134	0	4.35
R	Mike Krukow	8-114	0	106	1	4.40
R	Bruce Sutter	7-3	31	129	0	1.35

January 6 - The Cubs trade outfielder Rick Monday to the Dodgers for first baseman Bill Buckner and shortstop Ivan DeJesus.

January 19 - The Baseball Writers Association elects Ernie Banks to the Hall of Fame.

February 11 - The Cubs trade Bill Madlock and second baseman Rod

Sperring to the Giants for outfielder Bobby Murcer, third baseman Steve Ontiveros, and a minor leaguer.

April 7 - The Mets beat the Cubs 5-3 in the season opener at Wrigley.

April 12 - Cubs owner Phil Wrigley dies at the age of 82. William Wrigley succeeds his father as chairman.

May 17 - The Cubs crush the Padres 23-6 at Wrigley Field, hitting seven home runs. In the fifth, Larry Biittner, Jerry Morales, and Bobby Murcer hit consecutive homers.

May 28 - Reliever Ramon Hernandez is traded to the Red Sox for pitcher Danny Darwin.

The Cubs beat the Pirates, 6-3, moving into first place. Bruce Sutter pitches three scoreless innings for the save.

June 6 - Rick Reuschel retires 17 in a row during one stretch of a 3-1 victory over Los Angeles.

June 16 - Kerry Wood is born in Irving, Texas.

June 25 - The Cubs score four in the ninth to beat the Mets, 5-4. Manny Trillow beats out a double play attempt with the bases full for the winner.

July 4 - Outfielder Larry Biittner pitches the last inning and a third of a 19-3 loss to the Expos, fanning three but allowing six runs on three homers and a walk. Biittner will also be fined $50 by the NLfor throwing a brush-back pitch after surrendering the third home run.

WORTH NOTING - Bill Buckner was the fourth player to get 200 hits in one season in each league, joining Nap Lajoie, George Sisler, and Al Oliver.

July 7 - Rick Reuschel improves to 12-2 with a 2-0 shutout of the Dodgers. Reuschel has not given up an earned run, except a homer, since June 1.

July 12 - After giving up a game-winning homer to Steve Henderson in a 4-2 Mets victory, Bruce Sutter complains of a sore arm, asking to sit out the All-Star Game. Sutter will sit out another week as well.

July 27 - Rick Reuschel tosses his second straight shutout, beating the Reds 3-0.

July 28 - The wind is blowing out as Chicago and Cincinnati combine for 11 homers, tying an ML record, in a 16-15 Cubs triumph at Wrigley. The Cubs battle back from a 6-0 deficit to win it on Dave Rosello's RBI single. Rick Reuschel, who shut the Reds out the day before, hurls 2/3 of an inning for the victory.

September 8 - Bruce Sutter earns a 3-2 win over the Expos with two scoreless innings, striking out all six batters he faces, including three on nine pitches in the ninth.

October 31 - The Cubs trade Bill Bonham to the Reds for pitchers Woody Fryman and Bill Caudill.

1978

President: William Hagenah; **Manager:** Herman Franks; **Ballpark:** Wrigley Field; **Attendance:** 1,525,311; **Finish:** Third (79-83); **Recap:** The Cubs finish third despite winning two fewer games than the year before. Dave Kingman, signed as a free agent, leads the club with 28 homers and shortstop Ivan DeJesus finishes first in the NL in runs (104) and swipes 41 bases, the most by a Cub since Kiki Cuyler's 43 in

1929. Bill Buckner contributes a solid .323 as the Cubs leads the NL in hitting (.264).

Poor pitching sinks the club this year, as Rick Reuschel leads the club with 14 wins. Bruce Sutter in 1978 is somewhat vulnerable, posting a 3.15 ERA, nearly two full runs more than the year before, but still records 27 saves.

P	PLAYER	R	HR	RBI	SB	AVE
1B	Bill Buckner	47	5	74	7	.323
2B	Manny Trillo	53	4	55	0	.261
SS	Ivan DeJesus	104	3	35	41	.278
3B	Steve Ontiveros	34	1	22	0	.243
RF	Bobby Murcer	66	9	64	14	.281
CF	Greg Gross	34	1	39	3	.265
LF	Dave Kingman	65	28	79	3	.266
C	Dave Rader	29	3	36	1	.203
UT	Larry Biittner	32	4	50	0	.257
OF	Gene Clines	31	0	17	4	.258
UT	Rodney Scott	41	0	15	27	.282
UT	Mike Vail	15	4	33	0	.333
IF	Mick Kelleher	8	0	6	4	.253

T	PITCHER	W-L	SV	SO	SH	ERA
R	Dennis Lamp	7-15	0	73	3	3.29
R	Rick Reuschel	14-15	0	115	1	3.41
R	Ray Burris	7-13	1	94	1	4.75
R	Mike Krukow	9-3	0	81	1	3.91
R	Bruce Sutter	8-10	27	106	0	3.15

April 14 - The Cubs beat the Pirates 5-4 in front of 45,777 at Wrigley on Opening Day.

May 14 - Dave Kingman hits three homers and drives in eight runs in a 10-7 victory over the Dodgers.

May 24 - Manny Trillo hits a two-run homer in the 10th to give the Cubs a 6-4 win over the Phillies, moving Chicago into first place.

June 10 - The Cubs reacquire lefty Ken Holtzman from the Yankees for minor league pitcher Ron Davis. Holtzman will go 0-3 and retire.

Bill Buckner

September 5 - A record 45 players participate in a 10-8 Cubs loss to the Expos.

September 19 - The Cubs rally from an 11-2 defecit in the 7th to tie the Pirates but right fielder Dave Parker homers off Bruce Sutter in the 11th to give the Bucs a 12-11 triumph. In the game, 38-year old first baseman Willie Stargell attempts to steal second base. When he sees Ivan DeJesus waiting for him with the ball, he slides about 10 feet short of the bag and signals "time out." The ploy doesn't work but the play becomes a fixture on blooper reels for decades after.

September 21 - The Cubs use a record 27 players during a 14-inning 3-2 loss to Pittsburgh. The Pirates win when second baseman Rennie Stennett walks in the 14th, pinch runner Matt Alexander steals second, sprints to third when catcher Dave Rader's throw goes into center field, and

WORTH NOTING - Dave Kingman holds the record for most home runs by a player (442) not in the Hall of Fame.

scores when Greg Gross' toss from center hits him in the back and caroms to the dugout.

1979

President: William Hagenah; **Manager:** Herman Franks / Joey Amalfitano; **Ballpark:** Wrigley Field; **Attendance:** 1,648,587; **Finish:** Fifth (80-82); **Recap:** The Cubs enter September just 5 1/2 games behind the Pirates but then lose 14 of 17 games and sink to fifth. Led by Dave Kingman, the club hits at a higher clip (.269), slugs more home runs (135) scores more runs (706) and records a lower ERA (3.88) than the year before. Kingman hits a league-leading 48 homers and drives in 115 runs. Rick Reuschel (18 wins) and Bruce Sutter (37) return to brilliant form. Sutter also wins six games and posts a 2.23 ERA, enough to win the NL's Cy Young Award.

P	Player	R	HR	RBI	SB	AVE
1B	Bill Buckner	72	14	66	9	.284
2B	Ted Sizemore	36	2	24	3	.248
SS	Ivan DeJesus	92	5	52	24	.283
3B	Steve Ontiveros	58	4	57	0	.285
RF	Scot Thompson	36	2	29	4	.289
CF	Jerry Martin	74	19	73	2	.272
LF	Dave Kingman	97	48	115	4	.288
C	Barry Foote	47	16	56	5	.254
UT	Larry Biittner	35	3	50	1	.290
IF	Steve Dillard	31	5	24	1	.283
UT	Mike Vail	28	7	35	0	.335
IF	Mick Kelleher	14	0	10	2	.254

T	Pitcher	W-L	SV	SO	SH	ERA
R	Rick Reuschel	18-12	0	125	1	3.62
R	Dennis Lamp	11-10	0	86	1	3.51
R	Lynn McGlothen	13-14	2	147	1	4.12
R	Mike Krukow	9-9	0	119	0	4.20
R	Bruce Sutter	6-6	37	110	0	2.23

February 23 - The Cubs trade second baseman Manny Trillo, catcher Dave Rader and outfielder Greg Gross to the Phillies for catcher Barry Foote, outfielder Jerry Martin, infielder Ted Sizemore, and two minor leaguers, including second baseman Ryne Sandberg.

March 7 - The Veterans Committee elects former Cubs slugger Hack Wilson to the Hall of Fame.

April 29 - Down 5-0 in the ninth in Atlanta, the Cubs load the bases with two out. Pinch hitter Tim Blackwell singles for two runs, Larry Biittner singles in another, and Bobby Murcer slams a three-run homer for a 6-5 victory.

May 10 - A 7-7 tie between the Reds and Cubs is suspended in the ninth because Chicago has to catch a plane. The contest will be made up on July 23.

May 17 - The Cubs and Phils hook up for the legendary 10-inning slugfest won by Philadelphia, 23-22. The Cubs (6) and Phillies (5) combine for a record-tying 11 homers and 97 total bases including three round-trippers by Dave Kingman, two by Mike Schmidt and a grand slam by Bill Buckner. Schmidt's second homer comes in the 10th off Bruce Sutter to provide the game-winning run. The Cubs battle back from a 7-0 Phils lead in the first and lead 15-6 after three innings, and 21-9 after five, but can't hold it. It's the largest scoring major league game since August 25, 1922, when the same two teams met. The Cubs won that one, 26-23.

May 23 - The Cubs acquire high-kicking reliever Dick Tidrow from the Yankees for Ray Burris.

June 26 - Bobby Murcer is shipped to the

Yanks for pitcher Paul Semall and cash.

June 30 - In the 11th inning of a 3-3 tie at Wrigley, the Mets score six runs, five of them charged to reliever Dick Tidrow, with four on two-run homers by outfielders Joel Youngblood and Lee Mazzilli. Steve Henderson's triple off Donnie Moore gives the Mets a 9-3 advantage going into the bottom of the frame. But New York reliever Dale Murray allows singles to Ken Henderson and Ivan DeJesus, a walk to Scot Thompson, an RBI single to Bill Buckner, and a pinch-grand slam to Mike Vail. Jerry Martin and Steve Ontiveros then connect for solo homers to give the Cubs a 9-8 win.

June 28 - The Cubs purchase outfielder Ken Henderson from the Reds.

June 30 - The Mets score six runs in the top of the 11th to break a 3-3 tie at Wrigley. The Cubs pound back with five in their half of the frame before succumbing, 9-8.

July 15 - In a New York-Penn League game, the Cubs' minor league Geneva team scores 15 runs in the ninth to cap a 29-4 assault on the Utica Blue Jays. Infielder Scott Fletcher leads the Cubs with five hits, including two homers, and eight RBI.

July 23 - The Cubs and Reds complete the May 10 suspended game, with Chicago coming out on top 8-7 on a run-scoring single in the 18th by Steve Ontiveros.

July 27 - Dave Kingman hits two home runs to lead the Cubs to a 4-2 victory over the Mets at Shea Stadium.

July 28 - Kingman hits three more home runs in a 6-4 loss to New York. It's Kong's second three-home run game of the season and he ties the MLrecord with five round-trippers in two games.

August 5 - Jack Brickhouse works his 5,000th televised Cubs broadcast, won by Chicago 3-2 over St. Louis.

August 17 - The Cubs swap Ted Sizemore to the Red Sox for cash and a player to be named later (catcher Mike O'Berry).

September 24 - Manager Herman Franks resigns. He'll be replaced by Dodgers coach Preston Gomez after the season.

November 7 - Bruce Sutter's 37 saves earns him the National League's Cy Young Award.

1980

President: William Hagenah; **Manager:** Preston Gomez / Joey Amalfitano; **Ballpark:** Wrigley Field; **Attendance:** 1,206,776; **Finish:** Sixth (64-98); **Recap:** The 1980 season begins with a thud as Dave Kingman dumps a pail of ice water on a reporter during spring training, launching a season-long battle with the press. Aside from the bickering, though, there isn't much else to write about in Chicago as the Cubs finish with 98 losses, 27 games out of first place.

Preston Gomez, who guided the Padres and Astros to last-place finishes, succeeds Herman Franks as the club's manager. He

WORTH NOTING - Catcher Barry Foote, who played for the Cubs from 1979-81, later became the highest-paid manager in minor league history. In 1984, Foote took over the Class A Fort Lauderdale club in the Yankee organization while under a playing contract for $400,000 a year.

Rick Reuschel

doesn't last the season, with Joey Amalfitano taking over again.

Bill Buckner and Bruce Sutter enjoy superb seasons, with Buckner winning the batting title at .324 and Sutter leading the league with 28 saves.

The Cubs'bullpen in 1980 is particularly outstanding, with middle man Dick Tidrow compiling a record-tying 84 appearances and three young relievers, Lee Smith, Bill Caudill, and Willie Hernandez, headed for future stardom.

P	PLAYER	R	HR	RBI	SB	AVE
1B	Bill Buckner	69	10	68	1	.324
2B	Mike Tyson	34	3	23	1	.238
SS	Ivan DeJesus	78	3	33	44	.259
3B	Lenny Randle	67	5	39	19	.276
RF	Mike Vail	30	6	47	2	.298
CF	Jerry Martin	57	23	73	8	.227
LF	Dave Kingman	31	18	57	2	.278
C	Tim Blackwell	24	5	30	0	.272
UT	Larry Biittner	21	1	34	1	.249
OF	Jesus Figueroa	20	1	11	2	.253
IF	Mick Kelleher	12	0	4	1	.146
UT	Scot Thompson	26	2	13	6	.212

T	PITCHER	W-L	SV	SO	SH	ERA
R	Rick Reuschel	13-13	0	140	0	3.40
R	Dennis Lamp	10-14	0	83	1	5.19
R	Mike Krukow	10-15	0	130	0	4.39
R	Lynn McGlothen	12-14	0	119	2	4.80
R	Bruce Sutter	5-8	28	76	0	2.65

April 10 - Just 12,219 frigid New York fans turn out for the season opener between the Mets and Cubs. The Mets win, 5-2.

April 17 - The Cubs return the favor, beating the Mets 4-1 on Opening Day at Wrigley. Dennis Lamp is the winner.

April 19 - Dave Kingman smacks a two-run homer in the sixth and a grand slam in a seven-run eighth to lead the Cubbies to a 12-9 victory over the Mets at Wrigley.

April 22 - Barry Foote hits a two-out grand slam in the ninth to give the Cubs a 16-14 Wrigley triumph over the Cardinals. Foote collects four hits in the game, driving in eight runs and Ivan DeJesus hits for the cycle.

June 14 - The Cubs host a special Old Timers Game, a two-inning game between the remaining members of the 1945 Cubs vs. the 1945 Tigers, a replay of the last World Series the Cubs were involved in. The Tigers beat them in this one, too, 4-1.

July 6 - Cubs relievers hold the Pirates hitless for 12 2/3 innings but Pittsburgh rallies in the 20th for a 5-4 win.

July 25 - The last-place Cubs fire manager Preston Gomez, replacing him with coach Joey Amalfitano.

October 17 - The Cubs peddle catcher Mike O'Berry to the Reds for pitcher Jay Howell.

December9 - The Cubs trade Bruce Sutter

to the Cardinals for third baseman Ken Reitz and first baseman Leon "Bull" Durham.

December 13 - Right fielder Mike Vail is sent to the Reds for outfielder Heity Cruz.

1981

President: William Hagenah; **Manager:** Joey Amalfitano; **Ballpark:** Wrigley Field; **Attendance:** 565,637; **Finish:** Eighth / Fifth (15-37 / 23-28); **Recap:** The 1981 season is a year of transition for Chicago. The team is an also-ran in both halves of the strike-interrupted season, and the club is sold to the Chicago Tribune Company after generations of Wrigley ownership. But newcomers Leon Durham, Jody Davis, and Mike Krukow emerge as quality players and Dallas Green, manager of the World Champion Phillies, is hired to mold the team into a contender.

Green begins by hiring his former coach at Philadelphia, Lee Elia, to manager the club, then obtains former Phillies Keith Moreland, Larry Bowa, and rookie Ryne Sandberg. The new GM then declares his intention of installing lights at Wrigley Field, setting off a storm of protest that sweeps Chicago quicker than the fire of 1871.

P	Player	R	HR	RBI	SB	AVE
1B	Bill Buckner	45	10	75	5	.311
2B	Pat Tabler	11	1	5	0	.188
SS	Ivan DeJesus	49	0	13	21	.194
3B	Ken Reitz	10	2	28	0	.215
RF	Leon Durham	42	10	35	25	.290
CF	Jerry Morales	27	1	25	1	.286
LF	Steve Henderson	32	5	35	5	.293
C	Jody Davis	14	4	21	0	.256
C	Tim Blackwell	21	1	11	2	.234
UT	Scot Thompson	8	0	8	2	.165
UT	Steve Dillard	18	2	11	0	.218
UT	Heity Cruz	15	7	15	2	.229
IF	Mike Tyson	6	2	8	1	.185

WORTH QUOTING - "The announcer says, 'Will the lady who lost her nine children at the ballpark please pick them up immediately. They are beating the Cubs, 10-0, in the seventh.'"

-Tom Dressen, 1981

T	Pitcher	W-L	SV	SO	SH	ERA
R	Mike Krukow	9-9	0	101	1	3.69
R	Randy Martz	5-7	6	32	0	3.67
R	Rick Reuschel	4-7	0	53	0	3.45
R	Doug Bird	4-5	0	34	1	3.60
R	Dick Tidrow	3-10	9	39	0	5.04

February 28 - The Cubs rid themselves of moody slugger Dave Kingman, sending him to the Mets for outfielder Steve Henderson and $100,000.

April 9 - Rick Reuschel loses his fourth straight Opening Day assignment, to the Mets 2-0.

April 29 - The Cubs snap a 12-game losing streak by scoring five runs with two outs in the ninth to beat the Cardinals 6-1.

May 4 - Hector and Houston's Jose Cruz square each homer in a battle of the brothers won by the Astros, 5-4. Jose hits a three-run dinger in the first off Mike Krukow and Hector answers with a solo shot off Joaquin Andujar in the sixth.

June 4 - It's been that kind of season: veteran outfielder Bobby Bonds, recently acquired by the Cubs, trips on a seam in the outfield carpet at Pittsburgh's Three Rivers Stadium in his first game with Chicago and breaks his hand. He'll go on the 21-day disabled list.

June 6 - Mike Tyson hits a three-run pinch-home run in the fourth to knock Dodger rookie sensation Fernando Valenzuela out

Bruce Sutter

of the box in an 11-5 Cubs win at Wrigley.

June 11 - The Cubs win their final game before the walkout, 6-1 over the Giants. Just 5,017 unhappy Wrigley fans attend.

June 16 - William Wrigley announces that he is selling the ballclub to the Tribune Company for $20.5 million(!), ending 64 years of family ownership.

October 15 - Phillies manager Dallas Green, who led his team to a World Championship in 1980, jumps the club to become the Cubs'new general manager.

October 22 - Green hires one of his old coaches at Philadelphia, Lee Elia, as the Cubs'new manager.

November 15 - Infielder Steve Macko, who played for the Cubs in 1979-80, dies of cancer at age 27.

December 8 - The Cubs trade Mike Krukow to the Phillies for pitchers Dickie Noles and Dan Larsen and catcher/outfielder, Keith Moreland.

WORTH QUOTING - "There's nothing wrong with this team that more pitching, more fielding, and more hitting couldn't help."

-Bill Buckner, 1981

1982

President: Andrew McKenna; **Manager:** Lee Elia; **Ballpark:** Wrigley Field; **Attendance:** 1,249,278; **Finish:** Fifth (73-89); **Recap:** The Cubs begin slowly, suffering through a 13-game losing streak in May, but the club rebounds in August and September to avoid the cellar.

Rookie Ryne Sandberg, playing third base, recovers from a 1-for-31 beginning to hit .271 and score 103 runs. Leon Durham slugs 22 homers and Jody Davis, Keith Moreland and Bill Buckner all produce steady years. Big Lee Smith proves to be the real deal, saving 17 games, and 38-year-old Ferguson Jenkins returns to his old team to post 14 wins.

P	PLAYER	R	HR	RBI	SB	AVE
1B	Bill Buckner	93	15	105	15	.306
2B	Bump Wills	64	6	38	35	.272
SS	Larry Bowa	50	0	29	8	.246
3B	Ryne Sandberg	103	7	54	32	.271
RF	Jay Johnstone	39	10	43	0	.249
CF	Leon Durham	84	22	90	28	.312
LF	Keith Moreland	50	15	68	0	.261
C	Jody Davis	41	12	52	0	.261
OF	Gary Woods	28	4	30	3	.269
IF	Junior Kennedy	22	2	25	1	.219
OF	Steve Henderson	23	2	29	6	.233
OF	Jerry Morales	14	4	30	1	.284
OF	Bob Molinaro	6	1	12	1	.197

T	PITCHER	W-L	SV	SO	SH	ERA
R	Ferguson Jenkins	14-15	0	134	1	3.15
R	Doug Bird	9-14	0	71	1	5.14
R	Dickie Noles	10-13	0	85	2	4.42
R	Randy Martz	11-10	1	40	0	4.21
R	Lee Smith	2-5	17	99	0	2.69

January 12 - So much for scouting: the Cubs select catcher Troy Afenir with the second overall pick in the first round of the January amateur draft. Afenir will play in just 45 major league games with three different teams, but the third overall pick, Kirby Puckett (Twins) and the fourth overall pick, Randy Myers (Reds) will see plenty of action.

April 9 - Fergie Jenkins, back with the Cubs, thrills the Wrigley faithful with a 5-0 Opening Day shutout of the Mets.

April 28 - Dickie Noles beats Tom Seaver and the Reds on a one-hitter in his first career complete game, winning 6-0. Eddie Milner's fourth-inning single is Cincy's only safety.

May 13 - The Cubs tally their 8,000th victory, a 5-0 whitewashing of the Astros in Houston.

May 25 - Fergie Jenkins fans the Padres' Garry Templeton in the third to become just the seventh pitcher in ML history to record 3,000 career strikeouts. The Cubs lose 2-1.

June 7 - Shawon Dunston, who hit an astonishing .790 this year for Brooklyn's Thomas Jefferson High School, is selected by the Cubs as the first pick in the June amateur draft.

June 14 - The Cubs snap a 13-game losing streak, tying their all-time record set in 1944, with a 12-11 victory over the Phillies. Chicago makes six errors in the contest.

WORTH NOTING - In 1981, Bill Buckner became one of only five National Leaguers to drive in more than 21 percent of their team's runs. Two of the four others are also Cubs: Bill Nicholson (1943), and Ernie Banks (1959). The other two are Wally Berger of the Braves (1935) and Nate Colbert of the Padres (1972).

October3 - The Cubs lose to the Cardinals in 14 innings, 5-4. Starter Doug Bird, who gets a no-decision in the game, finishes 9-14 for his first losing season in nine years. The streak ties him with Carl Erskine, Whitey Ford, Milt Pappas, Tom Seaver, Juan Marichal, Orel Hershiser, and Roger Clemens.

1983

President: Andrew McKenna; **Manager:** Lee Elia / Charlie Fox; **Ballpark:** Wrigley Field; **Attendance:** 1,479,717; **Finish:** Fifth (71-91); **Recap:** Another fifth-place finish and a season-long battle with the city of Chicago over whether or not to install lights at Wrigley Field or demolish the center-field scoreboard breeds hostility in the Friendly Confines when the losses begin to mount up in August. Manager Lee Elia burns a bridge when he is quoted to say, "85 percent of the people in this country work and the other 15 percent come out to Wrigley to boo my players" and is fired. The blame for the team's poor play could be aimed squarely at the pitching staff, since the offense finishes second in the NL in runs scored (701), second in homers

WORTH QUOTING - "I'd rather hit home runs. You don't have to run as hard."
-Dave Kingman

Leon Durham

(140), first in slugging (.401) and first in fielding (.982).

Closer Lee Smith, more than anyone, saves the ballclub from a cellar finish by compiling a league-leading 29 saves (with a 1.65 ERA) despite not having many games to save.

P	PLAYER	R	HR	RBI	SB	AVE
1B	Bill Buckner	79	16	66	12	.280
2B	Ryne Sandberg	94	8	48	37	.261
SS	Larry Bowa	73	2	43	7	.267
3B	Ron Cey	73	24	90	0	.275
RF	Keith Moreland	76	16	70	0	.302
CF	Mel Hall	60	17	56	6	.283
LF	Leon Durham	58	12	55	12	.258
C	Jody Davis	56	24	84	0	.271
UT	Gary Woods	25	4	22	5	.242
OF	Jay Johnstone	16	6	22	1	.257
OF	Jerry Morales	11	0	11	0	.195

T	PITCHER	W-L	SV	SO	SH	ERA
R	Chuck Rainey	14-13	0	84	1	4.48
L	Steve Trout	10-14	0	80	0	4.65
R	Ferguson Jenkins	6-9	0	96	1	4.30
R	Lee Smith	4-10	29	91	0	1.65

January 19 - The Cubs acquire third baseman Ron Cey from the Dodgers for minor leaguers Vance Lovelace and Dan Cataline.

January 26 - The Cubs trade pitchers Randy Martz and Dick Tidrow and infielders Scott Fletcher and Pat Tabler to the White Sox for pitchers Steve Trout and Warren Brusstar.

April 6 - Montreal's Steve Rogers shuts out the Cubs 3-0 on Opening Day at Wrigley in front of 4,802 freezing fans. Ferguson Jenkins is the loser.

June 5 - Lee Smith fans four of the final five batters to earn his eighth save in a 3-1 victory over the Pirates.

August 22 - With the Cubs in fifth place, GM Dallas Green fires manager Lee Elia, naming his special assistant, Charlie Fox, interim skipper.

August 24 - Chuck Rainey takes a no-hitter into the ninth but loses it with two outs on Eddie Milner's single to center. The Cubs beat the Reds 3-0. It's Rainey's first complete game of the season.

October 6 - The Cubs hire Jim Frey as their new manager. Frey led the Royals to their first World Series in 1980.

December7 - The Cubs, Expos and Padres pull off a complicated trade involving five players. Chicago acquires pitcher Scott Sanderson from Montreal, sending reliever Craig Lefferts, outfielder Carmelo Martinez and infielder Fritz Connally to San Diego. The Padres then trade reliever Gary Lucas to Montreal.

1984

President: Jim Finks; **Manager:** Jim Frey;

Ballpark: Wrigley Field; **Attendance:** 2,107,655; **Finish:** First (96-65); **Recap:** The Cubs break the 2,000,000 mark in attendance for the first time as they march to their first title of any kind since 1945. Chicago begins the season 12-8 and at the end of April find themselves tied with the resurgent Mets for first place. The two battle back and forth until mid-May, when GM Dallas Green sends Mel Hall and Joe Carter to Cleveland for starter Rick Sutcliffe. Sutcliffe, 4-5 at the time of the trade, goes 16-1 the rest of the way and joins the rotation of Dennis Eckersley, Scott Sanderson, Dick Ruthven, and Steve Trout, outdistancing the Mets by 6 1/2 games.

Aside from the rotation and a solid bullpen anchored by hard-throwing Lee Smith, the lineup proves to be the NL's best, pacing the league in runs (762), led by Leon Durham (96 RBIs), Ron Cey (97 RBIs), Jody Davis (94 RBIs), Gary Matthews (82 RBIs) and Most Valuable Player Ryne Sandberg (84 RBIs, 114 runs).

P	Player	R	HR	RBI	SB	AVE
1B	Leon Durham	86	23	96	16	.279
2B	Ryne Sandberg	114	19	84	32	.314
SS	Larry Bowa	33	0	17	10	.233
3B	Ron Cey	71	25	97	3	.240
RF	Keith Moreland	59	16	80	1	.279
CF	Bob Dernier	94	3	32	45	.278
LF	Gary Matthews	101	14	82	17	.291
C	Jody Davis	55	19	94	5	.256
OF	Henry Cotto	24	0	9	9	.274
UT	Gary Woods	13	3	10	2	.235
OF	Thad Bosley	17	2	14	5	.296
OF	Jay Johnstone	8	0	3	0	.288
OF	Mel Hall	25	4	22	2	.280

T	Pitcher	W-L	SV	SO	SH	ERA
R	Rick Sutcliffe	16-1	0	155	3	2.69
L	Steve Trout	13-7	0	81	2	3.41
R	Dennis Eckersley	10-8	0	81	0	3.03
R	Scott Sanderson	8-5	0	76	0	3.14
R	Lee Smith	9-7	33	86	0	3.65

January 5 - The Cubs sign free agent slugger Richie Hebner.

WORTH NOTING - Ryne Sandberg had only one non-Cub base hit, as a Phillie in 1981. He collected it against Mike Krukow of the Cubs.

March 17 - Fergie Jenkins, 6-9 last season, is released by the Cubs.

April 13 - The Cubs beat the Mets 11-2 before 33,436 on Opening Day at Wrigley.

May 25 - The Cubs acquire pitcher Dennis Eckersley and minor leaguer Mike Brumley from the Red Sox for Bill Buckner.

May 27 - The Cubs lose a disputed game with the Reds at Wrigley, 4-3. In the third inning, Cincinnati protests a blow by Ron Cey down the third base line that is called a homer by umpire Steve Rippley, claiming it is foul. During the argument, Reds starter Mario Soto is ejected from the game for shoving Rippley. After a huddle, the ruling is, indeed, a foul. The Cubs immediately protest. Soto, still incensed, runs on the field and tackles third base coach Don Zimmer; both benches empty. Soto then runs into the stands with a bat when a soda vendor throws a bag of ice at him. Both teams officially protest the game; Soto will be suspended for five days.

June 10 - The Cubs pull off a triple steal in the ninth inning of a 2-0 victory over the Cardinals. Leon Durham steals home, Jody

WORTH QUOTING - "The latest diet is better than the Pritikin Diet. You eat only when the Cubs win."
-Pianist George Shearing, appearing on KTVN Radio, Las Vegas, 1982

WORTH NOTING- The Cubs' NLCS opponents in 1984 are the San Diego Padres, managed by **Dick Williams**. The Padres finish with a 92-70 (.568) record, leading the National League in shutouts (17).

P	PLAYER	R	HR	RBI	SB	BA
1B	Steve Garvey	72	8	86	1	.284
2B	Alan Wiggins	106	3	34	70	.258
SS	Garry Templeton	40	2	35	8	.258
3B	Graig Nettles	56	20	65	0	.228
RF	Tony Gwynn	88	5	71	33	.351
CF	Kevin McReynolds	68	20	75	3	.278
LF	Carmelo Martinez	64	13	66	1	.250
C	Terry Kennedy	54	14	57	1	.240

T	PITCHER	W	L	SV	SH	ERA
R	Eric Show	15	9	0	1	3.48
L	Mark Thurmond	14	8	0	1	2.97
R	Ed Whitson	14	8	0	0	3.24
L	Tim Lollar	11	13	0	2	3.91
R	Goose Gossage	10	6	25	0	2.90

Davis steals third and Larry Bowa takes second.

June 13 - The Cubs trade outfielders Mel Hall and Joe Carter to the Indians for catcher Ron Hassey and pitchers George Frazier and Rick Sutcliffe. Sutcliffe will go 16-1 for Chicago and win the Cy Young award.

June 23 - Ryne Sandberg goes 5-for-6 with seven RBI and two game-tying homers off former Cub Bruce Sutter in the ninth and tenth innings in a 12-11 victory over St. Louis. Dave Owens's single in the bottom of the 11th wins it. The Cardinals' Willie McGee hits for the cycle.

August 8 - The Cubs complete a four-game sweep of the second-place Mets at Wrigley Field with a 7-6 win. Keith Moreland goes 3-for-4 and drives in four to lead the way. Mets manager Davey Johnson is ejected in the seventh after Bob Dernier is hit by a pitch, the result of a beanball war that took place between the two clubs during a doubleheader sweep by the Cubs the day before. Cubs manager Jim Frey is then run in the ninth when a Lee Smith fastball comes a little too close to George Foster.

September 20 - The Cubs break two million in home attendance for the first time as 33,651 jam Wrigley to watch a 7-6 loss to the Pirates.

September 24 - The Cubbies clinch a title for the first time in almost 40 years as Rick Sutcliffe hurls a 4-1 two-hitter over Pittsburgh. It's Sutcliffe's 14th triumph in a row.

October 2 - NLCS Game 1

In the first League Championship Series game played with replacement umpires, the Cubs bomb the Padres 13-0 behind Rick Sutcliffe, who tosses a six-hitter and even hits a home run. The Cubs pound San Diego pitching for 16 hits and five homers, including two by Gary Matthews.

October 3 - NLCS Game 2

Steve Trout scatters five hits and Lee Smith gets the first save in Chicago's post-season history as the Cubs take Game 2, 4-2. Due to the league office demanding that three of the five games be played during prime time, the series will shift to San Diego for the final three games.

October 4 - NLCS Game 3

San Diego starter Ed Whitson shuts the Cubs down on five hits and Goose Gossage mops up in a 7-1 Padres victory.

October 6 - NLCS Game 4

The Cubs battle back from 2-0 and 5-3 deficits but first baseman Steve Garvey snaps a 5-5 tie by homering off Lee Smith in the bottom of the ninth to give the Padres a 7-5 win.

October 7 - NLCS Game 5
The Cubs lose a chance for a 1945 World Series rematch when they lose a 6-3 decision in Game 5 of the playoffs. Chicago jumps on Eric Show early, scoring three quick runs in the first two innings, but Dave Dravecky and Craig Lefferts shut them down the rest of the way and the Padres battle back for two off Rick Sutcliffe in the sixth and four more in the seventh, tying the game when Leon Durham boots an easy grounder to first. Tony Gwynn's double drives in the winning run and a two-run single by Steve Garvey puts the game away.

October 23 - Rick Sutcliffe is the unanimous choice for the National League's Cy Young Award.

November13 - Ryne Sandberg is voted the National League's Most Valuable Player.

1985

President: Dallas Green; **Manager:** Jim Frey; **Ballpark:** Wrigley Field; **Attendance:** 2,161,534; **Finish:** Fourth (77-84); **Recap:** The Cubs slip to fourth in 1985 thanks to a daunting epidemic of injuries that costs the club every one of its five starting pitchers at one point or another for extended periods. With only Lee Smith pitching well, the club finishes below .500 for the first of four straight seasons.

The team continues to hit well, again led by Ryne Sandberg but including solid seasons by Leon Durham (.282, 21 homers), Keith Moreland (106 RBIs) and veteran Davey Lopes (.284, 44 steals), who takes over in the outfield when Bob Dernier and Gary Matthews suffer extended slumps.

Ron Cey

P	Player	R	HR	RBI	SB	AVE
1B	Leon Durham	58	21	75	7	.282
2B	Ryne Sandberg	113	26	83	51	.305
SS	Shawon Dunston	40	4	18	11	.260
3B	Ron Cey	64	22	63	1	.232
RF	Keith Moreland	74	14	106	12	.307
CF	Bob Dernier	63	1	21	31	.254
LF	Gary Matthews	45	13	40	2	.235
C	Jody Davis	47	17	58	1	.232
OF	Thad Bosley	25	7	27	5	.328
IF	Chris Speier	16	4	24	1	.243
2B	Davey Lopes	52	11	44	47	.284
UT	Richie Hebner	10	3	22	0	.217
OF	Gary Woods	11	0	4	0	.244

WORTH NOTING - Ron Cey's beaning by Goose Gossage of the Yankees during the 1981 World Series led to a major league regulation requiring batters to wear helmets with earflaps.

WORTH NOTING - Ron Cey's 312 career homers rank him fifth on the All-Time list for third basemen.

T	Pitcher	W-L	SV	SO	SH	ERA
R	Dennis Eckersley	11-7	0	117	2	3.08
L	Steve Trout	9-7	0	44	1	3.39
L	Ray Fontenot	6-10	0	70	0	4.36
R	Rick Sutcliffe	8-8	0	102	3	3.18
R	Lee Smith	7-4	33	112	0	3.04

January 7 - Former Cub Lou Brock is elected to the Baseball Hall of Fame.

March 25 - The Cubs suffer a blow when an Illinois judge rules that state and city laws banning night baseball at Wrigley Field are constitutional. The Cubs lost home field advantage during the NLCS last year because of MLB's insistence that all championship games appear under the lights in order to get a higher share of the television audience.

April 9 - Rick Sutcliffe and Lee Smith combine to shut down the Pirates 2-1 on Opening Day in Chicago.

May 4 - The Cubs and Padres combine for seven home runs in a 12-8 Chicago win at Wrigley. Cubs shortstop Shawon Dunston hits his first major league homer.

May 8 - Ryne Sandberg's homer off San Francisco's Mike Krukow holds up as Rick Sutcliffe shuts out the Giants 1-0.

May 21 - A grand slam by slap-hitting Brian Dayett off Tom Browning in the sixth gives the Cubs a 7-4 win over Cincinnati. It'll be Dayett's only homer of the year.

June 3 - The Cubs select first baseman Mark Grace in the 24th round of the June Amateur Draft.

June 26 - The Cubs snap a club-record 13-game losing streak with a 7-3 win over the Mets.

July 5 - Davey Lopes is at bat with one out in the top of the first during a game at Wrigley when someone in the Cubs dugout notices that he is batting out of turn. After taking a strike, Ryne Sandberg replaces him in the box and singles. Lopes, scheduled to bat third, doubles Sandberg home. The Giants beat them anyway, 12-6.

September24 - Down 15-2, the Cubs rally for 13 runs, only to fall 17-15 to the Expos at Wrigley Field.

December 11 - Veteran infielder Manny Trillo returns to the Cubby fold, traded to Chicago from San Francisco for shortstop Dave Owen.

WORTH QUOTING - "Long relief is like being a plumber. Some days it's okay, but when thirty septic tanks back up, it's no fun at all."

-Cubs reliever George Frazier, 1984

1986

President: Dallas Green; **Manager:** Jim Frey / John Vukovich / Gene Michael; **Ballpark:** Wrigley Field; **Attendance:** 1,859,102; **Finish:** Fifth (70-90); **Recap:** All hopes that the Cubs' pitching would return to form in 1986 are shattered early, as the rotation continues to deteriorate and the Cubs slip to the bottom of the standings. Manager Jim Frey, as good a scapegoat as any, is replaced in June by the colorless Gene Michael. The biggest highlight of the season comes in July when the team fires one of its ballgirls for posing nude in *Playboy*.

P	PLAYER	R	HR	RBI	SB	AVE
1B	Leon Durham	66	20	65	8	.262
2B	Ryne Sandberg	68	14	76	34	.284
SS	Shawon Dunston	66	17	68	13	.250
3B	Ron Cey	42	13	36	0	.273
RF	Keith Moreland	72	12	79	3	.271
CF	Bob Dernier	32	4	18	27	.225
LF	Gary Matthews	49	21	46	3	.259
C	Jody Davis	61	21	74	0	.250
OF	Jerry Mumphrey	37	5	32	2	.304
IF	Chris Speier	21	6	23	2	.284
OF	Thad Bosley	15	1	9	3	.275
UT	Terry Francona	13	2	8	0	.250
IF	Manny Trillo	22	1	19	0	.296

T	PITCHER	W-L	SV	SO	SH	ERA
R	Dennis Eckersley	6-11	0	137	0	4.57
R	Scott Sanderson	9-11	1	124	1	4.19
R	Rick Sutcliffe	5-14	0	122	1	4.64
L	Steve Trout	5-7	0	69	0	4.75
R	Lee Smith	9-9	31	93	0	3.09

Rick Sutcliffe

April 18 - The Pirates spoil Opening Day at Wrigley, beating Rick Sutcliffe and the Cubs 4-0.

April 20 - The Cubs and Pirates play 13 innings before the game is called for darkness with the score knotted 8-8. The game will be finished August 11.

May 3 - Ron Cey hits his 300th and 301st career home runs and the Cubs push across four runs in the top of the ninth to beat the Giants 6-5.

June 12 - The Cubs, in fifth place, fire Jim Frey and third base coach Don Zimmer. Gene Michael, late of the Yankees, will take over.

June 23 - Chicago is pounded 19-1 by the Phillies, who set a club record with 11 doubles.

July 22 - The Cubs stir up controversy by firing ball girl Marla Collins after it is discovered that she posed nude for Playboy magazine. The photos, which will appear in the October issue, show Collins in her Cubs uniform and one of Harry Caray pointing to a tattoo on her right thigh.

Cubs pitcher Ed Lynch ties a National League record with three putouts in the first inning of a 6-4 triumph over the Padres.

August 11 - The Cubs use a record 10 pitchers during a 10-8 loss to Pittsburgh. The game is a continuation of the April 20 tie. Pirates Barry Jones, the winning pitcher, and Barry Bonds, who gets the game winning hit, were in the minors when the game started in April.

September 3 - The Astros and Cubs set a major legue record by using 53 players in an 18-inning, 8-7 Houston win at Wrigley.

WORTH NOTING - Lee Smith was the first pitcher to reach 400 saves.

1987

President: Dallas Green; **Manager:** Gene Michael / Frank Lucchesi; **Ballpark:** Wrigley Field; **Attendance:** 2,035,130; **Finish:** Sixth (76-85); **Recap:** Dallas Green makes his biggest and best (and cheapest) pickup when he signs free agent Andre Dawson, who so wants to play on Wrigley's soft grass he signs a blank check to do it. But aside from Dawson's 49 homers and 137 RBIs (earning him an MVP nod) and Rick Sutcliffe's comeback year (18 victories), there isn't much to cheer about in the 1987 campaign. The team continues to pitch poorly and play badly.

P	Player	R	HR	RBI	SB	AVE
1B	Leon Durham	70	27	63	2	.273
2B	Ryne Sandberg	81	16	59	21	.294
SS	Shawon Dunston	40	5	22	12	.246
3B	Keith Moreland	63	27	88	3	.266
RF	Andre Dawson	90	49	137	11	.287
CF	Dave Martinez	70	8	36	16	.292
LF	Jerry Mumphrey	41	13	44	1	.333
C	Jody Davis	57	19	51	1	.248
IF	Manny Trillo	27	8	26	0	.294
OF	Brian Dayett	20	5	25	0	.277
OF	Bob Dernier	38	8	21	16	.317
UT	Rafael Palmeiro	32	14	30	2	.276
IF	Paul Noce	17	3	14	5	.228

T	Pitcher	W-L	SV	SO	SH	ERA
R	Rick Sutcliffe	18-10	0	174	1	3.68
L	Jamie Moyer	12-15	0	147	0	5.10
R	Greg Maddux	6-14	0	101	1	5.61
R	Scott Sanderson	8-9	2	106	0	4.29
R	Lee Smith	4-10	36	96	0	3.12

January 30 - The Cubs trade Ron Cey to the Athletics for infielder Luis Quinones.

March 6 - Captivated by Wrigley Field, slugging free agent Andre Dawson invites GM Dallas Green to fill in a salary on a one-year blank contract so that he can play for the Cubs. Dawson will hit 49 home runs and win the MVPaward at the bargain price of $650,000.

March 30 - The Cubs acquire catcher Jim Sundberg from the Royals for outfielder Thad Bosley and pitcher Dave Gumpert.

April 3 - Another OOPS for the Cubs as they trade veteran Dennis Eckersley to the Athletics for three minor leaguers. Eck will go on to become baseball's premier closer.

April 7 - The Cards beat the Cubs 9-3 on Opening Day at Wrigley Field.

April 13 - Jamie Moyer sets a club record for strikeouts by a lefty with 12 versus the Phillies. He takes a no-hitter into the ninth, when it's broken up by Juan Samuel. The Cubs hold on to win, 5-2.

April 29 - Andre Dawson hits for the cycle and goes 5-for-5 in an 8-4 win over the Giants.

June 3 - Keith Moreland and Brian Dayett each hit grand slams in a 22-7 romp over the Astros at Wrigley. Billy Hatcher hits a grand slam for the Astros to equal a record set by the Orioles and Rangers on August 6, 1986.

June 9 - Iowa (AA) Cubs designated hitter Wade Rowdon leads his team to an 18-12 triumph over Louisville with four homers, six RBIs and five runs. He hits two homers during a nine-run second inning. Rowdon has a chance for five, but is walked intentionally; catcher Damon Berryhill then homers. Rowdon will hit just one homer in 78 plate appearances over five major league seasons.

June 26 - Paul Noce is thrown out trying to steal second base in the third inning of a 5-2 loss to Pittsburgh, but is ruled safe as the shortstop drops the ball. Noce is then thrown out trying to steal third.

July 12 - The Cubs acquire pitcher Bob Tewksbury, who just pitched back-to-back shutouts, from the Yankees for Steve Trout.

August 1 - Andre Dawson hits three home runs and drives in all the runs of a 5-3 victory over Philadelphia.

August 21 - Dawson hits homers 39 and 40 and Lee Smith picks up save No. 30 as the Cubs beat the Astros 7-5.

September 1 - During a 3-2 Cubs win in Houston, Astro Billy Hatcher's bat explodes when he makes contact with a pitch, raining rubber balls all over the infield. Hatcher is ejected for using a doctored bat and will be suspended for 10 games by the National League.

September 8 - The fifth-place Cubs fire manager Gene Michael, replacing him with Frank Lucchesi.

September 22 - Pitcher Dickie Noles is traded for himself. The Cubs send him to the Tigers for a player to be named later, which turns out to be Noles, who comes back on October 23.

September27 - Andre Dawson smacks his 47th homer of the year in his final plate appearance at Wrigley Field this season.

October 29 - GM Dallas Green, citing "philosophical differences" with the Tribune Company, resigns.

November 11 - Former manager Jim Frey is named GM. His first move is to hire his friend Don Zimmer as manager.

WORTH NOTING - Andre Dawson is one of only three players to win an MVP award in a losing season. The other two are Hank Sauer and Ernie Banks - also Cubs.

November 18 - Andre Dawson becomes the first player from a last-place team to win an MVPaward.

1988

President: John W. Madigan; **Manager:** Don Zimmer; **Ballpark:** Wrigley Field; **Attendance:** 2,089,034; **Finish:** Fourth (77-85); **Recap:** With the Cubs again also-rans, the Wrigley Field lights situation dominates the Chicago headlines throughout the summer. The Chicago Tribune Company, the team's owners, finally threaten to move the club to the suburbs if their demands aren't met, with the National League making it clear that no post-season games would be played during the daytime. Under the terms of an agreement hammered out during the season, the city council repeals the ban on lights, the Cubs agree to play only a "minimal amount" of night games, and the NL commits to an All-Star Game at the stadium.

As for the Cubs themselves, the 1988 season is remarkable if only for the development of a few key young players - first baseman Mark Grace, shortstop Shawon Dunston, outfielder Rafael Palmeiro and righthander Greg Maddux. A less satisfac-

WORTH QUOTING - "The Cubs striking is about as significant as the buggy-whip manufacturers going on strike. What difference does it make?"
-Mike Royko, Chicago Sun-Times, 1986

Andre Dawson

tory highlight is the trading of Lee Smith to the Red Sox for righthanders Calvin Schiraldi and Al Nipper.

P	PLAYER	R	HR	RBI	SB	AVE
1B	Mark Grace	65	7	57	3	.296
2B	Ryne Sandberg	77	19	69	25	.264
SS	Shawon Dunston	69	9	56	30	.249
3B	Vance Law	73	11	78	1	.293
RF	Andre Dawson	78	24	79	12	.303
CF	Dave Martinez	27	4	34	7	.254
LF	Rafael Palmeiro	75	8	53	12	.307
C	Damon Berryhill	19	7	38	1	.259
OF	Darrin Jackson	29	6	20	4	.266
C	Jody Davis	19	6	33	0	.229
IF	Manny Trillo	15	1	14	2	.250
OF	Mitch Webster	36	4	26	10	.265

T	PITCHER	W-L	SV	SO	SH	ERA
R	Greg Maddux	18-8	0	140	3	3.18
R	Rick Sutcliffe	13-14	0	144	2	3.86
L	Jamie Moyer	9-15	0	121	1	3.48
R	Calvin Schiraldi	9-13	1	140	1	4.38
R	Goose Gossage	4-4	13	30	0	4.33

February 12 - The Cubs acquire veteran reliever Goose Gossage from the Padres for Keith Moreland.

February 23 - The Chicago board of aldermen vote 7-2 to allow the Cubs to install lights at Wrigley Field. The team will be allowed to play up to 18 night games per season.

April 15 - Rick Sutcliffe blanks the Pirates 6-0 on Opening Day at Wrigley.

May 18 - To make room for rookie Mark Grace, the Cubs trade Leon Durham to the Reds for reliever Pat Perry.

May 31 - Rookie Jeff Pico hurls a four-hit shutout in his major league debut as the Cubs beat the Reds 4-0. He's the first Cub pitcher to debut with a shutout since Bill Lee did it in 1934.

July 4 - Umpire Lee Weyer, 51, suffers a heart attack and dies after working the Cubs' 3-2 win over the Giants in San Francisco.

July 19 - In the top of the ninth at Wrigley, San Francisco's Brett Butler wanders too far off the bag with a runner on second. Rick Sutcliffe runs at him and tags him out, credited with an unassisted pickoff. But Sutcliffe loses, 3-1.

July 29 - Sutcliffe steals home during an 8-3 win at Philadelphia, the first pitcher to do it since Pasqual Perez in 1984 and the first Cub hurler to do it since Hippo Vaughn in 1919.

August 6 - Goose Gossage posts his 300th career save, the second major leaguer to accomplish the feat, in a 7-4 Cubs win vs. Philadelphia. Reliever Pat Perry hits his only major league homer in the game, a two-run shot off Mike Maddux.

August 8 - The first night game ever at Wrigley Field, between the Cubs and Phils, is rained out in the fourth with Chicago leading 3-1.

August 9 - The Cubs beat the Mets 6-4 in the first official night game in Wrigley history. New York center fielder Lenny Dykstra hits the first night home run. Reliever Frank DiPino earns the first night victory.

September 29 - The Cubs trade Jody Davis to the Braves for pitchers Kevin Coffman and Kevin Blankenship.

September 30 - President Ronald Regan visits with Harry Caray in the Wrigley Field broadcast booth during a 10-9 Cubs loss to Pittsburgh.

December 5 - The Cubs send future star Rafael Palmeiro, along with pitchers Jamie Moyer and Drew Hall, to Texas in exchange for reliever Mitch "Wild Thing" Williams, pitchers Paul Kilgus and Steve Wilson, and infielder Curtis Wilkerson.

1989

President: Stanton Cook; **Manager:** Don Zimmer; **Ballpark:** Wrigley Field; **Attendance:** 2,491,942; **Finish:** First (93-69); **Recap:** A pre-season deal that sends budding star Rafael Palmeiro to the Rangers for closer Mitch Williams and strong performances by starters Greg Maddux, Mike Bielecki and Rick Sutcliffe result in an unexpected division title in 1989. The main offense comes from Ryne Sandberg (30 homers and a league-leading 104 runs), Mark Grace (.314), and Rookie of the Year Jerome Walton (.293 and 24 steals). Williams tallies 36 saves and leads the NL with 76 appearances.

WORTH QUOTING - "Oh, I get a little tired now and then, but knowing my lifestyle, that's only natural."
-Harry Caray, when asked about the effects of his 1987 stroke, quoted in *The Sporting News*

P	Player	R	HR	RBI	SB	AVE
1B	Mark Grace	74	13	79	14	.314
2B	Ryne Sandberg	104	30	76	15	.290
SS	Shawon Dunston	52	9	60	19	.278
3B	Vance Law	38	7	42	2	.235
RF	Andre Dawson	62	21	77	8	.252
CF	Jerome Walton	64	5	46	24	.293
LF	Dwight Smith	52	9	52	9	.324
C	Damon Berryhill	37	5	41	1	.257
OF	Mitch Webster	40	3	19	14	.257
UT	Lloyd McClendon	47	12	40	6	.286
IF	Domingo Ramos	18	1	19	1	.263
UT	Curtis Wilkerson	18	1	10	4	.244
OF	Gary Varsho	10	0	6	3	.184

T	Pitcher	W-L	SV	SO	SH	ERA
R	Greg Maddux	19-12	0	135	1	2.95
R	Rick Sutcliffe	16-11	0	153	1	3.66
R	Mike Bielecki	18-7	0	147	3	3.14
R	Scott Sanderson	11-9	0	86	0	3.94
L	Mitch Williams	4-4	36	67	0	2.76

April 4 - The Cubs beat the Phillies 5-4 on Opening Day in Chicago.

May 5 - Andre Dawson goes 4-for-4 in a 4-2 win over the Dodgers, giving him eight hits in his last eight at-bats.

May 10 - It's another long-term loss for the Cubs as Jerome Walton injures his hamstring while crawling back to third base in a 4-3 loss to the Giants. Walton's baserunning error stifles a ninth-inning comeback. He'll be out a month.

WORTH NOTING - Andre Dawson is one of only four players to hit 300 home runs and steal 300 bases.

Ryne Sandberg

July 23 - Cubs play-by-play man Harry Caray is inducted into the broadcaster's wing of the Hall of Fame.

July 30 - Mark Grace hits a two-out three run homer in the ninth to give the Cubs a 6-4 triumph over the Mets.

August 18 - Andre Dawson gets his 2,000th career hit during a 6-5 loss to the Astros.

August 21 - A 30-game hitting streak by Jerome Walton is snapped when he goes 0-for-4 in a 6-5, 10-inning loss to Cincinnati. It's the longest streak in modern Cubs history.

WORTH QUOTING - "If we went by tradition, we'd still be playing without gloves."
-Manager Jim Frey, on the installation of lights at Wrigley Field, 1988

August 29 - Dwight Smith comes in to play right field as a defensive replacement in the seventh inning and singles home a run in the bottom of the inning, throws out a runner at the plate in the eighth, ties the game with a sacrifice fly in the ninth, and singles home the game winner in the 10th. The Cubs beat Houston 10-9.

August 31 - Just minutes before the trading deadline, the Cubs acquire third baseman Luis Salazar and outfielder Marvelle Wynne from the Padres for pitcher Calvin Schiraldi, first baseman Phil Stephenson, and outfielder Darrin Jackson.

September 25 - The Cubs lose to the Expos 4-3 in 10 innings but clinch a tie for the Eastern Division title when St. Louis loses later in the day.

Andre Dawson hits an inside-the-park homer when his fly ball is allegedly dropped by Dave Martinez, who suffers a painful muscle pull while making the play and drops to the ground. Although the ball never touches the ground, the umpires' views are blocked by Martinez'teammates, who rush to his aid. Dawson is awarded home plate over Montreal's howls of protest.

September 26 - The Cubs clinch the division title with a 3-2 win over the Expos. Mitch Williams fans catcher Mike Fitzgerald to end the game.

October 4 - NLCS Game 1
The Giants pummel Greg Maddux and the Cubs 11-3 in Game 1, with Will Clark tagging the righthander for three hits and six RBIs. Mark Grace hits a two-run homer in the first, and Ryne Sandberg homers off starter Scott Garrelts in the third for all of Chicago's offense.

October 5 - NLCS Game 2
The Cubs rough up former teammate Rick Reuschel with five runs in 2/3 of an inning, then hang on for a 9-5 triumph. Mark Grace goes 3-for-4 with four RBIs. Les Lancaster hurls the final four innings for the win.

October 7 - NLCS Game 3
The Cubs take a 4-3 lead into the bottom of the seventh, when Robby Thompson hits a two-run homer off Les Lancaster that provides the margin in a 5-4 San Francisco victory.

October 8 - NLCS Game 4
Third baseman Matt Williams hits a two-run homer in the fifth off Steve Wilson as the Giants take Game 4. Greg Maddux struggles again, giving up four runs in less than four innings of work.

October 9 - NLCS Game 5
Eighteen-game winner Mike Bielecki allows just a pair of singles through six innings, carrying a 1-0 lead into the seventh, when Will Clark's sacrifice fly ties the score. In the eighth, after Bielecki loads the bases with three walks, Mitch Williams gets two quick strikes on Clark, then is tagged for a two-run single. The Cubs rally in the ninth on three two-out singles to make it 3-2, but Giants closer Steve Bedrosian gets Ryne Sandberg on a grounder to end the game.

November 8 - Jerome Walton just edges Dwight Smith to win the National League Rookie of the Year Award. It's the first time NLteammates have finished 1-2 in Rookie of the Year voting. Walton is the first Cubby to win the honor since Billy Williams in 1961.

WORTH QUOTING -"WILL THE LAST PERSON TO LEAVE THE STADIUM PLEASE TURN OUTTHE LIGHTS?"
-Sign held up by a fan in the bleachers at the end of the first night game at Wrigley Field on August 9, 1988

1990

President: Stanton Cook; **Manager:** Don Zimmer; **Ballpark:** Wrigley Field; **Attendance:** 2,243,791; **Finish:** Fourth (77-85); **Recap:** Ryne Sandberg enjoys his finest season, pacing the NL in homers (40 - the first second baseman to lead the league since Rogers Hornsby in 1925) and runs (116) and driving in 100 runs, but the Cubs have little else on display in a fourth-place season. Greg Maddux slumps to 15-15 and Mitch Williams records only 16 saves, going 1-8.

The Cubs contend until the last half of September, when the Pirates come roaring back.

WORTH NOTING- The Cubs' NLCS opponents in 1989 are the San Francisco Giants, managed by **Roger Craig**. The Giants finish with a 92-70 (.568) record.

P	PLAYER	R	HR	RBI	SB	BA
1B	Will Clark	104	23	111	8	.333
2B	Robby Thompson	91	13	50	12	.241
SS	Jose Uribe	34	1	30	6	.221
3B	Matt Williams	31	18	50	1	.202
RF	Candy Muldonado	39	9	41	4	.217
CF	Brett Butler	100	4	36	31	.283
LF	Kevin Mitchell	100	47	125	3	.291
C	Terry Kennedy	19	5	34	1	.239

T	PITCHER	W	L	SV	SH	ERA
R	Rick Reuschel	17	8	0	0	2.94
R	Scott Garrelts	14	5	0	1	2.28
R	Don Robinson	12	11	0	1	3.43
R	Mike LaCoss	10	10	6	0	3.17
L	Craig Lefferts	2	4	20	0	2.69
R	Steve Bedrosian	1	4	17	0	2.65

P	PLAYER	R	HR	RBI	SB	AVE
1B	Mark Grace	72	9	82	15	.309
2B	Ryne Sandberg	116	40	100	25	.306
SS	Shawon Dunston	73	17	66	25	.262
3B	Luis Salazar	44	12	47	3	.254
RF	Andre Dawson	72	27	100	16	.310
CF	Jerome Walton	63	2	21	14	.263
LF	Dwight Smith	34	6	27	11	.262
C	Joe Girardi	36	1	38	8	.270
UT	Doug Descenzo	27	1	26	15	.253
IF	Domingo Ramos	22	2	17	0	.265
OF	Marvell Wynne	21	4	19	3	.204
OF	Dave Clark	22	5	20	7	.275
UT	Curtis Wilkerson	21	0	16	2	.220

T	PITCHER	W-L	SV	SO	SH	ERA
R	Greg Maddux	15-15	0	144	2	3.46
R	Mike Bielecki	8-11	1	103	0	4.93
R	Mike Harkey	12-6	0	94	1	3.26
R	Shawn Boskie	5-6	0	49	0	3.69
L	Mitch Williams	1-8	16	55	0	3.93

April 10 - The Cubs nip the Phillies 2-1 on Opening Day at Wrigley Field.

April 21 - The White Sox' Steve Lyons plays all nine positions in an exhibition game with the Cubs.

April 29 - Greg Maddux records seven putouts, a major league record for pitchers, in a 4-0 shutout of the Dodgers.

May 18 - Ryne Sandberg commits an error after 584 chances and 123 games, both major league records, during a 7-0 loss to the Astros.

May 22 - Andre Dawson is walked intentionally five times, another major league record, in a 2-1 Cubs win vs. Cincinnati.

July 28 - Shawon Dunston drives in five runs and collects a record-tying three triples during a 10-7 win vs. Montreal.

August 28 - Ryne Sandberg's home run in a 5-2 win over Houston makes him the first second baseman ever to post back-to-back 30-homer seasons. He'll finish with 40, the first since Rogers Hornsby in 1925 to lead the league in homers.

September 6 - Chicago's Eastern Division lead is shrunk to half a game over St. Louis when the last-place Phillies beat them 9-1.

September 9 - Luis Salazar singles home the tying run in the eighth and doubles home the winner in the ninth as the Cubs beat the Cardinals 3-2 and retain their 1/2 game lead.

September 10 - Rookie Steve Wilson fans 10 Cardinals in just five innings, and Cubs relievers add eight more Ks in a 4-1 victory at Wrigley. Dwight Smith hits a two-run homer.

December 6 - Free agent slugger George Bell signs with the Cubs.

WORTH NOTING - Greg Maddux is the only pitcher in history to win the Cy Young Award in three consecutive seasons (1992-1994).

1991

President: Stanton Cook; **Manager:** Don Zimmer / Joe Altobelli / Jim Essian; **Ballpark:** Wrigley Field; **Attendance:** 2,314,250; **Finish:** Fourth (77-83); **Recap:** Prior to the 1991 season, the ballclub spends lavishly to try to return to the postseason, signing pricey free agents George Bell, Dave Smith, and Danny Jackson. But all the team buys is a fourth-place finish, with Ryne Sandberg and Andre Dawson still going on strong but with Mark Grace and Jerome Walton noticeably slumping and Jackson and Smith spending most of the season on the disabled list.

Early in the campaign, Don Zimmer is

unexpectedly fired in favor of Jim Essian. After a few weeks of silence, the commissioner's office discloses that it has been probing the manager's race track betting habits. Zimmer will be absolved from any wrongdoing for lack of evidence.

P	PLAYER	R	HR	RBI	SB	AVE
1B	Mark Grace	87	8	58	3	.273
2B	Ryne Sandberg	104	26	100	22	.291
SS	Shawon Dunston	59	12	50	21	.260
3B	Luis Salazar	34	14	38	0	.258
RF	Andre Dawson	69	31	104	4	.272
CF	Jerome Walton	42	5	17	7	.219
LF	George Bell	63	25	86	2	.285
C	Rick Wilkins	21	6	22	3	.222
UT	Chico Walker	51	6	34	13	.257
UT	Doug Dascenzo	40	1	18	14	.255
IF	Jose Vizcaino	7	0	10	2	.262
OF	Dwight Smith	16	3	21	2	.228
UT	Hector Villanueva	23	13	32	0	.276

T	PITCHER	W-L	SV	SO	SH	ERA
R	Greg Maddux	15-11	0	198	2	3.35
R	Mike Bielecki	13-11	0	72	0	4.50
R	Shawn Boskie	4-9	0	62	0	5.23
R	Rick Sutcliffe	6-5	0	52	0	4.10
L	Paul Assenmacher	7-8	15	117	0	3.24

January 8 - Ferguson Jenkins is elected to the Baseball Hall of Fame. Fergie is one of only two men to be inducted into both the American and Canadian Halls of Fame. The other is Jackie Robinson.

April 7 - The Cubs acquire pitchers Chuck McElroy and Bob Scanlan from the Phillies for reliever Mitch Williams.

April 9 - The Cubs are on the losing end of a 4-1 decision to the Cardinals on Opening Day at Wrigley.

May 13 - Three generations of Carays take the mic during the Cubs' 5-3 loss to the Atlanta Braves - Harry, son Skip, and grandson Chip.

May 21 - Don Zimmer is fired as Cubs manager; Jim Essian replaces him.

Mark Grace

July 23 - During an 8-5 Cubs win at Wrigley, erratic Reds reliever Rob Dibble throws a ball at outfielder Doug Dascenzo as Dascenzo runs to first. Dibble will be fined but not suspended. Andre Dawson, who bumps umpire Joe West during an argument, will be both fined and suspended.

August 25 - Dascenzo's National League-record streak of 242 consecutive errorless games is snapped when he commits an error during a 12-9 loss to the Padres. He is two games short of the ML record.

October 6 - The Cubs beat the Cardinals 7-3 and curb an attempt by St. Louis to become the first team since the 1912 Washington Senators to have 10 players

WORTH QUOTING - "It'll be great not having to listen to two national anthems."
-Mitch Webster, after being traded to the Cubs from the Montreal Expos

WORTH QUOTING - "I pitch like my hair's on fire."

-Mitch Williams

with 10 or more steals when catcher Hector Villanueva throws out Tom Pagnozzi on two attempts.

October 18 - The Cubs fire manager Jim Essian. Jim Lefebvre will replace him.

1992

President: Stanton Cook; **Manager:** Jim Lefebvre; **Ballpark:** Wrigley Field; **Attendance:** 2,126,720; **Finish:** Fourth (78-84); **Recap:** The 1992 season almost mirrors the year before, with the Cubs winning just one more game than in 1991 thanks to the offensive efforts of Mark Grace, Ryne Sandberg and Andre Dawson. With Dave Smith spending most of the season on the disabled list, less-than-intimidating Bob Scanlon becomes Jim Lefebvre's closer, converting just 14 saves.

Early in 1992, GM Jim Frey is given the boot in favor of American League executive Larry Himes.

The biggest headline of the year is outside the lines, as baseball commissioner Fay Vincent attempts to put the Cubs and Cardinals into the Western Division of a newly realigned National League, due to the league's expansion into Denver and Miami. Although the plan is essentially welcomed by most clubs, the plan begins to go south when Chicago declares its opposition. The team's main point is that a shift to the west would inconvenience viewers of the Tribune Company's WGN superstation, the cable network that broadcasts Cubs games, forcing them to watch more games at the later Mountain and Pacific time zones. The Cubs also object to what they perceive as Vincent's strongarming tactics. When the commissioner refuses to budge, the Cubs go to court and secure a restraining order against the move. The result is that the Cubs and Cardinals both move into the newly-created Central Division, with the Braves moving west. Vincent resigns in the Fall.

WORTH QUOTING - "It's the fans that need spring training. You gotta get 'em interested. Wake 'em up. Let 'em know that their season is coming, the good times are gonna roll."

-Harry Caray, from the Hall of Fame Collection

P	PLAYER	R	HR	RBI	SB	AVE
1B	Mark Grace	72	9	79	6	.307
2B	Ryne Sandberg	100	26	87	17	.304
SS	Rey Sanchez	24	1	19	2	.251
3B	Steve Buechele	25	1	21	1	.276
RF	Andre Dawson	60	22	90	6	.277
CF	Sammy Sosa	41	8	25	15	.260
LF	Derrick May	33	8	45	5	.274
C	Joe Girardi	19	1	12	0	.270
OF	Doug Descenzo	37	0	20	6	.255
OF	Dwight Smith	28	3	24	9	.276
UT	Luis Salazar	20	5	25	1	.208
IF	Jose Vizcaino	25	1	17	3	.225
C	Rick Wilkins	20	8	22	0	.270

T	PITCHER	W-L	SV	SO	SH	ERA
R	Greg Maddux	20-11	0	199	4	2.15
R	Mike Morgan	16-8	0	123	1	2.55
R	Frank Castillo	10-11	0	135	0	3.46
L	Danny Jackson	4-9	0	51	0	4.22
R	Bob Scanlan	3-6	14	42	0	2.89

March 2 - The Cubs sign Ryne Sandberg to the richest contract in baseball history - four years at $28.4 million.

March 30 - The Cubs acquire outfielder Sammy Sosa, along with pitcher Ken Patterson, from the White Sox for George Bell.

April 10 - The Cards nip the Cubs 2-1 on

Opening Day in Chicago. Former Cub Lee Smith earns the save.

June 8 - Rookie pitcher Jim Bullinger hits a home run in his first major league at-bat, the 10th pitcher in history to do it, on the first pitch off Rheal Cormier in a 5-2 win over the Cardinals.

June 25 - The Mets' Vince Coleman nearly charges Greg Maddux on the mound when he and Maddux get into a shouting match, but Maddux regains his composure enough to fan 10 in a 3-1 victory.

July 5 - Maddux shuts out the Braves 8-0 behind homers from Kal Daniels, Andre Dawson, Ryne Sandberg, and Mark Grace. During the game, home plate umpire Bill Hohn ejects a Braves fan for making obscene gestures.

July 6 - Baseball commissioner Fay Vincent orders a realignment of the National League for 1993, putting the Cubs and Cardinals into the Western Division. The Cubs will block the move, though, in a suit that will lead to Vincent's resignation.

July 10 - The Cubs acquire third baseman Steve Buechele from the Pirates for lefty Danny Jackson.

July 16 - Greg Maddux announces that he will become a free agent after the season, frustrated with the lack of negotiations with the Cubs.

July 27 - Wrigley Field fans give Maddux a standing ovation in his first start since announcing his intention to file as a free agent. Maddux then beats the first-place Pirates 3-2, aided by leadoff batter Sammy Sosa's three hits, including a homer.

August 25 - Mike Harkey injures himself while warming up against the Pirates and has to be replaced by Jeff Robinson. He'll appear in the box score without having thrown a pitch. The Cubs lose 7-4.

WORTH NOTING - Ryne Sandberg's string of nine consecutive Gold Gloves was snapped in 1992. Pittsburgh's Jose Lind was the winner.

August 30 - Jim Bullinger one-hits the Giants in just his third major league start, beating them 3-1. The only hit he gives up is an eighth-inning homer by catcher Kirk Manwaring.

September 16 - Greg Maddux earns his 18th win in a 14-9 crushing of Philadelphia. Andre Dawson collects for hits, and Dawson, Ryne Sandberg and Rick Wilkins homer.

September20 - Shawn Boskie gives up six runs on six hits in the first and leaves without recording an out. The Cardinals win, 16-4.

September 30 - Greg Maddux becomes the first Cub 20-game winner in 15 years, blanking the Pirates 6-0.

November 17 - The Cubs swap infielders Alex Arias and Gary Scott to the new Florida Marlins for pitcher Greg Hibbard.

December 1 - The Cubs sign free agent Juan Guzman to a four-year deal. Guzman went 16-11 for the Rangers.

December 8 - Chicago signs free agent reliever Dan Plesac to a two-year contract.

December 9 - The Cubs sign free agent closer Randy Myers to a three-year deal.

Greg Maddux

December 11 - Outfielder Candy Maldonado returns to the Cubs, inked to a two-year pact.

1993

President: Stanton Cook; **Manager:** Jim Lefebvre; **Ballpark:** Wrigley Field; **Attendance:** 2,653,763; **Finish:** Fourth (84-78); **Recap:** Despite the defection of Greg Maddux and Andre Dawson, who leaves for Boston, Jim Lefebvre brings the team to its third winning season in 22 years. The team is led by new reliever Randy Myers, who sets a league record with 53 saves and who contributes to 65 percent of the team's victories, and outfielder Sammy Sosa, acquired from the cross-town White Sox, who slugs 33 homers and steals 36 bases. But instead of a pat on the back, Lefebvre is fired and replaced with Tom Trebelhorn.

P	Player	R	HR	RBI	SB	AVE
1B	Mark Grace	86	14	98	8	.325
2B	Ryne Sandberg	67	9	45	9	.309
SS	Rey Sanchez	35	0	28	1	.282
3B	Steve Buechele	53	15	65	1	.272
RF	Sammy Sosa	92	33	93	36	.261
CF	Dwight Smith	51	11	35	8	.300
LF	Derrick May	62	10	77	10	.295
C	Rick Wilkins	78	30	73	2	.303
IF	Jose Vizcaino	74	4	54	12	.287
OF	Willie Wilson	29	1	11	7	.258
OF	Candy Moldonado	8	3	15	0	.186
UT	Eric Yelding	14	1	10	3	.204
OF	Kevin Roberson	23	9	27	0	.189

T	Pitcher	W-L	SV	SO	SH	ERA
R	Mike Morgan	10-15	0	111	1	4.03
L	Greg Hibbard	15-11	0	82	0	3.96
R	Jose Guzman	12-10	0	163	1	4.34
R	Mike Harkey	10-10	0	67	0	5.26
L	Randy Myers	2-4	53	86	0	3.11

March 27 - Just before the end of spring training, Ryne Sandberg (broken hand) and Shawon Dunston (lower back pain) are put on the disabled list and will miss Opening Day for the first time in nine seasons.

April 5 - Atlanta's Greg Maddux comes back to haunt his old club, beating the Cubs 1-0 on Opening Day in Chicago.

April 6 - Juan Guzman, in his NL debut, takes a perfect game into the eighth inning and a no-hitter into the ninth before giving up a two-out single to Otis Nixon in a 1-0 one-hit victory over the Braves.

May 9 - Mark Grace hits for the cycle during the Cubs'5-4 loss to the Padres.

June 1 - Heathcliff Slocumb is traded to the Indians for shortstop Jose Hernandez.

WORTH QUOTING - "I've now got the starter to replace him."
-Cubs GM Larry Himes on Jose Guzman, after losing Greg Maddux to free agency

July 2 - Sammy Sosa collects six hits in an 11-8 win vs. Colorado.

July 30 - The Cubs acquire outfielder Tuffy Rhodes in a three-way deal that sees lefty Paul Assenmacher sent to the Yankees.

August 20 - The Cubs send Candy Maldonado to the Indians for outfielder Glenallen Hill.

September 6 - Ryne Sandberg's 17-game hitting streak is snapped.

September13 - Sandberg breaks his finger sliding during a 6-5 win over the Giants, ending his season.

October6 - Manager Jim Lefebvre is fired.

October 13 - Tom Trebelhorn is named manager.

1994

President: Stanton Cook; **Manager:** Tom Trebelhorn; **Ballpark:** Wrigley Field; **Attendance:** 1,845,208; **Finish:** Fifth (49-64); **Recap:** Tuffy Rhodes gets the Cubs off to a good start with three homers on Opening Day, but the team loses that game and many more, finishing fifth in the strike-shortened season. Depressed by the club's poor play and the crumbling of his marriage, All-Star Ryne Sandberg announces his retirement at the age of 34.

In September, wholesale changes are made to the front office, with Andy MacPhail coming over from Minnesota to become CEO, and Ed Lynch replacing Larry Himes as GM. Jim Riggleman then replaces Tom Trebelhorn as manager.

WORTH NOTING - Of Glenallen Hill's 30 hits in 1993, 17 of them were for extra bases. He is one of only three Cubs to have more extra-base hits than singles in a season. The others: Cliff Heathcote (1930) and Ned Williamson (1883).

P	PLAYER	R	HR	RBI	SB	AVE
1B	Mark Grace	55	6	44	0	.298
2B	Rey Sanchez	26	0	24	2	.285
SS	Shawon Dunston	38	11	35	3	.278
3B	Steve Buechele	33	14	52	1	.242
RF	Sammy Sosa	59	25	70	22	.300
CF	Tuffy Rhodes	39	8	19	6	.234
LF	Derrick May	43	8	51	3	.284
C	Rick Wilkins	44	7	39	4	.227
OF	Glenallen Hill	48	10	38	19	.297
UT	Eddie Zambrano	17	6	18	2	.259
IF	Ryne Sandberg	36	5	24	2	.238
UT	Jose Hernandez	18	1	9	2	.242
C	Mark Parent	8	3	16	0	.263

T	PITCHER	W-L	SV	SO	SH	ERA
R	Willie Banks	8-12	0	91	1	5.40
R	Steve Trachsel	9-7	0	108	0	3.21
R	Anthony Young	4-6	0	65	0	3.92
R	Mike Morgan	2-10	0	57	0	6.69
L	Randy Myers	1-5	21	32	0	3.79

February 25 - Leo Durocher is elected to the Hall of Fame by the Veterans Committee.

March 30 - The Cubs acquire pitcher Anthony Young from the Mets for shortstop Jose Vizcaino.

April 4 - Tuffy Rhodes becomes the first National Leaguer to hit three homers on Opening Day as the Cubs beat Dwight Gooden and the Mets 12-8 at Wrigley. He

WORTH QUOTING - "There ARE Cubs fans."

-Mitch Williams, when asked about the difference between fans at Wrigley Field and fans at Arlington Stadium in Texas

WORTH QUOTING - "The weather's cold, my club stinks, we can't win, my knees are killing me, I'm off my diet, I can't putt anymore, my wife's nagging me. Other than that, life's great."

-Don Zimmer, quoted in the *Boston Globe*, 1990

does it in his first three at-bats of the game.

May 2 - The Cubs, who have lost 10 in a row, wear blue, instead of white with pinstripes, for their home game vs. Cincinnati. It doesn't work, as they lose to John Smiley 9-0.

May 4 - The Cubs snap an 11-game losing streak, beating the Reds 5-2.

May 6 - Anthony Young snaps a record 27-game losing streak with a 10-1 win over Pittsburgh. The win is the Cubs' first at home this season, snapping a record 14-game home losing streak.

May 15 - Six Marlins pitchers combine to shut out the hapless Cubs, 3-0.

June 13 - Ryne Sandberg announces his retirement.

June 27 - Randy Myers notches his 200th career save, just the third lefty to reach the mark. The Cubs beat the Pirates 2-1.

July 20 - Mark Grace collects four hits, including thee doubles, in a 9-8 win over the Rockies.

October 21 - The Cubs announce that Jim Riggleman will be their manager in 1995.

1995

President: Andy MacPhail; **Manager:** Jim Riggleman; **Ballpark:** Wrigley Field; **Attendance:** 1,918,265; **Finish:** Third (73-71); **Recap:** The Cubs stay in contention for a Wild Card spot for most of 1995, thanks to strong efforts by Sammy Sosa (36 homers), Mark Grace (.326) and Randy Myers (38 saves). But glaring weaknesses shut them down in September.

P	Player	R	HR	RBI	SB	AVE
1B	Mark Grace	97	16	92	6	.326
2B	Rey Sanchez	57	3	27	6	.278
SS	Shawon Dunston	34	9	30	0	.227
3B	Todd Zeile	34	9	30	0	.227
RF	Sammy Sosa	89	36	119	34	268
CF	Brian McRae	92	12	48	27	.288
LF	Luis Gonzalez	34	7	34	5	.290
C	Scott Servais	31	12	35	2	.286
OF	Scott Bullett	19	3	22	8	.273
IF	Jose Hernandez	37	13	40	1	.245
UT	Howard Johnson	26	7	22	1	.195
OF	Ozzie Timmons	30	8	28	3	.263
UT	Rick Wilkins	24	6	14	0	.191

T	Pitcher	W-L	SV	SO	SH	ERA
R	Jaime Navarro	14-6	0	128	1	3.28
R	Frank Castillo	11-10	0	135	2	3.21
R	Steve Trachsel	7-13	0	117	0	5.15
R	Kevin Foster	12-11	0	146	0	4.51
L	Randy Myers	1-2	38	59	0	3.88

April 5 - The Cubs acquire outfielder Brian McRae from the Royals for pitchers Derek Wallace and Geno Morones.

April 26 - The Cubs defeat the Reds 7-1 in the delayed season opener at Cincinnati in front of 51,000 booing fans.

April 28 - The Cubs beat the Expos 4-3 on Opening Day at Wrigley.

May 16 - Jaimie Navarro's 2-0 blanking of the Giants at Candlestick Park is one of four National League shutouts tossed today - the first time it's happened since 1991.

May 21 - With a 2-1 win over the Dodgers, the Cubs become the first major league club to win 9,000 games.

June 28 - The Cubs trade Rick Wilkins to the Astros for outfielder Luis Gonzalez and catcher Scott Servais. If the Cubs had more patience, this deal would be a steal.

July 12 - During a 3-2 loss in Montreal, Mark Grace shares Expos first baseman David Segui's glove because his own is not delivered to the park on time. The players leave the mitt on the field between innings.

July 28 - Frank Castillo beats the Phillies 4-0 in just two and a half hours, thanks to baseball's new speed-up-the-game rules. "It wasn't the new rule about throwing a pitch in 12 seconds," says Castillo. "since I usually throw in five seconds."

August 14 - Sammy Sosa hits the 10,000th home run in Cubs history, off knuckleballer Tom Candiotti in Dodger Stadium.

August 18 - The Cubs muscle up and pound the Rockies 26-7 at Coors Field. The contest takes six hours to play because of a 2 1/2 hour rain delay. Sammy Sosa goes 4-for-4 with four RBIs and four runs scored; Luis Gonzalez drives in six. The Cubs set several major league records: nine Cubs score two or more runs; 26 RBIs are collected (tying the NL mark), and 14 Cubs collected hits. It's the 39th time in their history the Cubs have scored 20 or more runs, a major league record.

September 25 - Frank Castillo allows just one hit - a triple by Bernard Gilkey - in a 7-0 whitewashing of the Cardinals. Castillo fans 13 in the game.

September28 - The Cubs become the first team this century to fall behind six times before coming back each time to eventually notch a 12-11 win over the Astros at Wrigley Field. During the game, a fan runs onto the field toward Randy Myers on the mound. Myers decks him with one punch.

WORTH QUOTING - "I had nothing to lose, everything to gain. I gained a lot of losses."

-Mike Morgan, on signing with the Oakland A's right out of high school

September 29 - The Cubs come back to win again, 4-3 in 10 innings vs. Houston. This time they rally for three in the ninth to tie the game. The win is the eighth straight for Chicago, who still has playoff hopes. Houston will beat them tomorrow, however, 9-8, to knock them out of the race.

October 31 - Ryne Sandberg announces that he will return for the 1996 season.

1996

President: Andy MacPhail; **Manager:** Jim Riggleman; **Ballpark:** Wrigley Field; **Attendance:** 2,219,110; **Finish:** Fourth (76-86); **Recap:** Ryne Sandberg returns after a year's absence, slugging 25 homers and driving in 92 runs, and Sammy Sosa adds 40 homers, but the Cubs finish fourth in the Central Division again. Mark Grace also has a solid year, batting .331.

The Cubs finish third in the NLin scoring (a best-ever 831 runs) and slug a club-record 212 homers.

P	Player	R	HR	RBI	SB	AVE
1B	Mark Grace	88	9	75	2	.331
2B	Ryne Sandberg	85	25	92	12	.244
SS	Rey Sanchez	28	1	12	7	.211
3B	Leo Gomez	44	17	56	1	.238
RF	Sammy Sosa	84	40	100	18	.273
CF	Brian McRae	111	17	66	37	.276
LF	Luis Gonzalez	70	15	79	9	.271
C	Scott Servais	42	11	63	0	.265

Shawon Dunston

UT	Jose Hernandez	52	10	41	4	.242
OF	Scott Bullett	26	3	16	7	.212
IF	Dave Magadan	23	3	17	0	.257
OF	Ozzie Timmons	18	7	16	1	.200
OF	Doug Glanville	10	1	10	2	.241

T	PITCHER	W-L	SV	SO	SH	ERA
R	Jaime Navarro	15-12	0	158	1	3.92
R	Frank Castillo	7-16	0	139	1	5.28
R	Steve Trachsel	13-9	0	132	2	3.03
R	Jim Bullinger	6-10	1	90	1	6.54
R	Turk Wendell	4-5	18	75	0	2.84

April 1 - The Cubs beat the Padres 5-4 in 10 innings before 38,734 on Opening Day in Chicago.

April 19 - At Wrigley, Brian McRae, Ryne Sandberg and Mark Grace hit consecutive homers in the sixth to lead the Cubs to a 10-6 win vs. San Francisco. McRae's shot is a grand slam. Losing pitcher Mike Watson says, "I hate this place. They should burn it down."

May 11 - On John Franco Day at Shea Stadium, Franco is ejected in the fifth following a bench-clearing incident between the Mets and Cubs. The brawl is launched when the Mets' Pete Harnisch punches Cubs catcher Scott Servais while the pitcher is at bat. There are nine ejections, including Harnisch and Servais; Harnisch will get an eight-game suspension and fine for the punch. The Mets win 7-6.

May 13 - Steve Trachsel allows a leadoff double to Houston's Brian Hunter, then does not allow a hit after to win 6-0.

May 16 - Sammy Sosa connects for two homers in one inning, during an eight-run seventh for Chicago at Wrigley Field. The Cubs pound the Astros 13-1.

June 5 - Sammy Sosa drives in five runs on three homers as the Cubs rally from a 4-0 deficit to beat the Phillies 9-6.

Shortstop Rey Sanchez will miss the next eight weeks after undergoing an operation on his wrist today.

June 11 - Reserve outfielder Scott Bullett, who will bat just .212 for the season, collects five hits and drives in four as the Cubs beat the Phils 9-2.

June 18 - Brant Brown, recalled three days prior to fill in for injured Mark Grace, rips three homers in a doubleheader with the Dodgers. Brown will return to the club's Triple-AIowa club 10 days later. The Cubs split the twinbill, losing the opener 9-6 and winning the nightcap 7-4.

July 26 - Tyler Houston singles, doubles, homers, and drives in six in a 17-4 triumph over Colorado. Sammy Sosa hits his 34th round-tripper; he leads the NL with 34.

August 20 - Sosa notches his 100th RBI

when he is plunked by a Mark Hutton pitch with the bases loaded during an 8-1 win over Florida. The pitch, though, breaks Sosa's wrist and he'll miss four weeks, snapping his streak of 304 consecutive games played.

August 24 - Minor league prospect Kerry Wood combines on his second no-hitter, beating Vero Beach 3-0. He pitches eight innings; he tossed seven of a no-hitter July 28 vs. Tampa.

September 10 - The Expos use a record nine pitchers in a 10-3 Cubs victory at Wrigley. The mark matches the record set by the 1949 Browns for a nine-inning game.

November 1 - Sammy Sosa joins a major league All-Star team that opens an eighth-game series in Japan with a 6-5 loss to the Japan All-Stars. Sosa is joined by Cal Ripken, Alex Rodriguez, Brady Anderson, Barry Bonds, Mike Piazza, and Gary Sheffield.

December 2 - The Cubs bring Shawon Dunston back to the Windy City, signed as a free agent.

December 13 - The Cubs sign free agent righthander Kevin Tapani to a three-year deal.

December 10 - Reliever Mel Rojas is signed to a three-year contract.

1997

President: Andy MacPhail; **Manager:** Jim Riggleman; **Ballpark:** Wrigley Field; **Attendance:** 2,190,308; **Finish:** Fifth (68-94); **Recap:** The Cubs slide to fifth place, losing 94 games despite some hitting hero-ics by Sammy Sosa (36 homers, 119 RBIs), a precursor of things to come in 1998. Ryne Sandberg, playing his final season, drives in 64 runs with 12 homers, batting .254. The Cubs' struggle to find a closer continues, with righthander Terry Adams saving 18 but going 2-9. Free agent righthander Kevin Tapani, signed after last season, spends most of the year on the disabled list.

P	Player	R	HR	RBI	SB	AVE
1B	Mark Grace	87	13	78	2	.319
2B	Ryne Sandberg	54	12	64	7	.264
SS	Shawon Dunston	57	9	41	29	.284
3B	Kevin Orie	40	8	44	2	.275
RF	Sammy Sosa	90	36	119	22	.251
CF	Brian McRae	63	6	28	14	.240
LF	Doug Glanville	79	4	35	19	.300
C	Scott Servais	36	6	45	0	.260
UT	Jose Hernandez	33	7	26	2	.273
OF	Dave Clark	19	5	32	1	.301
IF	Rey Sanchez	14	1	12	4	.249
IF	Dave Hansen	19	3	21	1	.311
UT	Tyler Houston	15	2	28	1	.260

T	Pitcher	W-L	SV	SO	SH	ERA
R	Steve Trachsel	8-12	0	160	0	4.51
R	Kevin Foster	10-7	0	118	0	4.61
L	Terry Mulholland	6-12	0	74	0	4.07
R	Jeremi Gonzalez	11-9	0	93	1	4.25
R	Terry Adams	2-9	18	64	0	4.62

April 8 - The Cubs lose to the Marlins 5-3 on Opening Day at Wrigley Field.

April 16 - The Cubs drop to 0-12 on the season with a 4-0 loss to Colorado, breaking the National League record for starts set by the 1884 Detroit Wolverines.

April 21 - The Cubs post their first win of the year, beating the Mets 6-4 behind Frank Castillo.

April 26 - Ryne Sandberg hits his 267th home run as a second baseman, breaking the record set by Joe Morgan, in the Cubs' 7-6 triumph over Pittsburgh.

April 29 - The Cubs win their fourth in five games, beating the Expos 14-8. Brooks Kieschnick hits two homers and drives in six runs.

May 10 - The Cubs take advantage of San Francisco win to roll the first triple play of the season. With two on, Giant Stan Javier flies to shallow center field and second base umpire Bob Davidson waits before calling the infield fly rule. The ball glances off center fielder Brian McRae as three Cubs dive for the ball, hitting the ground; Davidson calls an infield fly and Javier out. Pitcher Kirk Reuter, on second, tries for third but is thrown out by McRae. Darryl Hamilton tries for second but Jose Hernandez throws to Ryne Sandberg, who tags him out. The Cubs lose anyway, 4-2.

May 15 - The Cubs hit three triples in the seventh, and four in the game, defeating the visiting Padres 8-2.

May 16 - Sammy Sosa goes four-for-four with six RBIs to lead a 21-hit attack as the Cubs crush the Padres 16-7.

May 26 - Sosa and Pittsburgh's Tony Womack both hit inside-the-park home runs in the sixth inning of a 2-1 Cubs win at Three Rivers Stadium. It's the first time two inside-the-park homers have been hit in an NL game since Lou Brock and Heity Cruz of the Cardinals did it in a game vs. San Diego on June 18, 1976.

June 3 - The Cubs select high school pitcher Jon Garland in the June Amateur Draft. They'll trade him to the White Sox in July.

June 15 - The Cubs complete their first interleague series, with Milwaukee, with a 4-3 win to take the three-game set two games to one. In three games the teams draw 112,690 - just 7,638 shy of the Wrigley Field record of 120,328 for a three-game series, set in 1994 vs. the Reds.

June 16 - The Cubs beat the White Sox 8-3 in the first interleague game between the city rivals, the first official contest between the two teams since the 1906 World Series. Both teams wear replica uniforms - the Cubs wearing the 1908 outfits, the Sox wearing the 1917 gear.

June 17 - The White Sox defeat the Cubs 5-3 before 44,249 at Comiskey Park. It's the largest regular-season crowd at Comiskey this year.

June 18 - The Sox take the city series 2-1 with a 3-0 shutout of the Cubs behind Wilson Alvarez.

July 16 - Sammy Sosa's diving catch in the seventh and Scott Servais's pickoff throw to first in the eighth preserve a 6-5 win over the Mets.

August 4 - Kevin Tapani, sidelined since April after surgery on his index finger, beats the Braves 3-1 in his Cubs debut.

August 8 - The Cubs swap Brian McRae and relievers Mel Rojas and Turk Wendell to the Mets for outfielder Lance Johnson, infielder Manny Alexander and pitcher Mark Clark.

August 31 - Shawon Dunston is traded to the Pirates in exchange for a player to be named later.

September16 - Kevin Tapani allows just a single to Bret Boone in the sixth in a 5-0 shutout of Cincinnati. Sammy Sosa breaks a scoreless tie with a two-run homer in the sixth.

September 21 - Ryne Sandberg, who will retire after the season, goes 2-for-3 in his final game at Wrigley Field, leaving for a pinch-runner in the fifth.

December 9 - The Cubs sign free agent infielder Jeff Blauser to a two-year deal.

December 12 - The Cubs trade pitcher Miguel Batista to the Expos for slugging outfielder Henry Rodriguez.

December 23 - Mickey Morandini is obtained from the Phillies for outfielder Doug Glanville.

1998

President: Andy MacPhail; **Manager:** Jim Riggleman; **Ballpark:** Wrigley Field; **Attendance:** 2,623,000; **Finish:** Second - Wild Card (90-73); **Recap:** The Wrigley faithful are both saddened and euphoric in 1998 with beloved Hall of Fame broadcasters Jack Brickhouse and Harry Caray pass away but with the club pushing toward a playoff spot and Sammy Sosa battling the Cardinals' Mark McGwire in a home run duel that ends with both players breaking Roger Maris's 1961 home run record.

The ballclub is also bolstered by the additions of veteran infielders Mickey Morandini and Jeff Blauser, the slugging of third baseman Jose Hernandez and Henry Rodriguez, and the slick play of center fielder Lance Johnson. In fact, aside from Scott Servais, Mark Grace and Sosa, the entire lineup is overhauled, and it pays off. Kevin Tapani, after almost a year on the disabled list, wins 19 games and Steve Trachsel wins 15. Closer Rod Beck, obtained from San Francisco, records 51 saves in a well-balanced bullpen that also includes veteran lefties Terry Mulholland and Bob Patterson.

Chicago battles San Francisco for the Wild Card playoff spot for most of August and September before finally clinching on September 28.

Righthander Kerry Wood, who possesses a 98 mph fastball and sharp breaking ball, earns Rookie of the Year honors with 13 victories and 233 strikeouts in 167 innings pitched.

P	Player	R	HR	RBI	SB	AVE
1B	Mark Grace	92	17	89	4	.309
2B	Mickey Morandini	93	8	53	13	.296
SS	Jeff Blauser	49	4	26	2	.219
3B	Jose Hernandez	76	23	75	4	.254
RF	Sammy Sosa	134	66	158	18	.308
CF	Lance Johnson	51	2	21	10	.280
LF	Henry Rodriguez	56	31	85	1	.251
C	Scott Servais	35	7	36	1	.222
UT	Brant Brown	56	14	48	4	.291
UT	Manny Alexander	34	5	25	4	.227
UT	Tyler Houston	26	9	33	2	.255
OF	Matt Mieske	16	1	12	0	.299
IF	Kevin Orie	24	2	21	1	.181

T	Pitcher	W-L	SV	SO	SH	ERA
R	Kevin Tapani	19-9	0	136	2	4.85
R	Steve Trachsel	15-8	0	149	0	4.46
R	Mark Clark	9-14	0	161	1	4.84
R	Kerry Wood	13-6	0	233	1	3.40
R	Rod Beck	3-4	51	81	0	3.02

January 15 - The Cubs sign free agent closer Rod Beck to a one-year contract.

February 18 - Beloved broadcaster Harry Caray, 84, dies after collapsing four days earlier at a Valentine's Day dinner. The Cubs will wear a patch with a caricature of Caray's face on their uniforms this season. A video rendition of his "Take Me Out to the Ballgame" will be broadcast on scoreboards around baseball for years.

March 3 - Retired Cubs broadcaster Jack Brickhouse undergoes surgery to remove a tumor in his brain.

April 3 - The Cubs defeat the Expos 6-2 behind Steve Trachsel on Opening Day in

Sammy Sosa

Chicago.

April 10 - Henry Rodriguez collects five hits and drives in three to lead the Cubs to a 13-0 win over the Expos. Kevin Tapani tosses a three-hitter.

April 15 - Sammy Sosa's 210th career home run breaks Bob Horner's major league record for most home runs without a grand slam. The Cubs lose 2-1 to the Mets.

May 6 - Rookie righthander Kerry Wood pitches perhaps the most dominant game in history, fanning 20 Astros and tossing a one-hit, 2-0 shutout at Wrigley Field. The 20 strikeouts ties the record set by Roger Clemens, who performed the feat twice. Wood, against his nature, doesn't walk a batter and allows just an infield single to Ricky Gutierrez in the third. Wood becomes just the second pitcher in history whose strikeout total matches his age (Bob Feller fanned 17 when he was 17 in 1936).

May 11 - Wood strikes out 13 Diamondbacks in a 4-2 victory, setting a major league record with 33 strikeouts over two games.

May 12 - Mark Grace becomes the first player to hit a home run into the swimming pool during a 7-6 win at Arizona's Bank One Ballpark.

June 2 - The Cubs select high school outfielder Corey Patterson with the third pick in the June Amateur Draft.

June 15 - Sammy Sosa hits three home runs, giving him 15 in his last 16 games, to lead the Cubs to a 6-5 win over the Brewers.

June 18 - Brant Brown ropes three homers in a 12-5 win vs. Philadelphia. He also singles and drives in five runs.

June 20 - Sammy Sosa hits his 21st homer in 30 days, a major league record, in a 9-4 triumph over the Phillies.

June 25 - Sosa snaps the major league record for home runs in a calendar month with his 19th in June during a 6-4 loss to the Tigers.
June 30 - Sosa' 20th of the month is his 34th of the year, but the Cubs lose 5-4 to Arizona. Sammy goes 34-for-114 (.298) in Junne with 20 homers, 40 RBIs, 25 runs, and slugs an astonishing .860. Not surprisingly, he is voted NLPlayer of the Month.

July 27 - Sosa finally hits his first career grand slam, on his 248th career homer, in a 6-2 victory over the D'Backs. The four RBIs gives him 100 for the year.

July 28 - Sosa hits his second grand slam in four at-bats but the Cubs lose 7-5 to Arizona. He's the first Cub to hit grand slams in consecutive games and the 18th major leaguer to do it.

July 31 - The Cubs trade Kevin Orie and pitchers Todd Noel and Justin Speier to the Marlins for relievers Felix Heredia and Steve Hoff.

August 6 - Jack Brickhouse dies at the age of 82 after complications from brain surgery. Brickhouse was the play-by-play announcer from 1941-81, before Harry Caray joined the team.

August 26 - Sammy Sosa bangs homer No. 52 to lead the Cubs to a 9-2 win over Cincinnati.

August 28 - Sosa sends homer No. 53 over the wall in a 10-5 win vs. Colorado.

August 30 - Sosa's 54th gives the Cubs a 4-3 win over the Rockies.

August 31 - Sammy's 55th ties the Cardinals' Mark McGwire in the race for Roger Maris's single season home run record. Sosa ties Ernie Banks for second place on the Cubs' all-time list with 30 homers at Wrigley, three short of the record held by Hack Wilson.

September 2 - Sosa hits his 56th as the Cubs defeat the Reds, 4-2 but falls behind in the race as Mark McGwire hits homer No. 59 against the Marlins.

September 4 - Sosa's 57th breaks the Cub record set by Hack Wilson 68 years ago. The Cubs beat Pittsburgh 5-2.

September5 - Sammy hits his 58th to help the Cubs beat the Pirates 8-4 and maintain their lead in the National League's Wild

WORTH NOTING- The Cubs' NLDS opponents in 1998 are the Atlanta Braves, managed by **Bobby Cox**. The Braves finish with a 106-56 (.654) record, leading the National League in complete games (24), strikeouts (1,232), shutouts (23) and ERA(3.25).

P	PLAYER	R	HR	RBI	SB	BA
1B	Andres Galarraga	103	44	121	7	.305
2B	Keith Lockhart	50	9	37	2	.257
SS	Walt Weiss	64	0	27	7	.280
3B	Chipper Jones	123	34	107	16	.313
RF	Michael Tucker	54	13	46	8	.244
CF	Andruw Jones	89	31	90	27	.271
LF	Ryan Klesko	69	18	7	5	.274
C	Javy Lopez	73	34	106	5	.284

T	PITCHER	W	L	SV	SH	ERA
L	Tom Glavine	20	6	0	3	2.47
R	Greg Maddux	18	9	0	5	2.22
R	John Smoltz	17	3	0	2	2.90
R	Kevin Millwood	17	8	0	1	4.08
R	Kerry Ligtenberg	3	2	30	0	2.71

Card race.

September 8 - Steve Trachsel serves up Mark McGwire's record-setting 62nd home run of the season, in the fourth inning of a 6-3 Cardinals victory at Busch Stadium. Sosa, in right field when Big Mac rips the line drive over the left field wall, joins the celebration at home plate.

September 12 - Sosa becomes the fourth player in MLhistory to reach the 60-homer mark when he hits No. 60 off Valerio De Los Santos of Milwaukee during a 15-12 Cubs victory.

September 13 - Sammy hits homers No. 61 and 62 in an 11-10 win vs. Milwaukee, tying the NL record with 10 multi-home run games in a single season, set by Pittsburgh's Ralph Kiner in 1-47. Sosa is now tied with McGwire for the league lead.

September 16 - Sosa hits a grand slam in the eighth to power the Cubs to a 6-3 win over San Diego. It's his 63rd of the year.

September 23 - It's a good day and a bad day for the Cubs as Sosa hits his 64th and 65th of the year but the Brewers battle back from a 7-0 deficit, aided in part by a dropped fly ball by left fielder Brant Brown, to win the game 8-7. The Cubs remain tied for the Wild Card spot with the Mets. Sosa tops the 400 mark in total bases with three today.

September25 - Sosa crushes his 66th, and final, homer of the year in the fourth inning of a 6-2 loss to Houston. Sosa's homer puts him in the lead over Mark McGwire in the home run chase, but Big Mac ties it again with a shot in the fifth inning of the Cardinals'game in St. Louis.

September28 - The Cubs hold off a three-run rally by San Francisco in the ninth to win a one-game playoff for the National League's Wild Card spot in the playoffs. Rod Beck gets the white-knuckle save.

September 30 - NLDS Game 1
John Smoltz handcuffs the Cubs on five hits and one run, that on a solo homer by Tyler Houston in the eighth. The Braves take the lead on Michael Tucker's home run in the second. A grand slam by Ryan Klesko in the seventh puts the game out of reach as the Braves win 7-1.

October 1 - NLDS Game 2
The Cubs take a 1-0 lead into the ninth but manager Jim Riggleman allows tiring starter Kevin Tapani to start the ninth despite having a rested Rod Beck waiting in the bullpen. Catcher Javy Lopez homers to left to tie the game with one out. In the 10th, Terry Mulholland relieves but misses the first base bag on a bunt play to put runners on first and second and Chipper Jones singles home the winning run.

October 3 - NLDS Game 3
Greg Maddux returns to Wrigley Field and pitches the Braves past the Cubs 6-2. Maddux scores the first run himself when he stretches a single into a double and, after moving to third on a groundout, scores on a passed ball. In the top of the eighth, Gerald Williams singles in Atlanta's second run, and Eddie Perez rips a grand slam off of Rod Beck to put the game away.

November 6 - Kerry Wood wins the National League's Rookie of the Year Award.

November 8 - Sammy Sosa edges Mark McGwire in National League MVPvoting.

December 1 - The Cubs sign free agent

pitcher Scott Sanders.

December 7 - Free agent third baseman Gary Gaetti is signed. The Cubs also sign outfielder Glenallen Hill.

December8 - Continuing their tradition of signing marginal free agent veterans, the Cubs sign catcher Benito Santiago. Santiago played just 15 games for the Blue Jays this season.

December 14 - The Cubs trade Brant Brown to the Pirates for pitcher Jon Lieber.

1999

President: Andy MacPhail; **Manager:** Jim Riggleman; **Ballpark:** Wrigley Field; **Attendance:** 2,813,854; **Finish:** Sixth (67-95); **Recap:** Jim Riggleman remains at the Cubs' helm throughout the season, but the team finishes sixth in the six-team division, losing 95 games. Sammy Sosa becomes one of only two players (with Mark McGwire) to post back-to-back 60-homer seasons by hitting 63. Sosa also drives in 141 runs and scores 114. Mark Grace hits a steady .309 and scores 107 runs. But the Cubs' pitching is catastrophic, with Steve Trachsel losing a league-leading 18 games and just one starter, Dan Serafini (3-2), posting a winning record.

Riggleman is fired in October, replaced by Atlanta hitting coach Don Baylor.

P	Player	R	HR	RBI	SB	AVE
1B	Mark Grace	107	16	91	3	.309
2B	Mickey Morandini	60	4	34	6	.241
SS	Jose Hernandez	57	15	43	7	.272
3B	Gary Gaetti	22	9	46	0	.204
RF	Sammy Sosa	114	63	141	7	.288
CF	Lance Johnson	46	1	21	13	.260
LF	Henry Rodriguez	72	26	87	2	.304
C	Benito Santiago	28	7	36	1	.249
UT	Jeff Blauser	41	9	26	2	.240
UT	Tyler Houston	26	9	27	1	.233
OF	Glenallen Hill	43	20	55	5	.300

T	Pitcher	W-L	SV	SO	SH	ERA
R	Steve Trachsel	8-18	0	149	0	5.56
R	Jon Lieber	10-11	0	186	1	4.07
R	Kevin Tapani	6-12	0	73	0	4.83
R	Kyle Farnsworth	5-9	0	70	1	5.05
R	Terry Adams	6-3	13	57	0	4.02

March 16 - Kerry Wood tears a ligament in his right elbow. He'll require surgery that will sideline him the entire season.

March 31 - The Cubs purchase pitcher Dan Serafini from the Twins.

April 11 - Glenallen Hill collects five hits, including a double and a home run, but the Cubs lose to the Pirates 9-6.

April 12 - The Reds better the Cubs 7-2 in front of 39,092 on Opening Day at Wrigley Field.

April 24 - Terry Mulholland hurls 6 2/3 inning of scoreless relief as the Cubs beat the Mets 2-0.

May 4 - Mark Grace hits a grand slam in the third inning of a 12-11 loss to Colorado. It's his first bases-loaded homer in 6,136 at-bats.

May 5 - The Rockies become the first team in 35 years, and third this century, to score in all nine innings as they defeat the Cubs 13-6.

May 18 - A three-run homer by Mark Grace in the 11th un-ties a 1-1 deadlock and gives the Cubs a 4-1 victory over the Marlins in Miami.

June 15 - Brewers pitcher Jim Abbott, born without a right hand, gets his first major league hit during a 7-4 Cubs win in Milwaukee.

June 22 - The Cubs overcome an eight-run

deficit to beat Colorado, 13-12.

June 28 - Sixty-nine years later, the commissioner's office awards another RBI to Hack Wilson's record total of 190, set in 1930. The missing RBI came from the nightcap of a doubleheader between the Cubs and the Reds on July 28, 1930 when Charlie Grimm was erroneously credited with an RBI that should have been awarded to Wilson. "There is no doubt that Hack Wilson's RBI total should be 191," says commissioner Bud Selig. "I am sensitive to the historical significance that accompanies the correction of such a prestigious record, especially after so many years have passed, but it is important to get it right." The commissioner's office also awards Babe Ruth six additional walks, raising his record career total to 2,062.

June 30 - With President Bill Clinton in attendance, Sammy Sosa whacks his 30th homer in a 5-4 triumph over Milwaukee at Wrigley. Of Sosa's last 13 hits, nine are home runs.

July 1 - The Brewers outslug the Cubs 19-12. Steve Trachsel allows 10 runs in 3 2/3 innings for his league-leading 11th loss.

July 3 - Third baseman Gary Gaetti takes the mound in the ninth for Chicago during a 21-8 loss to the Phillies.

August 26 - Kevin Tapani, 0-9 in his last 10 starts, is put on the disabled list for the remainder of the season. The Cubs beat the Giants 11-10 today; Sammy Sosa swats his 53rd home run.

August 31 - The Cubs trade Rod Beck to the Red Sox for lefty Mark Guthrie.

September1 - The Padres hold the Cubs to just two hits, but two hits are enough for Steve Trachsel in a 1-0 win. Sammy Sosa's 56th homer is the difference.

September 7 - The Cubs split a pair with the Reds, winning the first one 2-1 and losing the second 10-3. When Chicago puts Brian McNichol on the mound in game two, he becomes the 25th pitcher the Cubs have used this season.

September 9 - With his 59th home run, Sammy Sosa now has more homers than the Cubs have wins (56).

September 18 - Sosa becomes the first major leaguer to hit 60 homers in two seasons during a 7-4 loss to the Brewers. The Cardinals' Mark McGwire will slug his 60th on September 26th, joining Sosa in the double-60 club.

October 4 - Jim Riggleman is fired as Cubs manager.

October 7 - Major League Baseball announces that the Cubs and Mets will hook up in the first regular-season game outside North American when they open the 2000 season in Tokyo, Japan on March 29.

October 8 - It is discovered that Kerry Wood has atria septal defect, a small hole in his heart. The condition will be treated, but doctors say his baseball career is not in jeopardy.

November 1 - The Cubs sign Don Baylor as their new manager.

December 10 - Catcher Joe Girardi is signed to a three-year contract.

December 11 - The Cubs trade infielder Manny Alexander to the Red Sox for outfielder Damon Buford.

December 11 - The Cubs acquire second baseman Eric Young and pitcher Ismael Valdes from the Dodgers for pitchers Terry Adams and Chad Ricketts.

December 20 - Shortstop Ricky Gutierrez is signed to a two-year contract.

2000

President: Andy MacPhail; **Manager:** Don Baylor; **Ballpark:** Wrigley Field; **Attendance:** 2,789,511; **Finish:** Sixth (65-97); **Recap:** Don Baylor's first season as Cubs manager is less than eventful, with Sammy Sosa providing most, if not all, of the fireworks with another 50-homer season to lead the league. Kerry Wood develops a sore arm mid-season and Jon Lieber paces another shoddy pitching staff with a 12-11 mark. Reliever Rick Aguilera, acquired last season from Minnesota, somehow posts 29 saves.

Mark Grace, in a season-long tussle with the front office over a new contract, signs with the Arizona Diamondbacks over the winter.

P	Player	R	HR	RBI	SB	AVE
1B	Mark Grace	75	11	82	1	.280
2B	Eric Young	98	6	47	54	.297
SS	Ricky Gutierrez	73	11	56	8	.276
3B	Willie Greene	34	10	37	4	.289
RF	Sammy Sosa	106	50	138	7	.320
CF	Damon Buford	64	15	48	4	.251
LF	Henry Rodriguez	37	18	51	1	.251
C	Joe Girardi	47	6	40	1	.278
C	Jeff Reed	26	4	25	0	.214
IF	Jose Nieves	17	5	24	1	.212
IF	Shane Andrews	25	14	39	1	.229
OF	Glenallen Hill	23	11	29	0	.262
T	**Pitcher**	**W-L**	**SV**	**SO**	**SH**	**ERA**
R	Jon Lieber	12-11	0	192	1	4.41
R	Kevin Tapani	8-12	0	150	0	5.01
R	Kerry Wood	8-7	0	132	0	4.80
L	Scott Downs	4-3	0	63	0	5.17
R	Rick Aguilera	1-2	29	38	0	4.91

WORTH NOTING - Don Baylor holds the major league career record for getting hit by a pitch - 267 times.

March 29 - The Cubs and Mets square off in the first big league game played outside North America, in the Tokyo Dome in Tokyo, Japan. The Cubs win 5-3. Shane Andrews hits the first home run of the new millennium; Mark Grace adds another.

March 30 - The Mets beat the Cubs 5-1 in the second game of the two-game series in Tokyo.

April 10 - The Cubs beat the Braves 4-3 on Opening Day in Chicago. Mark Guthrie earns the victory in relief.

April 27 - Four Cubs homer in the top of the first at Houston's new Enron Field in a 12-3 victory over the Astros.

May 2 - Kerry Wood hurls six shutout innings in his first start since 1999, as the Cubs defeat the Astros 11-1 at Wrigley.

May 11 - The Cubs and Brewers play the longest nine-inning game in history, a four hour, 22-minute 14-8 Milwaukee victory. Glenallen Hill slugs a 490-foot homer that lands on the roof of a house on Waveland Avenue.

May 12 - The Cubs re-acquire outfielder Dave Martinez, from the Devil Rays for pitcher Mark Guthrie.

May 14 - Henry Rodriguez blasts two homers and drives in seven and Sammy Sosa gets five hits and five RBIs but the Cubs lose to Montreal, 16-15. Eric Young steals five bases in the game.

May 16 - A brawl between several

Dodgers on the bullpen bench and unruly Wrigley Field fans is instigated in the ninth inning of a 6-5 Cubs loss when a fan steals Chad Kreuter's hat and hits him on back of the head. Several L.A. players go into the stands after the fans before police break up the fight. Sixteen Dodgers and three coaches will be suspended for going into the stands, the most suspensions ever handed out for one incident.

June 2 - Rick Aguilera earns his 300th career save in a 2-0 Cubs win over Detroit.

June 5 - The Cubs select Miami high school shortstop Luis Montanez in the third overall pick of the June Amateur Draft.

June 9 - The Cubs acquire pitcher Chuck Smith in a three-way trade involving the Rangers and Marlins. Chicago sends Dave Martinez to Texas.

July 10 - Sammy Sosa defeats defending champ Ken Griffey Jr. in the All-Star Game Home Run Derby contest finals.

July 19 - Cubs GM Ed Lynch resigns. Team president Andy MacPhail will take over.

July 26 - The Cubs send moody pitcher Ismael Valdes back to the Dodgers for a pair of minor leaguers, Jamie Arnold and Jorge Piedra.

July 31 - Outfielder Rondell White is obtained from the Expos for pitcher Scott Downs. The Cubs then send Henry Rodriguez to the Marlins for outfielder Russ Gload and pitcher Dave Noyce.

August 6 - Mark Grace goes five-for-five in front of friends and family in home-town San Diego, but the Padres beat the Cubs 8-6.

August 8 - Rookie Phil Norton, making his major league debut, becomes the first pitcher in Cubs history to surrender four homers in an inning, in the fourth inning of a 7-5 Dodgers triumph.

September 12 - Kerry Wood hurls just his second career complete game, beating the Reds 2-1.

September 16 - Sammy Sosa becomes the second player to hit 50 or more homers in three consecutive years, joining Mark McGwire, in a 7-6 loss to the Cardinals.

September 23 - Mark Grace tallies his 1,000th career RBI in a 6-5 loss to St. Louis at Wrigley.

September 24 - Outfielder Corey Patterson, called up just six days before, becomes the first Cub since Ryne Sandberg in 1991 to hit an inside-the-park homer during a 15-5 triumph over the Cardinals.

October 1 - The Cubs beat the Pirates 10-9 in the final game to be played at Three Rivers Stadium in Pittsburgh. The Bucs load the bases with none out in the ninth but can't push the tying run across. Mark Grace, who makes the final putout, is hugged by his teammates - it's his last game in a Cubs uniform.

November 16 - The Cubs sign free agent pitcher Julian Tavarez to a two-year deal.

November 19 - Chicago sends reliever Tim Worrell to the Giants for third baseman Bill Mueller.

December8 - Free agent lefty Jeff Fassero is signed to a two-year contract.

Wrigley Field

2001

President: Andy MacPhail; **Manager:** Don Baylor; **Ballpark:** Wrigley Field; **Attendance:** 2,780,465; **Finish:** Third (88-74); **Recap:** The Cubs right themselves in 2001 and are seemingly on the road to recovery, finishing third with an 88-74 record, their best since 1989. With Sammy Sosa hitting 60+ homers for a record third year, driving in a career-best (and league-leading) 160 runs and scoring 146 and Jon Lieber posting 20 wins, Wrigley Fans are treated to a winning season for the first time in a long time.

First baseman Fred McGriff joins the team mid-season and provides 12 homers over the final two months and Tom Gordon stays off the disabled list long enough to record 27 saves for Chicago. Kerry Wood rebounds from arm troubles to post 12 wins and 217 strikeouts.

The Cubs do not have a pitcher throw a complete game against them all season, a major league record, and Cubs pitchers strike out 1,344 batters, another MLmark.

P	Player	R	HR	RBI	SB	AVE
1B	Fred McGriff	27	12	41	0	.282
2B	Eric Young	98	6	42	31	.279
SS	Ricky Gutierrez	76	10	66	4	.290
3B	Bill Mueller	38	6	23	1	.295
RF	Sammy Sosa	146	64	160	0	.328
CF	Gary Matthews Jr.	41	9	30	5	.217
LF	Rondell White	43	17	50	1	.307
C	Todd Hundley	23	12	31	0	.187
UT	Ron Coomer	25	8	53	0	.261
UT	Matt Stairs	48	17	61	2	.250
C	Joe Girardi	22	3	25	0	.253
UT	Michael Tucker	31	5	31	4	.263

T	Pitcher	W-L	SV	SO	SH	ERA
R	Jon Lieber	20-6	0	148	1	3.80
R	Jason Bere	11-11	0	175	0	4.31
R	Kevin Tapani	9-14	0	149	0	4.49
R	Kerry Wood	12-6	0	217	1	3.36
R	Tom Gordon	1-2	27	67	0	3.38

April 2 - The Expos defeat the Cubs 5-4 on

Opening Day in Chicago.

April 5 - Kevin Tapani hurls a two-hitter as the Cubs beat Montreal 2-1.

April 6 - Reliever Todd Van Poppel fans all five batters he faces to help preserve a 3-2 win at Philadelphia.

April 18 - Jeff Fassero earns both saves in a doubleheader vs. Philadelphia, becoming the first Cub since Bruce Sutter in 1979 to do so.

April 21 - Todd Hundley's second homer of the game leading off the ninth inning gives the Cubs a 4-3 win over the Pirates in Pittsburgh.

April 27 - Kerry Wood fans 14 in a 7-3 victory over San Francisco.

May 5 - The Cubs celebrate Cinco de Mayo with a 20-1 pummeling of the Los Angeles Dodgers, scoring 16 runs in the seventh and eighth innings.

May 6 - Tom "Flash" Gordon earns his first victory in 2 1/2 years, pitching an inning of perfect relief in a 3-2 win over the Dodgers.

May 16 - Sammy Sosa hits the 400th home run of his career, during a 6-2 loss to the Astros at Wrigley.

May 18 - Mark Grace, now a member of the Arizona Diamondbacks, returns to Wrigley and contributes to a win with a two-run single in the sixth. He's given a standing ovation each time he approaches the plate.

May 24 - Jon Lieber hurls a one-hit, 3-0 victory over the Reds, needing just 78 pitches to do it. Lieber allows just two baserunners, but gets two double plays to face the minimum 27 batters.

May 25 - Kerry Wood follows with a one-hitter of his own, stopping the Brewers. It's just the eighth time in major league history that teammates throw back-to-back one-hitters.

June 3 - A 12-game Cubs winning streak is snapped by the Brewers, 6-5 in 10 innings.

June 5 - Pinch-hitter Julio Zuleta hits a pinch-grand slam and Matt Stairs and Rondell White hit back-to-back homers in a 12-6 victory vs. St. Louis.

June 20 - The Cubs win their first game in 13 tries at Busch Stadium, as Sammy Sosa hits two homers in a 9-4 victory.

July 3 - Kerry Wood combines with two relievers on a five-hitter as the Cubs post their first win at Shea Stadium in more than three years, 3-0 over the Mets.

July 5 - Pitcher Jason Bere collects two singles in the third inning of a 13-4 rout of the Mets.

July 7 - The Cubs move into first place with a 10-6 victory over the Detroit Tigers.

July 21 - Sammy Sosa homered twice to become the eighth player with at least 50 multihomer games in a 5-4 victory over the Astros.

July 27 - The Cubs obtain veteran first baseman Fred McGriff from Tampa Bay for pitcher Manny Aybar.

July 30 - The Cubs acquire reliever David Weathers from Milwaukee for three minor leaguers.

August 30 - Fred McGriff hits a three-run homer in the seventh and Bill Mueller adds a solo shot in the ninth as the Cubs rally from a 4-1 defecit to defeat the Marlins 5-4.

September18 - Due to the terrorist attacks on September 11, Jon Lieber becomes the first Cub since Scott Sanderson in 1986 to start consecutive games.

September 19 - Kerry Wood allows just two hits over seven innings and Rondell White and Michael Tucker drive in four runs apiece as the Cubs batter the Reds 10-0.

September 27 - After mashing his 59th homer of the season, SammySosa grabs a small American flag given to him by first base coach Billy Williams and holds it high as he rounds the bases during a 6-5 Cubs loss to Houston. He waves it again after crossing the plate and once more during a curtain call, showing support for his adopted country during the national terrorist crisis.

September 29 - Fred McGriff, Rondell White and Todd Hundley homer on successive pitches from Houston's Dave Mlicki in the first inning of a 6-2 Cubs win at Wrigley Field. It' the eighth time in club history that players have hit thee consecutive home runs.

October2 - Sammy Sosa becomes the first player in ML history with three 60-homer seasons as he hits one off Cincinnati lefty Lance Davis in a 5-4 Cubs loss.

October 3 - Jon Lieber becomes the first Cub to win 20 games in nine years when he pitches six innings of a 13-7 victory vs. the Reds. Sammy Sosa hits his 61st homer.

October 6 - Julian Tavarez takes a no-hitter into the eighth inning before Pittsburgh's Mendy Lopez gets a one-out single in a 13-2 Cubs win at Wrigley. Sammy Sosa hits his 63rd homer.

October7 - Sosa hits his 64th in a 4-3 loss to the Pirates in the season-ender. He finishes with a .328 average, the highest for a Cubs right-handed hitter since Bill Madlock hit .339 in 1976. His 1,621 total bases over a four-year period breaks by five Chuck Klein's 69-year-old MLrecord.

November 2 - The Cubs obtain infielder Mark Bellhorn from the Athletics for minor league infielder Adam Morrissey.

December 11 - The Cubs trade reliever Felix Heredia to the Blue Jays in exchange for shortstop Alex Gonzalez.

December 20 - Free agent outfielder Moises Alou is signed to a three contract.

2002

President: Andy MacPhail; **Manager:** Don Baylor / Bruce Kimm; **Ballpark:** Wrigley Field; **Attendance:** 2,693,096; **Finish:** Fifth (67-95); **Recap:** Don Baylor doesn't survive the season, a drop to fifth despite the lofty production of Fred McGriff (30 homers, 103 RBIs) and Sammy Sosa (49 homers, 108 RBIs) and the addition of pricey free agent Moises Alou. The pitching is surprisingly effective in a 95-loss season, with four starters posting ERAs under 4.00, but the hitting's deplorable, with only McGriff (.273), Sosa (.288) and Alou (.275) finishing above .270. But the bullpen is a disaster, anchored by Antonio Alfonseca, who records just 19 saves.

The Cubs lead the majors in strikeouts both as a pitching staff (1,333) and at the plate (1,269), the first time a team has led the majors in both categories in the same season since 1884 when the Union Association's Boston club did it.

P	PLAYER	R	HR	RBI	SB	AVE
1B	Fred McGriff	67	30	103	1	.273
2B	Mark Bellhorn	86	4	27	7	.258
SS	Alex Gonzalez	58	18	61	5	.248
3B	Bill Mueller	51	7	37	0	.266
RF	Sammy Sosa	122	49	108	2	.288
CF	Corey Patterson	71	14	54	18	.253
LF	Moises Alou	50	15	61	8	.275
C	Todd Hundley	32	16	35	0	.211
C	Joe Girardi	19	1	13	1	.226
OF	Roosevelt Brown	14	3	23	2	.211
IF	Chris Stynes	25	5	26	1	.241
OF	Bobby Hill	26	4	20	6	.253
UT	Delino DeShields	20	3	10	10	.192

T	PITCHER	W-L	SV	SO	SH	ERA
R	Kerry Wood	12-11	0	217	1	3.66
R	Matt Clement	12-11	0	215	2	3.60
R	Jon Lieber	6-8	0	87	0	3.70
R	Mark Prior	6-6	0	147	0	3.32
R	Antonio Alfonseca	2-5	19	61	0	4.00

April 1 - The Reds beat the Cubs 5-4 in Cinergy Field's last season opener. The club will be playing in a nearby ballpark starting in 2003.

April 5 - In a 2-1 Opening Day loss at Wrigley, Sammy Sosa hits a low line drive to the opposite field that hits off the top of the fence and bounces back. Umpires initially rule that the ball did not clear the fence and Sosa's hit is only a single, but after a discussion with manager Don Baylor, crew chief Larry Young reverses the ruling and gives Sosa a home run.

Cubs legend Ron Santo throws out the first pitch, walking to the mound with the aid of a cane do to a prosthetic leg. He lost the leg in December, 2001 due to diabetes. His old teammate, Randy Hundley, is the catcher.

April 12 - Sammy Sosa hits a 484-foot homer, the longest ever hit at PNC Park in Pittsburgh, in a 7-3 Cubs win over the Pirates.

April 19 - Pitcher Matt Clement, who was acquired by Chicago on the last day of spring training, fans 12 in a 5-2 win over Cincinnati.

April 25 - The Cubs win their 15th consecutive Wrigley Field game started by Jon Lieber, beating the Giants 2-1. Lieber is 14-0 in his last 15 home starts.

May 2 - Sammy Sosa homers in two consecutive at-bats, giving him four in two games, as the Cubs beat the Padres 6-1 and end a five-game losing streak.

May 6 - Third baseman Bill Mueller, playing his first game of the season after undergoing knee surgery March 11, hits a game-tying homer in the ninth in a 6-5 victory over the Cardinals at Wrigley.

May 22 - Celebrated rookie pitcher Mark Prior allows two runs on four hits over six innings in his major league debut, a 7-4 win vs. Pittsburgh.

May 28 - Matt Clement takes a no-hitter into the seventh before Pittsburgh outfielder Brian Giles singles, settling for a two-hitter in his first complete game, 3-0.

June 7 - Sammy Sosa hits his 21st home run and Mark Prior allows four hits over seven innings as the Cubs win their first-ever game vs. the Seattle Mariners, in an interleague game at Safeco Field.

June 14 - Sosa hits his 25th homer of the season, and 475th of his career, in an 8-4 interleague win over the crosstown White Sox. Sosa's homer ties him with Stan Musial and Willie Stargell for 19th on the all-time list.

June 18 - Alex Gonzalez homers off reliever John Rocker in the bottom of the ninth to give the Cubs a 4-3 victory over the Texas Rangers. The contest is the first in history to feature four 400-homer players: Sammy Sosa (475), Rafael Palmeiro (460), Fred McGriff (459), and Juan Gonzalez (401).

June 19 - Jeff Fassero uncorks a bases-loaded wild pitch that lets the go-ahead run score in the 10th inning of a 7-4 Cubs loss to Texas.

June 21 - It takes only an hour and 49 minutes for a 2-1 Cubs victory over the Cardinals. Fred McGriff supplies the offense with two homers; John Lieber supplies the defense with a three-hitter.

June 22 - Today's game with St. Louis is cancelled due to the death of Cardinals pitcher Darryl Kile, who had a heart attack in his hotel room sometime overnight.

June 23 - The Cubs beat the still-stunned Cards 8-3 at Wrigley; Kile's No. 57 is on display all around Wrigley Field, including on the players' jerseys, the umpires' hats, and on the message board in center field.

July 5 - The Cubs fire manager Don Baylor, replacing him in the interim with coach Bruce Kimm.

July 12 - The Cubs start off the second half of the season with a 5-4 win when Marlins center fielder Preston Wilson runs into the Wrigley Field wall and drops pinch-hitter Angel Echevarria's fly ball in the 16th inning.

July 22 - Sammy Sosa hits a game-tying single off Phillies closer Jose Mesa and Fred McGriff follows with a game-winning double in the ninth as the Cubs beat the Phillies 7-6.

August 2 - Moises Alou hits a two-run, game-winning home run in the 12th and Kerry Wood fans 13 in a 6-4 win vs. Colorado.

August 4 - Mark Prior strikes out 13 and pitches his first career complete game, beating the Rockies 4-1.

August 10 - Sammy Sosa puts together perhaps his greatest offensive game, swatting three homers and driving in nine runs to lead the Cubs to a 15-1 win vs. Colorado. The nine ribbies ties the club mark set by Heinie Zimmerman in 1911. Sosa misses a chance for a record-tying four home runs when he unselfishly takes himself out of the game in the sixth to allow at-bats for other players.

August 11 - Sosa sets a National League record for RBIs in consecutive games (14) as he drives in five, four on a grand slam, in a 12-9 Chicago win over the Rockies.

August 15 - Mark Prior fans 12, including a club-record-tying seven in a row, in a 6-4 win vs. Houston.

August 24 - Matt Clement hurls a three-hit shutout over the Diamondbacks in Phoenix.

August 27 - Alan Benes tosses 5 1/3 shutout innings in his first major league start since September, 2001 to help the Cubs beat the Brewers 6-2.

August 29 - Mark Bellhorn becomes the first player in National League history to homer from both sides of the plate in the same inning in a 13-10 victory over the Brewers in Milwaukee.

September 2 - Kerry Wood ties a major

league record with four strikeouts in the fourth inning and hits a two-run homer in a 17-4 rout of the Brewers. A wild pitch allows the third batter in the inning, Paul Bako, to reach base after he strikes out. Wood then fans pitcher Andrew Lorraine for the fourth K of the frame.

September 13 - Fred McGriff hits a two-run homer for his 1500th career RBI in a 7-6 win vs. Cincinnati. He's the 40th player to reach the milestone.

September 15 - Sammy Sosa rips a three-run homer in the eighth inning of a 6-0 Cubs win over Cincinnati to surpass the 100-RBI plateau for the eighth straight year. He joins Hall of Famers Mel Ott and Willie Mays as the only NL players to record eight consecutive 100-RBI seasons.

September 29 - Sosa hits his 49th homer of the year, and 499th of his career, stopping one short of 500 in the Cubs' last game of the season, a 7-3 victory vs. Pittsburgh.

November 14 - The Cubs acquire catcher Damian Miller from the Diamondbacks for minor leaguers David Noyce and Gary Johnson.

December 3 - Free agent lefty Mike Remlinger is signed to a three-year deal.

December4 - The Cubs trade catcher Todd Hundley and outfielder Chad Hermansen to the Dodgers for first baseman Eric Karros, second baseman Mark Grudzielanek, and cash.

2003

President: Andy MacPhail; **Manager:** Dusty Baker; **Ballpark:** Wrigley Field; **Attendance:** 2,962,630; **Finish:** First (88-74); **Recap:** In the end, it's probably the tiring of pitchers Mark Prior and Kerry Wood that ultimately cost the Cubs their first World Series berth in 58 seasons, not the interference of a fan or the fumbling of a ground ball. Whatever the reason, the Cubs once again find themselves at the doorstep of the October Classic, only to fall short.

The greatest addition to the Cubs' roster during a very busy offseason is the signing of Dusty Baker as the team's new skipper. Baker, who led the Giants to a National League pennant in 2002, works his magic again and leads an almost completely overhauled squad to an division championship, the Cubs' first since 1989.

The ballclub starts slow, as usual, with a patchwork infield and an inexperienced mound staff. After an injury to outfielder Corey Patterson, who appears to be coming into his own, and the slumping of first baseman Hee Seop Choi, it looks like another long season at Wrigley.

Luckily, though, neither the Houston Astros nor St. Louis Cardinals seem to want the division crown either, enabling the Cubs to hang close through July and August. By then, the club has improved itself demonstrably due to the acquisition of Kenny Lofton, Aramis Ramirez and Randall Simon from Pittsburgh, and the emergence of Matt Clement and Carlos Zambrano as formidable moundsmen.

Zambrano, in his third year with the Cubs, is excellent this season at keeping opponents in the park. He allows just nine home runs in 214 innings, an average of one every 23.8 innings. He and Boston Red Sox ace Pedro Martinez are the only regular starters in single digits this season.

Led by Kerry Wood and Prior, who rebounds from injury to go 11-1 down the stretch, the Cubs win 19 games in September, the most in that month since 1945 (the last time they were in the World

Series), and overtake the Astros in an exciting final week to snatch the Central Division title.

The Cubs have four 13 game winners in 2003 for the first time since '45 - Prior, Wood, Clement and Zambrano - and the pitching staff registers a record 1404 strikeouts. Wood becomes the first Cub to lead the majors in strikeouts since Grover Cleveland Alexander in 1920. Relievers Joe Borowski, Kyle Farnsworth and Mike Remlinger tally 241 strikeouts in 213 2/3 innings.

P	PLAYER	R	HR	RBI	SB	AVE
1B	Eric Karros	37	12	40	1	.286
2B	Mark Grudzielanek	73	3	38	6	.314
SS	Alex Gonzalez	71	20	59	3	.228
3B	Aramis Ramirez	75	27	106	2	.272
LF	Moises Alou	83	22	91	3	.280
CF	Corey Patterson	49	13	55	16	.298
RF	Sammy Sosa	99	40	103	0	.279
C	Damian Miller	34	9	36	1	.233
2B	Ramon Martinez	30	3	34	0	.283
OF	Kenny Lofton	97	8	46	9	.296
1B	Randall Simon	47	16	72	0	.276
1B	Hee Seop Choi	31	8	28	1	.218
C	Paul Bako	19	0	17	0	.229

T	PITCHER	W-L	SV	SO	SH	ERA
R	Mark Prior	18-6	0	245	1	2.43
R	Kerry Wood	14-11	0	266	2	3.20
R	Matt Clement	14-12	0	171	1	4.11
R	Carlos Zambrano	13-11	0	168	1	3.11
L	Shawn Estes	8-11	0	103	1	5.73
R	Joe Borowski	2-2	33	66	0	2.63

March 31 - The Cubs pummel Tom Glavine and the New York Mets 15-2 in the season opener at Shea Stadium. Corey Patterson drives in seven runs for Chicago in the most lopsided opener in the majors since the White Sox beat the St. Louis Browns 17-3 on April 17, 1951.

April 4 - Sammy Sosa slams his 500th career homer, a solo shot off reliever Scott Sullivan, during a 10-9 loss at Cincinnati. Sosa is the 18th player to reach the mark.

Cubs reliever Juan Cruz fans the first two major league batters he faces, setting a club record with eight straight strikeouts (he struck out six Mets in the season opener).

WORTH NOTING - In 2003, Joe Borowski became the first Cub with 30 saves since Rod Beck had 51 in 1998.

April 8 - The Cubs beat the Montreal Expos 3-1 on Opening Day at frigid Wrigley Field. Matt Clement allows three hits over 7 1/3 innings. The Cubs were originally to open their home season the day before, but were snowed out.

April 9 - Mark Prior fans 12 in his first major league shutout, a 3-0 gem over the Expos.

April 12 - Kerry Wood strikes out 13 in eight impressive innings of a 4-0 Cubs win over the Pirates at Wrigley.

April 17 - The Cubs defeat the Reds 16-3, finishing off a four-game series with Cincinnati with 40 total runs, the first time Chicago has scored tha many since August 1894.

April 20 - Sammy Sosa swats his 504th career homer, then gets beaned in the head for his trouble, in an 8-2 loss to the Pirates in Pittsburgh. A pitch by fellow Dominican Salomon Torres shatters Sosa's helmet but Sosa stays in the game.

April 29 - Manager Dusty Baker celebrates his return to San Francisco with a 4-2 victory behind Kerry Wood.

May 10 - Alex Gonzalez delivers his third 10th-inning homer of the season to give the Cubs a 3-2 win over the St. Louis Cardinals at Wrigley Field.

Mark Prior

May 15 - Corey Patterson's 17th-inning homer gives the Cubs a 4-2 triumph over Milwaukee. Cubs pitchers strike out a record 24 Brewers on the day, two more than the previous NLmark set by the New York Mets on May 31, 1964, and tied by Cincinnati on August 8, 1972. Starter Kerry Wood fans 13 of them.

May 19 - Matt Morris of the Cardinals takes just two hours and five minutes to shut out the Cubs 2-0.

May 26 - The lowly Pittsburgh Pirates score nine runs in the eighth inning and blank the Cubs 10-0 in Chicago.

June 3 - Say it ain't Sosa! The Cubs'slugger is caught using a corked bat in the first inning of an interleague game against the Tampa Bay Devil Rays and is ejected. Sosa, who claims he grabbed the bat he normally uses for batting practice only, shatters the bat while grounding out with runners on second and third. After the game, Sosa apologizes to fans, his teammates, and the commissioner of baseball. All of Sosa's bats are confiscated by security personnel. The Cubs beat the Rays 3-2.

June 6 - New York's David Wells pitches his team to a 5-3 victory in the first game between the Yankees and Cubs since the 1938 World Series. Sammy Sosa, who learns before the game that he's to receive an eight-game suspension for using a corked bat, immediately files an appeal so that he can play the series. He goes 1-for-4 in the loss.

June 7 - Kerry Wood outpitches New Yorker Roger Clemens in a 5-2 Cubs triumph in Game 2 of the historic interleague series. Sammy Sosa homers off Clemens in the fifth.

In the fourth inning, Wood and first baseman Hee Seop Choi collide while trying to catch a popup off the bat of New York's Jason Giambi; Choi lands hard on his head, knocking him out. The big first baseman lays motionless for more than 10 minutes before trainers and doctors revive him. He is taken off the field in an ambulance. He'll be held overnight at a hospital before being released. Choi will be put on the 15-day disabled list with a concussion.

June 8 - Mark Prior earns a win versus the team that drafted him as the Cubs edge the Yankees in the final game of the series, 8-7. Sammy Sosa drives in a run with his 2,000th career hit.

June 10 - A Baltimore fan runs onto the field, throws cork at Sammy Sosa, then removes his shirt and bows before security personnel escort him off in the eighth inning of the Cubs' 4-0 victory over the

Orioles at Camden Yards.

June 11 - Sammy Sosa is given a seven-game suspension, whittled down from eight, which he begins before the team's 7-6 win over the Orioles.

June 18 - Sosa is booed but delivers a two-run homer in his first game back from suspension, leading the Cubs to a 4-1 victory over the Reds in Cincinnati.

June 20 - The White Sox crush the Cubs 12-3 at Wrigley in the first game of the annual interleague series between the two Chicago clubs.

June 22 - The Cubs come from behind for a 2-1 win, averting an embarrassing three-game sweep at the hands of the White Sox.

July 2 - Sammy Sosa homers on the first pitch of the ninth inning to give the Cubbies a 1-0 victory in Philadelphia.

July 4 - Moises Alou celebrates Independence Day at Wrigley by swatting three home runs, but it's the Cardinals who do most of the partying with an 11-8 win. It's the Cubs' eighth loss in 10 games, dropping them two games behind St. Louis.

July 5 - Alex Gonzalez singles with the bases loaded in the ninth to give the Cubs a 6-5 win over the arch-rival Cards.

July 8 - Manager Dusty Baker makes news with an unfortunate comment when asked his opinion of the "day vs. night" Wrigley Field controversy. Baker is quoted as saying that most minorities like to play in the heat, while most caucasians prefer to play at night. Despite the hoopla over the allegedly racist remarks, Baker will never apologize for his statement.

July 11 - During a 9-5 Cubs loss at Wrigley, Mark Prior collides with Atlanta second baseman Marcus Giles, injuring his arm and sending him to the disabled list. He'll be sidelined until August.

July 12 - Sammy Sosa helps the Cubs snap a five-game losing streak, going 2-for-4 with a homer in a 7-3 win over Atlanta. Sosa's homer gives him seven hits in his last seven at-bats. The Chicago slugger is batting .344 with 12 homers and 23 RBI since returning from suspension June 18.

July 19 - Kerry Wood tosses a two-hit 1-0 victory over the Florida Marlins. The righthander fans eight to increase his major league-leading strikeout total to 164.

July 20 - The Cubs pound Florida pitching for 20 hits in a 16-2 rout.

July 21 - The Cubs continue to pound the next day, pummeling the Braves 15-6 in Atlanta.

July 23 - The Cubs get a boost for the stretch drive, acquiring veteran outfielder Kenny Lofton and third baseman Aramis Ramirez from the Pittsburgh Pirates for third baseman Jose Hernandez and a couple of minor leaguers. The trade reunites Lofton with Dusty Baker, his manager in San Francisco in 2002.

July 27 - Sammy Sosa ties Ted Williams and Willie McCovey for 12th on the all-time home run list with his 521st during a 5-3 Cubs win in Houston.

July 31 - Sosa's 23rd homer of the season, a three-run shot in the first, gives him sole possession of 12th place on the all-time list. The Cubs beat the Giants 9-4 in San Francisco.

August 1 - New third sacker Aramis Ramirez knocks an RBI single in the 14th inning to give the Cubs a 4-3 win over Arizona. The marathon game is also extended by a three-hour rain delay, finishing 7 hours and 36 minutes after the first pitch.

August 5 - Mark Prior returns from the disabled list and allows just two hits over six innings in the Cubs'3-0 win in San Diego.

August 12 - Carlos Zambrano, 5-0 since the All-Star break, tosses a five-hitter to beat the first-place Houston Astros 3-0.

August 14 - The Cubs find themselves in a first place tie with the Astros by beating them 7-1 at Wrigley Field.

August 16 - The Cubs trade minor league outfielder Ray Sadler to the Pirates for first baseman Randall Simon, who is batting .274 with 10 homers and 51 RBIs. He'll be a great addition for Chicago down the stretch.

August 17 - Rock's Ozzy Osborne sings a bearly-recognizable rendition of "Take Me Out to the Ballgame" during the seventh inning stretch of a game against the Dodgers. The rendition is so muddled that the Chicago Tribune feels obliged to publish a transcript of the song the next day.

August 19 - The Cubs acquire veteran infielder Tony Womack from the Rockies for minor league pitcher Emmanuel Ramirez, strengthening their infield depth for the stretch drive. Womack has hit .225 with two homers and 20 RBIs for Colorado and Arizona this year.

August 20 - Mark Prior takes a no-hitter into the sixth inning, finishing with four hits in a 6-0 victory over first-place Houston.

August 22 - Red-hot Carlos Zambrano takes a no-hitter into the eighth inning, losing it on an infield single by third baseman Shea Hillenbrand, in a 4-1 win over the Diamondbacks.

August 26 - A three-hitter by Mark Prior kicks off a three-game series at Busch Stadium in St. Louis as the Cubs beat the Cardinals 7-4. It's just the third win in 14 games at Busch for Chicago.

August 27 - Kerry Wood is in top form, fanning 11 in seven shutout innings but the bullpen can't hold the 2-0 lead as the Cardinals rally for a 4-2 win.

August 28 - A solo homer by light-hitting outfielder Kerry Robinson off Mike Remlinger in the ninth gives the Cards a 3-2 win and 2-games-to-1 advantage in the three-game series.

September 1 - The Cubs begin a five-game showdown at Wrigley with the Cardinals, beating the 7-0 in the opener behind Mark Prior. Chicago will win four of the five games.

September 2 - Sammy Sosa hits a two-run homer in the bottom of the 15th to give the Cubbies a 4-2 win over the Redbirds.

September 4 - A 7-6 win over St. Louis pushes the Cubs to within half a game of first-place Houston.

September 7 - The Cubs beat the Brewers 9-2 in Milwaukee to take a 1/2 game lead in the National League Central Division.

September 9 - Outfielder Moises Alou hits a tie-breaking two-run single to beat the Expos 4-3 in San Juan, Puerto Rico. It's the first-place Cubs'sixth straight victory.

September 12 - The Cubs blow a 5-1 lead when the Reds score five runs in the seventh against relievers Mark Guthrie and Antonio Alfonseca, but they rally back and win 7-6 on Tom Goodwin's pinch-hit, two-run single in the ninth. With the win, Chicago remains just a game behind Houston.

September 16 - Sammy Sosa drives in all of the Cubs'runs and Mark Prior wins his 16th game, 3-2 over the New York Mets. Joe Barowski pitches the ninth for his 30th save; he's the first Cub with 30 saves since Rod Beck had 51 in 1998. Chicago remains one game behind Houston in the NL Central.

September 17 - A four-hit 2-0 shutout by Kerry Wood completes a three-game sweep of the Mets.

Kerry Wood

September 19 - The Cubs split a doubleheader in Pittsburgh, winning the first game 10-9 but losing the nightcap 10-6, dropping them to 1 1/2 behind the Astros.

September 21 - Mark Prior fans 14 during a 4-1 win over Pittsburgh, giving Cubs pitchers a major league-record 1,352 strikeouts for the season. The win pushes the Cubs to within 1/2 game of first place.

September 23 - Lo and behold, the Cubbies find themselves in sole possession of first place as Kerry Wood flirts with a no-hitter and beats the Cincinnati Reds 6-0. Wood takes the no-no into the seventh when, with one out, outfielder Wily Mo Pena chops an infield single. Wood fans 12 on the night. Houston loses to San Francisco 10-3.

September 24 - Sammy Sosa ties Mickey Mantle for 10th place on the all-time homer list and Shawn Estes tosses a four-hit shutout as the Cubs beat the Cincinnati Reds 8-0 to preserve their one-game lead over Houston, who beats San Francisco 2-1.

September 25 - Sosa homers twice, moving past Mantle into tenth place on the all-time list with 538, but the Reds rally back from a 3-0 defecit for an 8-4 triumph. With the loss, Chicago slips back into a first-place tie with Houston, who defeats Milwaukee 2-1. Sosa also collects his 100th RBI, becoming the first player in NL history to reach the mark in nine consecutive seasons.

September 27 - After a rainout forces a Saturday doubleheader, the Cubbies clinch a division title for the first time since 1989, sweeping the twinbill from the Pirates 4-2 and 7-2 while Houston loses to Milwaukee 5-2. Sammy Sosa hits his 40th home run, becoming the first National Leaguer to reach the mark six straight times, and Mark

WORTH NOTING- The Cubs' NLDS opponents in 2003 are the Atlanta Braves, managed by **Bobby Cox**. The Braves finish with a 101-61 (.623) record, leading the National League in runs scored (902), home runs (235) and batting average (.283).

P	PLAYER	R	HR	RBI	SB	BA
1B	Robert Fick	51	11	78	1	.266
2B	Marcus Giles	101	21	69	14	.318
SS	Rafael Furcal	130	15	60	25	.294
3B	Vinny Castilla	65	22	76	1	.277
RF	Gary Sheffield	126	39	131	18	.329
CF	Andruw Jones	101	36	116	4	.275
LF	Chipper Jones	101	27	106	2	.303
C	Javy Lopez	88	43	109	0	.327

T	PITCHER	W	L	SV	SH	ERA
R	Russ Ortiz	21	7	0	1	3.81
R	Greg Maddux	15	11	0	0	3.97
L	Mike Hampton	14	8	0	0	3.84
L	Horacio Ramirez	12	4	0	0	4.00
R	John Smoltz	0	2	45	0	1.12

Prior and Matt Clement turn in strong starts before a crowd of 40,121 fans at Wrigley Field. It's the first time the Northsiders reach the playoffs since 1998, when they beat Dusty Baker and his Giants in a one-game playoff for the NL Wild Card.

September 29 - Cubs broadcaster and former All-Star third baseman Ron Santo's number is retired at a Wrigley Field ceremony, just before the season finale with the Pirates. Santo's No. 10 joins Ernie Banks' No. 14 and Billy Williams'No. 26.

September 30 - NLDS Game 1

On a night when Cubs fans seem to outnumber Braves fans at Atlanta's Turner Field, Kerry Wood leads Chicago to a 4-2 victory, the first postseason win outside of Wrigley Field for the club since Game 3 of the 1945 World Series.

The game is scoreless until the third inning, when Atlanta second baseman Marcus Giles hits a solo homer off Wood, giving the Braves a 1-0 lead.

Righthander Russ Ortiz works out of all sorts of trouble, including a bases-loaded jam in the fourth by fanning Alex Gonzalez and Paul Bako and getting Wood to pop up, until the Cubs finally break through in the sixth. Chicago again loads the bases with no outs on consecutive singles by Moises Alou, Aramis Ramirez and Eric Karros. After pinch-hitter Randall Simon strikes out, Bako slaps a grounder that first baseman Robert Fick boots, tying the score 1-1, then Wood rips a drive off the wall in left center to give the Cubs a 3-1 lead. Kenny Lofton follows with a bloop hit to center, scoring Wood.

Wood continues to dominate the mighty Braves lineup until tiring in the eighth. Atlanta scores on a double play, cutting the lead to 4-2 with two out, but Kyle Farnsworth retires catcher Javy Lopez on a bases-loaded grounder to short. Closer Joe Borowski retires the side in order in the ninth for the save.

Wood allows just two hits over 7-plus innings, striking out 11. He becomes the first Cubs pitcher to drive in the game-winning run in a postseason game since Orval Overall in the 1907 World Series.

October 1 - NLDS Game 2

Carlos Zambrano takes the mound for Game 2, hoping to give the Cubs a 2-0 advantage in the best-of-five playoff.

The Cubs blow a chance to break the game open against Atlanta lefty Mike Hampton in the first inning. It's mostly downhill from there. After Sammy Sosa drives in two runs with a shot that banks off the center field wall, missing a home run by inches, the Cubs load the bases with nobody out. But Hampton regroups and fans Eric Karros, Ramon Martinez and Damian Miller in order to wriggle out of the jam.

The Braves cut the lead to 2-1 in the bottom half of the first. Left fielder Chipper Jones drives in the run with a fielder's choice grounder. Center fielder Andruw Jones ties the game in the fourth with an RBI single.

Pinch-hitter Marcus Giles gives the Braves a 3-2 advantage with a run-scoring single in the sixth, forcing manager Dusty Baker to replace Zambrano with Kyle Farnsworth and then Dave Veres.

The Cubs battle back to tie the game against Braves closer John Smoltz in the top of the eighth, scoring on a pair of singles by Karros and pinch-hitter Randall Simon and a sacrifice fly by pinch-hitter Tom Goodwin. Simon, however, commits a baserunning blunder that forfeits a chance for Chicago to go ahead.

With two on in the bottom of the eighth, Baker elects to walk lefty-swinging Rafael Furcal so that righty Veres (whom opponents battered to the tune of .290 this season) can pitch to rookie second baseman Mark DeRosa. The strategy backfires when Veres allows a two-run double that gives the Braves a 5-3 lead and win.

October 3 - NLDS Game 3

Game 3 is billed as Cy Young vs. Cy Old as Chicago wunderkind Mark Prior faces former Cub Greg Maddux in a must-win for both clubs. The last time the Cubs were involved in a pitching showdown of this magnitude was on October 8, 1908, when Three-Finger Brown beat Christy Mathewson 4-2 in a game that decided the NLpennant.

Prior lives up to the challenge, allowing just two hits in a complete-game 3-1 win that pushes the Braves to the brink of elimination. It's the first post-season complete game by a Cub since Claude Passeau beat the Tigers on a one-hitter in Game 3 of the 1945 World Series.

The Cubs get all the runs they need in the first on a two-out, two-run single by Randall Simon. Aramis Ramirez provides an insurance run in the eighth with a run-scoring double to right-center.

The Braves spoil the shutout in their half of the eighth when rookie second baseman Mark DeRosa slaps a pinch-hit double, moves to third on a groundout and scores on a sacrifice fly.

Maddux lasts six innings, allowing six hits and two runs. It's his 31st playoff appearance and 29th start.

October 4 - NLDS Game 4

With their backs against the wall, and with a raucous Wrigley Field crowd of 39,983 mocking Atlanta's Tomahawk Chop each step of the way, the Braves manage stave off elimination with a 6-4 triumph led by the pitching of Russ Ortiz and the hitting of left fielder Chipper Jones.

Ortiz, pitching on three days' rest, allows just two runs on seven hits through five innings and Jones swats two two-run homers to provide the margin of difference. The switch-hitting Jones homers from both sides of the plate, the first player to do it in the postseason since the Yankees' Bernie Williams did it against Seattle in 1995.

Eric Karros also hits two homers, but both are solo shots. The Cubs strand eight runners on base, including a runner in scoring position in each of the first five innings.

Cubs starter Matt Clement struggles with his command throughout the game, giving up four runs on eight hits and four walks.

October 5 - NLDS Game 5

There's joy in Wrigleyville as the Cubs win their first postseason series in 95 years, beating the Braves 5-1 behind Kerry Wood.

Wood hurls his second dominating game of the NLDS, allowing just five hits through eight innings.

Kenny Lofton leads off the game with a

double and comes around to score the first run. Alex Gonzalez leads off the second with a homer off Atlanta starter Mike Hampton, making it 2-0.

Aramis Ramirez puts the Cubs up 4-0 with a two-run shot in the sixth.

A disputed call in the sixth leads to the Braves'only run. With two on and no one out, Gary Sheffield sends a liner to center that Lofton slides for and appears to catch. But left field umpire Dale Scott rules the ball a trap; the Cubs get a force at second but shortstop Rafael Furcal scores.

The Cubs add an unearned run off reliever Will Cunnane in the sixth. Closer Joe Borowski fans center fielder Andruw Jones to end the game.

It's Chicago's first postseason series victory since the club beat the Detroit Tigers in the 1908 World Series.

October 7 - NLCS Game 1

The Cubs take on the scrappy Florida Marlins, the NL Wild Card winner, in the National League Championship Series beginning at Wrigley Field. Carlos Zambrano faces righthander Josh Beckett in Game 1 before a crowd of 39,567.

The Cubs get to Beckett early, as Moises Alou hits a two-run homer to lead a four-run rally in the first. But the Marlins respond with five runs in the third, thanks to homers by catcher Ivan Rodriguez, third baseman Miguel Cabrera and right fielder Juan Encarnacion.

Florida pads their lead in the sixth as left fielder Jeff Conine plates Cabrera with a sacrifice fly.

But Chicago storms right back in their half of the frame as Alex Gonzalez hits a two-run homer to right, tying the game 6-6.

Rodriguez continues a hot postseason by lining a two-run single off Joe Borowski in the ninth, putting the Marlins ahead 8-6.

But Sammy Sosa, 5-for-31 with no homers and 1 RBI in postseason play, ties the game with a mammoth two-run shot off closer Ugueth Urbina that clears the ballpark and bounces on Waveland Avenue, sending the Wrigley Field crowd into momentary euphoria.

Unfortunately, Sosa's homer only ties the game, and pinch-hitter Mike Lowell provides the winning margin for the Marlins with a solo homer off lefthander Mark Guthrie in the 11th.

The two clubs combine for 17 extra-base hits, a postseason record.

October 8 - NLCS Game 2

The Cubs don't take long to rebound from their opening loss, burying the Marlins 12-3 behind seven strong innings from Mark Prior.

The fun begins in the first inning when the Cubs load the bases against Florida starter Brad Penny and Randall Simon swats a single to left, scoring Kenny Lofton and Mark Grudzielanek.

In the second, Lofton bounces an RBI single up the middle. With two on, Sammy Sosa drives a Penny fastball 495 feet to center field that caroms near the scoreboard for a three-run homer, putting the Cubs up 5-0.

It's all Chicago from there as Alex Gonzalez launches two homers, giving him three for the series, and Aramis Ramirez adds another for seven more runs.

Prior cruises into the sixth with an 11-0 lead until Marlins first baseman Derek Lee and third baseman Miguel Cabrera lead off the inning with consecutive homers, cutting the lead to 11-2. Prior, though, composes himself and works into the eighth inning before being removed. Reliever Mark Guthrie, who gave up Mike Lowell's game-winning pinch-homer in Game 1, gets the final two outs in the ninth.

October 10 - NLCS Game 3

The action shifts to Florida with Kerry

Wood, dominant over the Marlins this season, takes on soft-throwing lefty Mark Redman in what will be a thriller to remember.

The Cubs strike first on a humid night at Pro Player Stadium. Kenny Lofton singles to lead off the game and Sammy Sosa follows an out later with a liner off the left field wall, a shot so hard Sosa is held to a single, scoring Lofton.

Wood helps himself in the second with a sacrifice fly that scores Eric Karros, giving the Cubs a 2-0 lead.

But the Marlins chip back in the bottom half of the inning on two singles and an RBI double by shortstop Alex Gonzalez.

Redman and Wood hold the offense at bay until the seventh, when a single off the bat of red-hot catcher Ivan Rodriguez scores two to give the Fist a 3-2 lead.

A two-run homer by Randall Simon, who is fast becoming a Chicago darling, gives the Cubbies a 4-3 advantage in the eighth. But pinch-hitter Todd Hollandsworth makes it 4-4 in the Marlins'half with a run-scoring single off closer Joe Borowski.

After two more tense scoreless innings, Lofton singles with one out in the 11th off Florida reliever Braden Looper. Doug Glanville, the last Cub to make the roster this season, bats for Borowski and rifles a liner into left-center that glances off the glove of a diving Jeff Conine, rolling to the wall and scoring Lofton.

Things get even more tense after that, when Mike Remlinger takes the mound in the bottom half of the inning looking for just his second save in three years. With one out, Luis Castillo strikes out with one out but reaches first as the ball bounces past catcher Paul Bako's legs for a wild pitch. Castillo makes it to second on a ground out, bringing up first baseman Derek Lee with two outs and a crowd of more than 65,000 standing and screaming.

WORTH NOTING- The Cubs' NLCS opponents in 2003 are the Florida Marlins, managed by **Jack McKeon**. The Marlins finish with a 91-71 (.562) record.

P	PLAYER	R	HR	RBI	SB	BA
1B	Derek Lee	91	31	92	21	.271
2B	Luis Castillo	99	6	39	21	.314
SS	Alex Gonzalez	52	18	77	0	.256
3B	Mike Lowell	76	32	105	3	.276
RF	Juan Encarnacion	80	19	94	19	.270
CF	Juan Pierre	100	1	41	65	.305
LF	Miguel Cabrera	39	12	62	0	.268
C	Ivan Rodriguez	90	16	85	10	.297

T	PITCHER	W	L	SV	SH	ERA
R	Brad Penny	14	10	0	0	4.13
L	Mark Redman	14	9	0	0	3.59
L	Dontrelle Willis	14	6	0	2	3.30
R	Carl Pavano	12	13	0	0	4.30
R	Braden Looper	6	4	28	0	3.68

Lee promptly bounces a grounder to Aramis Ramirez at third, who boots it. But Castillo, inexplicably, is caught off the bag at third and is run down for the third out.

October 11 - NLCS Game 4

Game 5 is over almost as quickly as it begins. Marlins rookie starter Dontrelle Willis, a rookie, walks the bases loaded with one out in the first inning. Aramis Ramirez then lifts a high fly ball that sails over the left field fence for a grand slam - the first postseason slam in Cubs history - and a quick commanding lead.

Ramirez adds an RBI single in the third, chasing Willis, and a run-scoring hit by Moises Alou gives the Cubs a 7-0 lead in the fourth.

Starter Matt Clement, who was traded, ironically, for Willis a year ago, sails into the fifth before running into trouble. An RBI groundout by shortstop Alex Gonzalez and a run-scoring single by pinch-hitter Todd Hollandsworth cuts the lead to 7-2.

But Ramirez continues his productive

night with a solo homer in the seventh that gives the Cubs an 8-2 advantage.

The Marlins mount a rally against Clement in the eighth, scoring once more on a double by Ivan Rodriguez, but Kyle Farnsworth relieves and gets the final four outs without allowing a hit.

October 12 - NLCS Game 5

The Marlins need a solid outing from a starting pitcher as they face elmination in the eye - and they get it from Josh Beckett. Beckett shuts down the Cubs' offense on two hits, hurling a 4-0 shutout.

Cubs starter Carlos Zambrano wriggles out of trouble in the first couple of innings, and actually looks like he's up to the battle, but gives up a back-breaking two-run homer to third baseman Mike Lowell in the fourth, the only runs Beckett needs. The Florida righthander fans 11 and retires the first batter in all nine innings, with seven of the nine outs coming on strikeouts.

The series is sent back to Chicago with the Cubs still in command.

October 14 - NLCS Game 6

Curses. The Cubs are five outs away from their first World Series berth in 58 years, then...it happens. Again.

Mark Prior sails into the eighth inning with a 3-0 lead, thanks to a Sammy Sosa RBI double, a Dontrelle Willis wild pitch, and a Mark Grudzielanek run-scoring single, then begins to tire.

With one out, Florida leadoff hitter Juan Pierre doubles and Luis Castillo lifts a fly ball down the left field line. Moises Alou races to the brick wall and jumps high over the left-field railing to make the catch - only his glove is knocked away by a fan reaching for the ball. Instead of a clear out, the Marlins have a last-chance gasp. And make the most of it.

As security officers escort the fan from his seat - under a shower of beer - Florida mounts a comeback that they will ride through Game 7 and into the World Series.

To be fair, the incident does not cost the Cubs the game. But the momentum shifts so quickly - and so clearly - that the Wrigley crowd can sense that all is lost even before Ivan Rodriguez lines an RBI single to left and Alex Gonzalez next bobbles a sure double-play ball that loads the bases.

First baseman Derek Lee then steps up and delivers a drive into the left-field corner that ties the game 3-3. Left fielder Jeff Conine then lifts a sacrifice fly to right off reliever Kyle Farnsworth that plates Cabrera for the go-ahead run, and pinch-hitter Mike Mordecai breaks the game open with a three-run double off the wall in left-center. The Marlins sock it to the Cubs for eight runs before the inning's over.

Florida reliever Chad Fox gets the 8-3 win.

October 15 - NLCS Game 7

The Cubs'riveting playoff run, and season, ends in a 9-6 slugfest. Kerry Wood, who won the pivotal Game 5 of the NLDS, is roughed up for six runs as Florida completes its stunning comeback from a three-games-to-one deficit.

A three-run homer by rookie Miguel Cabrera gives the Marlins a quick first-inning lead. The Cubs tie it with an RBI groundout by Damian Miller and two-run homer by Wood in the second, sending the nearly 40,000 Wrigley faithful into a frenzy.

A two-run homer by Moises Alou puts the Cubs up 5-3 in the third, but Wood,

WORTH QUOTING - "I felt I let the team down, the organization down, and the city of Chicago down. I choked."

-Kerry Wood, after Game 7
of the 2003 NLCS

clearly tiring after a long season, gives up three more runs in the fifth, thanks to an RBI single by Luis Castillo and a two-run double by shortstop Alex Gonzalez.

Josh Beckett, who threw a two-hit shutout in Game 5, relieves and hurls four innings of one-hit ball on two days of rest, allowing just a pinch-homer by Troy O'Leary. Ugueth Urbina shuts the door in the ninth, sending the Wrigley crowd home disappointed and the Marlins to the World Series.

Still, Cubs fans have reason to rejoice. A complete turnaround from the 2002 95-loss season, and a nucleus of young pitching talent that should keep the club in the hunt for years. Will the Cubbies reverse the curse in 2004?

The chronology continues...

Bibliography

American League, The. Written by Donald Honig. (Crown, 1983).

American League Story, The. Written by Lee Allen. (Hill and Wang, 1961).

Babe: The Legend Comes to Life. Written by Robert Creamer. (Simon and Schuster, 1974).

Ball Clubs, The. Written by Donald Dewey and Nicholas Acocella. (HarperCollins, 1996).

Ballplayers, The. Edited by Mike Shatzkin. (William Morrow, 1990).

Baseball. Produced by Ken Burns. Narrative written by Geoffrey C. Ward. (Alfred A. Knopf, 1994).

Baseball Anecdotes. Written by Daniel Okrent. (Oxford University Press, 1989).

Baseball Between the Wars: A Pictorial Tribute To The Men Who Made the Game In Chicago From 1909 to 1947. Written by Bill Hageman. (Contemporary Books, 2001)

Baseball Encyclopedia, The. Edited by Jeanine Bucek, Traci Cothran, Bill Deane, Bob Kerler, Maria Massey, Bob Tiemann, Richard Topp and Ken Samelson. (Macmillan, 1996).

Baseball Hall of Shame, The. Written by Bruce Nash and Allan Zullo. (Pocket Books, 1985).

Baseball Memories 1900-1909. Written by Marc Okkonen. (Sterling, 1992).

Baseball Memories 1950-1959. Written by Marc Okkonen. (Sterling, 1993).

Baseball Reader, The. Edited by Charles Einstein. (McGraw-Hill, 1983).

Baseball's Top 100. Edited by John Benson and Tony Blengino. (Diamond Library, 1995).

Baseball's 25 Greatest Pennant Races. Written by Lowell Reidenbaugh. (The Sporting News, 1987).

Baseball When the Grass Was Real. Written by Donald Honig. (Berkely Publishing, 1975).

Bill James Guide to Baseball Managers. Written by Bill James. (Scribner, 1997).

Biographical Encyclopedia of Baseball, The. Written by Donald Dewey and Nicholas Acocella. (Carroll & Graf, 1995).

Biographical Encyclopedia of the Negro Baseball Leagues, The. Written by James A. Wriley. (Carroll & Graf, 1994).

Boston Globe, The. Selected editions: 1918.

Boys of Summer, The. Written by Roger Kahn. (Harper & Row, 1971).

Branch Rickey. Written by Murray Polner. (Signet, 1983).

Branch Rickey: American in Action. Written by Arthur William Mann. (Houghton, 1957).

Branch Rickey's Little Blue Book: Wit and Strategy from Baseball's Last Wise Man. Written by Branch Rickey. (Macmillan, 1995).

Bums. Written by Peter Golenbock. (Putnam's, 1984).

Cardinals, The. Written by John Davenport. (Collier Books, 1983).

Cardinals Encyclopedia, The. Written by Mike Eisenbath. (Temple University Press, 1999).

Celebrating 70; Mark McGwire's Historic Season. Edited by Ron Smith. (The Sporting News, 1998).

Chicago Cubs, The. Written by Warren Brown. (Putnam's, 1946).

Chicago Cubs: An Illustrated History, The. Written by Donald Honig (Prentice Hall, 1991)

Chicago Tribune, The. Selected editions: 1903-2003.

Cubs of '69: Recollections of the Team That Should Have Been, The. Written by Rick Talley. (Contemporary Books, 1989).

Diz. Written by Robert Gregory. (Penguin Books, 1992).

Durocher's Cubs: The Greatest Team That Didn't Win. Written by David Claerbaut. (Taylor Publishing, 2000).

Essential Cubs. Written by Doug Meyers (Contemporary Books, 1999).

Game Is Never Over: An Appreciative History of the Chicago Cubs, 1948-1980, The. Written by Jim Langford. (Icarus, 1980).

Glory of Their Times, The. Written by Lawrence S. Ritter. (Random House, 1985).

Glory Years of the St. Louis Cardinals, The. Written by Mel Freese. (Palmerston & Reed, 1999).

Great Encyclopedia of 19th-Century Major League Baseball, The. Written by David Nemec. (Penguin Books, 1997).

Green Cathedrals. Written by Philip J. Lowry. (SABR, 1986).

Hardball. Written by Bowie Kuhn. (McGraw-Hill, 1988).

High and Inside: Orlando Cepeda's Story. Written by Orlando Cepeda. (Icarus, 1983).

Holy Cow! Written by Harray Caray and Bob Verdi. (Villard Books, 1989).

John McGraw. Written by Charles Alexander (Penguin Books, 1988).

Kansas City Star, The. Selected editions: 1985.

Los Angeles Times, The. Selected editions: 1965, 1985.

Lost Ballparks. Written by Lawrence S. Ritter. (Penguin Books, 1992).

Major Leagues. Written by David Pietruza. (McFarland & Company, 1991).

My Baseball Scrapbook. Written by Bob Broeg. (River City, 1983).

National League, The. Written by Donald Honig. (Crown, 1983).

New York Times, The. Selected editions: 1883, 1888, 1926, 1927, 1928, 1942, 1943, 1964, 1969, 1973.

Nice Guys Finish Last. Written by Leo Durocher and Ed Linn. (Simon and Schuster, 1975).

Ol'Diz. Written by Vince Staten. (HarperCollins, 1992).

Pennant Race. Written by Jim Brosnan. (Penguin Books, 1962).

Phillies Encyclopedia, The. Written by Frank Bilovsky and Richard Westcott. (Leisure Press, 1984).

Rogers Hornsby. Written by Charles C. Alexander. (Henry Holt & Company, 1995).

Sporting News, The. Selected editions 1886-1999.

Sports Encyclopedia: Baseball, The. Written by David S. Net and Richard M. Cohen. (St. Martin's Press, 1994, 1996, 1999).

St. Louis Cardinals, The. Written by Bruce Chadwick and David M. Spindel. (Abbeville Press, 1995).

St. Louis Cardinals Encyclopedia, The. Written by Bob Broeg and Jerry Vickery. (Masters Press, 1998).

St. Louis Globe-Democrat, The. Selected editions: 1876-1980

St. Louis Post-Dispatch, The. Selected editions: 1876-2003

Total Baseball. Edited by John Thorn, Pete Palmer, Michael Gershman and David Pietrusza. (Total Sports, 1999).

Voices from Cooperstown. Written by Anthony J. Connor. (Collier Books, 1982).

World Series, The. Written by Richard M. Cohen and David S. Neft. (Collier Books, 1986).

Yankee Encyclopedia, The. Written by Mark Gallagher. (Leisure Press, 1982).

ABOUT THE AUTHOR

Tim Steele grew up a fan of the Anaheim Angels in Placentia, California, a quiet suburb of Los Angeles and just a cumquat's throw from Anaheim Stadium. A graduate of El Dorado High School, which has coughed up such notable major league talent as Dan Petry, Bret Boone, Brett Tomko and Phil Nevin, Tim studied art, literature and slacking at Point Loma College in San Diego. A lefthanded pitcher, he joined the school's division-champion varsity baseball team his freshman year, leading the club in walks, earned runs, and home runs allowed, which was remarkable in that he appeared in only three games. Having had enough of that, Tim moved to Kansas City to attend Mid-America Nazarene College, where he continued his diamond ineptitude.

Tim has spent more than 17 years as a graphic designer and art director. He lives in Chesterfield, Missouri with his long-suffering wife, Suzi, and sons Dane, 19, and Blake, 15.

This is his third book.